SCRAMBLES

AMONGST THE ALPS IN THE

YEARS 1860-69

BY

EDWARD WHYMPER

WITH MAPS AND ILLUSTRATIONS

Toil and pleasure, in their natures opposite, are yet linked together in a kind
of necessary connection.—LIVY.

1871

FOG-BOW SEEN FROM THE MATTERHORN ON JULY 14, 1865.

"THE TAUGWALDERS THOUGHT THAT IT HAD SOME CONNECTION WITH THE ACCIDENT"

See Chap. XXII.

PREFACE.

In the year 1860, shortly before leaving England for a long continental tour, a certain eminent London publisher requested me to make for him some sketches of the great Alpine peaks. At this time I had only a literary acquaintance with mountaineering, and had even not seen—much less set foot upon—a mountain. Amongst the peaks which were upon my list was Mont Pelvoux, in Dauphiné. The sketches that were required of it were to celebrate the triumph of some Englishmen who intended to make its ascent. They came—they saw—but they did not conquer. By a mere chance I fell in with a very agreeable Frenchman who accompanied this party, and was pressed by him to return to the assault. In 1861 we did so, with my friend Macdonald—and we conquered. This was the origin of my scrambles amongst the Alps.

The ascent of Mont Pelvoux (including the disagreeables) was a very delightful scramble. The mountain air did *not* act as an emetic; the sky did *not* look black, instead of blue ; nor did I feel tempted to throw myself over precipices. I hastened to enlarge my experience, and went to the Matterhorn. I was urged towards Mont Pelvoux by those mysterious impulses which cause men to peer into the unknown. Not only was this mountain reputed to be the highest in France, and on that account was worthy of attention, but it was the dominating point of a most picturesque district of the highest interest, which, to this day, remains almost unexplored ! The Matterhorn attracted me simply by its grandeur. It was considered to be the most thoroughly inaccessible of all mountains, even by those who ought to have known better. Stimulated to make fresh exertions by one repulse after another, I returned, year after year, as I had opportunity, more and more determined to find a way up it, or to *prove* it to be really inaccessible.

A considerable portion of this volume is occupied by the history of these attacks on the Matterhorn, and the other excursions that are described have all some connection, more or less remote, with that mountain or with Mont Pelvoux. All are new excursions (that is, excursions made for the first time), unless the contrary is pointed out. Some have been passed over very briefly, and entire ascents or descents have been disposed of in a single line. If they had been worked out at full length, three volumes, instead of one, would have been required. Generally speaking, the salient points alone have been dwelt upon, and the rest has been left to the imagination. This treatment has spared the reader from much useless repetition.

In endeavouring to make the book of some use to those who may wish to go mountain-scrambling, whether in the Alps or elsewhere, undue prominence, perhaps, has been given to our mistakes and failures ; and it will doubtless be pointed out that our practice must have been bad if the principles which are laid down are sound, or that the principles must be unsound if the practice was good. It is maintained in an early chapter that the positive, or unavoidable, dangers of mountaineering are very small, yet from subsequent pages it can be shown that very considerable risks were run. The reason is obvious—we were not immaculate. Our blunders are not held up to be admired, or to be imitated, but to be avoided.

These scrambles amongst the Alps were holiday excursions, and as such they should be judged. They are spoken of as sport, and nothing more. The pleasure that they gave me cannot, I fear, be transferred to others. The ablest pens have failed, and must always fail, to give a true idea of the grandeur of the Alps. The most minute descriptions of the greatest writers do nothing more than convey impressions that are entirely erroneous—the reader conjures up visions, it may be magnificent ones, but they are infinitely inferior to the reality. I have dealt sparingly in descriptions, and have employed illustrations freely, in the hope that the pencil may perhaps succeed where the pen must inevitably have failed.

The preparation of the illustrations has occupied a large part of my time during the last six years. With the exception of the views upon pp. 21, 23, and 33, the whole of the illustrations have been engraved expressly for the book, and, unless it is otherwise specified, all are from my own sketches. About fifty have been drawn on the wood by Mr. James Mahoney, and I am much indebted to that artist for the care and fidelity with which he has followed my slight memoranda, and for the spirit that he has put into his admirable designs. Most of his drawings will be identified by his monogram. Twenty of the remainder are the work of Mr. Cyrus Johnston, and out of these I would draw especial attention to the view of the Matterhorn facing p. 84, the striated rock upon p. 141, and the bits from the Mer de Glace upon pp. 355-6. The illustrations have been introduced as illustrations, and very rarely for ornamental purposes. We have subordinated everything in them to accuracy, and it is only fair to the artists who have honoured me by their assistance to say that many of their designs would have ranked higher as works of art if they had been subjected to fewer restrictions. Most of the subjects have required very fine and finished engraving, and this, in its turn, has compelled the use of paper of unexceptionable quality. The whole of the paper in the book has been made expressly for it by Messrs. Dickinson, who assure me that it is the finest paper they have ever produced—it is certainly the most perfectly manufactured paper that has come under my notice. Mr. Clark's printing will speak for itself.

It is now my pleasant duty to acknowledge assistance that has been rendered, directly or indirectly, by friends and strangers, at home or abroad. First of all, my thanks are due to my companions for having placed their journals and sketches freely at my disposal. I am particularly obliged to Mr. J. Longridge, to Mr. T. F. Mitchell, and to Mr. W. Cutbill, for the facilities that they granted me when examining the Fell railway in 1869. From the Rev. T. G. Bonney (of St. John's Coll., Cambridge), and Mr. Rob. H. Scott, F.R.S., I have received many friendly hints and much valued criticism ; and aid, in a variety of ways, from Mr. Budden, Prof. Gastaldi and Sig. Giordano, in Italy ; from M. Emile Templier and the Maréchal Canrobert, in France ; and from Mr. Gosset of Berne. I am indebted to Mr. William Longman for being allowed to reproduce the Ascent of Mont Pelvoux * and three of its accompanying illustrations, and to the Messrs. Longman for the use of a portion of their map of the Western Alps ; to the English Alpine Club for the use of a part of Mr. Reilly's map of the Valpelline and Val Tournanche ; and especially to the Federal Council of Switzerland for having granted the unusual favour of a transfer from two of the valuable plates of the Dufour map. The two remaining maps are original. That of Mont Blanc is based upon the Government maps of France and Switzerland, and the survey of Mr. Reilly ; and that of the Matterhorn and its glaciers (excluding some corrections which I have taken the liberty of making) is an enlargement of a portion of the Dufour map.

HASLEMERE, *May* 1871.

---

* From *Peaks, Passes, and Glaciers*, 2d series. With this exception, almost the whole of the text is now published for the first time.

CONTENTS.

——◆——

1860
CHAPTER I.
INTRODUCTORY.

1861
CHAPTER II.
THE ASCENT OF MONT PELVOUX.

CHAPTER III.
THE MONT CENIS PASS AND THE FELL RAILWAY—THE GREAT TUNNEL THROUGH THE ALPS.

CHAPTER IV.

MY FIRST SCRAMBLE ON THE MATTERHORN.

1862

CHAPTER V.

RENEWED ATTEMPTS TO ASCEND THE MATTERHORN.

1863

CHAPTER VI.

THE VAL TOURNANCHE—THE BREUILJOCH—ZERMATT—ASCENT
OF THE GRAND TOURNALIN.

CHAPTER VII.

OUR SIXTH ATTEMPT TO ASCEND THE MATTERHORN.

1864

CHAPTER VIII.

FROM ST. MICHEL TO LA BÉRARDE BY THE COL DES AIGS. D'ARVE, COL DE MARTIGNARE, AND THE BRÈCHE DE LA MEIJE.

CHAPTER IX.

THE ASCENT OF THE POINTE DES ECRINS.

CHAPTER X.

FROM VAL LOUISE TO LA BÉRARDE BY THE COL DE PILATTE.

CHAPTER XI.

PASSAGE OF THE COL DE TRIOLET, AND ASCENTS OF MONT DOLENT, AIGUILLE DE TRÉLATÊTE, AND AIGUILLE D'ARGENTIÈRE.

CHAPTER XII.

THE MOMING PASS—ZERMATT.

1865

CHAPTER XIII.

THE ASCENT OF THE GRAND CORNIER.

CHAPTER XIV.

THE ASCENT OF THE DENT BLANCHE.

CHAPTER XV.

LOST ON THE COL D'HÉRENS—SEVENTH ATTEMPT TO ASCEND THE MATTERHORN.

b

CHAPTER XXI.

THE ASCENT OF THE MATTERHORN.

CHAPTER XXII.

THE DESCENT OF THE MATTERHORN.

APPENDIX.

LIST OF ILLUSTRATIONS.

The Drawings were made on the Wood by
H. J. Boot, C. Johnson, J. Mahoney, J. W. North, P. Skelton, W. G. Smith, and C. J. Staniland;
and were Engraved by J. W. and Edward Whymper.

* *From Photographs.*   ** *Designs.*

FULL PAGE ILLUSTRATIONS.

IN THE TEXT.

MAPS.

To be placed at the end of the Volume.

The body of the Work is printed by R. CLARK, Edinburgh ; the separate Plates
have been printed by the AUTHOR.

ERRATA.

Page 20, line 6 from top, "Col de Lantaret" to read "Col de Lautaret."

,, 29, ,, 13-15 ,, "Pie des Arcines" ,, "Pic de Arcines."

,, 45, note† "See Chap. 23" ,, "See Appendix."

,, 147, line 1 from top, "early and coarse" ,, "early, or a coarse."

,, 215, note, "referred to in Chapter xx." ,, "referred to in Chapter xxi.

SCRAMBLES AMONGST THE ALPS

BEACHY HEAD.

CHAPTER I.

On the 23d of July 1860, I started for my first tour in the Alps. As we steamed out into the Channel, Beachy Head came into view, and recalled a scramble of many years ago. With the impudence of ignorance, my brother* and I, schoolboys both, had tried to scale that great chalk cliff. Not the head itself—where sea-birds circle, and where the flints are ranged so orderly in parallel lines—but at a place more to·the east, where the pinnacle called the Devil's Chimney had fallen down. Since that time we have been often in dangers of different kinds, but never have we more nearly broken our necks than upon that occasion.

In Paris I made two ascents. The first to the seventh floor of

---

* The author of *Travels in Alaska*.

a house in the Quartier Latin—to an artist friend, who was engaged, at the moment of my entry, in combat with a little Jew. He hurled him with great good-will, and with considerable force, into some of his crockery, and then recommended me to go up the towers of Notre Dame. Half-an-hour later I stood on the parapet of the great west front, by the side of the leering fiend which for centuries has looked down upon the great city. It looked over the

Hotel Dieu to a small and commonplace building, around which there was always a moving crowd. To that building I descended. It was filled with chattering women and eager children, who were struggling to get a good sight of three corpses, which were exposed to view. It was the Morgue. I quitted the place disgusted, and overheard two women discussing the spectacle. One of them concluded with " But that it is droll;" the other answered approvingly, " But that it is droll," and the Devil of Notre Dame, looking down upon them,[*] seemed to say, " Yes, your climax—the cancan, your end—not uncommonly that building ; it is droll, but that it is droll."

I passed on to Switzerland; saw the sunlight lingering on the giants of the Oberland; heard the echoes from the cow-horns in the Lanterbrunnen valley and the avalanches rattling off the Jungfrau ; and then crossed the Gemmi into the Valais, resting for a time by the beautiful Oeschinen See, and getting a forcible illustration of glacier-motion in a neighbouring valley—the Gasteren Thal. The upper end of this valley is crowned by the Tschingel glacier, which, as it descends, passes over an abrupt cliff that is in the centre of its course. On each side the continuity of the glacier is maintained, but in the centre it is cleft in twain by the cliff. Lower down it is consolidated again. I scrambled on to this lower portion, advanced

---

[*] The position of the Morgue has been changed since 1860.

towards the cliff, and then stopped to admire the contrast of the brilliant pinnacles of ice with the blue sky. Without a warning, a huge slice of the glacier broke away, and fell over the cliff on to the lower portion with a thundering crash. Fragments rolled beyond me ; although, fortunately, not in my direction. I fled, and did not stop until off the glacier ; but before it was quitted learned another lesson in glacial matters : the terminal moraine, which seemed to be a solid mound, broke away underneath me, and showed that it was only a superficial covering resting on a slope of glassy ice.

On the steep path over the Gemmi there were opportunities for observing the manners and customs of the Swiss mule. It is  not perhaps in revenge for generations of ill-treatment that the mule grinds one's legs against fences and stone walls, and pretends to stumble in awkward places, particularly when coming round corners and on the brinks of precipices ; but their evil habit of walking on the outside edges of paths (even in the most unguarded positions) is one that is distinctly the result of association with man. The transport of wood from the mountains into the valleys occupies most of the mules during a considerable portion of the year ; the faggots into which the wood is made up project some distance on each side, and it is said that they walk intuitively to the outside of paths having rocks on the other side to avoid the collisions which would otherwise occur. When they carry tourists they behave in a similar manner ; and, no doubt, when the good time for mules arrives, and they no longer carry burdens, they will still continue, by natural selection, to do the same. This habit frequently gives rise to scenes; two mules meet; each wishes to pass on the outside, and neither will give way. It requires considerable persuasion, through the medium of the tail, before such difficulties are arranged.

I visited the baths of Leuk, and saw the queer assemblage of men, women, and children, attired in bathing-gowns, chatting, drinking, and playing at chess in the water. The company did not seem to be perfectly sure whether it was decorous in such a situation and in such attire for elderly men to chase young females from one corner to another, but it was unanimous in howling at the advent of a stranger who remained covered, and literally yelled when I departed without exhibiting my sketch.

I trudged up the Rhone valley, and turned aside at Visp to go up the Visp Thal, where one would expect to see greater traces of glacial action, if a glacier formerly filled it, as one is said to have done.*

I was bound for the valley of Saas, and my work took me high up the Alps on either side; far beyond limit of trees and the tracks of tourists. The view from the slopes of the Wiessmies, on the eastern side of the valley, 5000 or 6000 feet above the village of Saas, is perhaps the finest of its kind in the Alps. The full height of the three-peaked Mischabel (the highest mountain in Switzerland) is seen at one glance; 11,000 feet of dense forests, green alps, pinnacles of rock, and glittering glaciers. The peaks seemed to me then to be hopelessly inaccessible from this direction.

I descended the valley to the village of Stalden, and then went up the Visp Thal to Zermatt, and stopped there several days. Numerous traces of the formidable earthquake-shocks of five years before still remained, particularly at St. Nicholas, where the inhabitants had been terrified beyond measure at the destruction of

---

* And to have supplied from high up the valley of Saas "the well-known blocks of gabbro, which are recognised so extensively over the plains of Switzerland." J. D. Forbes, *Tour of Mont Blanc and Monte Rosa*, p. 295.

their churches and houses. At this place, as well as at Visp, a large part of the population was obliged to live under canvas for several months. It is remarkable that there was hardly a life lost on this occasion, although there were about fifty shocks, some of which were very severe.

At Zermatt I wandered in many directions, but the weather was bad, and my work was much retarded. One day, after spending a long time in attempts to sketch near the Hornli, and in futile endeavours to seize the forms of the peaks as they for a few seconds peered out from above the dense banks of woolly clouds, I determined not to return to Zermatt by the usual path, but to cross the Gorner glacier to the Riffel hotel. After a rapid scramble over the polished rocks and snowbeds which skirt the base of the Theodule glacier, and wading through some of the streams which flow from it, at that time much swollen by the late rains, the first difficulty was arrived at, in the shape of a precipice about three hundred feet high. It seemed that there would be no difficulty in crossing the glacier if the cliff could be descended ; but higher up, and lower down, the ice appeared, to my inexperienced eyes, to be impassable for a single person. The general contour of the cliff was nearly perpendicular, but it was a good deal broken up, and there was little difficulty in descending by zigzagging from one mass to another. At length there was a long slab, nearly smooth, fixed at an angle of about forty degrees between two wall-sided pieces of rock ; nothing, except the glacier, could be seen below. It was an awkward place, but being doubtful if return were possible, as I had been dropping from one ledge to another, passed it at length by lying across the slab, putting the shoulder stiffly against one side, and the feet against the other, and gradually wriggling down, by first moving the legs and then the back. When the bottom of the slab was gained a friendly crack was seen, into which the point of the baton could be stuck, and I dropped down to the next piece. It took a long time coming down that little bit of cliff, and for a few seconds it was satisfactory to see the ice close at hand.. In another moment a second difficulty presented itself. The glacier swept round an angle of the cliff, and as the ice was not of the nature of treacle or thin putty, it kept away from the little bay, on the edge of which I stood. We were not widely separated, but the edge of the ice was higher than the opposite edge of rock; and worse, the rock was covered with loose earth and stones which had fallen from above. All along the side of the cliff, as far as could be seen in both directions, the ice did not touch it, but there was this marginal crevasse, seven feet wide, and of unknown depth.

All this was seen at a glance, and almost at once I concluded that I could not jump the crevasse, and began to try along the cliff lower down; but without success, for the ice rose higher and higher, until at last further progress was stopped by the cliffs becoming perfectly smooth. With an axe it would have been possible to cut up the side of the ice; without one I saw there was no alternative but to return and face the jump.

It was getting towards evening, and the solemn stillness of the High Alps was broken only by the sound of rushing water or of falling rocks. If the jump should be successful,—well; if not, I fell into that horrible chasm, to be frozen in, or drowned in that gurgling, rushing water. Everything depended on that jump. Again I asked myself, "Can it be done?" It *must* be. So, finding my stick was useless, I threw it and the sketch-book to the ice, and first retreating as far as possible, ran forward with all my might, took the leap, barely reached the other side, and fell awkwardly on my knees.* Almost at the same moment a shower of stones fell on the spot from which I had jumped.

The glacier was crossed without further trouble, but the Riffel,†

* This would of course have been nothing to a practised gymnast in a room. The difficulty lay chiefly in jumping from bad footing on to worse. The incident would not have occurred if the cliffs had been descended a little more to the east.

† The Riffel hotel (the starting-point for the ascent of Monte Rosa), a deservedly popular inn, belonging to Monsieur Seiler, the proprietor of the hotels at Zermatt, is situate at a height of 3100 feet above that village (8400 above the sea), and commands a superb panoramic view.

which was then a very small building, was crammed with tourists, and could not take me in. As the way down was unknown to me, some of the people obligingly suggested getting a man at the chalets, otherwise the path would be certainly lost in the forest. On arriving at the chalets no man could be found, and the lights of Zermatt, shining through the trees, seemed to say, " Never mind a guide, but come along down ; I'll show you the way ;" so off I went through the forest, going straight towards them. The path was lost in a moment, and was never recovered ; I was tripped up by pine-roots, tumbled over rhododendron bushes, fell over rocks. The night was pitch dark, and after a time the lights of Zermatt became obscure, or went out altogether. By a series of slides, or falls, or evolutions more or less disagreeable, the descent through the forest was at length accomplished ; but torrents of formidable character had still to be passed before one could arrive at Zermatt. I felt my way about for hours, almost hopelessly ; by an exhaustive process at last discovering a bridge, and about midnight, covered with dirt and scratches, re-entered the inn which I had quitted in the morning.

Others besides tourists got into difficulties. A day or two afterwards, when on the way to my old station,

near the Hornli, I met a stout curé who had essayed to cross the Theodule pass. His strength or his wind had failed, and he was being carried down, a helpless bundle and a ridiculous spectacle, on the back of a lanky guide, while the peasants stood by with folded hands, their reverence for the church almost overcome by their sense of the ludicrous.

I descended the valley, diverging from the path at Randa to mount the slopes of the Dom,* in order to see the Weisshorn face to face. The latter mountain is the noblest in Switzerland, and

* The highest of the Mischabelhörner.

from this direction it looks especially magnificent. On its north there is a large snowy plateau that feeds the glacier of which a portion is seen from Randa, and which on more than one occasion has destroyed that village. From the direction of the Dom— that is, immediately opposite, this Bies glacier[*] seems to descend nearly vertically ; it does not do so, although it is very steep. Its size is much less than formerly, and the lower portion, now divided into three tails, clings in a strange, weird-like manner to the cliffs, to which it seems scarcely possible that it can remain attached.

Unwillingly I parted from the sight of this glorious mountain, and went down to Visp. A party of English tourists had passed up the valley a short time before with a mule. The party numbered nine— eight young women and a governess. The mule carried their luggage, and was ridden by each in turn. The peasants— themselves not unaccustomed to overload their beasts—were struck with astonishment at the unwonted sight, and made comments, more free than welcome to English ears, on the nonchalance with which young miss sat, calm and collected, on the miserable beast, while it was struggling under her weight, combined with that of the luggage. The story was often repeated ; and it tends to sustain some of the hard things which have been

* Ball's *Alpine Guide* speaks of this incorrectly as the small Bies glacier. It is about half-a-mile wide.

said of late about young ladies from the ages of twelve or fourteen to eighteen.

Arriving once more in the Rhone Valley, I proceeded to Viesch, and from thence ascended the Eggischorn; on which unpleasant eminence I lost my way in a fog, and my temper shortly afterwards. Then, after crossing the Grimsel in a severe thunderstorm, passed on to Brienz, Interlachen, and Bern; and thence to Fribourg and Morat, Neuchâtel, Martigny, and the St. Bernard. The massive walls of the convent were a welcome sight as I waded through the snow-beds near the summit of the pass,

 and pleasant also was the courteous salutation of the brother who bade me enter. He wondered at the weight of my knapsack, and I at the hardness of their bread. The saying that the monks make the toast in the winter that they give to tourists in the following season is not founded on truth; the winter is their most busy time of the year. But it *is* true they have exercised so much hospitality, that at times they have not possessed the means to furnish the fuel for heating their chapel in the winter.*

Instead of descending to Aosta, I turned aside into the Val Pelline, in order to obtain views of the Dent d'Erin. The night had come on before Biona was gained, and I had to knock long and loud upon the door of the curé's house before it was opened. An old woman, with querulous voice, and with a large goître, answered the summons, and demanded rather sharply what was wanted; but became pacific—almost good-natured—when a five-franc piece was held in her face, and she heard that lodging and supper were requested in exchange.

* The temperature at the St. Bernard in the winter is frequently 40° Fahr. below freezing point. January is their coldest month. See Dollfus-Ausset's *Matériaux pour l'étude des Glaciers,* vols. vi. and vii.

My directions asserted that a passage existed from Prerayen, at the head of this valley, to Breuil,* in the Val Tournanche, and the old woman, now convinced of my respectability, busied herself to find a guide. Presently she introduced a native, picturesquely attired in high-peaked hat, braided jacket, scarlet waistcoat, and indigo pantaloons, who agreed to take me to the village of Val Tournanche. We set off early on the next morning, and got to the summit of the pass without difficulty. It gave me my first experience of considerable slopes of hard steep snow, and, like all beginners, I endeavoured to prop myself up with my stick, and kept it *outside,* instead of holding it between myself and the slope, and leaning upon it, as should have been done. The man enlightened me ; but he had, properly, a very small opinion of his employer, and it is probably on that account that, a few minutes after we had passed the summit, he said he would not go any further and would return to Biona. All argument was useless; he stood still, and to everything that was said answered nothing but that he would go back. Being rather nervous about descending some long snow-slopes, which still intervened between us and the head of the valley, I offered more pay, and he went on a little way. Presently there were some cliffs down which we had to scramble. He called to me to stop, then shouted that he would go back, and beckoned to me to come up. On the contrary, I waited for him to come down ; but instead of doing so, in a second or two he turned round, clambered deliberately up the cliff, and vanished. I supposed it was only a ruse to extort offers of more money, and waited for half-an-hour, but he did not appear again. This was rather embarrassing, for he carried off my knapsack. The choice of action lay between chasing him and going on to Breuil, risking the loss of my knapsack. I chose the latter course, and got to Breuil the same evening. The landlord of the inn, suspicious of a person entirely innocent of luggage, was doubtful if he could admit me, and eventually thrust me into a kind of loft, which was already oc-

* There was not a pass between Prerayen and Breuil. See note to chap. vi.

cupied by guides and by hay.   In later years we became good
friends, and he did not hesitate to give credit and even to advance
considerable sums.

My sketches from Breuil were made under difficulties ; my
materials had been carried off—nothing better than fine sugar-
paper could be obtained, and the pencils seemed to contain more
silica than plumbago.   However, they *were* made, and the pass*
was again crossed, this time alone.   By the following evening the
old woman of Biona again produced the faithless guide.   The
knapsack was recovered after the lapse of several hours, and then
I poured forth all the terms of abuse and reproach of which I was
master.   The man smiled when called a liar, and shrugged his
shoulders when referred to as a thief, but drew his knife when
spoken of as a pig.

The following night was spent at Cormayeur, and the day after
I crossed the Col Ferrex to Orsières, and on the next the Tête
Noir to Chamounix.   The Emperor Napoleon arrived the same
day, and access to the Mer de Glace was refused to tourists ; but,
by scrambling along the Plan des Aiguilles, I managed to outwit
the guards, and to arrive at the Montanvert as the Imperial party
was leaving : the same afternoon failing to get to the Jardin, but
very nearly succeeding in breaking a leg by dislodging great rocks
on the moraine of the glacier.

From Chamounix I went to Geneva, and thence by the Mont
Cenis to Turin and to the Vaudois valleys.   A long and weary day
had ended when Paesana was reached.   The inn was full, and I
was tired, and about to go to bed, when some village stragglers
entered and began to sing.   They sang to Garibaldi !   The tenor,
a ragged fellow, whose clothes were not worth a shilling, took the
lead with wonderful expression and feeling.   The others kept their

---

* This pass is called usually the Va Cornère.   It is also known as the Gra
Cornère ; which is, I believe, patois for Grand Cornier.   It is mentioned in the first
volume of the second series of *Peaks, Passes, and Glaciers,* and in chapters six and
twenty of this volume.

places, and sang in admirable time.   For hours I sat enchanted ;
and, long after I retired, the sound of their melody could be
heard, relieved at times by the treble of the girl who belonged to
the inn.

GARIBALDI !

The next morning I passed the little lakes, which are the
sources of the Po, on my way into France.   The weather was
stormy, and misinterpreting the patois of some natives—who in
reality pointed out the right way—I missed the track, and found
myself under the cliffs of Monte Viso.   A gap that was occasionally seen, in the ridge connecting it with the mountains to the
east, tempted me up ; and, after a battle with a snow-slope of
excessive steepness, I reached the summit.   The scene was extraordinary, and, in my experience, unique.   To the north there was
not a particle of mist, and the violent wind coming from that
direction blew one back staggering.   But on the side of Italy, the
valleys were completely filled with dense masses of cloud to a
certain level ; and there—where they felt the influence of the
wind—they were cut off as level as the top of a table, the ridges
appearing above them.

I raced down to Abries, and went on through the gorge of the
Guil to Mont Dauphin.   The next day found me at La Bessée, at
the junction of the Val Louise with the Valley of the Durance,
in full view of Mont Pelvoux ; and by chance I walked into a

cabaret where a Frenchman was breakfasting, who, a few days before, had made an unsuccessful attempt to ascend that mountain with three Englishmen and the guide Michel Croz of Chamounix ;* a right good fellow, by name Jean Reynaud.

The same night I slept at Briançon, intending to take the courier on the following day to Grenoble ; but all places had been secured several days beforehand, so I set out at two P.M. on the next day for a seventy-mile walk. The weather was again bad ; and on the summit of the Col de Lautaret I was forced to seek shelter in the wretched little hospice. It was filled with workmen who were employed on the road, and with noxious vapours which proceeded from them. The inclemency of the weather was preferable to the inhospitality of the interior. Outside, it was disagreeable, but grand ; inside, it was disagreeable and mean.† The walk was continued under a deluge of rain, and I felt the way down—so intense was the darkness—to the village of La Grave, where the people of the inn detained me forcibly. It was perhaps fortunate that they did so ; for, during that night, blocks of rock fell at several places from the cliffs on to the road with such force that they made large holes in the macadam, which looked as if there had been explosions of gunpowder. I resumed the walk at half-past five the next morning, and proceeded, under steady rain, through Bourg d'Oysans to Grenoble, arriving at the latter place soon after seven P.M., having accomplished the entire distance from Briançon in about eighteen hours of actual walking.

This was the end of the Alpine portion of my tour of 1860, on which I was introduced to the great peaks, and acquired the passion for mountain-scrambling, the development of which is described in the following chapters.

---

* It was to illustrate this ascent that I had been sent to the Val Louise.

† Since that time a decent house has been built on the summit of this pass. The old vaulted hospice was erected for the benefit of the pilgrims who formerly crossed the pass *en route* for Rome.—Joanne's *Itinéraire du Dauphiné.*

BRIANÇON.

CHAPTER II.

THE ASCENT OF MONT PELVOUX.

"Thus fortune on our first endeavour smiles."
VIRGIL.

THE district of which Mont Pelvoux and the neighbouring summits are the culminating points,* is, both historically and topographically, one of the most interesting in the Alps.   As the nursery and the home of the Vaudois, it has claims to permanent attention: the names of Waldo and of Neff will be remembered when men

* See the map in chap. ix., and the general map.

more famous in their time will be forgotten; and the memory of the heroic courage and the simple piety of their disciples will endure as long as history lasts.

This district contains the highest summits in France, and some of its finest scenery. It has not perhaps the beauties of Switzerland, but has charms of its own; its cliffs, its torrents, and its gorges are unsurpassed; its deep and savage valleys present pictures of grandeur, and even sublimity, and it is second to none in the boldness of its mountain forms.

The district includes a mass of valleys which vie with each other in singularity of character and dissimilarity of climate. Some the rays of the sun can never reach, they are so deep and narrow.* In others the very antipodes may be found; the temperature more like that of the plains of Italy than of Alpine France. This great range of climate has a marked effect on the flora of these valleys: sterility reigns in some; stones take the place of trees; débris and mud replace plants and flowers: in others, in the space of a few miles, one passes vines, apple, pear, and cherry trees, the birch, alder, walnut, ash, larch, and pine, alternating with fields of rye, barley, oats, beans, and potatoes.

The valleys are for the most part short and erratic. They are not, apparently, arranged on any definite plan; they are not disposed, as is frequently the case elsewhere, either at right angles to, or parallel with, the highest summits; but they wander hither and thither, taking one direction for a few miles, then doubling back, and then perhaps resuming their original course. Thus, long perspectives are rarely to be seen, and it is difficult to form a general idea of the disposition of the peaks.

The highest summits are arranged almost in a horse-shoe form. The highest of all, which occupies a central position, is the Pointe

---

* The depth of the valleys is so great that the sun not only is not seen for more than a few hours per day during the greatest portion of the year, but in some places —at Villard d'Arène and at Andrieux for example—it is not seen at all for one hundred days.—Ladoucette's *Hautes-Alpes*, p. 599.

des Ecrins ; the second in height, the Meije,* is on the north ; and the Mont Pelvoux, which gives its name to the entire block, stands almost detached by itself on the outside.

The district is still very imperfectly known ; there are probably many valleys, and there are certainly many summits which have never been trodden by the feet of tourists or travellers ; but in 1861 it was even less known. Until quite recently there was, practically, no map of it ;† General Bourcet's, which was the best that was published, was completely wrong in its delineation of the mountains, and was frequently incorrect in regard to paths or roads.

The mountainous regions of Dauphiné, moreover, are not supplied, like Switzerland, the Tyrol, or even the Italian valleys, with accommodation for travellers. The inns, when they exist, are filthy to an indescribable extent ; rest is seldom obtained in their beds, or decent food found in their kitchens, and guides there are none. The tourist is thrown very much on his own resources, and it is not therefore surprising that these districts are less visited and less known than the rest of the Alps.

Most of the statements current in 1861 respecting these mountains had been derived from two authors ‡—M. Elie de Beaumont

* Sometimes called the Aiguille du Midi de la Grave, or the Aiguille de la Medje.

† The maps of the Dauphiné Alps to Ball's *Guide to the Western Alps*, and to Joanne's *Itinéraire du Dauphiné* (both engraved from the unpublished sheets of the map of France) must be excepted. These maps are, however, on too small a scale for travelling purposes.

‡ " Faits pour servir à l'Histoire des Montagnes de l'Oisans," by Elie de Beaumont, in the *Annales des Mines.*

Norway and its Glaciers ; followed by Excursions in the High Alps of Dauphiné. By J. D. Forbes.

The following works also treat more or less of the districts referred to in this chapter :—

Histoire des Hautes-Alps, by J. C. F. Ladoucette.

Itinéraire du Dauphiné, by Adolphe Joanne (2d part).

Tour du Monde, 1860, edited by Ed. Charton.

The Israel of the Alps, by Alexis Muston.

A Memoir of Felix Neff, by W. S. Gilly.

Good pictures of Dauphiné scenery are to be found in *Voyages Pittoresques dans*

and the late Principal J. D. Forbes. Their works, however, contained numerous errors in regard to the identification of the peaks, and, amongst others, they referred the supremacy to the Mont Pelvoux, the highest point of which they termed the Pointe des Arcines, or des Ecrins. Principal Forbes erroneously identified the high peak seen from the valley of St. Christophe, with that seen from the valley of the Durance, and spoke of both as the Mont Pelvoux, and M. de Beaumont committed similar mistakes. In point of fact, at the time when M. de Beaumont and Forbes wrote their respective memoirs, the proper relation of the Mont Pelvoux to the neighbouring summits had been determined by the engineers employed on the survey for the map of France, but their observations were not then accessible to the public, although they had evidently been seen by M. de Beaumont. This party of surveyors, led by Captain Durand, made the ascent of Mont Pelvoux from the side of the Val d'Ailefroide—that is, from the direction of Val Louise—in 1828. According to the natives of the Val Louise, they got to the top of the second peak in height, and remained upon it, lodged in a tent for several days, at a height of 12,904 feet. They took numerous porters to carry wood for fires, and erected a large cairn on the summit, which has caused the name of Pic de la Pyramide to be given to their summit.

In 1848, M. Puiseux made the ascent from the same direction, but his Val Louisan guide stopped short of the summit, and allowed this courageous astronomer to proceed by himself.[*]

In the middle of August 1860, Messrs. Bonney, Hawkshaw, and Mathews, with Michel Croz of Chamounix, tried to ascend the Pelvoux, likewise from the same direction. These gentlemen spent

l'ancienne France, by Ch. Nodier, J. Taylor, and A. de Cailleux, and in Lord Monson's *Views in the Departments of the Isère and the High Alps.*

[*] M. Puiseux took for guide a man named Pierre Bornéoud, of Claux in the Val Louise; who had accompanied Captain Durand in 1828. In 1861, the expedition of M. Puiseux was quite forgotten in the Val Louise. I am indebted to M. Puiseux for the above and other details.

several days and nights upon the mountain; and, encountering bad weather, only attained a height of 10,430 feet.

M. Jean Reynaud, of whom mention has been made in the preceding chapter, accompanied the party of Mr. Mathews, and he was of opinion that the attempt had been made too late in the season. He said that the weather was usually good enough for high mountain ascents *only* during the last few days of July, and the first ones of August,* and suggested that we should attempt to ascend the mountain in the following year at that time. The proposition was a tempting one, and Reynaud's cordial and modest manner made it irresistible, although there seemed small chance that we should succeed where a party such as that of Mr. Mathews had been beaten.

At the beginning of July 1861, I despatched to Reynaud from Havre, blankets (which were taxed as "prohibited fabrics"), rope, and other things desirable for the excursion, and set out on the tour of France; but, four weeks later, at Nîmes, found myself completely collapsed by the heat, then 94° Faht. in the shade, so I took a night train at once to Grenoble.

Grenoble is a town upon which a volume might be written. Its situation is probably the finest of any in France, and the views from its high forts are superb. The most noteworthy institution of the town is one which has acquired a deserved celebrity†—the Association Alimentaire. This institution, which was started nearly twenty years ago by some of the well-to-do inhabitants, was founded with the express object of giving to the working or needy population better food, better cooked and at a lower price, than could be

---

* This is a common saying in Dauphiné. It means that there is usually less snow on the mountains during these days than at any other time of the year. The natives have an almost childish dread of venturing upon snow or glaciers, and hence the period of minimum snow seems to them to be the most favourable time for excursions.

† "The model institution of the kind in France is admitted to be the 'Association Alimentaire' of Grenoble."—*Ten years of Imperialism in France;* Blackwood, 1862.

obtained at restaurants or at their own homes. Here the inhabitant of Grenoble can obtain a dinner of a quart of soup, meat or fish, vegetables, dessert, bread, and a quarter of a litre of sound wine, for the sum of sixpence halfpenny. Membership is acquired by the payment of a small sum—I believe two francs ; but dinner-tickets must be bought in advance, and no credit is given. The lower orders have not been slow in recognising the advantages to be derived from connection with the Association Alimentaire, which is said to have produced the happiest results among them. It is creditable to the management that this institution not only pays its expenses, but yields a small profit.

Although Grenoble may fairly be proud of this association, in other matters it has cause to be ashamed. Its streets are narrow, ill-paved, and tortuous; and its smells, and the improprieties to be seen in its houses, must be known to be appreciated.*

I lost my way in the streets of this picturesque but noisesome town, and having but a half-hour left in which to get a dinner and take a place in the diligence, was not well pleased to hear that an Englishman wished to see me. It turned out to be my friend Macdonald, who confided to me that he was going to try to ascend a mountain called Pelvoux in the course of ten days; but, on hearing of my intentions, agreed to join us at La Bessée on the 3d of August. In a few moments more I was perched in the banquette *en route* for Bourg d'Oysans, in a miserable vehicle which took nearly eight hours to accomplish less than 30 miles.

At five on a lovely morning I shouldered my knapsack and started for Briançon. Gauzy mists clung to the mountains, but melted away when touched by the sun, and disappeared by jerks (in the manner of views when focussed in a magic lantern), re-

* " Les maisons sont beaucoup plus malpropres que les rues. La plupart des allées et des escaliers ressemblent à des dépôts publics d'immondices. Dans la vieille ville, les maisons n'ont pas de concierge. Les habitants de la ville, affligés de déplorables habitudes, y entrent incessament sans scruple et sans pudeur, et rarement les propiétaires ou les locataires s'associent entre eux pour faire disparaître les ordures qui déshonorent leur demeure."—Joanne's *Itinéraire du Dauphiné*, vol. i. p. 118.

vealing the wonderfully bent and folded strata in the limestone cliffs behind the town.   Then I entered the Combe de Malval, and heard the Romanche eating its way through that wonderful gorge, and passed on to Le Dauphin, where the first glacier came into view, tailing over the mountain side on the right.   From this place until the summit of the Col de Lantaret was passed, every gap in the mountains showed a glittering glacier or a soaring peak ; the finest view was at La Grave, where the Meije rises by a series of tremendous precipices 8000 feet above the road.*   The finest distant view of the pass is seen after crossing the Col, near Monêtier. A mountain, commonly supposed to be Monte Viso, appears at the end of the vista, shooting into the sky ;† in the middle distance, but still ten miles off, is Briançon with its interminable forts, and in the foreground, leading down to the Guisane, and rising high up the neighbouring slopes, are fertile fields, studded with villages and church spires.   The next day I walked over from Briançon to La Bessée, to my worthy friend Jean Reynaud, the surveyor of roads of his district.

All the peaks of Mont Pelvoux are well seen from La Bessée, the highest point, as well as that upon which the engineers erected their cairn.   Neither Reynaud nor any one else knew this.   The natives knew only that the engineers had ascended one peak, and had seen from that a still higher point, which they called the Pointe des Arcines or des Ecrins.   They could not say whether this latter could be seen from La Bessée, nor could they tell the peak upon which the cairn had been erected.   We were under the impression that the highest point was concealed by the peaks we saw, and would be gained by passing over them.   They knew nothing of the ascent of Monsieur Puiseux, and they confidently asserted that the highest point of Mont Pelvoux had not been attained by any one ; it was this point we wished to reach.

* See chapter viii.

† Monte Viso is not seen from the Lautaret Road.   That this is so is seen when one crosses the Col du Galibier, on the south side of which pass the Monte Viso is visible for a short time.

Nothing prevented our starting at once but the absence of Macdonald and the want of a bâton. Reynaud suggested a visit to the postmaster, who possessed a bâton of local celebrity. Down we went to the bureau; but it was closed : we hallooed through the slits, but no answer. At last the postmaster was discovered endeavouring (with very fair success) to make himself intoxicated. He was just able to ejaculate, " France ! 'tis the first nation in the

MONT PELVOUX FROM ABOVE LA BESSÉE.

world !" which is a phrase used by a Frenchman when in the state that a Briton begins to shout, " We won't go home till morning "— national glory being uppermost in the thoughts of one, and home in those of the other. The bâton was produced ; it was a branch of a young oak, about five feet long, gnarled and twisted in several directions. " Sir," said the postmaster, as he presented it, " France ! 'tis the first—the first nation in the world, by its "—he stuck. " Bâtons ?" I suggested. " Yes, yes, sir ; by its bâtons, by its— its," and here he could not get on at all. As I looked at this

young limb, I thought of my own ; but Reynaud, who knew
everything about everybody in the village, said there was not a
better one, so off we went with it, leaving the official staggering
in the road and muttering, "France! 'tis the first nation in the
world!"

The 3d of August came, but Macdonald did not appear, so we
started for the Val Louise ; our party consisting of Reynaud, myself, and a porter, Jean Casimir Giraud, nicknamed "little nails,"
the shoemaker of the place.   An hour and a half's smart walking
took us to La Ville de Val Louise, our hearts gladdened by the
glorious peaks of Pelvoux shining out without a cloud around
them.   I renewed acquaintance with the mayor of "La Ville."
His aspect was original, and his manners were gracious, but the
odour which proceeded from him was dreadful.   The same may be
said of most of the inhabitants of these valleys.*

Reynaud kindly undertook to look after the commissariat, and
I found to my annoyance, when we were about to leave, that I had
given tacit consent to a small wine-cask being carried with us,
which was a great nuisance from the commencement.   It was excessively awkward to handle ; one man tried to carry it, and then
another, and at last it was slung from one of our bâtons, and was
carried by two, which gave our party the appearance of a mechanical diagram to illustrate the uses of levers.

* Their late préfet shall tell why.   "The men and women dress in sheepskins,
—which have been dried and scoured with salt, of which the feet are used as clasps,
the fore feet going round the neck, and the hinder ones round the loins.   Their arms
are naked, and the men are only distinguished from the women by the former wear-
ing wretched drawers, and the latter a sort of gown, which only covers them to just
below the knees.   They sleep without undressing upon straw, and have only sheepskins for coverings. . . . The nature of their food, combined with their dirtiness,
makes them exhale a strong odour from their bodies, which is smelt from afar, and
which is almost insupportable to strangers. . . . They live in a most indifferent
manner, or rather they linger in dreadful misery; their filthy and hideous countenances announce their slovenliness and their stink."—Ladoucette's *Histoire des
Hautes-Alpes*, pp. 656-7.   The sheepskins are now worn only by the poorest of the
natives, but the rest of the description is sufficiently accurate.

At " La Ville " the Val Louise splits into two branches—the Val d'Entraigues on the left and the Vallon d'Alefred (or Ailefroide) on the right ; our route was up the latter, and we moved steadily forwards to the village of La Pisse, where Pierre Sémiond lived, who was reputed to know more about the Pelvoux than any other man. He looked an honest fellow, but unfortunately he was ill and could not come.   He recommended his brother, an aged creature, whose furrowed and wrinkled face hardly seemed to announce the man we wanted ; but having no choice, we engaged him and again set forth.

Walnut and a great variety of other trees gave shadow to our path and fresh vigour to our limbs; while below, in a sublime gorge, thundered the torrent, whose waters took their rise from the snows we hoped to tread on the morrow.

The mountain could not be seen at La Ville, owing to

IN THE VAL D'ALEFRED.

a high intervening ridge ; we were now moving along the foot of this to get to the châlets of Alefred, or, as they are sometimes called, Aléfroide, where the mountain actually commences. From this direction the subordinate, but more proximate peaks appear considerably higher than the loftier ones behind, and

sometimes completely conceal them. But the whole height of the
peak, which in these valleys goes under the name of the "Grand
Pelvoux," is seen at one glance from its summit to its base, six
or seven thousand feet of nearly perpendicular cliffs.

THE GRAND PELVOUX DE VAL LOUISE.

The châlets of Alefred are a cluster of miserable wooden huts
at the foot of the Grand Pelvoux, and are close to the junction of
the streams which descend from the glacier de Sapenière (or du
Selé) on the left, and the glaciers Blanc and Noir on the right.
We rested a minute to purchase some butter and milk, and Sémiond
picked up a disreputable looking lad to assist in carrying, pushing,
and otherwise moving the wine-cask.

Our route now turned sharply to the left, and all were glad that
the day was drawing to a close, so that we had the shadows from
the mountains. A more frightful and desolate valley it is scarcely
possible to imagine; it contains miles of boulders, débris, stones,
sand, and mud; few trees, and they placed so high as to be almost
out of sight; not a soul inhabits it; no birds are in the air, no fish
in its waters; the mountain is too steep for the chamois, its slopes
too inhospitable for the marmot, the whole too repulsive for the
eagle. Not a living thing did we see in this sterile and savage valley

during four days, except some few poor goats which had been driven there against their will.

It was a scene in keeping with the diabolical deed perpetrated here about four hundred years ago—the murder of the Vaudois of Val Louise, in the cavern which was now in sight, though high above us. Their story is very sad. Peaceful and industrious, for more than three centuries they had inhabited these retired valleys in tranquil obscurity. The Archbishops of Embrun endeavoured, but with little success, to get them within the pale of their church ; their efforts were aided by others, who commenced by imprisonments and torture,* and at last adopted the method of burning them by hundreds at the stake.†

In the year 1488, Albert Cattanée, Archdeacon of Cremona and legate of Pope Innocent VIII., would have anticipated the barbarities which at a later date roused the indignation of Milton and the fears of Cromwell ;‡ but, driven everywhere back by the Waldenses of Piedmont, he left their valleys and crossed the Mont Genèvre to attack the weaker and more thinly populated valleys of the Vaudois in Dauphiné. At the head of an army which is said to have been composed of vagabonds, robbers, and assassins (who had been tempted to his banner by promises of absolution beforehand, of being set free from the obligation of vows which they might have made, and by the confirmation of property to them which they might have wrongfully acquired), as well as regular troops, Cattanée poured down the valley of the Durance. The inhabitants of the Val Louise fled before a host that was ten times their number, and took up their abode in this cavern, where they had collected pro-

---

* It became a regular business. " We find amongst the current accounts of the Bailiff of Embrun this singular article—' *Item, for persecuting the Vaudois, eight sols and thirty deniers of gold.'*"—Muston, vol. i. p. 38.

† On the 22d of May 1393, eighty persons of the valleys of Freissinières and Argentière, and one hundred and fifty persons of the Val Louise, were burnt at Embrun.—Muston, vol. i. p. 41.

‡ See Morland's *History of the Evangelical Churches of Piedmont,* 1658 ; Cromwell's *Acts,* 1658 ; and Burton's *Diary,* 1828.

E

visions sufficient for two years. But intolerance is ever pains-taking ; their retreat was discovered. Cattanée had a captain who combined the resources of a Herod to the cruelty of a Pelissier, and, lowering his men by ropes, fired piles of brushwood at the entrance to the cavern, suffocated the majority, and slew the remainder. The Vaudois were relentlessly exterminated, without distinction of age or sex. More than three thousand persons, it is said, perished in this frightful massacre ; the growth of three hundred and fifty years was destroyed at one blow, and the valley was completely depopulated. Louis XII. caused it to be re-peopled, and after another three centuries and a half, behold the result—a race of monkeys.*

We rested a little at a small spring, and then hastened onwards till we nearly arrived at the foot of the Sapenière glacier, when Sémiond said we must turn to the right, up the slopes. This we did, and clambered for half-an-hour through scattered pines and fallen boulders. Then evening began to close in rapidly, and it was time to look for a resting-place. There was no difficulty in getting one, for all around it was a chaotic assemblage of rocks. We selected the under side of one, which was more than fifty feet long by twenty high, cleared it of rubbish, and then collected wood for a fire.

That camp-fire is a pleasant reminiscence. The wine-cask had got through all its troubles ; it was tapped, and the Frenchmen seemed to derive some consolation from its execrable contents. Reynaud chanted scraps of French songs, and each contributed his

---

* The commune of the Val Louise contains at the present time about 3400 inhabi-tants. This cretin population has been aptly described by M. Elisée Reclus in the Tour du Monde, 1860. He says—"They attain the highest possible development of their intelligence in their infancy, and—abundantly provided with majestic goîtres, which are lengthened and swollen by age—are in this respect like to the ourang-outangs, who have nothing more to acquire after the age of three years. At the age of five years the little cretins have already the placid and mature expression which they ought to keep all their lives. . . . They wear trousers, and coats with tails, and a large black hat."

share of joke, story, or verse. The weather was perfect, and our prospects for the morrow were good. My companions' joy culminated when a packet of red fire was thrown into the flames. It hissed and bubbled for a moment or two, and then broke out into a grand flare. The effect of the momentary light was magnificent; all around the mountains were illuminated for a second, and then relapsed into their solemn gloom. One by one our party dropped off to sleep, and at last I got into my blanket-bag. It was hardly necessary, for, although we were at a height of at least 7000 feet, the minimum temperature was above 40° Fahrenheit.

We roused at three, but did not start till half-past four. Giraud had been engaged as far as this rock only, but as he wished to go on, we allowed him to accompany us. We mounted the slopes and quickly got above the trees, then had a couple of hours' clambering over bits of precipitous rock and banks of *débris*, and, at a quarter to seven, got to a narrow glacier—Clos de l'Homme—which streamed out of the plateau on the summit, and nearly reached the glacier de Sapenière. We worked as much as possible to the right, in hopes that we should not have to cross it, but were continually driven back, and at last we found that it was necessary to do so. Old Sémiond had a strong objection to the ice, and made explorations on his own account to endeavour to avoid it; but Reynaud and I preferred to cross it, and Giraud stuck to us. It was narrow—in fact, one could throw a stone across it—and was easily mounted on the side; but in the centre swelled into a steep dome, up which we were obliged to cut. Giraud stepped forward and said he should like to try his hand, and having got hold of the axe, would not give it up; and here, as well as afterwards when it was necessary to cross the gullies filled with hard snow, which abound on the higher part of the mountain, he did all the work, and did it admirably.

Old Sémiond of course came after us when we got across. We then zigzagged up some snow-slopes, and shortly afterwards commenced to ascend the interminable array of buttresses which are the great peculiarity of the Pelvoux.* They were very steep in many places, but on the whole afforded good hold, and no climbing should be called difficult which does that. Gullies abounded among them, sometimes of great length and depth. *They* were frequently rotten, and would have been difficult for a single man to pass. The uppermost men were continually abused for dislodging rocks and for harpooning those below with their batons. However, without these incidents the climbing would have been dull—they helped to break the monotony.

We went up chimneys and gullies by the hour together, and always seemed to be coming to something, although we never got to it. The outline sketch will help to explain the situation. We stood at the foot of a great buttress—perhaps about 200 feet high—and looked up. It did not go to a point as in the diagram, because we could not see the top; although we felt convinced that behind the fringe of pinnacles we did see there was a top, and that it was the

BUTTRESSES OF MONT PELVOUX.

edge of the plateau we so much desired to attain. Up we mounted, and reached the pinnacles; but, lo! another set was seen,—and another,—and yet more—till at last we reached the top, and found it was only a buttress, and that we had to descend 40 or 50 feet before we could commence to mount again. When this operation had been performed a few dozen times it began to be wearisome, especially as we were in the dark as to our whereabouts. Sémiond, however, encouraged us, and said he knew we were on the right route,—so away we went once more.

It was now nearly mid-day, and we seemed no nearer the summit of the Pelvoux than when we started. At last we all joined

---

* "The nucleus of the 'massif' is a fine protogine, divided by nearly vertical cracks."—*Dollfus-Ausset.*

together and held a council. "Sémiond, old friend, do you know where we are now?" "Oh yes, perfectly, to a yard and a half." "Well, then, how much are we below this plateau?" He affirmed we were not half-an-hour from the edge of the snow. "Very good; let us proceed." Half-an-hour passed, and then another, but we were still in the same state,—pinnacles, buttresses, and gullies were in profusion, but the plateau was not in sight. So we called him again—for he had been staring about latterly, as if in doubt—and repeated the question. "How far below are we now?" Well, he thought it might be half-an-hour more. "But you said that just now; are you sure we are going right?" "Yes, he believed we were." Believed! that would not do. "Are you sure we are going right for the Pie des Arcines?" "Pie des Arcines!" he ejaculated in astonishment, as if he had heard the words for the first time. "Pie des Arcines; no! but for the pyramid, the celebrated pyramid he had helped the great Capitaine Durand," etc.

Here was a fix;—we had been talking about it to him for a whole day, and now he confessed he knew nothing about it. I turned to Reynaud, who seemed thunderstruck. "What did he suggest?" He shrugged his shoulders. "Well," we said, after explaining our minds pretty freely to Sémiond, "the sooner we turn back the better, for we have no wish to see your pyramid."

We halted for an hour, and then commenced the descent. It took us nearly seven hours to come down to our rock; but I paid no heed to the distance, and do not remember anything about it. When we got down we made a discovery which affected us as much as the footprint in the sand did Robinson Crusoe: a blue silk veil lay by our fireside. There was but one solution,—Macdonald had arrived; but where was he? We soon packed our baggage, and tramped in the dusk, through the stony desert, to Alefred, where we arrived about half-past nine. "Where is the Englishman?" was the first question. He was gone to sleep at La Ville.

We passed that night in a hay-loft, and in the morning, after settling with Sémiond, we posted down to catch Macdonald. We

had already determined on the plan of operation, which was to get him
to join us, return, and be independent of all guides, simply taking
the best man we could get as a porter. I set my heart on Giraud,—
a good fellow, with no pretence, although in every respect up to the
work. But we were disappointed; he was obliged to go to Briançon.

The walk soon became exciting. The natives inquired the
result of our expedition, and common civility obliged us to stop.
But I was afraid of losing my man, for it was said he would wait
only till ten o'clock, and that time was near at hand. At last I
dashed over the bridge,—time from Alefred an hour and a quarter ;
but a cantonnier stopped me, saying that the Englishman had just
started for La Bessée. I rushed after him, turned angle after angle
of the road, but could not see him ; at last, as I came round a corner, he was also just turning another, going very fast. I shouted,
and luckily he heard me. We returned, re-provisioned ourselves
at La Ville, and the same evening saw us passing our first rock, *en
route* for another. I have said we determined to take no guide ;
but, on passing La Pisse, old Sémiond turned out and offered his
services. He went well, in spite of his years and disregard of
truth. "Why not take him?" said my friend. So we offered him
a fifth of his previous pay, and in a few seconds he closed with the
offer ; but this time came in an inferior position,—we were to lead,
he to follow. Our second follower was a youth of twenty-seven
years, who was not all that could be desired. He drank Reynaud's
wine, smoked our cigars, and quietly secreted the provisions when
we were nearly starving. Discovery of his proceedings did not at
all disconcert him, and he finished up by getting several items
added to our bill at La Ville, which, not a little to his disgust, we
disallowed.

This night we fixed our camp high above the tree line, and
indulged ourselves in the healthy employment of carrying our fuel
up to it. The present rock was not so comfortable as the first, and,
before we could settle down, we were obliged to turn out a large
mass which was in the way. It was very obstinate, but moved at

length ; slowly and gently at first, then faster and faster, at last taking great jumps in the air, striking a stream of fire at every touch, which shone out brightly as it entered the gloomy valley below, and long after it was out of sight we heard it bounding downwards, and then settle with a subdued crash on the glacier beneath. As we turned back from this curious sight, Reynaud asked if we had ever seen a torrent on fire, and told us that in the spring, the Durance, swollen by the melting of the snow, sometimes brings down so many rocks, that, where it passes through a narrow gorge at La Bessée, no water whatever is seen, but only boulders rolling over and over, grinding each other into powder, and striking so many sparks that the stream looks as if it were on fire.

We had another merry evening with nothing to mar it ; the weather was perfect, and we lay backward in luxurious repose, looking at the sky spangled with its ten thousand brilliant lights.

> . . . . "The ranges stood
> Transfigured in the silver flood,
> Their snows were flashing cold and keen,
> Dead white, save where some sharp ravine
> Took shadow, or the sombre green
> Of hemlocks turned to pitchy black,
> Against the whiteness at their back."*

Macdonald related his experiences over the café noir. He had travelled day and night for several days in order to join us, but had failed to find our first bivouac, and had camped a few hundred yards from us under another rock, higher up the mountain. The next morning he discerned us going along a ridge at a great height above him, and as it was useless to endeavour to overtake us, he lay down and watched with a heavy heart until we had turned the corner of a buttress, and vanished out of sight.

* J. G. Whittier, "Snow-Bound."

Nothing but the heavy breathing of our already sound asleep comrades broke the solemn stillness of the night.   It was a silence to be felt.   Nothing?   Hark! what is that dull booming sound above us?   Is that nothing?   There it is again, plainer—on it comes, nearer, clearer ; 'tis a crag escaped from the heights above! What a fearful crash!   We jump to our feet.   Down it comes with awful fury ; what power can withstand its violence?   Dancing, leaping, flying ; dashing against others ; roaring as it descends. Ah, it has passed!   No ; there it is again, and we hold our breath, as, with resistless force and explosions like artillery, it darts past, with an avalanche of shattered fragments trailing in its rear!   'Tis gone, and we breathe more freely as we hear the finale on the glacier below.*

We retired at last, but I was too excited to sleep.   At a quarter-past four every man once more shouldered his pack and started. This time we agreed to keep more to the right, to see if it were not possible to get to the plateau without losing any time by crossing the glacier.   To describe our route would be to repeat what has been said before.   We mounted steadily for an hour and a half, sometimes walking, but more frequently climbing, and then found, after all, that it was necessary to cross the glacier.   The part on which we struck came down a very steep slope, and was much crevassed.   The word crevassed hardly expresses its appearance—it was a mass of formid-able séracs.   We found, however, more difficulty in getting on than across it ; but, thanks to the rope, it was passed somehow ; then the interminable buttresses began again.   Hour after hour we proceeded upwards, frequently at fault, and obliged to descend.   The ridge behind us had sunk long ago, and we looked over it, and all others, till our eyes rested on the majestic Viso.   Hour after hour passed, and monotony was the order of the day ; when twelve o'clock came we lunched, and contemplated the scene with satisfaction ; all the

---

* M. Puiseux, on his expedition of 1848, was surprised, when at breakfast on the side of the mountain, by a mass of rock of more than a cubic yard falling like a bomb at his side, which threw up splinters in all directions.

summits in sight, with the single exception of the Viso, had given
in, and we looked over an immense expanse—a perfect sea of peaks
and snow-fields.   Still the pinnacles rose above us, and opinions
were freely uttered that we should see no summit of Pelvoux that
day.   Old Sémiond had become a perfect bore to all ; whenever
one rested for a moment to look about, he would say, with a com-
placent chuckle, "Don't be afraid, follow me."   We came at last to

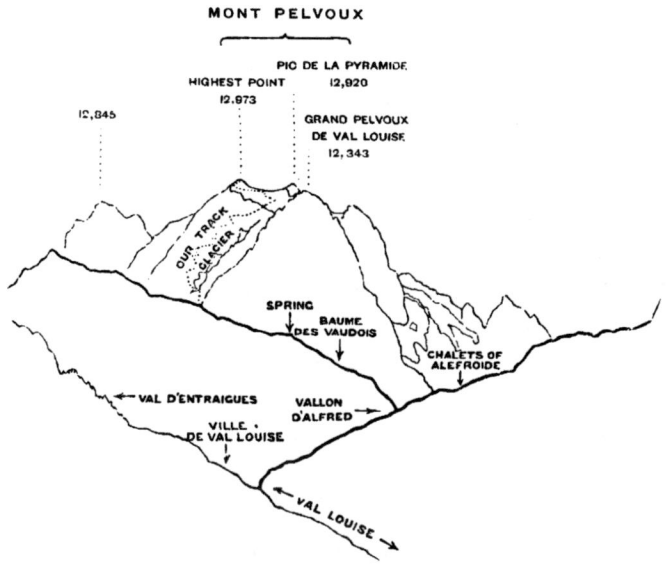

a very bad piece, rotten and steep, and no hold.   Here Reynaud
and Macdonald confessed to being tired, and talked of going to
sleep.   A way was discovered out of the difficulty ; then some one
called out, "Look at the Viso," and we saw that we almost looked
over it.   We worked away with redoubled energy, and at length
caught sight of the head of the glacier as it streamed out of the
plateau.   This gave us fresh hopes ; we were not deceived ; and
with a simultaneous shout we greeted the appearance of our long-
wished-for snows.   A large crevasse separated us from them ; but
a bridge was found ; we tied ourselves in line, and moved safely
over it.   Directly we got across there rose before us a fine snow-

F

capped peak. Old Sémiond cried, "The pyramid! I see the pyramid!" "Where, Sémiond, where?" "There; on the top of that peak."

There, sure enough, was the cairn he had helped to erect more than thirty years before. But where was the Pic des Arcines which we were to see? It was nowhere visible, but only a great expanse of snow, bordered by three lower peaks. Somewhat sadly we moved towards the pyramid, sighing that there was no other to conquer; but hardly had we gone two hundred paces, before there rose a superb white cone on the left, which had been hidden before by a slope of snow. We shouted—"The Pic des Arcines!" and inquired of Sémiond if he knew whether that peak had been ascended. As for him, he knew nothing, except that the peak before us was called the pyramid, from the cairn he had, etc. etc., and that it had not been ascended since. "All right then—face about," and we immediately turned at right angles for the cone, the porter making faint struggles for his beloved pyramid. Our progress was stopped, in the sixth of a mile, by the edge of the ridge connecting the two peaks, and we perceived that it curled over in a lovely volute. We involuntarily retreated. Sémiond, who was last in the line, took the opportunity to untie himself, and refused to come on; said we were running dangerous risks, and talked vaguely of crevasses. We tied him up again, and proceeded. The snow was very soft; we were always knee-deep, and sometimes floundered in up to the waist; but a simultaneous jerk before and behind always released one. By this time we had arrived at the foot of the final peak. The left-hand ridge seemed easier than that upon which we stood, so we curved round to get to it. Some rocks peeped out 150 feet below the summit, and up these we crawled, leaving our porter behind, as he said he was afraid. I could not resist the temptation, as we went off, to turn round and beckon him onwards, saying, "Don't be afraid—follow me," but he did not answer to the appeal, and never went to the top. The rocks led to a short ridge of ice—our plateau on one side, and a nearly vertical

ALÉFROIDE
(12,878?)

PIC SANS NOM
(12,845)

MONT PELVOUX
(12,973)

THE DURANCE.

MONT PELVOUX AND THE ALEFROIDE, FROM NEAR MONT-DAUPHIN, IN THE VALLEY OF THE DURANCE.

precipice on the other. Macdonald cut up it, and at a quarter to two we stood shaking hands on the loftiest summit of the conquered Pelvoux.

The day still continued everything that could be desired, and, far and near, countless peaks burst into sight, without a cloud to hide them. The mighty Mont Blanc, full seventy miles away, first caught our eyes, and then, still farther off, the Monte Rosa group; while, rolling away to the east, one unknown range after another succeeded in unveiled splendour; fainter and fainter in tone, but still perfectly defined, till at last the eye was unable to distinguish sky from mountain, and they died away in the far-off horizon. Monte Viso rose up grandly, but it was less than forty miles away, and we looked over it to a hazy mass we knew must be the plains of Piedmont. Southwards a blue mist seemed to indicate the existence of the distant Mediterranean; to the west we looked over to the mountains of Auvergne. Such was the panorama; a view extending in nearly every direction for more than one hundred miles. It was with some difficulty we wrenched our eyes from the more distant objects to contemplate the nearer ones. Mont Dauphin was very conspicuous, but La Bessée was not readily perceived. Besides these not a human habitation could be seen; all was rock, snow, or ice; and, large as we knew were the snow-fields of Dauphiné, we were surprised to find that they very far surpassed our most ardent imagination. Nearly in a line between us and the Viso, immediately to the south of Chateau Queyras, was a splendid group of mountains of great height. More to the south an unknown peak seemed still higher; while close to us we were astonished to discover that there was a mountain which appeared even higher than that on which we stood. At least this was my opinion; Macdonald thought it not so high, and Reynaud much about the same as our own.

This mountain was distant a couple of miles or so, and was separated from us by a tremendous abyss, the bottom of which we could not see. On the other side rose this mighty wall-sided peak, too steep for snow, black as night, with sharp ridges and pointed summit. We were in complete ignorance of its whereabouts, for none of us had been on the other side; we imagined that La Bérarde was in the abyss at our feet, but it was in reality beyond the other mountain.*

We left the summit at last, and descended to the rocks and to our porter, where I boiled some water, obtained by melting snow. After we had fed, and smoked our cigars (lighted without difficulty from a common match), we found it was ten minutes past three, and high time to be off. We dashed, waded, and tumbled for twenty-five minutes through the snow, and then began the long descent of the rocks. It was nearly four o'clock, and, as it would be dark at eight, it was evident that there was no time to be lost, and we pushed on to the utmost. Nothing remarkable occurred going down. We kept rather closer to the glacier, and crossed at the same point as in the morning. Getting *off* it was like getting *on* it—rather awkward. Old Sémiond had got over—so had Reynaud; Macdonald came next, but, as he made a long stretch to get on to a higher mass, he slipped, and would have been in the bowels of a crevasse in a moment had he not been tied.

It was nearly dark by the time we had crossed, but I still hoped that we should be able to pass the night at our rock. Macdonald was not so sanguine, and he was right; for at last we found ourselves quite at fault, and wandered helplessly up and down for an hour, while Reynaud and the porter indulged in a little mutual abuse. The dreary fact that, as we could not get down, we must stay where we were, was now quite apparent.

---

* This mountain is the culminating point of the group, and is named on the French map Pointe des Ecrins. It is seen from the Val Christophe, and from that direction its ridges completely conceal Mont Pelvoux. But on the other side—that is, from the direction of La Bessée or the Val Louise—the reverse is the case: the Pelvoux completely conceals it.

Unaware that this name was going to be applied to it, we gave the name Pic des Arcines, or des Ecrins, to our summit, in accordance with the traditions of the natives.

We were at least 10,500 feet high, and if it commenced to rain or snow, as the gathering clouds and rising wind seemed to threaten, we might be in a sore plight. We were hungry, having eaten little since 3 A.M., and a torrent we heard close at hand, but could not discover, aggravated our thirst. Sémiond endeavoured to get some water from it; but, although he succeeded in doing so, he was wholly unable to return, and we had to solace him by shouting at intervals through the night.

A more detestable locality for a night out of doors it is difficult to imagine. There was not shelter of any kind ; it was perfectly exposed to the chilly wind which began to rise, and it was too steep to promenade. Loose rubbly stones covered the ground, and had to be removed before we could sit with any comfort. This was an advantage, although we hardly thought so at the time, as it gave us some employment, and, after an hour's active exercise of that interesting kind, I obtained a small strip about nine feet long, on which it was possible to walk. Reynaud was furious at first, and soundly abused the porter, whose opinion as to the route down had been followed rather than that of our friend, and at last settled down to a deep dramatic despair, and wrung his hands with frantic gesture, as he exclaimed, " Oh, malheur, malheur! Oh misérables!"

Thunder commenced to growl, and lightning to play among the peaks above, and the wind, which had brought the temperature down to nearly freezing-point, began to chill us to the bones. We examined our resources. They were six and a half cigars, two boxes of vesuvians, one-third of a pint of brandy-and-water, and half-a-pint of spirits of wine: rather scant fare for three fellows who had to get through seven hours before daylight. The spirit-lamp was lighted, and the remaining spirits of wine, the brandy and some snow was heated by it. It made a strong liquor, but we only wished for more of it. When that was over, Macdonald endeavoured to dry his socks by the lamp, and then the three lay down under my plaid to pretend to sleep. Reynaud's woes were aggravated by toothache; Macdonald somehow managed to close his eyes.

The longest night must end, and ours did at last. We got down to our rock in an hour and a quarter, and found the lad not a little surprised at our absence. He said he had made a gigantic fire to light us down, and shouted with all his might; we neither saw the fire nor heard his shouts. He said we looked a ghastly crew, and no wonder; it was our fourth night out.

We feasted at our cave, and performed some very necessary ablutions. The persons of the natives are infested by certain agile creatures, whose rapidity of motion is only equalled by their numbers and voracity. It is dangerous to approach too near them, and one has to study the wind, so as to get on their weather-side : in spite of all such precautions my unfortunate companion and myself were being rapidly devoured alive. We only expected a temporary lull of our tortures, for the interiors of the inns are like the exteriors of the natives, swarming with this species of animated creation.

It is said that once, when these tormentors were filled with an unanimous desire, an unsuspecting traveller was dragged bodily from his bed! This needs confirmation. One word more, and I have done with this vile subject. We returned from our ablutions, and found the Frenchmen engaged in conversation. "Ah!" said old Sémiond, "as to fleas, I don't pretend to be different to anyone else,—*I have them.*" This time he certainly spoke the truth.

We got down to La Ville in good time, and luxuriated there for several days; played many games of bowls with the natives, and were invariably beaten by them. At last it was necessary to part, and I walked southwards to the Viso, while Macdonald went to Briançon.

I have not attempted to conceal that the ascent of Mont Pelvoux is of a rather monotonous character; the view from its summit can, however, be confidently recommended. A glance at the map will show that with the single exception of the Viso, whose position is unrivalled, it is better situated than any other mountain of considerable height for viewing the whole of the Western Alps.

Our discovery that the peak which is to be called the Pointe des Ecrins was a separate and distinct mountain from Mont Pelvoux—and not its highest point—gave us satisfaction, although it was also rather of the nature of a disappointment.*

On our return to La Bessée we wrongly identified it with the peak which is seen from thence to the left of the Pelvoux. The two mountains bear a considerable resemblance to each other, so the mistake is not, perhaps, unpardonable. Although the latter mountain is one that is considerably higher than the Wetterhorn or Monte Viso, it has no name; we called it the Pic Sans Nom.

It has been observed by others that it is improbable the French surveyors should have remained for several days upon the Pic de la Pyramide without visiting the other and loftier summit. If they did, it is strange that they did not leave some memorial of their visit. The natives who accompanied them asserted that they did not pass from one to the other; we therefore claimed to have made the ascent of the loftiest point for the first time. The claim, however, cannot be sustained, on account of the ascent of M. Puiseux. It is a matter of little moment; the excursion had for us all the interest of a first ascent; and I look back upon this, my first serious mountain scramble, with more satisfaction, and with as much pleasure as upon any that is recorded in this volume.

After parting from my agreeable companions, I walked by the gorge of the Guil to Abries, and made the acquaintance at that place of an ex-harbour-master of Marseilles,—a genial man, who spoke English well. Besides the ex-harbour-master and some fine trout in the neighbouring streams, there was little to invite a stay at Abries. The inn—l'Etoile, chez Richard—is a place to be avoided. Richard, it may be observed, possessed the instincts of a robber. At a later date, when forced to seek shelter in his house,

* We afterwards learned that Mr. M'Culloch had announced the fact a long time before in his *Geographical Dictionary*.

he desired to see my passport, and, catching sight of the words
John Russell, he entered that name instead of my own in a report
to the gendarmerie, uttering an exclamation of joyful surprise at
the same time.   I foolishly allowed the mistake to pass, and had to
pay dearly for it ; for he made out a lordly bill, against which all
protest was unavailing.

His innocent and not unnatural mistake was eclipsed by a
gendarme of Bourg d'Oysans, who took the passport, gravely held
it *upside down* for several minutes, pretended to read it, and handed
it back, saying it was all right.

Round about Abries the patois of the district is more or less
Italian in character, and the pronunciation of the natives reminds
one of a cockney who attempts to speak French for the first time,
Here bread is pronounced pane, and cheese, fromargee.   There are
a considerable number of dialects in use in this corner of France ;
and sometimes in the space of only a few miles one can find several,
all of which are as unintelligible to the natives of the surrounding
districts as they are to the traveller.   In some districts the spelling
of the patois is the same ; but the pronunciation is different—in this
resembling the Chinese.   It is not easy for the stranger to understand the dialects, either written or spoken ; and this will be
readily perceived from the samples given below, which are different
versions of the parable of the prodigal son.*

I quitted the abominations of Abries to seek a quiet bundle of
hay at Le Chalp—a village some miles nearer to the Viso.   On

* " Un sarten homme aïe dous garçous ; lou pus jouve dissec à soun païre :—
' Moun païre, beila me la pourtiou d'ou ben que me reven.' Et lou païre fec en
chascu sa part.   Et paou de tens après, lou cadet, quant aguec fachs sa pacoutilla,
se mettec en routo et s'en anec dinc un païs eiloigna, ounte mangec tout ce qu'aïé enbe
les fumelles.   Et quant aguec tout fricassa l'y aguec dinc aqueou païs-acqui une
grande famine, et coumensec à aver famp."

The above is a specimen of the patois of the neighbourhood of Gap ; the following
is that of Monêtier :—

" Un home avas dou bos.   Lou plus giouve de isou disse à son pere :—' Moun pere,
moun pere, douna-me soque me duou reveni de vatre be.' Et lou pere lour faze ou par-
tage de soun be.   Paouc de giours apres, lou plus giouve deiquelou dou bos, apres aveira

approaching the place the odour of sanctity* became distinctly perceptible ; and on turning a corner the cause was manifested ; there was the priest of the place, surrounded by some of his flock. I advanced humbly, hat in hand, but almost before a word could be said, he broke out with, "Who are you ?" " What are you?" "What do you want ?" I endeavoured to explain. "You are a deserter; I know you are a deserter ; go away, you can't stay here ; go to Le Monta, down there ; I won't have you here," and he literally drove me away. The explanation of his strange behaviour was that Piedmontese soldiers who were tired of the service had not unfrequently crossed the Col de la Traversette into the valley, and trouble had arisen from harbouring them. However, I did not know this at the time, and was not a little indignant that I, who was marching to the attack, should be taken for a deserter.

So I walked away, and shortly afterwards, as it was getting dark, encamped in a lovely hole—a cavity or kind of basin in the earth, with a stream on one side, a rock to windward, and some broken pine branches close at hand. Nothing could be more perfect : rock, hole, wood, and water. After making a roaring fire, I nestled in my blanket bag (an ordinary blanket sewn up, double round the legs, with a piece of elastic riband round the open end), and slept, but not for long. I was troubled with dreams of the Inquisition ; the tortures were being applied—priests were forcing fleas down my nostrils and into my eyes—and with red-hot pincers were taking out bits of flesh, and then cutting off my ears and tickling the soles of my feet. This was too much ; I yelled a great yell and awoke, to find myself covered with innumerable crawling bodies ; they were ants ; I had camped by an ant-hill, and, after making its inhabitants mad with the fire, had coolly lain down in their midst.

The night was fine, and as I settled down in more comfortable

amassa tout so que aou lavie, sen ane diens un païs etrangie ben leigu, aount aous dissipe tout soun be diens la grande deipensa et en deibaucha. Apres qu'aou lague tout deipensa, larribe una grand famina diens iquaou païs ilai, et aou cheique diens lou besoign."—Ladoucette's *Histoire des Hautes-Alpes,* pp. 613, 618.

* See p. 22.

G

quarters, a brilliant meteor sailed across full 60° of the cloudless sky, leaving a trail of light behind which lasted for several seconds. It was the herald of a splendid spectacle.   Stars fell by hundreds ;

THE BLANKET BAG.

and not dimmed by intervening vapours, they sparkled with greater brightness than Sirius in our damp climate.

The next morning, after walking up the valley to examine the Viso, I returned to Abries, and engaged a man from a neighbouring hamlet, for whom the ex-harbour-master had sent ; an inveterate smoker, and thirsty in proportion, whose pipe never left his mouth except to allow him to drink.   We returned up the valley together and slept in a hut of a shepherd, whose yearly wage was almost as small as that of the herdsman spoken of in Hyperion by Longfellow ; and the next morning, in his company, proceeded to the summit of the pass which I had crossed in 1860 ; but we were baffled in our attempt to get near the mountain ; a deep notch *

* There are three cols or passes close to Monte Viso on its northern side, which lead from the valley of the Po into that of the Guil.   The deep notch spoken of above is the nearest to the mountain, and although it is by far the lowest gap in that part of the chain, and would seem to be the true Col Viso, it does not appear to be used as

with precipitous cliffs cut us off from it ; the snow slope, too, which existed in the preceding year on the Piedmontese side of the pass, was now wanting, and we were unable to descend the rocks which lay beneath. A fortnight afterwards the mountain was ascended for the first time by Messrs. Mathews and Jacomb, with the two Croz's of Chamounix. Their attempt was made from the southern side, and the ascent, which was formerly considered a thing totally impossible, has become one of the most common and favourite excursions of the district.

We returned crest-fallen to Abries. The shepherd, whose boots were very much out of repair, slipped upon the steep snow-slopes and performed wonderful, but alarming, gyrations, which took him to the bottom of the valley, more quickly than he could otherwise have descended. He was not much hurt, and was made happy by a few needles and a little thread to repair his abraded garments ; the other man, however, considered it wilful waste to give him brandy to rub in his cuts, when it could be disposed of in a more ordinary and pleasant manner.

The night of the 14th of August found me at St. Veran, a village made famous by Neff, but in no other respect remarkable, saving that it is supposed to be the highest in Europe.* The Protestants *now* form only a miserable minority ; in 1861 there were said to be 120 to 780 Roman Catholics. The poor inn† was kept by one of the former, and it gave the impression of great poverty. There was no meat, no bread, no butter or cheese ; almost the only things that could be obtained were eggs. The manners of the natives were primitive ; the woman of the inn, without the least sense of impropriety, staid in the room until I was fairly in bed, and her bill for supper, bed, and breakfast, amounted to one and sevenpence.

a pass. The second, which I crossed in 1860, has the name Col del Color del Porco given to it upon the Sardinian map ! The third is the Col de la Traversette ; and this, although higher than at least one of those mentioned above, is that which is used by the natives who pass from one valley to the other.

* Its height is about 6600 feet above the sea.

† Ball's *Guide* is in error in saying there is no inn.

In this neighbourhood, and indeed all round about the Viso, the chamois still remain in considerable numbers. They said at St. Veran that six had been seen from the village on the day I was there, and the innkeeper declared that he had seen fifty together in the previous week! I myself saw in this and in the previous season several small companies round about the Viso. It is perhaps as favourable a district as any in the Alps for a sportsman who wishes to hunt the chamois, as the ground over which they wander is by no means of excessive difficulty.

The next day I descended the valley to Ville Vieille, and passed

NATURAL PILLAR NEAR MOLINES (WEATHER ACTION).

near the village of Molines, but on the opposite side of the valley, a remarkable natural pillar, in form not unlike a champagne bottle, about seventy feet high, which had been produced by the action of the weather, and, in all probability, chiefly by rain. In this case a " block of euphotide or diallage rock protects a friable limestone;"* the contrast of this dark cap with the white base, and the singularity of the form, made it a striking object. These natural pillars are among the most remarkable examples of the potent effects produced by the long-continued action of quiet-working forces. They are found in several other places in the Alps,† as well as elsewhere.

The village of Ville Vieille boasts of an inn with the sign of the Elephant ; which, in the opinion of local amateurs, is a proof that Hannibal passed through the gorge of the Guil. I remember the place, because its bread, being only a month old,‡ was unusually soft, and, for the first time during ten days, it was possible to eat some, without first of all chopping it into small pieces and soaking it in hot water, which produced a slimy paste on the outside, but left a hard untouched kernel.

The same day I crossed the Col Isoard to Briançon. It was the 15th of August, and all the world was *en fête;* sounds of revelry proceeded from the houses of Servières as I passed over the bridge upon which the pyrrhic dance is annually performed,§ and natives in all degrees of inebriation staggered about the paths. It was late before the lights of the great fortress came into sight ; but unchallenged I passed through the gates, and once more sought shelter under the roof of the Hotel de l'Ours.

* J. D. Forbes.

† In the gorge of the Dard, near Aosta ; near Euseigne, in the Val d'Hérens ; near Stalden, in the Visp Thal ; near Ferden, in the Lotschen Thal ; and, on a grander scale, near Botzen, in the Tyrol ; and in America on the Colorado river of the west.— See chap. 23.

‡ "An ancient and solemn custom wills that each family makes its bread in advance for a whole year, in order to show to the envious that corn is not wanting. The *poor* only eat new bread now and then, and do so because they are unable to make it at once for a whole year. But they are ashamed of their poverty, and when they are making it, hide from the sight of their neighbours."—Elisée Reclus, *Tour du Monde,* 1860.

§ See Ladoucette's *Hautes-Alpes,* p. 596.

CROSSING MONT CENIS (1861).

CHAPTER III.

THE MONT CENIS—THE FELL RAILWAY—THE GREAT TUNNEL THROUGH THE ALPS.

GUIDE-BOOKS say that the pass of the Mont Cenis* is dull. It is long, certainly, but it has a fair proportion of picturesque points, and it is not easy to see how it can be dull to those who have eyes. In the days when it was a rude mountain-track, crossed by trains of mules, and when it was better known to smugglers than to tourists, it may have been dull; but when Napoleon's road changed the rough path into one of the finest highways in Europe, mounting in grand curves and by uniform grades, and rendered the trot possible throughout its entire distance, the Mont Cenis became one of the most interesting passes in the Alps. The diligence service which was established was excellent, and there was little or nothing

* See the general map.

to be gained by travelling in a more expensive manner. The horses were changed as rapidly as on the best lines in the best period of coaching in England, and the diligences themselves were as comfortable as a "milord" could desire. The most exciting portion of the route was undoubtedly that between Lanslebourg and Susa. When the zig-zags began, teams of mules were hooked on, and the driver and his helpers marched by their side with long whips, which they handled skilfully. Passengers dismounted, and stretched their legs by cutting the curves. The pace was slow but steady, and scarcely a halt was made during the rise of 2000 feet. Crack! crack! went the whips as the corners of the zig-zags were turned. Great commotion among the mules! They scrambled and went round with a rush, tossing their heads and making music with their bells. The summit was gained, the mules were detached and trotted back merrily, while we, with fresh horses, were dragged at the gallop over the plain to the other side. The little postilion

seated on the leader smacked his whip lustily as he swept round the corners cut through the rock, and threw his head back, as the echoes returned, expectant of smiles and of future centimes.

The air was keen and often chilly, but the summit was soon passed, and one quickly descended to warmth again. Once more there was a change. The horses, reduced in number to three, or perhaps two, were the sturdiest and most sure of foot, and they raced down with the precision of old stagers. Woe to the diligence if they stumbled! So thought the conductor, who screwed down the breaks as the corners were approached. The horses, held well in hand, leant inwards as the top-heavy vehicle, so suddenly checked, heeled almost over ; but in another moment the break was released, and again they swept down, urged onwards by whip, "hoi," and "ha" of the driver.

All this is changed. The Victor Emmanuel railway superseded a considerable portion of Napoleon's road, and the "Fell" railway has the rest. In a few years more the great tunnel of the Alps will be completed, and that will bring about another change.

The Fell railway, which has been open about eighteen months, is a line that well deserves attention. Thirty-eight years ago Mr. Charles Vignolles, the eminent engineer, and Mr. Ericsson, patented the idea which is now an accomplished fact on the Mont Cenis. Nothing was done with it until Mr. Fell, the projector of the railway which bears his name, took it up, and to him much credit is due for bringing an admirable principle into operation.

The Fell railway follows the great Cenis road very closely, and diverges from it either to avoid villages or houses, or, as at the summit of the pass on the Italian side, to ease the gradients. The line runs from St. Michel to Susa. The distance between those two places is, as the crow flies, almost exactly equivalent to the distance from London to Chatham; but by reason of the numerous curves and detours the length of the line is nearly brought up to the distance of London from Brighton. From St. Michel to the summit of the pass it rises 4460 feet, or 900 feet more than the highest point of Snowdon is above the level of the sea ; and from the summit of the pass to Susa, a distance less than that from London to Kew, it descends no less than 5211 feet !

The railway itself is a marvel. For fifteen miles and three-quarters it has steeper gradients than one in fifteen. In some places it is one in twelve and a half ! An incline at this angle, starting from the base of the Nelson Column in Trafalgar Square, would reach the top of St. Paul's Cathedral if it were placed at Temple Bar ! A straight piece of railway constructed on such a gradient seems to go up a steep hill. One in eighty, or even one in a hundred, produces a very sensible diminution in the pace of a light train drawn by an ordinary locomotive ; how then is a train to be taken up an incline that is *six* times as steep ? It is accomplished by means of a third rail placed midway between the two ordinary ones, and elevated above them.* The engines are provided

* This third rail, or, as it is termed, "the centre rail," is laid on all the steep por-

with two pairs of horizontal driving-wheels as well as with the ordinary coupled vertical ones, and the power of the machine is thus enormously increased ; the horizontal wheels gripping the centre rail with great tenacity by being brought together, and being almost incapable of slipping, like the ordinary wheels when on even a moderate gradient.*

The third rail is the ordinary double-headed rail, and is laid horizontally; it is bolted down to wrought iron chairs, three feet apart, which are fixed by common coach-screws to a longitudinal sleeper, laid

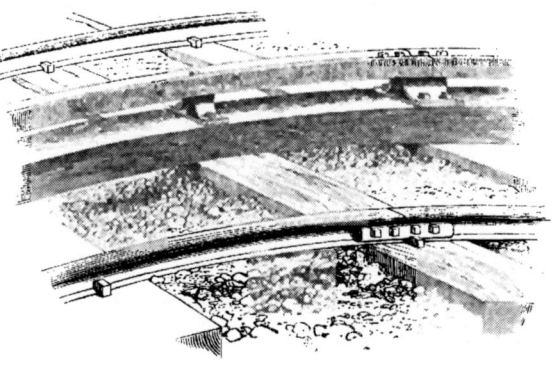

THE CENTRE RAIL ON A CURVE.

upon the usual transverse ones : the sleepers are attached to each other by fang-bolts. The dimensions of the different parts will be seen by reference to the annexed cross section :—

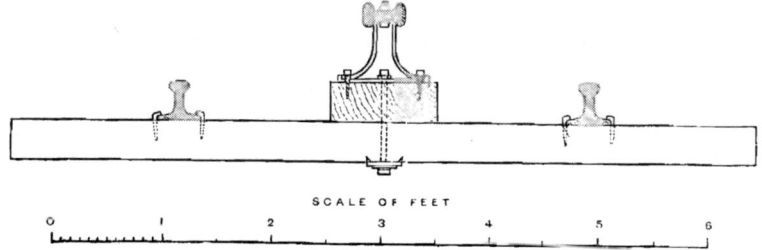

SCALE OF FEET

0   1   2   3   4   5   6

Let us now take a run on the railway, starting from St. Michel. For some distance from that place the gradients are not of an ex-

tions of the line, and round all except the mildest curves. Thirty miles, in all, of the road have the centre rail.

* These engines are described in the reports by Captain Tyler to the Board of Trade.

H

traordinary character, and a good pace is maintained. The first severe piece is about two miles up, where there is an incline of one in eighteen* for more than half-a-mile;—that is to say, the line rises at one step one hundred and sixty-four feet. From thence to Modane the gradients are again moderate (for the Fell railway) and the distance—about ten miles and a half from St. Michel— is accomplished without difficulty in an hour. Modane station is 1128 feet above St. Michel, so that on this *easy* portion of the line there is an average rise of 110 feet per mile, which is equal to a gradient of one in forty-eight ; an inclination sufficiently steep to bring an ordinary locomotive very nearly to a halt.

Just after passing Modane station there is one of the steepest inclines on the line, and it seems preposterous to suppose that any train could ascend it. A stoppage of ten minutes is made at Modane, and on leaving that station, the train goes off at the hill with a rush. In a few yards its pace is reduced, and it comes down and down to about four miles an hour, which speed is usually maintained until the incline is passed, without a diminution of the steam-pressure. I say usually, because, if it should happen that there is not suffi-cient steam, or should the driver happen to make a slip, the train would most likely come back to Modane ; for, although the break-power on the train is much more than sufficient to prevent it running back, the driver could hardly start with the breaks on, and the train would inevitably run back if they were off.

After this incline is passed, the line mounts by comparatively easy gradients towards Fort Lesseillon; it is then at a great height above the Arc, and as one winds round the faces of the cliff out of which the Napoleon road was cut, looking down upon the foaming stream below, without a suspicion of a parapet between the rail-way and the edge of the precipice, one naturally thinks about what would happen if the engine should leave the rails. The speed, however, that is kept up at this part is very gentle, and

* The inclination of the steepest part of Old Holborn Hill.—Roney's *Rambles on Railways.*

there is probably much less risk of an accident than there was in the days of diligences.

The next remarkable point on this line is at Termignon. The valley turns somewhat abruptly to the east, and the course of the railway is not at first perceived. It makes a great bend to the left, then doubles back, and rises in a little more than a mile no less than three hundred and thirty-four feet. This is, perhaps, the most striking piece of the whole line.

Lanslebourg station, 25½ miles from, and 2220 feet above, St. Michel, is arrived at in two hours and a quarter from the latter place. The engines are now changed. Thus far we have been traversing the easy portion of the route, but here the heavy section begins. From Lanslebourg the line rises continuously to the summit of the Mont Cenis pass, and accomplishes an ascent of 2240 feet in six miles and a third of distance.

It is curious and interesting to watch the ascent of the trains from Lanslebourg. The puffs of steam are seen rising above the trees, sometimes going in one direction, and sometimes directly the contrary, occasionally concealed by the covered ways—for over two miles out of the six the line is enclosed by planked sides and a corrugated iron roof to keep out the snow—and then coming out again into daylight. A halt for water has to be made about half-way up; but the engines are able to start again, and to resume their rate of seven miles an hour, although the gradient is no less than one in fourteen and a half. The zigzags of the old Cenis road are well known as one of the most remarkable pieces of road-engineering in the Alps. The railway follows them, and runs parallel to the road on the outside throughout its entire distance, with the exception of the turns at the corners, where it is carried a little further out, to render the curves less sharp. Nevertheless they are sufficiently sharp (135 feet radius), and would be impracticable without the centre rail.

The run across the top of the pass, from the Summit station to the Grande Croix station—a distance of about five miles—is soon accomplished, and then the tremendous descent to Susa is commenced. This, as seen from the engine, is little less than terrific. A large part of this section is covered in,* and the curves succeed one another in a manner unknown on any other line. From the outside the line looks more like a monstrous serpent than a railway.

THE COVERED WAYS ON THE "FELL" RAILWAY (ITALIAN SIDE OF THE MONT CENIS).

Inside one can see but a few yards ahead, the curves are so sharp, and the rails are nearly invisible. The engine vibrates, oscillates, and bounds; it is a matter of difficulty to hold on. Then, on emerging into the open air, one looks down some three or four thousand feet of precipice and steep mountain-side. The next moment the engine turns suddenly to the left, and driver and stoker have to grip firmly to avoid being left behind; the next, it turns as suddenly to the right; the next there is an accession or diminution of speed, from a change in the gradient. An ordinary engine, moving at fifty miles an hour, with a train behind it, is not usually very steady, but its motion is a trifle compared with that of a Fell engine when running down hill.

It may be supposed from this that travelling over the Fell rail-

---

* On the Italian side there are about three-quarters of a mile of strongly-built avalanche galleries, and more than three miles of covered way.

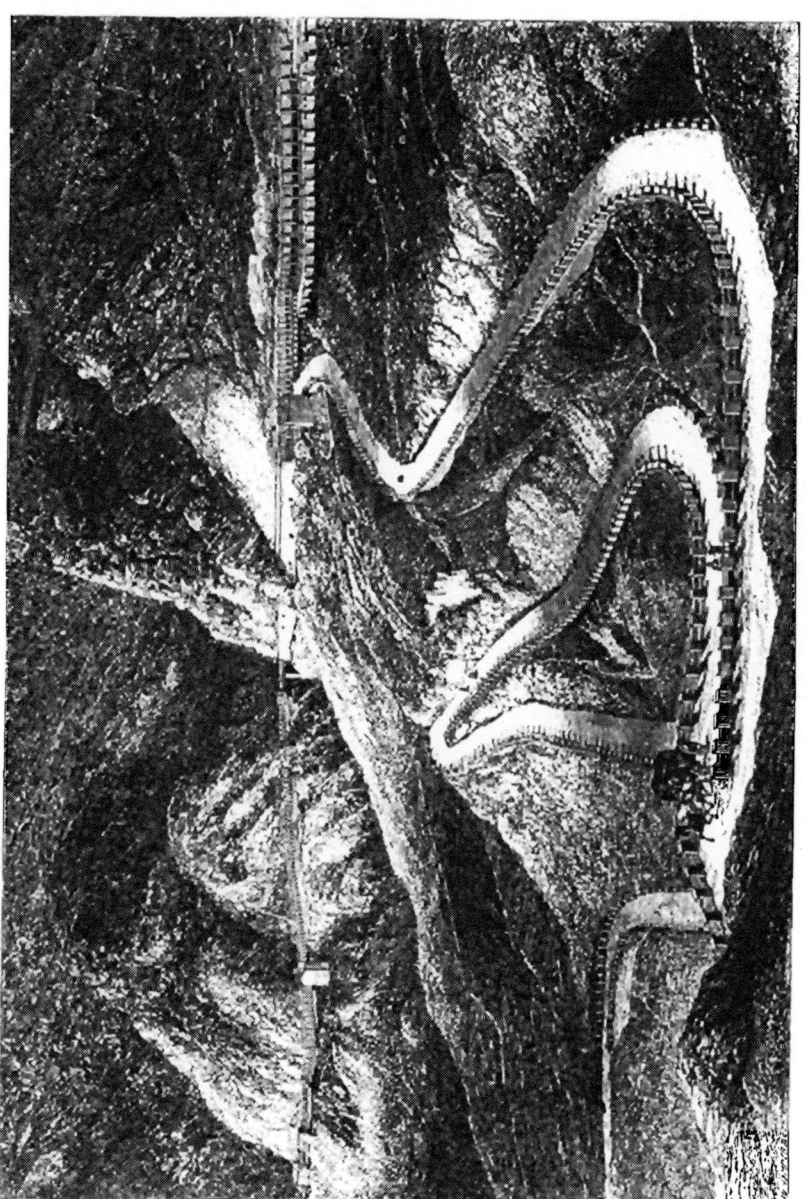

THE MONT CENIS ROAD AND THE FELL RAILWAY, NEAR THE SUMMIT OF THE PASS, ON THE ITALIAN SIDE.

way is disagreeable rather than pleasant. It is not so ; the train is steady enough, and the carriages have remarkably little motion. Outside they resemble the cars on the Swiss and American lines ; they are entered at the end, and the seats are arranged omnibus-fashion, down the length of the carriage. Each carriage has a guard and two breaks,—an ordinary one, and a centre rail break ; the handles of these come close together to the platform at one end, and are easily worked by one man. The steadiness of the train is chiefly due to these centre rail breaks. The flat face A, and the corresponding one on the opposite side, are brought together against the two sides of the centre rail by the shaft B being turned, and they hold it as in a vice. This greatly diminishes the up-and-down motion, and renders oscillation almost im-

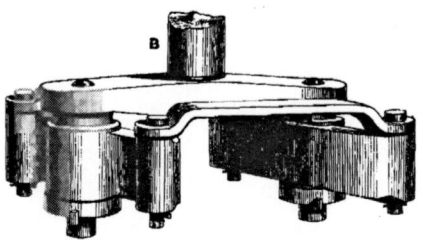

CENTRE RAIL BREAK.

possible. The steadiness of the train is still further maintained by pairs of flanged guide-wheels under each of the carriages, which, on a straight piece of line, barely touch the centre rail, but press upon it directly there is the least deviation towards either side.* There is no occasion to use the other breaks when the centre rail breaks are on ; the wheels of the carriages are not stopped, but revolve freely, and consequently do not suffer the deterioration which would otherwise result.

The steam is shut off, and the breaks are applied, a very few minutes after beginning the descent to Susa. The train might then run down for the entire distance by its own weight. In practice, it is difficult to apply the proper amount of retardation ; the breaks have frequently to be whistled off, and sometimes it is necessary to

---

* The carriages are not coupled in the ordinary way, and although there are no buffers, properly speaking, and in spite the speed of the train being changed incessantly, there is a freedom from the jarring which is so common on other lines. The reason is simply that the carriages are coupled up tightly.

steam down against them. Theoretically, this ought not of course to occur ; it only happens occasionally, and ordinarily the train goes down with the steam shut off, and with the centre rail breaks screwed up moderately. When an average train—that is, two or three carriages and a luggage-van—is running down at the maximum speed allowed (fifteen miles an hour), the breaks can pull it up dead within seventy yards. The pace is properly kept down to a low point in descending, and doing so, combined with the knowledge that the break-power can easily lessen it, will tend to make the public look favourably on what might otherwise be considered a dangerous innovation. The engines also are provided with the centre rail break, on a pattern somewhat different from those on the carriages, and the flat sides which press against the rails are renewed *every journey.* It is highly desirable that they should be, for a single run from Lanslebourg to Susa grinds a groove into them about three-eighths of an inch in depth.

Driving the trains over the summit section requires the most constant attention, and no small amount of nerve, and the drivers, who are all English, have well earned their money at the end of their run. Their opinion of the line was concisely and forcibly expressed to me by one of them in last August. " Yes, mister, they told us as how the line was very steep, but they didn't say that the engine would be on one curve, when the fourgon was on another, and the carriages was on a third. Them gradients, too, mister, they says they are one in twelve, but I think they are one in *ten, at the least,* and they didn't say as how we was to come down them in that snakewise fashion. It's worse than the G. I. P.,* mister ; there a fellow could jump off ; but here, in them covered ways, there ain't no place to jump to."

The Fell railway is of the nature of an experimental line, and

---

* The Great Indian Peninsula Railway, the line with the celebrated Bhore Ghaut incline, sixteen miles long, on an average gradient of one in forty-eight, which is said to have cost £800,000, or about double the entire cost of the Mount Cenis Railway, and six times its cost mile for mile. The Fell railway cost £8000 per mile.

as such it is a success.   It has reduced the time that was formerly occupied in passing from St. Michel to Susa by nearly one-half ;* it has lessened the cost and increased the comfort to the passengers. The gauge (3 feet 7⅜ inches) is a mistake, inasmuch as it loses time and causes trouble by the transference of the passengers, limits the power of the engines, and renders the rolling stock unfit for general use, should the line be pulled up,—which, according to the terms of the concession which was granted to the promoters, is to be done when the great tunnel of the Alps is open for traffic.

The covered ways have been made too low, and the steam and smoke are driven down by the roof in an unpleasant manner.† If, however, the doors of the carriages are shut, but little inconvenience is experienced on this account.

The engines are not anchored as firmly to the line as the carriages, and their motions are very violent.   There is, too, a certain vibration in the working parts of their machinery, which indicates that they are not perfect.   In ordinary locomotives the oscillatory movements which are acquired (even at moderate speeds) from the inequalities of the road, are less likely to cause injury to the machinery than the same motion is to the locomotives on the Fell railway.   With the former a certain amount of lateral play is possible over the base of the engine, but in the latter case it is impossible when the horizontal wheels and breaks are gripping the centre rail.   Many of the working parts of these locomotives must be subjected to sudden and violent strains, which do not occur to others on ordinary lines.

The engines are admitted to be imperfect, and new ones are in course of construction.   It is to be regretted there is a probability that the line will be pulled up at no very distant date, as improvements are thus prevented from being carried out ; otherwise there

* The trains take 5½ hours one way and 5¼ hours the other.   These times are inclusive of an hour and a half of stoppages.

† It is said that a number of railway directors were nearly suffocated on one of the early experimental trips, and that peremptory orders were given to remove portions of the roof.

would be no doubt it might become a thoroughly practical and profitable one. Let us now turn to the great tunnel of the Alps, the completion of which is to be death to the Fell railway.

When M. Medail of Bardonnêche—thirty years ago—pointed out that a shorter tunnel could be constructed beneath the Alps between his village and Modane than at any other place in the Sardinian States having a similar elevation above the level of the sea, neither he, nor any other person, had the least idea how the project could be executed.

The first step was taken by the geologists Signor Sismonda and M. Elie de Beaumont. They pointed out, about twenty years ago, that calcareous schists and quartzite rocks would form a large proportion of the strata through which the tunnel would pass. It takes a miner one hour and a half to two hours to make an ordinary hole for blasting (28 inches deep) in the calcareous schist, and not less than eight hours to make one 20 inches deep in the quartzite.[*] When would the tunnel have been finished if the ordinary processes had been alone employed?

The ordinary processes were clearly unavailable. The tunnel would be not only of prodigious length,[†] but it would have to be constructed without shafts. At no place where a shaft would have been of any use would it have been possible to make one less than 1000 feet deep! If one had been made about midway between the two ends, it would have been no less than 5315 feet deep. "I

* These are the times actually occupied in the tunnel.
† The Mont Cenis Tunnel will be 13,364 yards long. The lengths of some of the better known tunnels in England are given below, for the sake of comparison.

Shakespeare .	(South-Eastern Railway)	1430 yards .	7 shafts.
Kilsby . .	(North-Western Railway)	2398 ,,	. 2 ,,
Box . . .	(Great Western Railway)	3123 ,,	. 11 ,,
Woodhead .	(Man., Sheffield, and Linc. Railway)	5300 ,,	. ? ,,

The last-named is the longest railway tunnel in England.—*Enc. Brit.*, Art. "Railways."
The longest canal tunnel in England is the Marsden, on the Huddersfield Canal.—Roney's *Rambles on Railways*.

estimate," says M. Conte,* "that the sinking of a shaft a mile in depth would occupy not less than forty years. I do not know that a depth of 1000 feet has been hitherto passed."†

"Several projects were presented to the Sardinian government, some proposing to shorten the length of the tunnel by raising its level, and others to accelerate the boring of the holes for blasting ; but they were all put aside as impossible, or as having been insufficiently studied. The first one seriously considered by the government was that of M. Maus, a Belgian engineer. He proposed to construct a tunnel of 12,230 mètres between Bardonnêche and Modane, with a ruling gradient of 19 in 1000. The advance of the small gallery in front was to be made by means of a machine with chisels, put in motion by springs, that would have cut the rock into blocks—leaving them attached only at the back—which were afterwards to be brought down by means of wedges."

" M. Colladon of Geneva suggested moving the tools of the machine of M. Maus by means of compressed air, but he neither pointed out the means of compressing the air, nor how it was to be applied as a motive power."

" The government had constructed the railway from Turin to Genoa, and engineers were studying how to tug the trains up the incline at Busalla, which has a gradient of 1 in 29. MM. Grandis, Grattoni, and Sommeiller proposed to compress air by means of the 'compresseur à choc,' which is now used on the works of the Cenis tunnel, and to employ it for the traction of the trains."

" Mr. Bartlett, an English engineer on the Victor Emmanuel Railway,‡ had invented a machine for making holes for blasting,

* M. Conte, a well-known French engineer, was a member of a commission appointed to examine the progress of this tunnel in 1863. His report is the most accurate and the most complete account of it that has been published.

† M. Conte refers to tunnel-shafts.

‡ The Victor Emmanuel Railway Company has ceased to exist. The section in France is joined to the Paris, Lyons, and Mediterranean Railway, and that in Italy to the Alta Italia system. The railway from the French mouth of the tunnel to St. Michel will be made at the cost of the Paris, Lyons, and Mediterranean Company.

which was put in motion by steam. The machine was imperfect, and while experiments were being made with it (by means of compressed air), M. Sommeiller invented the boring-machine which is now used in the tunnel."

" The problem then appeared to be solved. The inventors joined themselves to M. Ranco—who had taken part in their experiments on the Genoa Railway—prepared a scheme, and presented it with confidence to the government, after having found out that they could compress air to a high pressure, that this air could be led from closed reservoirs and transmitted to great distances without a sensible diminution of its pressure, and that it could be employed to move the boring-machine which was intended to make the holes for blasting. A commission was appointed to examine the project, and its members satisfied themselves that the scheme was feasible. The Act of August 15, 1857, authorised the government to construct the section of the Victor Emmanuel Railway between Susa and Modane. MM. Grandis, Grattoni, and Sommeiller, were appointed to direct the works."

" M. Medail indicated the general direction of the tunnel between Modane and Bardonnêche. M. Maus drew his line a little more to the east, nearer to Modane. The engineers who direct the work have approached the latter course, and have selected that which seemed to them to be the shortest, the most easy to come out at, and, especially, the most convenient to lay out."

" It is needless to insist on the importance of the tracing of the course of the tunnel. It was necessary—1st, To establish upon the mountain a sufficient number of marks in order to determine the vertical plane passing through the axis of the gallery ; 2. To measure exactly the distance between the two mouths ; 3. To determine the difference of level between the two mouths, in order to arrange the gradients of the tunnel."

" These delicate operations were entrusted to MM. Borelli and Copello. M. Grandis undertook the control of the work."

" After the two mouths had been determined upon, they set out from Fourneaux to trace a line in the supposed direction of Bardonnêche. This first line came out in the valley of Rochemolles at a point too far off from that fixed upon, but with its help a second line was drawn which came sufficiently near to the proposed entry. These lines were subsequently still further corrected. These operations occupied the months of August and September 1857."

" The observations were made with a theodolite which had been constructed with the greatest care, and which read to 10" on the vernier. The line has been verified several times by different observers, and the results show that a straight line has been laid out. Supposing that the greatest error" (due to the instrument) " had been made, the deviation from the straight line would not amount to more than one foot.   MM. Borelli and Copello make—personally —the observations for the direction and for the verification of the actual course of the tunnel, and we may imagine that they will not readily leave to others such delicate work, upon which the success of the enterprise depends.   All the marks on the southern side, and the most important ones on the northern side, were fixed by the first days of October 1857 ; snowfalls and 'tourmentes' retarded the work, but it was nevertheless completed by the end of the month."

" In 1858 the triangulations and levellings were undertaken, and they were terminated at the end of the year."

" The trigonometrical work has for a base one of the sides of the triangles of the Etat Major, and upon it two sets of triangles have been constructed, one towards the southern and the other towards the northern side. The two systems are formed of twenty-eight triangles, and the number of angles measured is eighty-six. The majority of the angles have been repeated at least twenty times ; those of the principal triangles have been taken fifty times, and, of the small ones, at least ten times. The theodolite employed read to 5"."

" One can hardly give an idea of the difficulties that the observers have experienced in the course of their work. At heights like those from which they worked, meteorological changes occur with the greatest rapidity ; violent winds overturned their instruments, and mists or clouds concealed the points at the moments they wished to observe them. A single fact will give some notion of the nature of their work. Seven angles had to be measured from the summit of La Pelouse, 10,170 feet above the sea. The observers —who were lodged in the chalets of La Rionda, had to ascend to the summit for seven successive days, and it was seldom possible to measure two angles in the same day."

" The importance of these observations is readily comprehended, and I have described them at some length, because they form the base of the enterprise. One thing is notable. It is the personal care that the engineers have taken. M. Grandis directed the tracing of the line, the triangulation, and the levellings ; he assisted at these operations; he selected the bases and points at which 'signals' were to be placed; and all was done under his eye by the engineers, Borelli, Copello, Mella, and Mondino."

On account of the peculiar situation of the ends of the tunnel, two small, connecting, curved tunnels will have to be made. "The construction of these terminal curves is naturally neglected for the establishment of the two false mouths in the direction of the general line."

" The length between the two false mouths is 12,220·00 mètres. The entry on the side of Italy is at a height of 1335·38 ,,

,,   ,,   France   ,,   1202·82   ,,

Difference of level   132·56   ,,

This difference of level is overcome by a gradient of 222 in 10,000, which rises from the French entry to the centre *   .   .   .   = 135·64   ,,

A gradient of 1 in 2000, which rises from the Italian entry to the centre*   .   .   =   3·06   ,,

132·58   ,,

_____

* The summit will be a few feet higher than M. Conte states, the gradients having been increased since the commencement of the works.

If a single gradient had ruled throughout, rising from the French to the Italian side, it would have been reduced to 217 in 20,000 ; but although this would have been of the greatest advantage in working the line, it would have added one more difficulty to the construction of the tunnel. There were enough difficulties without adding another."

"It is, besides, evident that driving the tunnel to a summit doubles the chances of the two ends meeting, and negatives, to a certain extent, the possibilities of error from the two operations upon which the least dependence could be placed,—the triangulation and the levelling. Provided that the two axes are in the same direction, they must meet sooner or later ; whether this happens a few yards more to the north or to the south is of no importance."*

At the commencement of the tunnel in 1857, there was no accommodation at either end for those employed on the works ; and for a long time both engineers and workmen had to submit to numerous privations. Roads had to be made, and barracks to be erected ; one after another, houses and shops were added, and at the present time the tunnel-buildings alone form considerable villages at the two ends.†

The situations of the two mouths are essentially different from each other. That at Bardonnêche comes out at the bottom of the valley of Rochemolles ; that at Fourneaux 300 feet above the Cenis road. At the latter end the debris has been shot out at the mouth down the mountain-side ; and, large as the tip (in the language of

* Conte. *Conférences faites à l'Ecole Impériale des Ponts et Chaussées.* 1864.

† It is sufficient to indicate those at Bardonnêche only. The principal ones are : 1. Close to the tunnel-mouth — lodgings for the miners, the principal storehouses, stables, forges for repairing the drills. 2. At Bardonnêche, half-a-mile distant from the mouth — large barracks for the workmen ; six other buildings for workmen ; one house for other employées ; repairing-shops for the machinery ; storehouses ; a foundry ; the building containing the "compresseurs à choc," and the reservoirs for feeding the same ; a gasworks ; a building containing an infirmary, washhouses, etc. ; two buildings for "compresseurs à pompe ;" one building for new reservoirs of compressed air ; a cantine and a porter's lodge. An enumeration of the buildings at Fourneaux (Modane) would be nearly a repetition of the above.

navvies) undoubtedly is, it is difficult to believe one sees all the material that has been extracted from more than two miles and a half of tunnel. It is interesting as showing the greatest angle at which debris will stand. Its faces have, as nearly as possible, an angle of 45.°

During four years the ordinary means of excavation were alone employed, and but 1300 yards were driven. In this time the machines were being constructed which were destined to supersede a large part of the manual labour; at the beginning of 1861 they were sufficiently complete to be put to work, and in the summer of that year I went to Bardonnêche to see them in operation.*

The clocks of the Oulx had just struck twelve on the night of the 16th of August, as the diligence crawled into the village from Briançon, conveying a drunken driver, a still more intoxicated conducteur, and myself. The keeper of the inn at which we stopped declined to take me in, so I sought for repose in a neighbouring oatfield, and the next morning mightily astonished a native when I rose enveloped in my blanket-bag. He looked aghast for a moment at the apparition which seemed to spring out of the ground, and then turning round in a nervous, twitching manner, dropped his spade and fairly bolted, followed by hearty shouts of laughter. Bardonnêche—a little Alpine village whose situation is not unlike that of Zermatt, was about an hour distant. A strange banging noise could be heard a long way off, and a few minutes after my arrival, I stood in one of the shops by the side of the machine which was causing it, and by the side of M. Sommeiller, the inventor of the machine. They were experimenting with one of his famous "perforatrices," and a new form of boring-rod, upon a huge block of rock which

* In the previous year I had visited Modane, and favoured by introductions from M. Ch. Lafitte, at that time President of the Victor Emmanuel Railway, had been shown all that there was to be seen. I visited Modane again recently, and, for the third time, went to the end of the advanced gallery. I have to thank M. Mella and Sig. Borelli, the directors of the works in 1861 at Modane and Bardonnêche respectively, for their attention in 1860-1, and particularly Signor Copello, the present director at Modane, for the facilities given and for the information afforded by him.

was already riddled by more than a hundred holes, varying from one inch to four and a half in diameter. The perforatrice—a simple-looking cylinder fixed in a square frame, and connected with a few pipes and stop-cocks—was placed in a fresh position in front of the rock, and, at a sign from the engineer, was set in motion. A boring-rod darted out like a flash of lightning, went with a crash against a new part of the rock, chipped out several fragments at a blow, and withdrew as quickly as it had advanced. Bang, bang, it went again with the noise of a gong. In ten seconds the head of the borer had eaten itself a hole; in a minute it had all but disappeared; in twelve it had drilled a hole nearly a yard deep, as cleanly as a carpenter could in a piece of wood. The rod not only moved backwards and forwards, and advanced as the hole grew deeper, but turned gently round the whole time; a jet of water, projected with great force, cooled the chisel, and washed out the chips. More *air* was turned on; the sound of the blows could no longer be distinguished one from another, they made a continuous rattle, and the rate was increased from two hundred to no less than three hundred and forty strokes per minute, or about half as fast again as the motion of the piston-rod of an ordinary express locomotive when going sixty miles an hour.

The pipes are seen which conduct the compressed air for the working of these boring-machines on approaching the tunnel-mouths. They are eight inches in diameter, and are supported by pillars of masonry. As these pipes, outside the tunnel, are exposed to constant variations of temperature—sometimes to as much as 54° Fahr. in a single day—it has been necessary to guard against their expansion and contraction. They have been fixed accordingly at stated intervals by means of iron rods, the lower ends of which are carried through the masonry and bolted to plates on the outside. The intermediate pipes are carried on rollers (D) on the tops of the pillars, and between each of the fixed points there is one pipe having an enlarged mouth — terminated by a cheek — which receives the end (A) of the ordinary pipe. A circular

pipe of leather (c) is secured to the cheek by means of a metal
washer, and, pressed down by the compressed air on the end

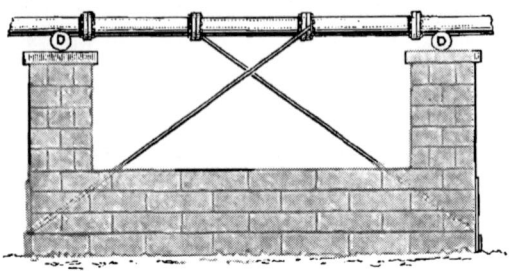

of the ordinary pipe,
makes the joint suffici-
ently air-tight, although
it does not hinder the
advance or the retreat
of the pipe.   In the
tunnel itself—where the
temperature is not sub-
ject to such fluctuations
—these precautions are
not necessary, and the
pipes are carried along
the walls, supported by

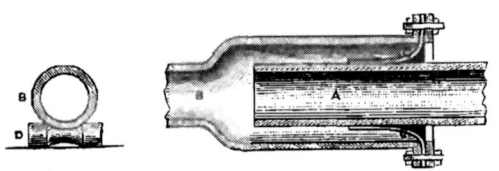

brackets, as far as the end of the finished work.   Through these
pipes highly compressed air is conducted, and is delivered at the
end of the "advanced gallery" where the boring-machines are at
work, with only a slight diminution in its pressure, notwithstanding
the escapes which occur at the joints.

On entering the tunnel one is struck by its size.   The Italians,
with a magnificent disregard of expense, or from regard to the
future, have constructed it not only with two pairs of rails,* but
with a footpath on each side.   From the rails to the crown of the
arch its height is just 20 feet, and its width is 26 feet 6 inches.
The next thing that is noticed is that it is almost everywhere lined
with masonry; a small fraction only of the rock is left unsupported.
The stone that is used is not obtained from the tunnel itself, but
is quarried several miles away, near to St. Michel.†   Not observed,

---

* The lines which will connect it with existing railways are to be only single
lines.

† Here, and in the subsequent pages, the French side is alone referred to, unless
it is otherwise specified; but the description would serve almost equally for the
Italian side.

but nevertheless existing, is a covered way about 3 feet 4 inches high, and 4 feet wide, which is made in the floor of the tunnel

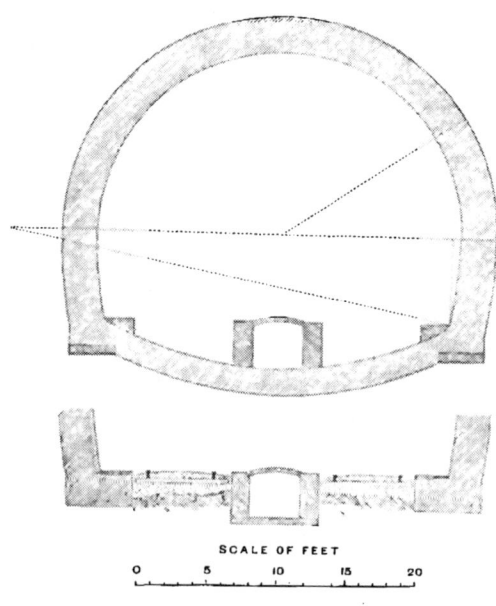

SCALE OF FEET

between the rails ; it is in fact a tunnel within a tunnel. Originally its dimensions were less, and it was intended merely as a subway in which the pipes conveying the compressed air might be placed, and as a drain ; it was found convenient to enlarge its size, and since that has been done, it has — on at least one occasion — served a purpose for which it was not originally intended. On the 15th of September 1863, a sudden fall of rock occurred, which killed several miners and imprisoned about sixty others who were at work in the advanced gallery. They were greatly alarmed, and expected to be starved ; but at last one of them remembered this subway, and they escaped by its means. Since that time the miners, knowing they have this exit, have troubled themselves very little about éboulements.

The temperature of the tunnel remains tolerably uniform throughout the year, but it is much higher in some parts than it is in others. On the occasion of my last visit, the exterior temperature was $63\frac{1}{2}°$ Fahr. in the shade ; a mile from the entrance it was 65°, and the mouth looked like the sun on a misty November day. At two miles the thermometer showed 70°, the atmosphere had become foul, and the mouth was invisible. In two hundred and fifty paces more, it had risen to 75°, the tunnel was filled with dense clouds of smoke, the light of an ordinary miner's lamp could not be perceived at the distance of five or six yards, and respiration was difficult, for the atmosphere was vile. This was the end of the finished work : it is from hence that the air is drawn by the pumping-engines at the mouth, and it is hereabouts that all the foul vapours naturally accumulate and hang. The great vault was no longer overhead, but the way was reduced to a drift eight or nine feet wide and scarcely as much high, encumbered with waggons filled with débris, between which and the walls one could barely pass. In a hundred feet or so, we emerged—comparatively speaking—into a blaze of light. Two hundred greasy, smoky, but still light-giving lamps, hung from the walls. Drops of water flashed past them like gems. Two hundred men toiled at the enlargement of the gallery—bearded, grimy men, some on their backs, some on their sides, some working overhead, some half naked, some quite naked—all tapping laboriously at their mining-rods, and all perspiring profusely. The temperature had risen to $81\frac{1}{2}°$.[*] The multitude of the lights, the crowd of men, and the obscurity of the smoke, help to make the tunnel look an immense size—in fact, at this part, it is sometimes but little less than 30 feet high and 35 feet wide ; for not merely has the rock to be removed at the top and sides, which is afterwards replaced by masonry, but it is occasionally excavated for an inverted arch, which is placed wherever it is necessary.

The temperature is, as nearly as possible, the same at the roof of the gallery as it is on the floor ; for jets of compressed air are let off above. The work of the masons would otherwise be unendurable.

There was a difference then of 18° between the temperature at the mouth and at the end of the finished work. In winter this amount would be trebled or quadrupled. How much of the increase is due to the lights, men, and horses, and how much to the natural temperature of the rock ? If the heat increased in the tunnel,

---

[*] It is almost unnecessary to remark that no stout men are seen in the tunnel.

yard by yard, in the same proportion as it does when *descending* into the earth, the temperature in its centre should be about 90° higher than at its mouth. Although it is known that the rate of increase is very much less than this, the actual rate is not known. I believe it is correct to say that not a single observation has been made upon the natural temperature of the rock since the tunnel has been commenced. Four-fifths of it are now driven. The opportunity for observation has been lost; for, apart from the cooling which must inevitably have taken place, almost the whole of the tunnel has been lined with masonry, and it is not to be expected that any person, or any body of persons, will incur the expense, even if they were permitted, of removing this, and then making the necessary holes. It is to be hoped that some observations will be made on the remaining portion, for similar opportunities are not likely to occur very frequently.

About 2000 feet on the French side of the tunnel was undergoing the processes of enlargement and completion in the summer of 1869.* In some places portions of the advanced gallery remained untouched, and then one came to caverns, such as have been described above. This section was being completed faster than the advanced gallery was being driven. It was pleasant to get away from it farther into the bowels of the mountain ; the heat became less, and the atmosphere more pure. The noise of the hammers died gradually away, and at last no sound whatever could be heard, except of our own footsteps and of water running in the subway. After a time the banging of the chisels could be distinguished which were at work on the front of the attack. Five hundred paces took us to them.† The ponderous frame, technically called "l'affût," supported nine of the machines known as "perforatrices ;" each perforatrice propelled a boring-rod, and each boring-rod was striking the rock at the rate of 200 strokes per minute, with a force of 200

---

* The monthly advances which are sometimes quoted in English newspapers refer to the advanced gallery, not to the finished work.

† In addition to the 2000 feet of unfinished work mentioned above.

pounds.* The terrific din that these 1800 strokes per minute, given with such force, make in a rock-chamber that is only 8 ft. 3 in. high, and 9 ft. 2½ in. wide, can hardly be imagined ; neither can an adequate idea be given of the admirable manner in which the machines accomplish their work. In spite of the noise and the cramped position in which the men necessarily toil on account of the limited space, the work goes steadily forward day and night. Each man knows his part. The foremen direct by signs rather than by words ; the labourers guide the chisels ; the workmen regulate the supply of air ; the machinists are ready in case of accident ; slim boys, with long-nosed cans, oil the machinery. Order triumphs in the midst of apparent confusion. One sees now the results of years of perfecting and of practice. Things were very different at the beginning. Then, says M. Conte, " everything was new, not only to the workmen, but also to those who had the direction. . . . The work of perforation was commenced at Bardonnêche on January 12, 1861, but for several days only a single perforatrice was in action, then a second was added, and by the 20th a certain amount of useful work had been done. On the 26th the number of the perforatrices was increased to four, and by working eight hours per day, 10 or 12 holes were made about a yard in depth. On the 12th of February they had perfected about 32 yards of the advanced gallery, which had been left unfinished, and then arrived at the front of the attack. The whole difficulty was there. The number of the machines was again increased, but during ten days there was little result. On the 22d February the works were suspended, in order to make alterations suggested by experience ; and it was recommenced on the 2d of March. During the first half of this month an advance of half-a-mètre was accomplished in two days, by working seven hours a-day ; but towards the end of the month the work had become more easy, and it was possible to perform the whole of the operation in a single day, and to obtain a daily advance of 18 inches to two feet."

* The perforatrices are independent machines, and one can be stopped or removed without arresting the progress of the others.

"In April, the improvements introduced, and the practice acquired, caused better progress, and in the middle of the month the work of perforation was accomplished in eight or nine hours."

"In the month of May, when nine perforatrices were at length at work, progress was stopped by exterior causes, and was suspended for two months."

"From July to the 19th of August the work was continued, but only one attack per day was made, on account of there not being a sufficient number of instructed persons to carry on the work incessantly. Still it was carried on with regularity, and the advance was 28 inches to 3 feet per day. The perforation was generally accomplished in six hours."

"From the 19th of August the work was continued day and night, but at first, in consequence of the inexperience of some of the employées, the depth of the holes had to be reduced to two feet, and that depth occupied them twelve hours. Little by little this fresh band of workmen became as skilful as the first, and at the end of two months the two attacks were carried on with regularity." *

The best form of boring-rod for all kinds of rock, excepting such as are homogeneous, was hit upon in 1861, and it has been in use ever since. The head is in the form of a Z. For homogeneous

---

* On the Italian side, in order to advance *one* mètre :—

1862.	1863.
120 holes, each 30 to 32 inches in depth, had to be bored.	96 holes, 36 inches deep, were bored.
110 lbs. of powder were consumed.	94½ lbs. of powder were consumed.
200 mètres of match.	210 mètres of match.
190 drills were put *hors de combat*.	185 drills were used up.

On the French side, in order to advance *one* mètre :— ·
1863.
103 holes, 34 inches deep, were bored.
125¼ lbs. of powder were consumed.
200 mètres of match.
158 drills were used up.

Conte.

rock, the ordinary form of chisel is found best. Almost all the details of the machinery, the size of the gallery, the dimensions and number of the holes, and the manner of firing them, have been changed since the beginning ; the general principles alone remain unaltered. The present system is as follows. A hole $4\frac{3}{4}$ inches in diameter is made to a depth of about a yard, towards the centre of the drift, but rather nearer to the floor than to the roof. Fifty to sixty holes, according to circumstances, of less diameter, but of about equal depth, are then driven into the remainder of the face.

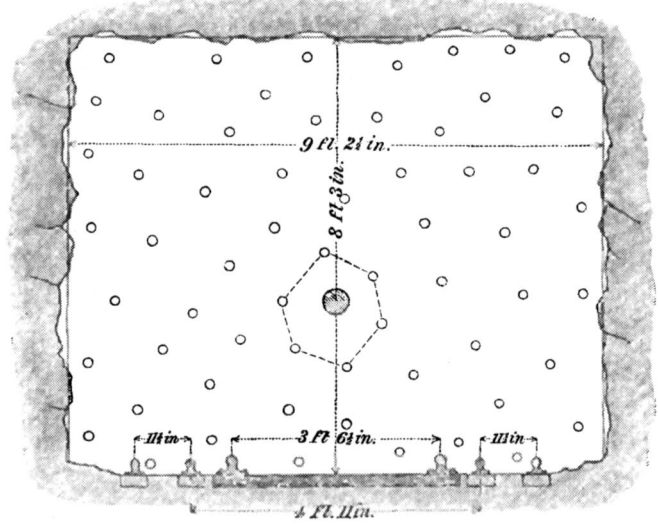

CROSS SECTION OF THE ADVANCED GALLERY.

All the holes are then dried and cleaned by a jet of compressed air, the "affût" is withdrawn behind strong iron-bound doors, and six of the small holes nearest to the large are charged and fired. The force of the explosion goes in the direction of least resistance, that is towards the central hole, and a breach is made such as is indicated in the longitudinal section by the thick dotted line. The remaining holes are then charged and fired in sets of six or eight at a time, those nearest to the breach being exploded first. This system has been found more economical than firing a larger number of shots at one time. The waggons are then advanced, and the débris is cleared away; the two pairs of rails at the sides, shown in the cross section, are for wag-gonets, whose contents are afterwards transferred to large waggons. The "affût" is then again advanced. These operations are now repeated with unvarying regularity twice every day.

The temperature at the working face of the advanced gallery is seldom higher than from 75° to 76°, and the atmosphere is as pure as can be de-sired, when the machines are at work.* This, it must be remem-bered, is notwithstanding the pre-sence of more than thirty men,† and almost as many lamps, in a space about nine feet wide, eight high, and

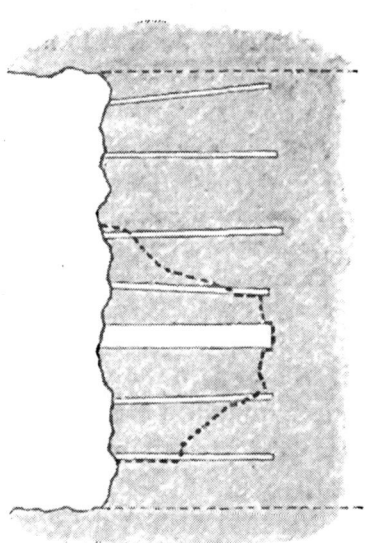

LONGITUDINAL SECTION OF THE END OF THE ADVANCED GALLERY.

fifty long. The comparative lowness of the temperature is of course due to the expansion of the compressed air.

At the distance of a hundred and sixty paces, the sound of the machines could not be distinguished, and the atmosphere again gradually deteriorated as we approached the region which may, not improperly, be termed infernal. Once more we passed through the foul vapours and by the army of miners. Laborious as the work of these men undoubtedly is, it is lighter and far less dangerous than that of our coal-cutters. The heat, although it seems considerable to one coming from a lower temperature, is not excessive, and this may be inferred from seeing how few men

* The temperature is raised to 80° or 86° after the mines are exploded.

† 1 chef; 4 machinists; 2 master miners, who determine the direction of the holes; 8 labourers, who guide the boring-rods; 9 workmen, who look after the per-foratrices; 5 boys; 8 labourers; 2 workmen, who keep up communication with the exterior, —in all, 39 persons.

are unclothed. They work readily enough for their three francs a-day,* and take to their labour cheerfully ; very few skulkers can be seen in the Mont Cenis tunnel. The following table shows how small is the risk to life.

FATAL ACCIDENTS which have occurred at the GREAT TUNNEL OF THE ALPS from the commencement of the works to August 1869 :—

Inside the Tunnel.		Outside the Tunnel.	
From falls of rock . . .	8	Falls from heights . . .	2
Accidents from waggons .	14	Accidents from waggons .	4
Premature explosions . .	3—25	Explosion of gunpowder .	5—11
	Total . 36		

It will be seen from this that one-half of the fatal accidents have arisen from men being run over by waggons. This has chiefly come from the impossibility of making the miners walk on the footways at the sides of the tunnel. They will walk on the rails. The result is that they are not unfrequently killed, although the greatest precautions are taken with the waggons descending with débris. The total is insignificant when one considers the number of men engaged and the length of time over which it is spread, and it compares favourably with almost any other enterprise of similar magnitude.

The waggons laden with débris run down, on the French side, by their own weight, on account of the gradient, and so did the truck on which I descended with my guide—the courteous engineer who directs the works. Fresh relays of miners were entering, and those whom they relieved were coming out with their arms around each others' waists " in the manner of schoolboys and lovers." The air seemed chilly, although it was a bright summer day ; and our nostrils, for hours after leaving the tunnel, yielded such supplies of carbon as to suggest that the manufacture of compressed soot might be profitably added to the already numerous industries of the works.

* The workmen in the advanced gallery receive five francs a-day, and a small bonus per mètre if they exceed a certain fixed distance.

About four thousand men are now employed on the tunnel,* and they complete ten to eleven feet every day. The average daily progress of the last five years is ten feet one inch. Each yard of progress costs at the present time abóut £200, or just double the average of railway tunneling in England.† There are many yards, however, which have cost infinitely more than £200 per yard. The work is now so far advanced that the engineers can estimate with some probability what the total expenditure will amount to. They place it at £3,000,000 (£224 per yard), which sum includes

* On the French side they are employed as follows (subdivisions are omitted for the sake of brevity) :—

   (1.) In the advanced gallery—

'Ajusteurs'	13	
Miners	14	
Labourers	140	
Boys	13	180

   (2.) Enlargement by manual labour—

Miners	510	
Labourers	180	
Boys	30	720

   Masonry—

Masons and dressers of stone .	58	
Labourers	170	
Boys	52	280

   (3.) Manufactories, machinery, stores (exterior works)—

Smiths, joiners, fitters, etc. .	120	
Labourers	440	
Boys	10	570

(4.) Overseers, foremen, clerks, etc.	60
(5.) Platelayers, transport of materials, etc. . .	180
Total . .	1990

Horse-power of machines—

Hydraulic wheels	480
Ventilating machines	300
Sundry ,, ...	80
Total horse-power of machinery .	860
Horses employed in clearing away débris	80

† *Encyclo. Brit.* art. " Railways."

L

the expense of the whole of the machinery and of the exterior works. This amount does not seem extravagant when we remember that for every yard of advance, never less—and frequently more —than seventy cubic yards of rock have to be excavated, and to be carried away (at the present time) a distance of three miles ; that about twenty-five cubic yards of masonry have to be built, the stone for which is conveyed twelve miles in a mountainous country ; that all the machinery employed has been constructed and invented expressly for the tunnel, and that the creation of two small towns has been necessary.

The strata which have been pierced agree very satisfactorily in their nature and in their thickness with the indications of the geologists.* The engineers therefore believe that no greater difficulties will be encountered than those which have been overcome. Remarkably little water has been met with : the miner's dreaded enemy seems to have fled before the engineer who has utilised its power. I have not entered into a description of the manner in which this has been accomplished, because it has been frequently done before ; but there is nothing more interesting in regard to the tunnel than

* Table of the strata which have been pierced on the French side of the great tunnel of the Alps : —

		Mètres.		Mètres.	Thickness of the Strata in Mètres.
1. Débris and pebbles	from	0	to	128	128
2. Anthracitic schists	,,	128	,,	2095·35	1967·35
3. Quartzite	,,	2095·35	,,	2476·75	381·40
4. Anhydrite	,,	2476·75	,,	2696·90	220·15
5. Compact calcareous rock	,,	2696·90	,,	2730·90	34·
6. Talcose schists	,,	2730·90	,,	2780·20	49·30
7. Compact calcareous rock	,,	2780·20	,,	2802·02	21·82
8. Anhydrite	,,	2802·02	,,	2831·75	29·73
9. Calcareous schists	,,	2831·75	,,	2852·95	21·20
10. Anhydrite	,,	2852·95	,,	2867·15	14·20
11. Calcareous schists	,,	2867·15	,,	3264·	396·85
12. Anhydrite	,,	3264·	,,	3334·45	70·45
13. Calcareous schist (the same as at Bardonnêche)	,,	3334·45	,,	continues	?

On the Bardonnêche side the tunnel passes through calcareous schist alone.

the way in which the waste power of nature has been applied for the reduction of the difficulties of the undertaking. There is not a single steam-engine on the works : everything is done with compressed air, or by hydraulic power. Just one half·of the tunnel was driven at the end of October 1866, after more than nine years of labour. The third quarter was finished by the end of 1868.* Unless extraordinary obstacles are encountered, the two ends will probably meet in February 1871 ;† but it will be long after that date before the tunnel will be used for traffic.‡

* The advanced gallery only.

† TABLE SHOWING THE PROGRESS OF THE ADVANCED GALLERY ON EACH SIDE,
FROM THE COMMENCEMENT UP TO 1ST NOVEMBER 1869.

	Year.	BARDONNÊCHE.		MODANE.		Total of the two sides per annum.	General Total.
		Advance in mètres.	Total.	Advance in mètres.	Total.		
By manual labour.	1857	27.28		10.80		38.08	
	1858	257.57		201.95		459.52	
	1859	236.35	725.00	132.75	921.00	362.10	1646.00
	1860	203.80		139.50		343.30	
	1861			193.00		193.00	
	1862			243.00		243.00	
By mechanical means.	1861	170.00		,, ,,		170.00	
	1862	380.00		,, ,,		380.00	
	1863	426.00		376.00		802.00	
	1864	621.20		466.65		1087.85	
	1865	765.30	5337.40	458.40	3407.00	1223.70	8744.40
	1866	812.70		212.29		1024.99	
	1867	824.30		687.81		1512.11	
	1868	638.60		681.55		1320.15	
	1869	699.30		·524.30		842.10	
Total advance at Bardonnêche			6062.40	Total advance at Modane.	4328.00	Total advance at both ends	10,390.40

Total length of the tunnel, 12,220 mètres.
Remained to be driven Nov. 1, 1869, $1829\frac{2}{5}$ mètres.

See Appendix for the progress of the work since this date.

‡ The railways which will connect the tunnel with existing lines will be difficult and costly works, with numerous tunnels and bridges. A good deal of the heavy work is done on the line between Susa and Bardonnêche, but on the French side the works are almost untouched.

Will the two ends meet? The engineers are confident that
they will. One important fact remains to be pointed out. The
two sides have not advanced with equal rapidity. On the Italian
side the summit is nearly gained—before these pages are published
it will have been passed; but on the French side they are nearly
2000 yards short of it. The work is still to be carried on simultaneously, and, consequently, on the Italian side they will shortly
begin to descend. M. Conte mentioned * that one of the reasons
which influenced the engineers to drive the tunnel to a summit,
was, that by so doing, any error in the determination of its length,
or in the levels, would be negatived. It was only necessary that
the two ends should be driven in the same line,—they would be
sure to meet sooner or later. This was on the supposition that the
two gradients would be maintained until the two ends met. The
whole of this advantage is going to be sacrificed. If there is any
material error in the determination of the length or of the levels,
the two ends may not meet. One has not to go farther than the
summit of the Mont Cenis pass itself to show that errors may creep
into trigonometrical work, even when it is conducted by distinguished engineers. The height of that pass has been obtained by
two independent surveys; one, carried through France from the
level of the sea, and the other carried through Italy from the level
of the sea; yet the Italians make the summit 59 feet higher than
the French.

When the great tunnel of the Alps is completed, will it be a
useless marvel? or will locomotives be able to work in it? Will
the trains arrive at the ends with cargoes of asphyxiated passengers
who will have to be revived with draughts of compressed air? or
will there be no trouble on account of ventilation? It must not
be argued that because it is impossible for locomotives to work in
the tunnel at present, it will be impossible for them to work in it
when it is completed. The temperatures of the two sides will frequently be different, and that alone will produce considerable

* See p. 61.

currents. The very passage of the trains will do a good deal. Besides this, there is already a large amount of ventilating power established at the two ends, and it can be kept in action at a small expense. I saw at the Fourneaux (Modane) mouth, on my last visit, the pumping-engines that had been set up about two years before. There were four cylinders, each 16 feet 4 inches in diameter, with a stroke of 6 feet 6 inches. Only two were at work, yet—at a distance of *two miles* from the mouth—they produced a very sensible current flowing into the tunnel, which was indicated by the miners' lamps that we carried. There is no reason to be afraid that the eminent engineer, who has hitherto shown himself equal to all the difficulties which have arisen, will be beaten by the ventilation.

M. Conte, at the conclusion of his pamphlet, pays a high tribute of praise to M. Sommeiller, and properly speaks of him as " the soul of the enterprise." " We may quote him as a model of courage and devotion. . . . . If one may believe the companions of his youth, he followed the idea, which he now realises, at the time he was studying at the university of Turin. This idea he has never abandoned." Englishmen ought to be amongst the first to recognise his boldness and perseverance, although they have played no part in the execution of the tunnel.* It is the grandest conception of its kind, and when it is completed, it will be not only— in a double sense—one of the highways of Europe, but it will most likely become the high road to India.

It is humiliating to compare the working of our coal-mines with the operations carried on in the great tunnel of the Alps. In the former we see the old, barbarous, wasteful methods still employed, with disregard of human life, and for the future. In the latter, mechanical power, skilfully applied, economises labour, and gives safety and comfort to those who are at work. The exhaustion of

---

* The machinery has been principally made in Belgium ; the engineers are French and Italians, and the subordinates, for the most part, Piedmontese and French.

our coal-fields, which recent inquiries have placed at a more distant date than was expected a few years ago, is a thing that is inevitable sooner or later. Actual exhaustion is not so much to be feared as inability to compete with foreign producers. The question is adjourned, but it will presently be forced upon public attention again. When it becomes too pressing to be neglected, then, possibly, there will be a chance of the condition of our miners being ameliorated; but it is improbable so long as gigantic public subscriptions pay for the effects of private neglect, which actually tend to perpetuate what they are intended to cure, that the chief sinners will take proper action. When they take alarm, then perhaps there will be salvation for the pitmen. The fact that two hundred of their men lose their lives every year by fire-damp explosions will not move British pit-owners so readily as the disagreeable truth that the time is rapidly approaching when they will be unable to compete with foreign markets, unless they work with greater economy. We have heard times without number that miners are careless ; that they *will* smoke their pipes where they ought not ; that they *will* carry forbidden matches, or even break open their safety-lamps to get a light. It is useless to combat such habits by repressive enactments, and childish to talk of double-locking lamps because single-locked ones are found ineffectual. The more difficulty there is in obtaining a light, the more men will struggle to get one. The only way to prevent explosions is to render them impossible, and that can be accomplished, to a large extent at least, by better ventilation. Coal can be got more economically, and the ventilation can be improved, by the use of one and the same means. Steam machinery cannot be used in coal-pits for the same reason that it could not in the great tunnel of the Alps ; but machines moved by compressed air can. A machine for coal-cutting worked by compressed air was patented so long ago as 1861, and has been successfully at work in a pit in Yorkshire * for a long time. Its action is an imitation of that of the miner's pick ; it cuts

* The West Ardsley.

a narrow groove 3 ft. 9 in. deep along the bottom of the coal, which is afterwards broken down in the usual way. Three times more coal can be got by four men with it in a day than they can get without it. The waste of coal in the operation of holing is reduced by *two-thirds.* That is to say, if this machine could be used in all the pits in the kingdom, there would be an actual saving of 8,000,000 to 9,000,000 tons of coal per annum! There are other (hydraulic) coal-cutting machines at work in collieries in the north of England, which are equally economical, and which will, like Mr. Firth's machine, work narrow seams at a profit which it would not pay to work by hand ; but they do not possess the important ventilating power, which is one of its chief recommendations. The expansion of the air not only lowers the temperature, but it drives all the gas away from the working-face. That this is done is sufficiently proved by the fact that there has not been a single explosion at West Ardsley since the machine has been in use, *although there were many minor ones before it was introduced.*

Who can say the condition of our coal-mines is satisfactory when such results are attainable? Yet who can touch the evil? The man who shall succeed in improving their ventilation will be a greater benefactor to his country than Sir Humphrey Davy, and will well deserve public reward; although, perhaps, he will be more likely to incur unmerited odium.

CHAPTER IV.

MY FIRST SCRAMBLE ON THE MATTERHORN.

" What power must have been required to shatter and to sweep away the missing parts of this pyramid ; for we do not see it surrounded by heaps of fragments ; one only sees other peaks—themselves rooted to the ground—whose sides, equally rent, indicate an immense mass of débris, of which we do not see any trace in the neighbourhood. Doubtless this is that débris which, in the form of pebbles, boulders, and sand, fills our valleys and our plains." DE SAUSSURE.

Two summits amongst those in the Alps which yet remained virgin had excited my admiration. One of these had been attacked numberless times by the best mountaineers without success ; the other, surrounded by traditional inaccessibility, was almost untouched. These mountains were the Weisshorn and the Matterhorn.

After visiting the great tunnel of the Alps in 1861, I wandered for ten days in the neighbouring valleys, intending, presently, to attempt the ascent of these two peaks. Rumours were floating about that the former had been conquered, and that the latter was shortly to be attacked, and they were confirmed on arrival at Chatillon, at the entrance of the Val Tournanche. My interest in the Weisshorn abated, but it was raised to the highest pitch on hearing that Professor Tyndall was at Breil, and intending to try to crown his first victory by another and still greater one.

Up to this time my experience with guides had not been fortunate, and I was inclined, improperly, to rate them at a low value. They represented to me pointers out of paths, and great consumers of meat and drink, but little more ; and, with the recollection of Mont Pelvoux, I should have greatly preferred the company of a couple of my countrymen to any number of guides. In answer to inquiries at Chatillon, a series of men came forward, whose faces expressed malice, pride, envy, hatred, and roguery of every description, but who seemed to be destitute of all good qualities. The arrival of two gentlemen with a guide, who they represented was the embodiment of every virtue, and exactly the man for the Matterhorn, rendered it unnecessary to engage any of the others. My new guide in *physique* was a combination of Chang and Anak ; and although in acquiring him I did not obtain exactly what was wanted, his late employers did exactly what *they* wanted, for I obtained the responsibility, without knowledge, of paying his back fare, which must have been a relief at once to their minds and to their purses.

When walking up towards Breil,* we inquired for another man of all the knowing ones, and they, with one voice, proclaimed that Jean-Antoine Carrel, of the village of Val Tournanche, was the cock of his valley. We sought, of course, for Carrel ; and found him a well-made, resolute-looking fellow, with a certain defiant air which was rather taking. Yes, he would go. Twenty francs a-day, whatever was the result, was his price. I assented. But I must take his comrade. " Why so ?" Oh, it was absolutely impossible to get along without another man. As he said this an evil countenance came forth out of the darkness and proclaimed itself the comrade. I demurred, the negotiations broke off, and we went up to Breil. This place will be frequently mentioned in subsequent chapters, and was in full view of the extraordinary peak, the ascent of which we were about to attempt.

It is unnecessary to enter into a minute description of the Matterhorn, after all that has been written about that famous mountain. Those by whom this book is likely to be read will know that that peak is nearly 15,000 feet high, and that it rises abruptly, by a series of cliffs which may properly be termed preci-

* Frequently spelt Breuil.

M

pices, a clear 5000 feet above the glaciers which surround its base. They will know too that it was the last great Alpine peak which remained unscaled,—less on account of the difficulty of doing so, than from the terror inspired by its invincible appearance. There seemed to be a *cordon* drawn around it, up to which one might go, but no farther. Within that invisible line gins and effreets were supposed to exist—the Wandering Jew and the spirits of the damned. The superstitious natives in the surrounding valleys (many of whom still firmly believe it to be not only the highest mountain in the Alps, but in the world) spoke of a ruined city on its summit wherein the spirits dwelt ; and if you laughed, they gravely shook their heads ; told you to look yourself to see the castles and the walls, and warned one against a rash approach, lest the infuriate demons from their impregnable heights might hurl down vengeance for one's derision. Such were the traditions of the natives. Stronger minds felt the influence of the wonderful form, and men who ordinarily spoke or wrote like rational beings, when they came under its power, seemed to quit their senses, and ranted, and rhapsodised, losing for a time all common forms of speech. Even the sober De Saussure was moved to enthusiasm when he saw the mountain, and—inspired by the spectacle—he anticipated the speculations of modern geologists, in the striking sentences which are placed at the head of this chapter.

The Matterhorn looks equally imposing from whatever side it is seen ; it never seems commonplace ; and in this respect, and in regard to the impression it makes upon spectators, it stands almost alone amongst mountains. It has no rivals in the Alps, and but few in the world.

The seven or eight thousand feet which compose the actual peak have several well-marked ridges and numerous others.* The most continuous is that which leads towards the north-east ; the summit is at its higher, and the little peak, called the Hörnli, is at its lower end. Another one that is well pronounced descends from

* See the map of the Matterhorn and its glaciers.

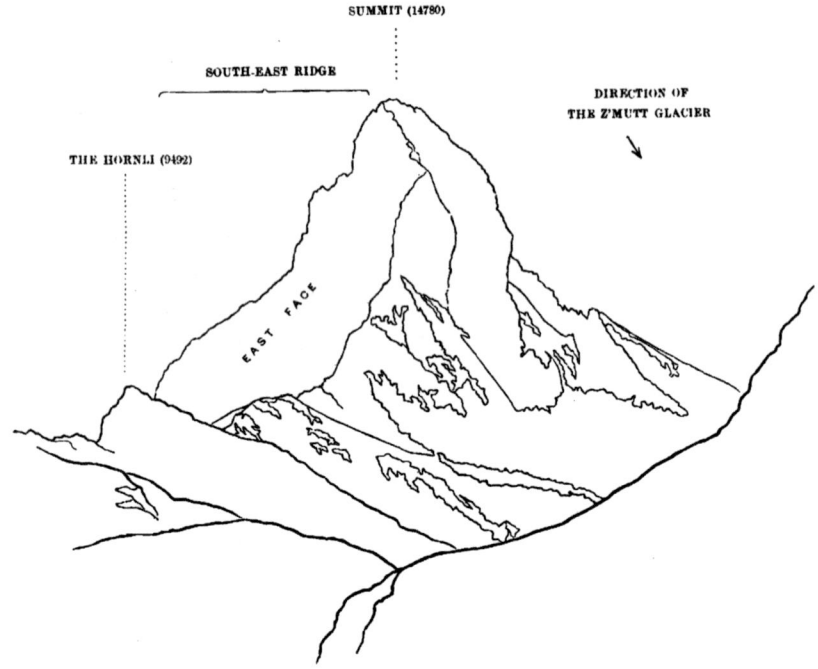

SUMMIT (14780)

SOUTH-EAST RIDGE

DIRECTION OF
THE Z'MUTT GLACIER

THE HORNLI (9492)

EAST FACE

THE MATTERHORN FROM THE NORTH-EAST.

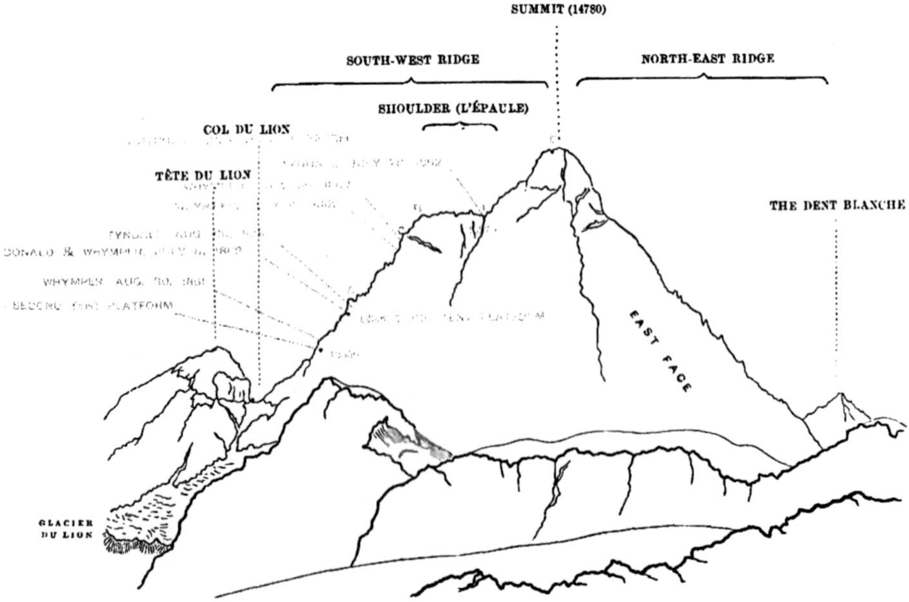

SUMMIT (14780)

SOUTH-WEST RIDGE

NORTH-EAST RIDGE

SHOULDER (L'ÉPAULE)

COL DU LION

TÊTE DU LION

THE DENT BLANCHE

TYNDALL
DONALD & WHYMPER
WHYMPER AUG. 20. 1861
SECOND TENT PLATFORM

EAST FACE

GLACIER
DU LION

THE MATTERHORN FROM THE SUMMIT OF THE THEODULE PASS.
(10,899 FEET)

the summit to the ridge called the Furgen Grat. The slope of the mountain that is between these two ridges will be referred to as the eastern face. A third, somewhat less continuous than the others, descends in a south-westerly direction, and the portion of the mountain that is seen from Breil is confined to that which is comprised between this and the second ridge. This section is not composed, like that between the first and second ridge, of one grand face ; but it is broken up into a series of huge precipices, spotted with snow-slopes, and streaked with snow-gullies. The other half of the mountain, facing the Z'Mutt glacier, is not capable of equally simple definition. There are precipices, apparent, but not actual ; there are precipices absolutely perpendicular ; there are precipices overhanging : there are glaciers, and there are hanging glaciers ; there are glaciers which tumble great *séracs* over greater cliffs, whose débris, subsequently consolidated, becomes glacier again : there are ridges split by the frost, and washed by the rain and melted snow into towers and spires : while, everywhere, there are ceaseless sounds of action, telling that the causes are still in operation which have been at work since the world began ; reducing the mighty mass to atoms, and effecting its degradation.

Most tourists obtain their first view of the mountain either from the valley of Zermatt, or from that of Tournanche. From the former direction the base of the mountain is seen at its narrowest, and its ridges and faces seem to be of prodigious steepness. The tourist toils up the valley, looking frequently for the great sight which is to reward his pains, without seeing it (for the mountain is first perceived in that direction about a mile to the north of Zermatt), when, all at once, as he turns a rocky corner of the path, it comes into view ; not, however, where it is expected ; the face has to be raised up to look at it ; it seems overhead. Although this is the impression, the fact is that the summit of the Matterhorn from this point makes an angle with the eye of less than 16°, while the Dom, from the same place, makes a larger angle, but is passed by unobserved. So little can dependence be placed on unaided vision.

The view of the mountain from Breil, in the Val Tournanche, is not less striking than that on the other side ; but, usually, it makes less impression, because the spectator grows accustomed to the sight while coming up or down the valley. From this direction the mountain is seen to be broken up into a series of pyramidal wedge-shaped masses ; on the other side it is remarkable for the large, unbroken extent of cliffs that it presents, and for the simplicity of its outline. It was natural to suppose that a way would more readily be found to the summit on a side thus broken up, than in any other direction. The eastern face, fronting Zermatt, seemed one smooth, impossible cliff, from summit to base ; the ghastly precipices which face the Z'Mutt glacier forbade any attempt in that direction. There remained only the side of Val Tournanche ; and it will be found that nearly all the earliest attempts to ascend the mountain were made on that side.

The first efforts to ascend the Matterhorn of which I have heard, were made by the guides, or rather by the chasseurs, of Val Tournanche.* These attempts were made in the years 1858-9, from the direction of Breil, and the highest point that was attained was about as far as the place which is now called the " Chimney " (cheminée), a height of about 12,650 feet. Those who were concerned in these expeditions were Jean-Antoine Carrel, Jean Jacques Carrel, Victor Carrel, the Abbé Gorret, and Gabrielle Maquignaz. I have been unable to obtain any further details about them.

The next attempt was a remarkable one; and of it, too, there is no published account. It was made by the Messrs. Alfred, Charles, and Sandbach Parker, of Liverpool, in July 1860. These gentlemen, *without guides*, endeavoured to storm the citadel by attacking its eastern face†—that to which reference was just now made as a smooth, impracticable cliff. Mr. Sandbach Parker

* There were no guides, properly speaking, in this valley at that time, with the exception of one or two Pessions and Pelissiers.

† This face is that on the right hand of the large engraving which accompanies this chapter. It is also represented, more prominently, in the engraving in Chapter xv.

THE MATTERHORN, FROM NEAR THE SUMMIT OF THE THEODULE PASS

informs me that he and his brothers went along the ridge between the Hörnli and the peak until they came to the point where the ascending angle is considerably increased. This place is marked on Dufour's map of Switzerland 3298 mètres (10,820 feet). They were then obliged to bear a little to the left to get on to the face of the mountain, and, afterwards, they turned to the right, and ascended about 700 feet further, keeping as nearly as was practicable to the crest of the ridge, but, occasionally, bearing a little to the left—that is, more on to the face of the mountain. The brothers started from Zermatt, and did not sleep out. Clouds, a high wind, and want of time, were the causes which prevented these daring gentlemen from going further. Thus, their highest point was under 12,000 feet.

The third attempt upon the mountain was made towards the end of August 1860, by Mr. Vaughan Hawkins,* from the side of the Val Tournanche. A vivid account of his expedition has been published by him in *Vacation Tourists;†* and it has been referred to several times by Professor Tyndall in the numerous papers he has contributed to Alpine literature. I will dismiss it, therefore, as briefly as possible.

Mr. Hawkins had inspected the mountain in 1859, with the guide J. J. Bennen, and he had formed the opinion that the south-west ridge‡ would lead to the summit. He engaged J. Jacques Carrel, who was concerned in the first attempts, and, accompanied by Bennen (and by Professor Tyndall, whom he had invited to take part in the expedition), he started for the gap between the little and the great peak.§

* Mr. Hawkins was unaware that any attempts had been made before his own, and spoke of it as the first. † *Macmillan,* 1861.

‡ This ridge is seen on the left of the large engraving accompanying this chapter ; and if the reader consults this view, the explanatory outlines, and the maps, he will be able to form a fair idea of the points which were attained on this and on the subsequent attempts.

§ Since this time the small peak has received the name Tête du Lion. The gap is now called the Col du Lion ; the glacier at its base, the Glacier du Lion ; and the gully which connects them, the Couloir du Lion.

Bennen was a guide who was beginning to be talked about. During the chief part of his brief career he was in the service of Wellig, the landlord of the inn on the Æggischhorn, and was hired out by him to tourists. Although his experience was limited, he had acquired a good reputation ; and his book of certificates, which is lying before me,* shows that he was highly esteemed by his employers. A good-looking man, with courteous,

J. J. BENNEN (1862).

gentlemanly manners, skilful and bold, he might, by this time, have taken a front place amongst guides if he had only been endowed with more prudence. He perished miserably, in the spring of 1864, not far from his home, on a mountain called the Haut de Cry, in the Valais.†

Mr. Hawkins' party, led by Bennen, climbed the rocks abutting against the Couloir du Lion, on its south side, and attained the Col du Lion, although not without difficulty. They then followed the south-west ridge, passed the place at which the

* By the kindness of its owner, Mr. F. Tuckett.   † See Appendix.

earliest explorers had turned back (the Chimney),* and ascended about 300 feet more. Mr. Hawkins and J. J. Carrel then stopped, but Bennen and Professor Tyndall mounted a few feet higher. They retreated, however, in less than half-an-hour, finding that there was too little time ; and, descending to the Col by the same route as they had followed on the ascent, proceeded thence to Breil, down the Couloir instead of by the rocks. The point at which Mr. Hawkins stopped is easily identified from his description. Its height is 12,992 feet above the sea. I think that Bennen and Tyndall could not have ascended more than 50 or 60 feet beyond this in the few minutes they were absent from the others, as they were upon one of the most difficult parts of the mountain. This party therefore accomplished an advance of about 350 or 400 feet.

Mr. Hawkins did not, as far as I know, make another attempt ; and the next was made by the Messrs. Parker, in July 1861. They again started from Zermatt ; followed the route they had struck out on the previous year, and got a little higher than before ; but they were defeated by want of time, shortly afterwards left Zermatt on account of bad weather, and did not again renew their attempts. Mr. Parker says—" In neither case did we go as high as we could. At the point where we turned we saw our way for a few hundred feet further ; but, beyond that, the difficulties seemed to increase." I am informed that both attempts should be considered as excursions undertaken with the view of ascertaining whether there was any encouragement to make a more deliberate attack on the north-east side.

My guide and I arrived at Breil on the 28th of August 1861, and we found that Professor Tyndall *had* been there a day or two before, but had done nothing. I had seen the mountain from nearly every direction, and it seemed, even to a novice like myself, far too much for a single day. I intended to sleep out upon it, as

---

* A view of this place accompanies Chapter v.

high as possible, and to attempt to reach the summit on the
following day. We endeavoured to induce another man to
accompany us, but without success. Matthias zum Taugwald
and other well-known guides were there at the time, but they
declined to go on any account. A sturdy old fellow—Peter
Taugwalder by name—said he would go! His price? "Two
hundred francs." "What, whether we ascend or not?" "Yes—
nothing less." The end of the matter was, that all the men who
were more or less capable showed a strong disinclination, or
positively refused, to go (their disinclination being very much in
proportion to their capacity), or else asked a prohibitive price.
This, it may be said once for all, was the reason why so many
futile attempts were made upon the Matterhorn. One first-rate
guide after another was brought up to the mountain, and patted
on the back, but all declined the business. The men who went
had no heart in the matter, and took the first opportunity to turn
back.* For they were, with the exception of one man, to whom
reference will be made presently, universally impressed with the
belief that the summit was entirely inaccessible.

We resolved to go alone, but, anticipating a cold bivouac, begged
the loan of a couple of blankets from the innkeeper. He refused
them ; giving the curious reason, that we had bought a bottle of
brandy at Val Tournanche, and had not bought any from him! No
brandy, no blankets, appeared to be his rule. We did not require
them that night, as it was passed in the highest cow-shed in the
valley, which is about an hour nearer to the mountain than is the
hotel. The cowherds, worthy fellows, seldom troubled by tourists,
hailed our company with delight, and did their best to make us
comfortable ; brought out their little stores of simple food, and, as
we sat with them round the great copper pot which hung over the
fire, bade us in husky voice, but with honest intent, to beware of
the perils of the haunted cliffs. When night was coming on, we
saw, stealing up the hill-side, the forms of Jean-Antoine Carrel and

* The guide Bennen must be excepted.

the comrade. "Oh ho!" I said, "you have repented?" "Not at all; you deceive yourself." "Why then have you come here?" "Because we ourselves are going on the mountain to-morrow." "Oh, then it is *not* necessary to have more than three." "Not for *us.*" I admired their pluck, and had a strong inclination to engage the pair; but, finally, decided against it. The comrade turned out to be the J. J. Carrel who had been with Mr. Hawkins, and was nearly related to the other man.

JEAN-ANTOINE CARREL (1869).

Both were bold mountaineers; but Jean-Antoine was incomparably the better man of the two, and he is the finest rock-climber I have ever seen. He was the only man who persistently refused to accept defeat, and who continued to believe, in spite of all discouragements, that the great mountain was not inaccessible, and that it could be ascended from the side of his native valley.

The night wore away without any excitement, except from the fleas, a party of whom executed a spirited fandango on my cheek, to the sound of music produced on the drum of my ear, by one of their fellows beating with a wisp of hay. The two Carrels crept noiselessly out before daybreak, and went off. We did not leave until nearly seven o'clock, and followed them leisurely, leaving all our properties in the cow-shed ; sauntered over the gentian-studded slopes which intervene between the shed and the Glacier du Lion, left cows and their pastures behind, traversed the stony wastes, and arrived at the ice. Old, hard beds of snow lay on its right bank (our left hand), and we mounted over them on to the lower portion of the glacier with ease. But, as we ascended, crevasses became numerous, and we were at last brought to a halt by some which were of very large dimensions ; and, as our cutting powers were limited, we sought an easier route, and turned, naturally, to the lower rocks of the Tête du Lion, which overlook the glacier on its west. Some good scrambling took us in a short time on to the crest of the ridge which descends towards the south ; and thence, up to the level of the Col du Lion, there was a long natural stair-case, on which it was seldom necessary to use the hands. We dubbed the place "The Great Staircase." Then the cliffs of the Tête du Lion, which rise above the Couloir, had to be skirted. This part varies considerably in different seasons, and in 1861 we found it difficult ; for the fine steady weather of that year had reduced the snow-beds abutting against it to a lower level than usual, and the rocks which were left exposed at the junction of the snow with the cliffs, had few ledges or cracks to which we could hold. But by half-past ten o'clock we stood on the Col, and looked down upon the magnificent basin out of which the Z'Mutt glacier flows. We decided to pass the night upon the Col, for we were charmed with the capabilities of the place, although it was one where liberties could not be taken. On one side a sheer wall overhung the Tiefenmatten glacier ; on the other, steep, glassy slopes of hard snow descended to the Glacier du Lion, furrowed by water and by falling stones ; on the north there was the great peak of the Mat-terhorn,* and on the south the cliffs of the Tête du Lion. Throw

---

* The engraving is made after a sketch taken from the rocks of the Matterhorn, just above the Col.

a bottle down to the Tiefenmatten—no sound returns for more than a dozen seconds.

      *   *   *   " how fearful

And dizzy 'tis, to cast one's eyes so low!"

THE COL DU LION: LOOKING TOWARDS THE TÊTE DU LION.

But no harm could come from that side. Neither could it from the other. Nor was it likely that it would from the Tête du Lion, for some jutting ledges conveniently overhung our proposed resting-place. We waited for a while, basked in the sunshine, and watched or listened to the Carrels, who were sometimes seen or heard, high above us, upon the ridge leading towards the summit; and, leaving at mid-day, we descended to the cow-shed, packed up the tent and other properties, and returned to the Col, although heavily laden, before six o'clock. This tent was constructed on a pattern suggested by Mr. Francis Galton, and it was not a success. It looked very pretty when set up in London, but it proved thoroughly useless in the Alps. It was made of light canvas, and opened like a book; had one end closed permanently and the other with flaps; it was supported by two alpenstocks, and had the canvas sides prolonged so as to turn in underneath. Numerous cords were sewn to the lower edges, to which stones were to be attached; but the main fastenings were by a cord which passed underneath the ridge and through iron rings screwed into the tops of the alpenstocks, and were secured by pegs. The wind, which playfully careered about the surrounding cliffs, was driven through our gap with the force of a blow-pipe; the flaps of the tent would not keep down, the pegs would not stay in, and it exhibited so marked a desire to go to the top of the Dent Blanche, that we thought it prudent to take it down and to sit upon it. When night came on we wrapped ourselves in it, and made our camp as comfortable as the circumstances would allow. The silence was impressive. No living thing was near our solitary bivouac; the Carrels had turned back and were out of hearing; the stones had ceased to fall, and the trickling water to murmur—

"The music of whose liquid lip
Had been to us companionship,
And, in our lonely life, had grown
To have an almost human tone."*

It was bitterly cold. Water froze hard in a bottle under my head. Not surprising, as we were actually on snow, and in a position where the slightest wind was at once felt. For a time we dozed, but about midnight there came from high aloft a tremendous

* J. G. Whittier.

explosion, followed by a second of dead quiet. A great mass of rock had split off, and was descending towards us. My guide started up, wrung his hands, and exclaimed, " O my God, we are lost ! " We heard it coming, mass after mass pouring over the precipices, bounding and rebounding from cliff to cliff, and the great rocks in advance smiting one another. They seemed to be close, although they were probably distant, but some small fragments, which dropped upon us at the same time from the ledges just above, added to the alarm, and my demoralised companion passed the remainder of the night in a state of shudder, ejaculating " terrible," and other adjectives.

We put ourselves in motion at daybreak, and commenced the ascent of the south-west ridge. There was no more sauntering with hands in the pockets ; each step had to be earned by downright climbing. But it was the most pleasant kind of climbing. The rocks were fast and unencumbered with débris ; the cracks were good, although not numerous, and there was nothing to fear except from one's-self. So we thought, at least, and shouted to awake echoes from the cliffs. · Ah ! there is no response. Not yet ; wait a while, everything here is upon a superlative scale ; count a dozen, and then the echoes will return from the walls of the Dent d'Herens, miles away, in waves of pure and undefiled sound ; soft, musical, and sweet. Halt a moment to regard the view ! We overlook the Tête du Lion, and nothing except the Dent d'Herens, whose summit is still a thousand feet above us, stands in the way ; the ranges of the Graian Alps—an ocean of mountains—are seen at a glance, governed by their three great peaks, the Grivola, Grand Paradis, and Tour de St. Pierre. How soft, and yet how sharp, they look in the early morning ! The mid-day mists have not begun to rise ; nothing is obscured ; even the pointed Viso, all but a hundred miles away, is perfectly defined.

Turn to the east, and watch the sun's slanting rays coming across the Monte Rosa snow-fields. Look at the shadowed parts, and see how even they—radiant with reflected light—are more brilliant than man knows how to depict. See, how—even there— the gentle undulations give shadows within shadows ; and how— yet again—where falling stones or ice have left a track, there are shadows upon shadows, each with a light and a dark side, with infinite gradations of matchless tenderness. Then, note the sun- light as it steals noiselessly along, and reveals countless unsuspected forms ;—the delicate ripple-lines which mark the concealed crevasse, and the waves of drifted snow ; producing each minute more lights and fresh shadows ; sparkling on the edges and glittering on the ends of the icicles ; shining on the heights and illuminating the depths, until all is aglow, and the dazzled eye returns for relief to the sombre crags.

Hardly an hour had passed since we left the Col before we arrived at the " Chimney." It proved to be the counterpart of the place to which reference has been made at p. 5 ; a smooth, straight slab of rock was fixed, at a considerable angle, between two others equally smooth.* My companion essayed to go up, and, after crumpling his long body into many ridiculous positions, he said that he would not, for he could not, do it. With some little trouble I got up it unassisted, and then my guide tied himself on to the end of our rope, and I endeavoured to pull him up. But he was so awkward that he did little for himself, and so heavy that he proved too much for me, and after several attempts he untied him- self, and quietly observed that he should go down. I told him he was a coward, and *he* mentioned his opinion of me. I requested him to go to Breil, and to say that he had left his " monsieur " on the mountain, and he turned to go ; whereupon I had to eat humble pie and ask him to come back ; for, although it was not very difficult to go up, and not at all dangerous with a man standing below, it was quite another thing to come down, as the lower edge overhung in a provoking manner.

The day was perfect ; the sun was pouring down grateful

* Mr. Hawkins referred to this place as one of excessive difficulty. He, however, found it coated with ice ; we found it free from ice.

warmth ; the wind had fallen ; the way seemed clear, no insuperable obstacle was in sight ; but what could one do alone? I stood on the top, chafing under this unexpected contretemps, and remained for some time irresolute ; but as it became apparent that the Chimney was swept more frequently than was necessary (it was a natural channel for falling stones), I turned at last, descended with the assistance of my companion, and returned with him to Breil, where we arrived about mid-day.

The Carrels did not show themselves, but we were told that they had not got to any great height,* and that the "comrade," who for convenience had taken off his shoes and tied them round his waist, had managed to let one of them slip, and had come down with a piece of cord fastened round his naked foot. Notwithstanding this, they had boldly glissaded down the Couloir du Lion, J. J. Carrel having his shoeless foot tied up in a pocket handkerchief.

The Matterhorn was not assailed again in 1861. I left Breil with the conviction that it was little use for a single tourist to organise an attack upon it, so great was its influence on the morals of the guides, and persuaded that it was desirable at least two should go, to back each other when required : and departed with my guide † over the Col Theodule, longing, more than before, to make the ascent, and determined to return, if possible with a companion, to lay siege to the mountain until one or the other was vanquished.

* I learned afterwards from Jean-Antoine Carrel that they got considerably higher than upon their previous attempts, and about 250 or 300 feet higher than Professor Tyndall in 1860. In 1862 I saw the initials of J. A. Carrel cut on the rocks at the place where he and his comrade had turned back.

† This man proved to be both willing and useful on lower ground, and voluntarily accompanied me a considerable distance out of his way, without fee or reward.

CHAPTER V.

" 'Tis a lesson you should heed,
        Try, try, try again.
If at first you don't succeed,
        Try, try, try again.
Then your courage should appear,
    For if you will persevere
    You will conquer, never fear.
        Try, try, try again."

                                    HICKSON.

THE year 1862 was still young, and the Matterhorn, clad in its
wintry garb, bore but little resemblance to the Matterhorn of the
summer, when a new force came to do battle with the mountain,
from another direction. Mr. T. S. Kennedy of Leeds conceived the
extraordinary idea that the peak might prove less impracticable in
January than in June, and arrived at Zermatt in the former month
to put his conception to the test. With stout Peter Perrn and
sturdy Peter Taugwalder he slept in the little chapel at the
Schwarzensee, and on the next morning, like the Messrs. Parker,
followed the ridge between the peak called Hörnli and the great
mountain. But they found that snow in winter obeyed the ordinary laws, and that the wind and frost were not less unkind than
in summer. " The wind whirled up the snow and spiculæ of ice
into our faces like needles, and flat pieces of ice a foot in diameter,
carried up from the glacier below, went flying past. Still no one
seemed to like to be the first to give in, till a gust fiercer than usual
forced us to shelter for a time behind a rock. Immediately it was
tacitly understood that our expedition must now end ; but we

determined to leave some memento of our visit, and, after descending a considerable distance, we found a suitable place with loose stones of which to build a cairn.   In half-an-hour a tower six feet high was erected ; a bottle, with the date, was placed inside, and we retreated as rapidly as possible."* This cairn was placed at the spot marked upon Dufour's Map of Switzerland 10,820 feet (3298 mètres), and the highest point attained by Mr. Kennedy was not, I imagine, more than two or three hundred feet above it.

Shortly after this Professor Tyndall gave, in his little tract *Mountaineering in* 1861, an account of the reason why he had left Breil, in August 1861, without doing anything.† It seems that he sent his guide Bennen to reconnoitre, and that the latter made the following report to his employer :—" Herr, I have examined the mountain carefully, and find it more difficult and dangerous than I had imagined.   There is no place upon it where we could well pass the night.   We might do so on yonder Col upon the snow, but there we should be almost frozen to death, and totally unfit for the work of the next day.   On the rocks there is no ledge or cranny which could give us proper harbourage ; and starting from Breuil it is certainly impossible to reach the summit in a single day."   " I was entirely taken aback," says Tyndall, " by this report.   I felt like a man whose grip had given way, and who was dropping through the air. . . .   Bennen was evidently dead against any attempt upon the mountain. ' We can, at all events, reach the lower of the two summits,' I remarked. ' Even that is difficult,' he replied ; ' but when you have reached it, what then ?   The peak has neither name nor fame.' "‡

* *Alpine Journal*, 1863, p. 82.   † See p. 87.

‡ *Mountaineering in* 1861, pp. 86-7.   Tyndall and Bennen were mistaken in supposing that the mountain has two summits ; it has only one.   They seem to have been deceived by the appearance of that part of the south-west ridge which is called " the shoulder " (l'épaule), as seen from Breil.   Viewed from that place, its southern end has certainly, through foreshortening, the semblance of a peak ; but when one regards it from the Col Theodule, or from any place in the same direction, the delusion is at once apparent.

I was more surprised than discouraged by this report by Bennen. One half of his assertions I knew to be wrong. The Col to which he referred was the Col du Lion, upon which we had passed a night less than a week after he had spoken so authoritatively ; and I had seen a place not far below the " Chimney,"—a place about 500 feet above the Col—where it seemed possible to construct a sleeping-place. Bennen's opinions seem to have undergone a complete change. In 1860 he is described as having been enthusiastic to make an attempt ; in 1861 he was dead against one. Nothing dismayed by this, my friend Mr. Reginald Macdonald, our companion on the Pelvoux—to whom so much of our success had been due, agreed to join me in a renewed assault from the south ; and, although we failed to secure Melchior Anderegg and some other notable guides, we obtained two men of repute, namely, Johann zum Taugwald and Johann Kronig, of Zermatt. We met at that place early in July, but stormy weather prevented us even from crossing to the other side of the chain for some time. We crossed the Col Theodule on the 5th, but the weather was thoroughly unsettled—it was raining in the valleys, and snowing upon the mountains. Shortly before we gained the summit we were made extremely uncomfortable by hearing mysterious, rushing sounds, which sometimes seemed as if a sudden gust of wind was sweeping along the snow, and, at others, almost like the swishing of a long whip : yet the snow exhibited no signs of motion, and the air was perfectly calm. The dense, black storm-clouds made us momentarily expect that our bodies might be used as lightning-conductors, and we were well satisfied to get under shelter of the inn at Breil, without having submitted to any such experience.*

* The late Principal Forbes was similarly situated while crossing the same pass in 1842. He described the sounds as rustling, fizzing, and hissing. See his *Travels in the Alps of Savoy*, second ed., p. 323. Mr. R. Spence Watson experienced the same upon the upper part of the Aletsch glacier in July 1863, and he spoke of the sounds as singing or hissing. See the *Athenæum*, Sept. 12, 1863. The respective parties seem to have been highly electrified on each occasion. Forbes says that his

We had need of a porter, and, by the advice of our landlord, descended to the chalets of Breil in search of one Luc Meynet. We found his house a mean abode, encumbered with cheese-making apparatus, and tenanted only by some bright-eyed children; but as they said that uncle Luc would soon be home, we waited at the door of the little chalet and watched for him. At last a speck was seen coming round the corner of the patch of pines below Breil, and then the children clapped their hands, dropped their toys, and ran eagerly forward to meet him. We saw an ungainly, wobbling figure stoop down and catch up the little ones, kiss them on each cheek, and put them into the empty panniers on each side of the mule, and then heard it come on carolling, as if this was not a world of woe: and yet the face of little Luc Meynet, the hunchback of Breil, bore traces of trouble and sorrow, and there was more than a touch of sadness in his voice when he said that he must look after his brother's children. All his difficulties were, however, at length overcome, and he agreed to join us to carry the tent.

In the past winter I had turned my attention to tents, and that which we had brought with us was the result of experiments to devise one which should be sufficiently portable to be taken over the most difficult ground, and which should combine lightness with stability. Its base was just under six feet square, and a section perpendicular to its length was an equilateral triangle, the sides of which were six feet long. It was intended to accommodate four persons. It was supported by four ash poles, six feet and a half long, and one inch and a quarter thick, tapering to the top to an inch and an eighth; these were shod with iron points. The order of proceeding in the construction of the tent was as follows: —Holes were drilled through the poles about five inches from their tops, for the insertion of two wrought-iron bolts, three inches long

---

fingers "yielded a fizzing sound;" and Watson says that his "hair stood on end in an uncomfortable but very amusing manner," and that "the veil on the wide-awake of one of the party stood upright in the air!"

and one quarter of an inch thick. The bolts were then inserted, 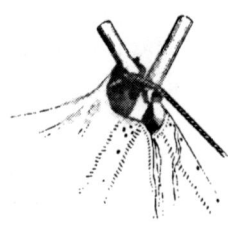 and the two pairs of poles were set out (and fixed up by a cord), to the proper dimensions. The roof was then put on. This was made of the rough, unbleached calico called forfar, which can be obtained in six-feet widths, and it was continued round for about two feet, on each side, on to the floor. The width of the material was the length of the tent, and seams were thus avoided in the roof. The forfar was sewn round each pole ; par-

ALPINE TENT.

ticular care being taken to avoid wrinkles, and to get the whole perfectly taut. The flooring was next put in and sewn down to the forfar. This was of the ordinary plaid mackintosh, about nine feet square ; the surplus three feet being continued up the sides to prevent draughts. It is as well to have two feet of this surplus on one side, and only one foot on the other ; the latter amount being sufficient for the side occupied by the feet. One end was then permanently closed by a triangular piece of forfar, which was sewn down to that which was already fixed. The other end was left open, and had two triangular flaps that overlapped each other, and which were fastened up when we were inside by pieces of tape. Lastly, the forfar was nailed down to the poles to prevent the tent getting out of shape. The cord which was used for climbing served for the tent ; it was passed over the crossed poles and underneath the ridge of the roof, and the two ends—one fore and the other aft—were easily secured to pieces of rock. Such a tent costs about four guineas, and its weight is about twenty-three pounds ; or, if the lightest kind of forfar is used, it need not exceed twenty pounds. When it was fastened up for transport it presented the appearance shown in the portrait of Meynet in Chapter XV., and it could be unrolled and set up by two persons in three minutes ; a point of no small importance during extreme weather.

This tent is intended, and adapted, for camping out at high altitudes, or in cold climates. It is not pretended that it is perfectly waterproof, but it can be made so by the addition of mackintosh to the roof; and this increases the weight by only two and a half pounds. It is then fit for general use.* It may be observed that the pattern of this tent is identical in all essential points with that arrived at (after great experience) by Sir Leopold M'Clintock for Arctic work, and frequent use by many persons, under varied conditions, has shown that the pattern is both practical and substantial.†

---

* I have described this tent at length, as frequent application has been made to me for information on the subject. I would strongly recommend any person who wishes to have one for long-continued use, to have one made under his own eye, and to be particularly careful to test the poles. My experience goes to show that poles which (when supported upon their extremities) will bear a dead weight of 100 lbs. suspended from their centres, will stand any wind to which they are likely to be submitted. Ash is, perhaps, the best wood that can be selected : lancewood is equally good, but heavier.

† It has been used, amongst others, by Messrs. Freshfield, Moore, and Tucker, in the Caucasus ; by the Rev. W. H. Hawker in Corsica ; and by myself in Greenland.

Sunday; the 6th of July, was showery, and snow fell on the Matterhorn, but we started on the following morning with our three men, and pursued my route of the previous year. I was requested to direct the way, as none save myself had been on the mountain before ; but I did not distinguish myself on this occasion, and led my companions nearly to the top of the small peak before the mistake was discovered. The party becoming rebellious, a little exploration was made towards our right, and we found that we were upon the top of the cliff overlooking the Col du Lion. The upper part of the small peak is of a very different character to the lower part ; the rocks are not so firm, and they are usually covered, or intermixed, with snow, and glazed with ice : the angle too is more severe. While descending a small snow-slope, to get on to the right track, Kronig slipped on a streak of ice, and went down at a fearful pace. Fortunately he kept on his legs, and, by a great effort, succeeded in stopping just before he arrived at some rocks that jutted through the snow, which would infallibly have knocked him over. When we rejoined him a few minutes later, we found that he was incapable of standing, much less of moving, with a face corpse-like in hue, and trembling violently. He remained in this condition for more than an hour, and the day was consequently far advanced before we arrived at our camping-place on the Col. Profiting by the experience of last year, we did not pitch the tent actually on the snow, but collected a quantity of débris from the neighbouring ledges, and after constructing a rough platform of the larger pieces, levelled the whole with the dirt and mud.

Meynet had proved invaluable as a tent-bearer ; for—although his legs were more picturesque than symmetrical, and although he seemed to be built on principle with no two parts alike—his very deformities proved of service ; and we quickly found he had spirit of no common order, and that few peasants are more agreeable companions, or better climbers, than little Luc Meynet, the hunchback of Breil. He now showed himself not less serviceable as a scavenger, and humbly asked for gristly pieces of meat, rejected by the others, or for suspicious eggs ; and seemed to consider it a peculiar favour, if not a treat, to be permitted to drink the coffee-grounds. With the greatest contentment he took the worst place at the door of the tent, and did all the dirty work which was put upon him by the guides, as gratefully as a dog—who has been well beaten—will receive a stroke.

A strong wind sprang up from the east during the night, and in the morning it was blowing almost a hurricane. The tent behaved nobly, and we remained under its shelter for several hours after the sun had risen, uncertain what it was best to do. A lull tempted us to move, but we had scarcely ascended a hundred feet before the storm burst upon us with increased fury. Advance or return was alike impossible ; the ridge was denuded of its débris ; and we clutched our hardest when we saw stones as big as a man's fist blown away horizontally into space. We dared not attempt to stand upright, and remained stationary, on all fours, glued, as it were, to the rocks. It was intensely cold, for the blast had swept along the main chain of the Pennine Alps, and across the great snow-fields around Monte Rosa. Our warmth and courage rapidly evaporated, and at the next lull we retreated to the tent ; having to halt several times even in that short distance. Taugwald and Kronig then declared that they had had enough, and refused to have anything more to do with the mountain. Meynet also informed us that he would be required down below for important cheese-making operations on the following day. It was therefore needful to return to Breil, and we arrived there at 2.30 P.M., extremely chagrined at our complete defeat.

Jean-Antoine Carrel, attracted by rumours, had come up to the inn during our absence, and after some negotiations agreed to accompany us, with one of his friends named Pession, on the first fine day. We thought ourselves fortunate ; for Carrel clearly considered the mountain a kind of *preserve,* and regarded our late attempt as an act of *poaching.** The wind blew itself out during

---

* A better feeling exists at the present time in the Val Tournanche in regard to strangers. In 1862 the jealousy of the natives towards their Swiss neighbours was oftentimes extremely amusing, although embarrassing.

the night, and we started again, with these two men and a porter, at 8 A.M. on the 9th, with unexceptionable weather. Carrel pleased us by suggesting that we should camp even higher than before ; and we accordingly proceeded, without resting at the Col, until we overtopped the Tête du Lion. Near the foot of the "Chimney," a little below the crest of the ridge, and on its eastern side, we found a protected place ; and by building up from ledge to ledge (under the direction of our leader, who was a mason by profession), we at length constructed a platform of sufficient size and of considerable solidity. Its height was about 12,550 feet above the sea ; and it exists, I believe, at the present time.* We then pushed on, as the day was very fine, and, after a short hour's scramble, got to the foot of the Great Tower upon the ridge (that is to say, to Mr. Hawkins' farthest point), and afterwards returned to our bivouac. We turned out again at 4 A.M., and at 5.15 started upwards once more, with fine weather and the thermometer at 28°. Carrel scrambled up the Chimney, and Macdonald and I after him. Pession's turn came, but when he arrived at the top he looked very ill, declared himself to be thoroughly incapable, and said that he must go back. We waited some time, but he did not get better, neither could we learn the nature of his illness. Carrel flatly refused to go on with us alone. We were helpless. Macdonald, ever the coolest of the cool, suggested that we should try what we could do without them ; but our better judgment prevailed, and, finally, we returned together to Breil. On the next day my friend started for London.

Three times I had essayed the ascent of this mountain, and on each occasion had failed ignominiously. I had not advanced a yard beyond my predecessors. Up to the height of nearly 13,000 feet there were no extraordinary difficulties ; the way so far might even become "a matter of amusement." Only 1800 feet remained ;

---

* The heights given on the outlines of the Matterhorn, accompanying Chap. iv., on the geological section in the Appendix, and quoted throughout the book, are after the barometric (mercurial) measurements of Signor F. Giordano in 1866 and 1868. I have ventured to differ from him only in regard to the height of the second tent-platform, and have assigned to it a somewhat lower elevation than his estimate.

but they were as yet untrodden, and might present the most formidable obstacles.   No man could expect to climb them by himself.   A morsel of rock only seven feet high might at any time
defeat him, if it were perpendicular.   Such a place might be possible to two, or a bagatelle to three men.   It was evident that a
party should consist of three men at least.   But where could the
other two men be obtained ?   Carrel was the only man who exhibited
any enthusiasm in the matter ; and he, in 1861, had absolutely
refused to go unless the party consisted of at least *four* persons.
Want of men made the difficulty, not the mountain.

The weather became bad again, so I went to Zermatt on the
chance of picking up a man, and remained there during a week of
storms.*   Not one of the good men, however, could be induced to
come, and I returned to Breil on the 17th, hoping to combine
the skill of Carrel with the willingness of Meynet on a new
attempt, by the same route as before ; for the Hörnli ridge, which
I had examined in the meantime, seemed to be entirely impracticable.   Both men were inclined to go, but their ordinary occupations prevented them from starting at once. †

My tent had been left rolled up at the second platform, and
whilst waiting for the men it occurred to me that it might have
been blown away during the late stormy weather ; so I started off
on the 18th to see if this were so or not.   The way was by this
time familiar, and I mounted rapidly, astonishing the friendly
herdsmen—who nodded recognition as I flitted past them and the
cows—for I was alone, because no man was available.   But more
deliberation was necessary when the pastures were passed, and
climbing began, for it was needful to mark each step, in case of mist,
or surprise by night.   It is one of the few things which can be said
in favour of mountaineering alone (a practice which has little besides to commend it), that it awakens a man's faculties, and makes
him observe.   When one has no arms to help, and no head to guide

---

* During this time making the ascent of Monte Rosa.

† They were not guides by profession.

him except his own, he must needs take note even of small things, for he cannot afford to throw away a chance ; and so it came to pass, upon my solitary scramble, when above the snow-line, and beyond the ordinary limits of flowering plants, when peering about noting angles and landmarks, that my eyes fell upon the tiny straggling plants—oftentimes a single flower on a single stalk— pioneers of vegetation, atoms of life in a world of desolation, which had found their way up—who can tell how ?—from far below, and were obtaining bare sustenance from the scanty soil in protected nooks ; and it gave a new interest to the well-known rocks to see what a gallant fight the survivors made (for many must have perished in the attempt) to ascend the great mountain. The Gentian, as one might have expected, was there, but it was run close by Saxifrages, and by *Linaria alpina,* and was beaten by *Thlaspi rotundifolium,* which latter plant was the highest I was able to secure, although it too was overtopped by a little white flower which I knew not, and was unable to reach.*

* Those which I collected were as follow :—*Myosotis alpestris,* Gm.; *Veronica alpina,* L. ; *Linaria alpina,* M.; *Gentiana Bavarica,* L. ; *Thlaspi rotundifolium,* Gaud. ; *Silene acaulis* L. (?) ; *Potentilla* sp.; *Saxifraga* sp.; *Saxifraga muscoides,* Wulf. I am indebted for these names to Mr. William Carruthers of the British Museum. The plants ranged from about 10,500 to a little below 13,000 feet, and are the highest which I have seen anywhere in the Alps. Three times this number of species might be collected, I have no doubt, within these limits. I was not endeavouring to make a *flora* of the Matterhorn, but to obtain those plants which attained the greatest height. Very few lichens are seen on the higher parts of this mountain ; their rarity is due, doubtless, to the constant disintegration of the rocks, and the consequent exposure of fresh surfaces. *Silene acaulis* was the highest plant found by De Saussure on his travels in the Alps. He mentions (§ 2018) that he found a tuft "near the place where I slept on my return (from the ascent of Mont Blanc), about 1780 toises (11,388 feet) above the level of the sea."

Mr. William Mathews and Mr. Charles Packe, who have botanised respectively for many years in the Alps and Pyrenees, have favoured me with the names of the highest plants that they have obtained upon their excursions. Their lists, although not extensive, are interesting as showing the extreme limits attained by some of the hardiest of Alpine plants. Those mentioned by Mr. Mathews are— *Campanula cenisia* (on the Grivola, 12,047 feet) ; *Saxifraga bryoides* and *Androsace glacialis* (on the summits of Mont Emilius, 11,677, and the Ruitor, 11,480) ; *Ranunculus*

The tent was safe, although snowed up ; and I turned to con-template the view, which, when seen alone and undisturbed, had all the strength and charm of complete novelty.* The highest peaks of the Pennine chain were in front—the Breithorn (13,685 feet), the Lyskamm (14,889), and Monte Rosa (15,217) ; then, turn-ing to the right, the entire block of mountains which separated the Val Tournanche from the Val d'Ayas was seen at a glance, with its dominating summit the Grand Tournalin (11,155†). Behind were the ranges dividing the Val d'Ayas from the Valley of Gres-soney, backed by higher summits. More still to the right, the eye wandered down the entire length of the Val Tournanche, and then rested upon the Graian Alps with their innumerable peaks, and upon the isolated pyramid of Monte Viso (12,643) in the extreme distance. Next, still turning to the right, came the mountains

glacialis, Armeria alpina, and *Pyrethrum alpinum* (on Monte Viso, from 10,000 to 10,500 feet) ; *Thlaspi rotundifolium,* and *Saxifraga biflora* (Monte Viso, about 9500 feet) ; and *Campanula rotundifolia* (?), *Artemisia spicata* (Wulf.), *Aronicum Doronicum,* and *Petrocallis Pyrenaica* (Col de Seylières, 9247).

Mr. Packe obtained, on or close to the summit of the Pic de Mulhahacen, Sierra Nevada, of Granada (11,600 to 11,700 feet), *Papaver alpinum* (var. *Pyrenaicum*), *Artemisia Nevadensis* (used for giving the flavour to the Manzanilla sherry), *Viola Nevadensis, Galium Pyrenaicum, Trisetum glaciale, Festuca Clementei, Saxifraga Grœnlandica* (var. *Mista*), *Erigeron alpinum* (var. *glaciale*) and *Arenaria tetra-quetra.* On the Picacho de Veleta (11,440 feet), and on the Alcazaba (11,350), the same plants were obtained, with the exception of the first named. At a height of 11,150 feet on these mountains he also collected *Ptilotrichum purpureum, Lepidium stylatum,* and *Biscutella saxatilis ;* and, at 10,000 feet, *Alyssum spicatum* and *Si-deritis scordiodes.* Mr. Packe mentions the following plants as occurring at 9000 to 10,000 feet in the Pyrenees :—*Cerastium latifolium, Draba Wahlenbergii, Hut-chinsia alpina, Linaria alpina, Oxyria reniformis, Ranunculus glacialis, Saxifraga nervosa, S. oppositifolia, S. Grœnlandica, Statice Armeria, Veronica alpina.*

Information on the botany of the Val Tournanche is contained in the little pam-phlet by the Canon G. Carrel, entitled *La Vallée de Valtornenche en* 1867 ; and a list of the plants which have hitherto been collected on the glacier-surrounded ridge (Furgen Grat) connecting the Matterhorn with the Col Theodule, will be found in Dollfus-Ausset's *Matériaux pour l'étude des Glaciers,* vol. viii. part first, 1868.

* See the map of the valley of Zermatt, etc. ; that of the Valpelline, etc. ; and the general route map.

† On the authority of Canon Carrel.

intervening between the Val Tournanche and the Val Barthelemy : Mont Rouss (a round-topped snowy summit, which seems so important from Breil, but which is in reality only a buttress of the higher mountain, the Château des Dames), had long ago sunk, and the eye passed over it, scarcely heeding its existence, to the Becca Salle (or, as it is printed on the map, Bec de Sale),—a miniature Matterhorn— and to other, and more important heights.   Then the grand mass of the Dent d'Hérens (13,714) stopped the way ; a noble mountain, encrusted on its northern slopes with enormous hanging glaciers, which broke away at mid-day in immense slices, and thundered down on to the Tiefenmatten glacier ; and lastly, most splendid of all, came the Dent Blanche (14,318), soaring above the basin of the great Z'Muttgletscher.   Such a view is hardly to be matched in the Alps, and *this* view is very rarely seen, as I saw it, perfectly unclouded.*

* I have already had occasion to mention the rapid changes which occur in the weather at considerable elevations in the Alps, and shall have to do so again in subsequent chapters.   No one can regret more than myself the variable weather which afflicts that otherwise delightful chain of mountains, or the necessity of speaking about it : its summits appear to enjoy more than their fair share of wind and tempests.   Meteorological disturbances, it would seem, are by no means necessary accompaniments of high regions.   There are some happy places which are said to be favoured with almost perpetual calm.   Take the case of the Sierra Nevada of California, for example, which includes numerous summits from 13,000 to 15,000 feet. Mr. Whitney, of San Francisco, says (in his *Guide-book to the Yosemite Valley, and the adjacent region*), " At high altitudes, all through the mountains, the weather during the summer is almost always the finest possible for travelling.   There are occasional storms in the high mountains ; but, in ordinary seasons, these are quite rare, and one of the greatest drawbacks to the pleasure of travelling in the Alps, the uncertainty of the weather, is here almost entirely wanting."   It is probable that a more thorough acquaintance with that region will modify this opinion ; for it must be admitted that it is very difficult to judge of the state of the atmosphere of great heights from the valleys, and it often occurs that a terrific storm is raging above when there is a dead calm below, at a distance perhaps of not more than three or four miles.   A case of this kind is described in Chapter vii., and another may be mentioned here.   At the very time that I was regarding the Dent Blanche from a height of 12,550 feet on the Matterhorn, Mr. T. S. Kennedy was engaged in making the first ascent of the former mountain, and he described his ascent in a very picturesque paper in the *Alpine Journal* (1863). I learn from it that he experienced severe weather.   " The wind roared over our ridge,

Time sped away unregarded, and the little birds which had built their nests on the neighbouring cliffs had begun to chirp their evening hymn before I thought of returning. Half mechanically I turned to the tent, unrolled it, and set it up; it contained food enough for several days, and I resolved to stay over the night. I had started from Breil without provisions, or telling Favre—the innkeeper, who was accustomed to my erratic ways—where I was going. I returned to the view. The sun was setting, and its rosy rays, blending with the snowy blue, had thrown a pale, pure violet far as the eye could see; the valleys were drowned in a purple gloom, while the summits shone with unnatural brightness : and as I sat in the door of the tent, and watched the twilight change to darkness, the earth seemed to become less earthy and almost sublime ; the world seemed dead, and I, its sole inhabitant. By and by, the moon as it rose brought the hills again into sight, and by a judicious repression of detail rendered the view yet more magnificent. Something in the south hung like a great glow-worm in the air ; it was too large for a star, and too steady for a meteor ; and it was long before I could realise the incredible fact that it was the moonlight glittering on the great snow-slope on the north side of Monte Viso, at a distance, as the crow flies, of 98 miles. Shivering, at last I entered the tent and made my coffee. The night was passed comfortably, and the next morning, tempted by the brilliancy of the weather, I proceeded yet higher in search of another place for a platform.

making fearfully wild music among the desolate crags. . . It rendered an ordinary voice inaudible," and "nothing at a distance greater than fifty yards could be seen at all. . . Thick mists and driving clouds of snow swept over and past us ;" the thermometer fell to 20° Fahr., and his companion's hair became a mass of white icicles. Now, at this time, Mr. Kennedy was distant from me only four and a half miles. With me, and in my immediate neighbourhood, the air was perfectly calm, and the temperature was agreeably warm ; even during the night it fell only two or three degrees below freezing point. During most of the day the Dent Blanche was perfectly unclouded, though, for a time, light fleecy clouds were hovering about its upper 2000 feet ; but no one would have supposed from appearances that my friend was experiencing a storm such as he has described.

Solitary scrambling over a pretty wide area had shown me that a single individual is subjected to many difficulties which do not trouble a party of two or three men, and that the disadvantages of being alone are more felt while descending than during the ascent. In order to neutralise these inconveniences, I devised two little appliances, which were now brought into use for the first time. One was a claw—a kind of grapnel —about five inches long, made of shear steel, one-fifth of an inch thick. This was of use in difficult places where there was no hold within arm's length, but where there were cracks or ledges some distance higher. It could be stuck on the end of the alpenstock and dropped into such places, or, on extreme occasions, flung up until it attached itself to something. The edges that laid hold of the rocks were serrated, which tended to make them catch more readily : the other end had a ring to which a rope was fastened. It must not be understood that this was employed for hauling one's-self up for any great distance, but that it was used in ascending, at the most, for only a few yards at a time. In descending, however, it could be prudently used for a greater distance at a time, as the claws could be planted firmly ; but it was necessary to keep the rope taut, and the pull constantly in the direction of the length of the implement, otherwise it had a tendency to slip away. The second device was merely a modification of a dodge practised by all climbers. It is frequently necessary for a single man (or for the last man of a party) during a descent, to make a loop in the end of his rope, which he passes over some rocks, and to come down holding the free end. The loop is then jerked off, and the process may be repeated. But as it sometimes happens that there are no rocks at hand which will allow a loose loop to be used, a slip-knot has to be resorted to, and the rope is drawn in tightly. Consequently it will occur that it is not possible to jerk the loop off, and the rope has to be cut and left behind. To prevent this, I had a wrought-iron ring (two and a quarter inches in diameter and three eighths of an inch thick) attached to one end of my rope, and a loop could be made in a moment by passing the other end of the rope through this ring, which of course slipped up and held tightly as I descended holding the free end. A strong piece of cord was also attached to the ring, and, on arriving at the bottom, this was pulled ; the ring slid back again, and the loop was whipped off readily. By means of these two simple appliances I was able to ascend and descend rocks, which otherwise would have been completely impassable.  The combined weight of these two things amounted to less than half-a-pound.

It has been mentioned (p. 93) that the rocks of the south-west ridge are by no means difficult for some distance above the Col du Lion. This is true of the rocks up to the level of the Chimney, but they steepen when that is passed, and remaining smooth and with but few fractures, and still continuing to dip outwards, present some steps of a very uncertain kind, particularly when they are glazed with ice. At this point (just above the Chimney) the climber is obliged to follow the southern (or Breil) side of the ridge, but, in a few feet more, one must turn over to the northern (or Z'Mutt) side, where, in most years, nature kindly provides a snow-slope. When this is surmounted, one can again return to the crest of the ridge, and follow it, by easy rocks, to the foot of the Great Tower. This was the highest point attained by Mr. Hawkins in 1860, and it was also our highest on the 9th of July.

This Great Tower is one of the most striking features of the ridge. It stands out like a turret at the angle of a castle. Behind it a

battlemented wall leads upwards to the citadel.*   Seen from the
Theodule pass, it looks only an insignificant pinnacle, but as one
approaches it (on the ridge) so it seems to rise, and, when one is at
its base, it completely conceals the upper parts of the mountain.
I found here a suitable place for the tent ; which, although not so
well protected as the second platform, possessed the advantage of
being 300 feet higher up ; and fascinated by the wildness of the
cliffs, and enticed by the perfection of the weather, I went on to see
what was behind.

The first step was a difficult one ; the ridge became diminished
to the least possible width—it was hard to keep one's balance—and
just where it was narrowest, a more than perpendicular mass barred
the way.   Nothing fairly within arm's reach could be laid hold of ;
it was necessary to spring up, and then to haul one's-self over the
sharp edge by sheer strength.   Progression directly upwards was
then impossible.   Enormous and appalling precipices plunged
down to the Tiefenmatten glacier on the left, but round the right-
hand side it was just possible to go.   One hindrance then succeeded
another, and much time was consumed in seeking the way.   I have
a vivid recollection of a gully of more than usual perplexity at the
side of the Great Tower, with minute ledges and steep walls ; of the
ledges dwindling down and at last ceasing ; and of finding myself,
with arms and legs divergent, fixed as if crucified, pressing against
the rock, and feeling each rise and fall of my chest as I breathed ;
of screwing my head round to look for hold, and not seeing any, and
of jumping sideways on to the other side.

'Tis vain to attempt to describe such places.   Whether they are
sketched with a light hand, or wrought out in laborious detail, one
stands an equal chance of being misunderstood.   Their enchantment to the climber arises from their calls on his faculties, in their
demands on his strength, and on overcoming the impediments which
they oppose to his skill.   The non-mountaineering reader cannot

* See the engraving " Crags of the Matterhorn," which accompanies Chap. vii.

feel this, and his interest in descriptions of such places is usually very small, unless he supposes that the situations are perilous. They are not necessarily perilous, but I think it is impossible to avoid giving such an impression if the difficulties are particularly insisted upon.

A painstaking writer is therefore liable to be misunderstood in at least two ways. If he skips the difficulties, fearing, perhaps, to be charged with tediousness, he lays himself open to the imputation of being unobservant, or simply stupid ; or, if he chronicles each step, and works out each difficulty, he is exposed to the risk of being accused either of frightful exaggeration, or of getting into utterly unjustifiable situations. I do not wish to be charged with one or the other of these things, and shall therefore explain myself more fully.

Places such as this gully have their charm, so long as a man feels that the difficulties are within his power ; but their enchantment vanishes directly they are too much for him, and when he feels this they are dangerous to him. The line which separates the difficult from the dangerous is sometimes a very shadowy, but it is not an imaginary, one. It is a true line, without breadth. It is often easy to pass and very hard to see. It is sometimes passed unconsciously, and the consciousness that it has been passed is felt too late ; but so long as a man undertakes that which is well within his power, he is not likely to pass this line, or, consequently, to get into any great danger, although he may meet with considerable difficulty. That which is within a man's power varies, of course, according to time, place, and circumstance, but, as a rule, he can tell pretty well when he is arriving at the end of his tether ; and it seems to me, although it is difficult to determine for another, even approximately, the limits to which it is prudent for him to go, that it is tolerably easy to do so for one's-self. But (according to my opinion) if the doubtful line is crossed consciously, deliberately, one passes from doing that which is justifiable to doing that which is unjustifiable, because it is imprudent.

Q

I expect that any intelligent critic will inquire, " But do you really mean to assert that dangers in mountaineering arise only from superlative difficulty ; and that the perfect mountaineer does not run any risks ?" I am not prepared to go quite so far as this, although there is only one risk to which the scrambler on the Higher Alps is unavoidably subject, which does not occur to pedestrians in London's streets. This arises from falling rocks, and I shall endeavour, in the course of this volume, to make the reader understand that it is a *positive* danger, and one against which skill, strength, and courage, are equally unavailing. It occurs at unexpected times, and may occur in almost any place. The critic may retort, " Your admission of this one danger destroys all the rest of the argument." I agree with him that it would do so if it were a *grave* risk to life. But although it is a real danger, it is not a very serious risk. Not many cases can be quoted of accidents which have happened through falling stones, and I do not know an instance of life having been lost in this way in the High Alps.* I suppose, however, few persons will maintain that it is unjustifiable to do anything, for sport or otherwise, so long as *any* risk is incurred ; else it would be unjustifiable to cross Fleet Street at mid-day. If it were one's bounden duty to avoid every risk, we should have to pass our lives indoors. I conceive that the pleasures of mountaineering outweigh the risks arising from this particular cause, and that the practice will not be vetoed on its account. Still, I wish to stamp it as a *positive* danger, and as one which may imperil the life of the most perfect mountaineer.

There is, then, only one positive danger in mountaineering, and that is little risk. There are, however, numerous negative dangers through which many lose their lives. The words positive and negative are used in the following sense. A positive danger is one which we are powerless to avoid, and a negative danger is one which

---

* The contrary is the case in regard to the Lower Alps. Amongst others, the case may be mentioned of a lady who (not very long ago) had her skull fractured while sitting at the base of the Mer de Glace.

requires action on our part to convert it into a positive one. A precipice is a negative danger, but it is a positive one to a man who falls over it : a steep snow-slope of new snow has dangerous qualities, but it is not positively dangerous until its equilibrium is disturbed, and it descends as an avalanche : the piled-up blocks on a shattered ridge may be dangerous, but they are not so until they are dislodged : and a concealed crevasse may be perilous to the last degree, but it is not so unless you tumble into it. This distinction is not hair-splitting, and it is essential to remember it, if one would come to a clear understanding about that which is right and wrong in mountaineering. If it were impossible to avoid tumbling into crevasses, or dislodging vast masses of débris, or starting avalanches, or falling over precipices, mountaineering, for the sake of sport, would be entirely unjustifiable ; and, according to the principles already laid down, it is unjustifiable if, through incompetence or recklessness, any one converts these negative slumbering dangers into active and positive ones.

It may be remarked parenthetically that the term foolhardiness is frequently used rather loosely in regard to accidents which occur in the Alps. The mere fact that a man loses his life, or sustains injury, whether it be on the mountains or elsewhere, is no proof that he was foolhardy ; and upon reviewing those accidents which have happened in late years, it seems to me that to the major part the word is inapplicable. If anything is undertaken for sport which there is good reason to suppose must fail, or will probably be fatal to life, that may be considered foolhardy. But if the unavoidable risks are almost inappreciable, and that which is undertaken is not clearly beyond the powers of those who undertake it, it seems to me that the use of this word is not advisable, even although a fatal accident should happen. A slip which arises from a momentary indiscretion, or an accident the consequence of exhaustion, should hardly be classed amongst those fatalities which are the direct results of imprudences that are entirely unjustifiable ; and it cannot be denied that accidents have happened for which no excuses can be offered.

The most capable men agree that there are two species of fool-hardiness which merit emphatic condemnation. The first is attempting to traverse the upper (snow-covered) portions of glaciers without using a rope, and the second is ignoring the instability of new snow. Lives are lost every year through one or the other of these imbecilities. In each case the dangers are perfectly well known, and the results may be predicted with tolerable certainty. A man who attempts to traverse the upper parts of glaciers by himself, or with others, unroped, does not necessarily take harm on the first attempt, but if he perseveres he is certain to come to grief sooner or later. He may go on with impunity for a considerable time, or he may perish on the first attempt ; but, whatever may be the case, he is foolhardy, because he incurs a risk which can only be incurred by the neglect of the simplest of precautions. In the second case one cannot, unfortunately, speak with the same precision, because there are three elements involved, all of which are subject to continual variation. The first is the quality of the snow, the second is its quantity, and the third is the angle at which it reposes. Still it is not very difficult in practice to determine when a new fall of snow is dangerous to traverse or not. For example, it may be laid down as a general rule that it is imprudent to meddle with any slope exceeding thirty degrees for several days after a heavy fall. It is equally certain that slopes considerably exceeding this angle are traversed, or attempted to be crossed, every year, by incompetent persons, within twenty-four hours of heavy falls.

It may be questioned whether those who commit these imprudences consider they are endangering their lives. In some cases such things have probably been done from mere ignorance, but in others the clamour and protestations against departure have at least taken it out of the power of those concerned to say that they were unaware of the opinion of those who were the most fit judges. Whether such things are done from ignorance or from conceit, it is not unfair to class them as acts of foolhardiness.

Three possible causes of accidents have now been mentioned. From the first there is small risk, but unavoidable danger so long as mountaineering is practised ; from the others there may be great risks, but they are easily avoided by the exercise of a little common sense. The largest part of the accidents, however, which occur in the Alps cannot be classed under these heads, but arise chiefly from momentary indiscretions, and from men trying to do that which is beyond their powers. It is not easy to find two cases exactly alike, although they principally come from the difficulty man experiences in keeping on his feet in slippery places. They come not from any dangers inherent to mountains, but from the frailties of the mountaineer. A volume might be filled with examples, and they would all be found to show that if *this* had been done, or *that* had not been done, the results would not have happened. In many cases some canon of mountaineering will be found to have been violated, and in all, the man rather than the mountain will be found to have been the offender.

I have now endeavoured to discriminate between that which is merely difficult and that which is absolutely dangerous ; secondly, to distinguish unavoidable from avoidable dangers ; and thirdly, to make a rough classification of the causes of accidents. If that which has been said is true, it follows that the dangers from the Alps themselves have been ridiculously overrated, and that the thing to be wished for is, not that the mountains should become easier, but that men should become wiser and stronger. It is too much to expect, however, so long as tyros attempt to imitate the doings of skilled mountaineers, and middle-aged gentlemen, with stiff knees, essay the things which are adapted only to the young and active, that accidents in the Alps will cease, or even diminish in number ; and, although these too daring persons should, perhaps, be pitied rather than censured, it is very much to be desired that they would pay a little more attention to the truth "That which is sport to one may be death to another," instead of applying to themselves the maxim "What man has done man can do."

This long digression has been caused by an innocent gully which I feared the reader might think was dangerous. It was an untrodden vestibule which led to a scene so wild that even the most sober description of it must seem an exaggeration. There was a change in the quality of the rock, and there was a change in the appearance of the ridge. The rocks (talcose gneiss) below this spot were singularly firm ; it was rarely necessary to test one's hold ; the way led over the living rock, and not up rent-off fragments. But here, all was decay and ruin. The crest of the ridge was shattered and cleft, and the feet sank in the chips which had drifted down ; while above, huge blocks, hacked and carved by the hand of time, nodded to the sky, looking like the grave-stones of giants. Out of curiosity I wandered to a notch in the ridge, between two tottering piles of immense masses, which seemed to need but a few pounds on one or the other side to make them fall ; so nicely poised that they would literally have rocked in the wind, for they were put in motion by a touch ; and based on support so frail that I wondered they did not collapse before my eyes. In the whole range of my Alpine experience I have seen nothing more striking than this desolate, ruined, and shattered ridge at the back of the Great Tower. I have seen stranger shapes,—rocks which mimic the human form, with monstrous leering faces—and isolated pinnacles, sharper and greater than any here ; but I have never seen exhibited so impressively the tremendous effects which may be produced by frost, and by the long-continued action of forces whose individual effects are imperceptible.

It is needless to say that it is impossible to climb by the crest of the ridge at this part ; still one is compelled to keep near to it, for there is no other way. Generally speaking, the angles on the Matterhorn are too steep to allow the formation of considerable beds of snow, but here there is a corner which permits it to accumu-late, and it is turned to gratefully, for, by its assistance, one can ascend four times as rapidly as upon the rocks.

The Tower was now almost out of sight, and I looked over

"THE CHIMNEY."

(ON THE SOUTH-WEST RIDGE OF THE MATTERHORN).

the central Pennine Alps to the Grand Combin, and to the chain of Mont Blanc. My neighbour, the Dent d'Hérens, still rose above me, although but slightly, and the height which had been attained could be measured by its help. So far, I had no doubts about my capacity to descend that which had been ascended ; but, in a short time, on looking ahead, I saw that the cliffs steepened, and I turned back (without pushing on to them, and getting into inextricable difficulties), exulting in the thought that they would be passed when we returned together, and that I had, without assistance, got nearly to the height of the Dent d'Hérens, and considerably higher than any one had been before.* My exultation was a little premature.

About 5 P.M. I left the tent again, and thought myself as good as at Breil. The friendly rope and claw had done good service, and had smoothened all the difficulties. I lowered myself through the Chimney, however, by making a fixture of the rope, which I then cut off, and left behind, as there was enough and to spare. My axe had proved a great nuisance in coming down, and I left it in the tent. It was not attached to the bâton, but was a separate affair, —an old navy boarding-axe. While cutting up the different snow-beds on the ascent, the bâton trailed behind fastened to the rope ; and, when climbing, the axe was carried behind, run through the rope tied round my waist, and was sufficiently out of the way ; but in descending, when coming down face outwards (as is always best where it is possible), the head or the handle of the weapon caught frequently against the rocks, and several times nearly upset me. So, out of laziness if you will, it was left in the tent. I paid dearly for the imprudence.

The Col du Lion was passed, and fifty yards more would have placed me on the " Great Staircase," down which one can run. But

---

* A remarkable streak of snow (marked " cravate " in the outline of the Matterhorn, as seen from the Theodule) runs across the cliff at this part of the mountain. My highest point was somewhat higher than the lowest part of this snow, and was consequently nearly 13,500 feet above the sea.

on arriving at an angle of the cliffs of the Tête du Lion, while skirting the upper edge of the snow which abuts against them, I found that the heat of the two past days had nearly obliterated the steps which had been cut when coming up. The rocks happened to be impracticable just at this corner, so nothing could be done except make the steps afresh. The snow was too hard to beat or tread down, and at the angle it was all but ice ; half-a-dozen steps only were required, and then the ledges could be followed again. So I held to the rock with my right hand, and prodded at the snow with the point of my stick until a good step was made, and then, leaning round the angle, did the same for the other side. So far well, but in attempting to pass the corner (to the present moment I cannot tell how it happened) I slipped and fell.

The slope was steep on which this took place, and was at the top of a gully that led down through two subordinate buttresses towards the Glacier du Lion—which was just seen, a thousand feet below. The gully narrowed and narrowed, until there was a mere thread of snow lying between two walls of rock, which came to an abrupt termination at the top of a precipice that intervened between it and the glacier. Imagine a funnel cut in half through its length, placed at an angle of 45 degrees, with its point below and its concave side uppermost, and you will have a fair idea of the place.

The knapsack brought my head down first, and I pitched into some rocks about a dozen feet below ; they caught something and tumbled me off the edge, head over heels, into the gully ; the bâton was dashed from my hands, and I whirled downwards in a series of bounds, each longer than the last ; now over ice, now into rocks ; striking my head four or five times, each time with increased force. The last bound sent me spinning through the air, in a leap of fifty or sixty feet, from one side of the gully to the other, and I struck the rocks, luckily, with the whole of my left side. They caught my clothes for a moment, and I fell back on to

"IN ATTEMPTING TO PASS THE CORNER I SLIPPED AND FELL."

the snow with motion arrested ; my head fortunately came the right side up, and a few frantic catches brought me to a halt, in the neck of the gully, and on the verge of the precipice. Bâton, hat, and veil skimmed by and disappeared, and the crash of the rocks—which I had started—as they fell on to the glacier, told how narrow had been the escape from utter destruction. As it was, I fell nearly 200 feet in seven or eight bounds. Ten feet more would have taken me in one gigantic leap of 800 feet on to the glacier below.

The situation was still sufficiently serious. The rocks· could not be left go for a moment, and the blood was spirting out of more than twenty cuts. The most serious ones were in the head, and I vainly tried to close them with one hand, while holding on with the other. It was useless ; the blood jerked out in blinding jets at each pulsation. At last, in a moment of inspiration, I kicked out a big lump of snow, and stuck it as a plaster on my head. The idea was a happy one, and the flow of blood diminished ; then, scrambling up, I got, not a moment too soon, to a place of safety, and fainted away. The sun was setting when consciousness returned, and it was pitch dark before the Great Staircase was descended ; but, by a combination of luck and care, the whole 4800 feet of descent to Breil was accomplished without a slip, or once missing the way. I slunk past the cabin of the cowherds, who were talking and laughing inside, utterly ashamed of the state to which I had been brought by my imbecility, and entered the inn stealthily, wishing to escape to my room unnoticed. But Favre met me in the passage, demanded "Who is it ? " screamed with fright when he got a light, and aroused the household. Two dozen heads then held solemn council over mine, with more talk than action. The natives were unanimous in recommending that hot wine (syn. vinegar), mixed with salt, should be rubbed into the cuts. I protested, but they insisted. It was all the doctoring they received. Whether their rapid healing was to be attributed to that simple remedy, or to a good state of health, is a question ; they closed up remarkably quickly, and in a few days I was able to move again.*

It was sufficiently dull during this time. I was chiefly occupied in meditating on the vanity of human wishes, and in watching

AT BREIL (GIOMEIN). .

my clothes being washed in the tub which was turned by the stream in the front of the house ; and I vowed that if an Englishman should at any time fall sick in the Val Tournanche, he should not feel so solitary as I did at this dreary time.†

* I received much attention from a kind English lady who was staying in the inn.

† As it seldom happens that one survives such a fall, it may be interesting to record what my sensations were during its occurrence. I was perfectly conscious of what was happening, and felt each blow ; but, like a patient under chloroform, experienced no pain. Each blow was, naturally, more severe than that which preceded it, and I distinctly remember thinking "Well, if the next is harder still, that will be the end !" Like persons who have been rescued from drowning, I remember that the recollection of a multitude of things rushed through my head, many of them trivialities or absurdities, which had been forgotten long before ; and, more remarkable, this bounding through space did not feel disagreeable. But I think that in no very great distance more, consciousness as well as sensation would have been lost, and upon that I base my belief, improbable as it seems, that death by a fall from a great height is as painless an end as can be experienced.

The battering was very rough, yet no bones were broken. The most severe cuts were one of four inches long on the top of the head, and another of three inches on the

The news of the accident brought Jean-Antoine Carrel up to Breil, and, along with the haughty chasseur came one of his relatives, a strong and able young fellow named Cæsar. With these two men and Meynet I made another start on the 23d of July. We got to the tent without any trouble, and on the following day had ascended beyond the Tower, and were picking our way cautiously over the loose rocks behind (where my traces of the week before were well apparent) in lovely weather, when one of those abominable and almost instantaneous changes occurred, to which the Matterhorn is so liable on its southern side. Mists were created out of invisible vapours, and in a few minutes snow fell heavily. We stopped, as this part was of excessive difficulty, and, unwilling to retreat, remained on the spot several hours, in hopes that another change would occur; but, as it did not, we at length went down to the base of the Tower, and commenced to make a third platform, at the height of 12,992 feet above the sea. It still continued to snow, and we took refuge in the tent. Carrel argued that the weather had broken up, and that the mountain would become so glazed with ice as to render any attempt futile; and I, that the change was only temporary, and that the rocks were too hot to allow ice to form upon them. I wished to stay until the weather improved, but my leader would not endure contradiction, grew more positive, and insisted that we must go down. We went down, and when we got below the Col his opinion was found to be wrong; the cloud was confined to the upper 3000 feet, and outside it there was brilliant weather.

right temple: this latter bled frightfully. There was a formidable-looking cut, of about the same size as the last, on the palm of the left hand, and every limb was grazed, or cut, more or less seriously. The tips of the ears were taken off, and a sharp rock cut a circular bit out of the side of the left boot, sock, and ankle, at one stroke. The loss of blood, although so great, did not seem to be permanently injurious. The only serious effect has been the reduction of a naturally retentive memory to a very common-place one; and although my recollections of more distant occurrences remain unshaken, the events of that particular day would be clean gone but for the few notes which were written down before the accident.

Carrel was not an easy man to manage. He was perfectly aware that he was the cock of the Val Tournanche, and he commanded the other men as by right. He was equally conscious that he was indispensable to me, and took no pains to conceal his knowledge of the fact. If he had been commanded, or if he had been entreated to stop, it would have been all the same. But, let me repeat, he was the only first-rate climber I could find who believed that the mountain was not inaccessible. With him I had hopes, but without him none ; so he was allowed to do as he would. His will on this occasion was almost incomprehensible. He certainly could not be charged with cowardice, for a bolder man could hardly be found ; nor was he turning away on account of difficulty, for nothing to which we had yet come seemed to be difficult to *him ;* and his strong personal desire to make the ascent was evident. There was no occasion to come down on account of food, for we had taken, to guard against this very casualty, enough to last for a week ; and there was no danger, and little or no discomfort, in stopping in the tent. It seemed to me that he was spinning out the ascent for his own purposes, and that although he wished very much to be the first man on the top, and did not object to be accompanied by any one else who had the same wish, he had no intention of letting one succeed too soon,—perhaps to give a greater appearance of *éclat* when the thing was accomplished. As he feared no rival, he may have supposed that the more difficulties he made the more valuable he would be estimated ; though, to do him justice, he never showed any great hunger for money. His demands were fair, not excessive ; but he always stipulated for so much per day, and so, under any circumstances, he did not do badly.

Vexed at having my time thus frittered away, I was still well pleased when he volunteered to start again on the morrow, if it was fine. We were to advance the tent to the foot of the Tower, to fix ropes in the most difficult parts beyond, and to make a push for the summit on the following day.

The next morning (Friday the 25th) when I arose, good little

Meynet was ready and waiting, and he said that the two Carrels had gone off some time before, and had left word that they intended marmot-hunting, as the day was favourable for that sport.* My holiday had nearly expired, and these men clearly could not be relied upon ; so, as a last resort, I proposed to the hunchback to accompany me alone, to see if we could not get higher than before, though of reaching the summit there was little or no hope. He did not hesitate, and in a few hours we stood—for the third time together—upon the Col du Lion ; but it was the first time Meynet had seen the view unclouded. The poor little deformed peasant gazed upon it silently and reverently for a time, and then, unconsciously, fell on one knee in an attitude of adoration, and clasped his hands, exclaiming in ecstasy, " Oh, beautiful mountains !" His actions were as appropriate as his words were natural, and tears bore witness to the reality of his emotion.

Our power was too limited to advance the tent, so we slept at the old station, and starting very early the next morning, passed the place where we had turned back on the 24th, and, subsequently, my highest point on the 19th. We found the crest of the ridge so treacherous that we took to the cliffs on the right, although most unwillingly. Little by little we fought our way up, but at length we were both spread-eagled on the all but perpendicular face, unable to advance, and barely able to descend. We returned to the ridge. It was almost equally difficult, and infinitely more unstable ; and at length, after having pushed our attempts as far as was prudent, I determined to return to Breil, and to have a light ladder made to assist us to overcome some of the steepest parts.† I expected, too, that by this time Carrel would have had enough marmot-hunting, and would deign to accompany us again.

* An incident like this goes far to make one look favourably upon the *règlements* of Chamounix and other places. This could not have occurred at Chamounix, nor here, if there had been a *bureau des guides.*

† This appeared to be the most difficult part of the mountain. One was driven to keep to the edge of the ridge, or very near to it ; and at the point where we turned back (which was almost as high as the *highest* part of the " cravate," and perhaps

We came down at a great pace, for we were now so familiar with the mountain, and with each other's wants, that we knew immediately when to give a helping hand, and when to let alone. The rocks also were in a better state than I have ever seen them, being almost entirely free from glaze of ice. Meynet was always merriest on the difficult parts, and, on the most difficult, kept on enunciating the sentiment, " We can only die once," which thought seemed to afford him infinite satisfaction. We arrived at the inn early in the evening, and I found my projects summarily and unexpectedly knocked on the head.

Professor Tyndall had arrived while we were absent, and he had engaged both Cæsar and Jean-Antoine Carrel. Bennen was also with him, together with a powerful and active friend, a Valaisan guide, named Anton Walter. They had a ladder already prepared, provisions were being collected, and they intended to start on the following morning (Sunday). This new arrival took me by surprise. Bennen, it will be remembered, refused point-blank to take Professor Tyndall on the Matterhorn in 1861. " He was dead against any attempt on the mountain," says Tyndall. He was now eager to set out. Professor Tyndall has not explained in what way this revolution came about in his guide. I was equally astonished at the faithlessness of Carrel, and attributed it to pique at our having presumed to do without him. It was useless to compete with the Professor and his four men, who were ready to start in a few hours, so I waited to see what would come of their attempt.

Everything seemed to favour it, and they set out on a fine morning in high spirits, leaving me tormented with envy and all uncharitableness. If they succeeded, they carried off the prize for which I had been so long struggling ; and if they failed, there was

100 feet higher than my scramble on the 19th) there were smooth walls seven or eight feet high in every direction, which were impassable to a single man, and which could only be surmounted by the assistance of ladders, or by using one's comrades as ladders.

A CANNONADE ON THE MATTERHORN. (1862)

no time to make another attempt, for I was due in a few days more in London. When this came home clearly to me, I resolved to leave Breil at once, but, when packing up, found that some necessaries had been left behind in the tent. So I went off about midday to recover them ; caught the army of the Professor before it reached the Col, as they were going very slowly ; left them there (stopping to take food), and went on to the tent. I was near to it when all at once I heard a noise aloft, and, on looking up, perceived a stone of at least a foot cube flying straight at my head. I ducked, and scrambled under the lee side of a friendly rock, while the stone went by with a loud buzz. It was the advanced guard of a perfect storm of stones, which descended with infernal clatter down the very edge of the ridge, leaving a trail of dust behind, with a strong smell of sulphur, that told who had sent them. The men below were on the look-out, but the stones did not come near them, and breaking away on one side went down to the glacier.*

I waited at the tent to welcome the Professor, and when he arrived went down to Breil. Early next morning some one ran to me saying that a flag was seen on the summit of the Matterhorn. It was not so, however, although I saw that they had passed the place where we had turned back on the 26th. I had now no doubt of their final success, for they had got beyond the point which Carrel, not less than myself, had always considered to be the most questionable place on the whole mountain. Up to it there was no choice of route,—I suppose that at no one point between it and the Col was it possible to diverge a dozen paces to the right or left,

---

* Professor Tyndall describes this incident in the following words :—"We had gathered up our traps, and bent to the work before us, when suddenly an explosion occurred overhead. We looked aloft and saw in mid-air a solid shot from the Matterhorn describing its proper parabola, and finally splitting into fragments as it smote one of the rocky towers in front. Down the shattered fragments came like a kind of spray, slightly wide of us, but still near enough to compel a sharp look-out. Two or three such explosions occurred, but we chose the back fin of the mountain for our track, and from this the falling stones were speedily deflected right or left."—*Saturday Review*, Aug. 8, 1863. Reprinted in *Macmillan's Magazine*, April, 1869.

but beyond it it was otherwise, and we had always agreed, in our
debates, that if it could be passed success was certain. The accompanying outline from a sketch taken from the door of the inn at
Breil will help to explain. The letter A indicates the position of
the Great Tower; C the "cravate" (the strongly-marked streak of
snow referred to on p. 119, and which we just failed to arrive at on

the 26th); B the place where we now saw something that looked
like a flag. Behind the point B a nearly level ridge leads up to the
foot of the final peak, which will be understood by a reference to
the outline facing p. 83, on which the same letters indicate the
same places. It was just now said, we considered that if the point
C could be passed, success was certain. Tyndall was at B very
early in the morning, and I did not doubt that he would reach the
summit, although it yet remained problematical whether he would
be able to stand on the very highest point. The summit was evidently formed of a long ridge, on which there were two points
nearly equally elevated—so equally that one could not say which
was the highest—and between the two there seemed to be a deep

notch, marked D on the outlines, which might defeat one at the very last moment.

My knapsack was packed, and I had drunk a parting glass of wine with Favre, who was jubilant at the success which was to make the fortune of his inn ; but I could not bring myself to leave until the result was heard, and lingered about, as a foolish lover hovers round the object of his affections, even after he has been contemptuously rejected. The sun had set before the men were descried coming over the pastures. There was no spring in their steps—they, too, were defeated. The Carrels hid their heads, but the others said, as men will do when they have been beaten, that the mountain was horrible, impossible, and so forth. Professor Tyndall told me they had arrived *within a stone's throw of the summit,* and admonished me to have nothing more to do with the mountain. I understood him to say that he should not try again, and ran down to the village of Val Tournanche, almost inclined to believe that the mountain was inaccessible ; leaving the tent, ropes, and other matters in the hands of Favre, to be placed at the disposal of any person who wished to ascend it, more, I am afraid, out of irony than for generosity. There may have been those who believed that the Matterhorn could be ascended, but, anyhow, their faith did not bring forth works. No one tried again in 1862.

Business took me into Dauphiné before returning to London, and a week after Tyndall's defeat I lay one night, after a sultry day, half-asleep, tossing about in one of the abominations which serve for beds in the inn kept by the Deputy-Mayor of La Ville de Val Louise ; looking at a strange ruddiness on the ceiling, which I thought might be some effect of electricity produced by the irritation of the myriads of fleas ; when the great bell of the church, close at hand, pealed out with loud and hurried clangour. I jumped up, for the voices and movements of the people in the house made me think of fire. It was fire ; and I saw from my window, on the other side of the river, great forked flames shooting high into the sky, black dots with long shadows hurrying towards the place, and the crests of the ridges catching the light and standing out like spectres. All the world was in motion, for the neighbouring villages—now aroused—rang out the alarm. I pulled on my shirt, and tore over the bridge. Three large chalets were on fire, and were surrounded by a mass of people, who were bringing all their pots and pans, and anything that would hold water. They formed themselves into several chains, each two deep, leading towards the nearest stream, and passed the water up one side, and the empty utensils down the other. My old friend the mayor was there, in full force, striking the ground-with his stick, and vociferating, "Work ! work !" but the men, with much presence of mind, chiefly ranged themselves on the sides of the empty buckets, and left the real work to their better halves. Their efforts were useless, and the chalets burnt themselves out.

The next morning I visited the still smouldering ruins, and saw the homeless families sitting in a dismal row in front of their charred property. The people said that one of the houses had been well insured, and that its owner had endeavoured to forestall luck. He had arranged the place for a bonfire, set the lower rooms on fire in several places, and had then gone out of the way, leaving his wife and children in the upper rooms, to be roasted or not as the case might be. His plans only partially succeeded, and it was satisfactory to see the scoundrel brought back in the custody of two stalwart gensdarmes. Three days afterwards I was in London.

" BUT WHAT IS THIS?"

CHAPTER VI.

THE VAL TOURNANCHE—DIRECT PASS FROM BREIL TO ZERMATT
(BREUILJOCH)—ZERMATT—ASCENT OF THE GRAND TOURNALIN, ETC. ETC.

" How like a winter hath my absence been
From thee, the pleasure of a fleeting year !"

W. SHAKESPEARE.

I CROSSED the Channel on the 29th of July 1863, embarrassed by
the possession of two ladders, each twelve feet long, which joined
together like those used by firemen, and shut up like parallel rulers.
My luggage was highly suggestive of housebreaking, for, besides these,
there were several coils of rope, and numerous tools of suspicious
appearance, and it was reluctantly admitted into France, but it
passed through the custom-house with less trouble then I anticipated, after a timely expenditure of a few francs.

I am not in love with the douane. It is the purgatory of travellers, where uncongenial spirits mingle together for a time, before
they are separated into rich and poor. The douaniers look upon
tourists as their natural enemies ; see how eagerly they pounce upon
the portmanteaux ! One of them has discovered something ! He
has never seen its like before, and he holds it aloft in the face of
its owner, with inquisitorial insolence. " But *what is* this?" The

explanation is but half satisfactory. " But what is *this* ?" says he, laying hold of a little box. " Powder." " But that it is forbidden to carry of powder on the railway." " Bah !" says another and older hand, " pass the effects of Monsieur ;" and our countryman—whose cheeks had begun to redden under the stares of his fellow-travellers —is allowed to depart with his half-worn tooth-brush, while the discomfited douanier gives a mighty shrug at the strange habits of those " whose insular position excludes them from the march of continental ideas."

My real troubles commenced at Susa. The officials there, more honest and more obtuse than the Frenchmen, declined at one and the same time to be bribed, or to pass my baggage until a satisfactory account of it was rendered ; and, as they refused to believe the true explanation, I was puzzled what to say, but was presently relieved from the dilemma by one of the men, who was cleverer than his fellows, suggesting that I was going ,to Turin to exhibit in the streets ; that I mounted the ladder and balanced myself on the end of it, then lighted my pipe and put the point of the bâton in its bowl, and caused the bâton to gyrate around my head. The rope was to keep back the spectators, and an Englishman in my company was the agent. " Monsieur is acrobat then ?" " Yes, certainly." " Pass the effects of Monsieur the acrobat !"

These ladders were the source of endless trouble. Let us pass over the doubts of the guardians of the Hotel d'Europe (Trombetta), whether a person in the possession of such questionable articles should be admitted to their very respectable house, and get to Chatillon, at the entrance of the Val Tournanche. A mule was chartered to carry them, and, as they were too long to sling across its back, they were arranged lengthways, and one end projected over the animal's head, while the other extended beyond its tail. A mule when going up or down hill always moves with a jerky action, and in consequence of this the ladders hit my mule severe blows between its ears and in its flanks. The beast, not knowing what strange creature it had on its back, naturally tossed its head and threw out its legs, and this, of course, only made the blows that it received more severe. At last it ran away, and would have perished by rolling down a precipice, if the men had not caught hold of its tail. The end of the matter was that a man had to follow the mule, holding the end of the ladders, which obliged him to move his arms up and down incessantly, and to bow to the hind quarters of the animal in a way that afforded more amusement to his comrades than it did to him.

I was once more *en route* for the Matterhorn, for I had heard in the spring of 1863 the cause of the failure of Professor Tyndall, and learnt that the case was not so hopeless as it appeared to be at one time. I found that he arrived as far only as the northern end of "the shoulder." The point at which he says,* they "sat down with broken hopes, the summit within a stone's-throw of us, but still defying us," was not the notch or cleft at D (which is literally within a stone's-throw of the summit), but another and more formidable cleft that intervenes between the northern end of "the shoulder" and the commencement of the final peak. It is marked E on the outline which faces p. 83. Carrel and all the men who had been with me knew of the existence of this cleft, and of the pinnacle which rose between it and the final peak ;† and we had frequently talked about the best manner of passing the place. On this we disagreed, but we were both of opinion that when we got to "the shoulder" it would be necessary to bear down gradually to the right or to the left, to avoid coming to the top of the notch. But Tyndall's party, after arriving at "the shoulder," was led by his guides along the crest of the ridge, and, consequently, when they got to its northern end, they came to the top of the notch, instead of the bottom—to the dismay of all but the Carrels. Dr. Tyndall's words are, " The ridge was here split by a deep cleft which separated it from the final precipice, and the case became more hopeless as we came more near." The Professor adds, " The mountain is 14,800

---

* *Saturday Review*, August 8, 1863.

† The pinnacle, in fact, had a name,—' L'ange Anbé.'

feet high, and 14,600 feet had been accomplished." He greatly deceived himself; by the barometric measurements of Signor Giordano the notch is no less than 800 feet below the summit. The guide Walter (Dr. Tyndall says) said it was impossible to proceed, and the Carrels, appealed to for their opinion (this is their own account), gave as an answer, "We are porters, ask your guides." Bennen, thus left to himself, "was finally forced to accept defeat." Tyndall had nevertheless accomplished an advance of about 400 feet over one of the most difficult parts of the mountain.

There are material discrepancies between the published narratives of Professor Tyndall* and the verbal accounts of the Carrels. The former says the men had to be "urged on," that "they pronounced flatly against the final precipice," "they yielded so utterly," and that Bennen said, in answer to a final appeal made to him, "'What could I do, sir? not one of them would accompany me.' It was the accurate truth." Jean-Antoine Carrel, says that when Professor Tyndall gave the order to turn he would have advanced to examine the route, as he did not think that further progress was impossible, but he was stopped by the Professor, and was naturally obliged to follow the others.† These disagreements may well be left to be

* *Saturday Review*, 1863, and *Macmillan's Magazine*, 1869.

† I have entered into this matter because much surprise has been expressed that Carrel was able to pass this place, without any great difficulty, in 1865, which turned back so strong a party in 1862. The cause of Professor Tyndall's defeat was simply that his second guide (Walter) did not give aid to Bennen when it was required, and that the Carrels *would not act as guides after having been hired as porters*. J. A. Carrel not only knew of the existence of this place before they came to it; but always believed in the possibility of passing it, and of ascending the mountain; and had he been leader to the party I do not doubt that he might have taken Tyndall to the top. But when appealed to to assist Bennen (a Swiss, and the recognised leader of the party), was it likely that he (an Italian, a porter), who intended to be the first man up the mountain by a route which he regarded peculiarly his own, would render any aid?

It is not so easy to understand how Dr. Tyndall and Bennen overlooked the existence of this cleft, for it is seen over several points of the compass, and particularly well from the southern side of the Theodule pass. Still more difficult is it to explain how the Professor came to consider that he was only a stone's-throw from the summit;

settled by those who are concerned.   Tyndall, Walter, and Bennen, now disappear from this history.*

The Val Tournanche is one of the most charming valleys in the Italian Alps ; it is a paradise to an artist, and if the space at my command were greater I would willingly linger over its groves of chestnuts, its bright trickling rills and its roaring torrents, its upland unsuspected valleys and its noble cliffs.   The path rises steeply from Chatillon, but it is well shaded, and the heat of the summer sun is tempered by cool air and spray which comes off the ice-cold streams.†   One sees from the path, at several places on the right bank of the valley, groups of arches which have been built high up against the faces of the cliffs.   Guide-books repeat—on whose authority I know not—that they are the remains of a Roman aqueduct.   They have the Roman boldness of conception, but the work has not the usual Roman solidity.   The arches have always seemed to me to be the remains of an *unfinished* work, and I learn

from Jean Antoine Carrel that there are other groups of arches, which are not seen from the path, all having the same appearance.   It may be questioned whether those seen near the village of Antey are Roman. Some of them are semicircular, whilst others are distinctly pointed.   Here is one of the latter, which might pass for fourteenth-
century work, or later ;—a two-centred arch, with mean voussoirs, and the masonry, in rough courses.   These arches are well worth the attention of an archæologist, but some difficulty will be found in approaching them closely.

for, when he got to the end of " the shoulder," he must have been perfectly aware that the whole height of the final peak was still above him.

   * Dr. Tyndall ascended the Matterhorn in 1868. See Appendix.

   † Information upon the Val Tournanche will be found in De Saussure's *Voyages dans les Alpes*, vol. iv. pp. 379-81, 406-9 ; in Canon Carrel's pamphlet, *La Vallée de Valtornenche en 1867* ; and in King's *Italian Valleys of the Alps*, pp. 220-1.

We sauntered up the valley, and got to Breil when all were asleep. A halo round the moon promised watery weather, and we were not disappointed, for, on the next day (August 1), rain fell heavily, and when the clouds lifted for a time, we saw that new snow lay thickly over everything higher than 9000 feet. J. A. Carrel was ready and waiting (as I had determined to give the bold cragsman another chance); and he did not need to say that the Matterhorn would be impracticable for several days after all this new snow, even if the weather were to arrange itself at once. Our first day together was accordingly spent upon a neighbouring summit, the Cimes Blanches; a degraded mountain, well known for its fine panoramic view. It was little that we saw; for, in every direction except to the south, writhing masses of heavy clouds obscured everything; and to the south our view was intercepted by a peak higher than the Cimes Blanches, named the Grand Tournalin.* But we got some innocent pleasure out of watching the gambolings of a number of goats, who became fast friends after we had given them some salt; in fact, too fast, and caused us no little annoyance when we were descending. " Carrel," I said, as a number of stones whizzed by which they had dislodged, " this must be put a stop to." " Diable !" he grunted, " it is very well to talk, but how will you do it ?" I said that I would try ; and sitting down, poured a little brandy into the hollow of my hand, and allured the nearest goat with deceitful gestures. It was one who had gobbled up the paper in which the salt had been carried— an animal of enterprising character—and it advanced fearlessly and licked up the brandy. I shall not easily forget its surprise. It stopped short, and coughed, and looked at me as much as to say, " Oh, you cheat !" and spat and ran away ; stopping now and then to cough and spit again. We were not troubled any more by those goats.

More snow fell during the night, and our attempt on the Matterhorn was postponed indefinitely. As there was nothing to

---

* I shall speak again of this mountain, and therefore pass it over for the present.

be done at Breil, I determined to make the tour of the mountain, and commenced by inventing a pass from Breil to Zermatt,* in place of the hackneyed Theodule. Any one who looks at the map will see that the latter pass makes a considerable detour to the east, and, apparently, goes out of the way. I thought that it was possible to strike out a shorter route, both in distance and in time, and we set out on the 3d of August, to carry out the idea. We followed the Theodule path for some time, but quitted it when it bore away to the east, and kept straight on until we struck the moraine of the Mont Cervin glacier. Our track still continued in a straight line up the centre of the glacier to the foot of a tooth of rock, which juts prominently out of the ridge (Furggengrat) connecting the Matterhorn with the Theodulehorn. The head of the glacier was connected with this little peak by a steep bank of snow ; but we were able to go straight up, and struck the Col at its lowest point, a little to the right (that is to say, to the east) of the above-mentioned peak. On the north there was a snow-slope corresponding to that on the other side, but half-an-hour took us to its base ; we then bore away over the nearly level plateau of the Furggengletscher, making a straight track to the Hörnli, from whence we descended to Zermatt by one of the well-known paths. This pass has been dubbed the Breuiljoch by the Swiss surveyors. It is a few feet higher than the Theodule, and it may be recommended to those who are familiar with that pass, as it gives equally fine views, and is accessible at all times. But it will never be frequented like the Theodule, as the snow-slope at its summit, at certain times, will require the use of the axe. It took us six hours and a quarter to go from one place to the other, which was an hour longer than we would have occupied by the Theodule, although the distance in miles is less.

It is stated in one of the MS. note-books of the late Principal J. D. Forbes, that this depression, now called the Breuiljoch, was formerly *the* pass between the Val Tournanche and Zermatt, and that it was abandoned for the Theodule in consequence of changes

* See the map of the Matterhorn and its glaciers.

T

in the glaciers.* The authority for the statement was not given. I presume it was from local tradition, but I readily credit it ; for, before the time that the glaciers had shrunk to so great an extent, the steep snow-slopes above mentioned, in all probability, did not exist ; but, most likely, the glaciers led by very gentle gradients up to the summit ; in which case the route would have formed the natural highway between the two places. It is far from impossible, if the glaciers continue to diminish at their present rapid rate,† that the Theodule itself, the easiest and the most frequented of all the higher Alpine passes, may, in the course of a few years, become somewhat difficult ; and if this should be the case, the prosperity of Zermatt will probably suffer.‡

* My attention was directed to this note by Mr. A. Adams-Reilly.

† The summit of the Theodule pass is 10,899 feet above the sea. It is estimated that of late about a thousand tourists have crossed it per annum. In the winter, when the crevasses are bridged over and partially filled up, and the weather is favourable, cows and sheep pass over it from Zermatt to Val Tournanche, and *vice versa*.

In the *middle of August*, 1792, De Saussure appears to have taken mules from Breil, over the Val Tournanche glacier to the summit of the Theodule ; and on a previous journey he did the same, also in the middle of August. He distinctly mentions (§ 2220) that the glacier was completely covered with snow, and that *no* crevasses were open. I do not think mules could have been taken over the same spot in any August during the past ten years without great difficulty. In that month the glacier is usually very bare of snow, and many crevasses are open. They are easily enough avoided by those on foot, but would prove very troublesome to mules.

A few days before we crossed the Breuiljoch in 1863, Mr. F. Morshead made a parallel pass to it. He crossed the ridge on the *western* side of the little peak, and followed a somewhat more difficult route than ours. In 1865 I wanted to use Mr. Morshead's pass (see Chap. xv.), but found that it was not possible to descend the Zermatt side ; for, during the two years which had elapsed, the glacier had shrunk so much that it was completely severed from the summit of the pass, and we could not get down the rocks that were exposed.

‡ The admirable situation of Zermatt has been known for, at least, thirty years, but it is only within the last twelve or fourteen that it has become an approved Alpine centre. Thirty years ago the Theodule pass, the Weissthor, and the Col d'Hérens were, I believe, the only routes ever taken from Zermatt across the Pennine Alps. At the present time there are (inclusive of these passes and of the valley road) no less than twenty-four different ways in which a tourist may go from Zermatt. The summits of some of these cols are more than 14,000 feet above the

Carrel and I wandered out again in the afternoon, and went, first of all, to a favourite spot with tourists near the end of the Gorner glacier (or, properly speaking, the Boden glacier), to a little verdant flat—studded with *Euphrasia officinalis*—the delight of swarms of bees, who gather there the honey which afterwards appears at the *table d'hôte.*

On our right the glacier-torrent thundered down the valley through a gorge with precipitous sides, not easily approached ; for the turf at the top was slippery, and the rocks had everywhere been rounded by the glacier,—which formerly extended far away. This gorge seems to have been made chiefly by the torrent, and to have been excavated subsequently to the retreat of the glacier. It seems so because not merely upon its walls are there the marks of running water, but even upon the rounded rocks at the top of its walls, at a height of seventy or eighty feet above the present level of the torrent, there are some of those queer concavities which rapid streams alone are known to produce on rocks.

A little bridge, apparently frail, spans the torrent just above the entrance to this gorge, and from it one perceives, being fashioned in the rocks below, concavities similar to those to which reference has just been made. The torrent is seen hurrying forwards. Not everywhere. In some places the water strikes projecting angles, and, thrown back by them, remains almost stationary, eddying round and round : in others, obstructions fling it up in fountains, which play perpetually on the *under* surfaces of overhanging masses ; and sometimes do so in such a way that the water not only works upon the under surfaces, but round the corner ; that is to say, upon

level of the sea, and a good many of them cannot be recommended either for ease, or as offering the shortest way from Zermatt to the valleys and villages to which they lead.

Zermatt itself is still only a village with 500 inhabitants (about thirty of whom are guides), with picturesque châlet dwellings, black with age. The hotels, including the inn on the Riffelberg, all belong to one proprietor (M. Alexandre Seiler), to whom the village and valley are very much indebted for their prosperity, and who is the best person to consult for information, or in all cases of difficulty.

the surfaces which are *not* opposed to the general direction of the current. In all cases *concavities* are being produced. Projecting angles are rounded, it is true, and are more or less convex, but they are overlooked on account of the prevalence of concave forms.

Cause and effect help each other here. The inequalities of the

WATER-WORN ROCKS IN THE GORGE BELOW THE GORNER GLACIER.

torrent bed and walls cause its eddyings, and the eddies fashion the concavities. The more profound the latter become, the more disturbance is caused in the water. The destruction of the rocks proceeds at an ever-increasing rate ; for the larger the amount of surface that is exposed, the greater are the opportunities for the assaults of heat and cold.

When water is in the form of glacier it has not the power of making concavities, such as these, in rocks, and of working upon surfaces which are not opposed to the direction of the current. Its nature is changed; it operates in a different way, and it leaves marks which are readily distinguished from those produced by torrent-action.

The prevailing forms which result from glacier-action are more

STRIATIONS PRODUCED BY GLACIER-ACTION (AT GRINDELWALD).

or less *convex*. Ultimately, all angles and almost all curves are obliterated, and large areas of flat surfaces are produced. This perfection of abrasion is rarely found, except in such localities as have sustained a grinding much more severe than that which has occurred in the Alps; and, generally speaking, the dictum of the veteran geologist Studer, quoted below, is undoubtedly true.* Not merely can the operations of extinct glaciers be traced in detail by means of the bosses of rock popularly termed *roches moutonnées*, but their effects in the aggregate, on a range of mountains or an entire country, can be recognised sometimes at a distance of fifteen or twenty miles from the incessant repetition of these convex forms.

It will not be uninteresting to consider, for a few moments, the way in which they are produced by glaciers; but first of all we must look back to the time when they had no existence.

§ 1. If ever the surface of the earth was as true as if it had been turned out from a lathe, it was certainly not so when the great glaciers —whose poor remnants we now see in the Alps—began to stretch far away from the mountains on to the lowlands of Switzerland and on to the plain of Piedmont,—unless geology is a lie. If geological reasoning is not a delusion and a snare, age upon age had passed away before this took place; rocks had crumbled into dust, and their particles had been re-arranged; lightning had struck the peaks; frost had cleft their ridges; avalanches had swept their slopes; earthquakes had fissured the soil; and torrents had transported the débris far and wide,—had eaten into the clefts, had scored the slopes, and had deepened the fissures for an indefinite length of time. It was, therefore, not a bran new world upon which the glaciers commenced to work—a globe which had been, as it were, just turned out of a mould; but it was scarred and weather-beaten; there were upon it hills and dales innumerable, cracks and chasms, asperities and depressions, which heat and cold had penetrated, and water had still further deepened. The world was incalculably old when this modern glacial period began its operations; and, although it continued for a long time, the glaciers

---

* " Un des faits les mieux constatés est que l'érosion des glaciers se distingue de celle des eaux en ce que la première produit des roches convexes ou moutonnées, tandis que la seconde donne lieu à des concavités."—Prof. B. Studer, *Origine des Lacs Suisses.*

were unable to obliterate the effects of the older and greater powers.   The *roches moutonnées* owe their peculiar form to the grinding of ice certainly, but they were blocked out anterior to the formation of the glaciers.   They were, when the ice quitted them, to what they were before the glaciers began to work, very much like what an old worn coin is to one that is newly struck.   The hollows were not so much affected, but the eminences were ground down ; the depressions of the modelling remained, but the parts in relief were taken away.   It requires, therefore, some little effort to imagine what the rock forms were like before the glaciers of the glacial period began to operate upon them, but we cannot be wrong in assuming that the forms were similar to those exhibited by weathered rocks at the present time.

§ 2. Glacier ice is plastic, and can be moulded by pressure to almost any form.   Hence, if a glacier could remain perfectly stationary, it would be moulded, by means of its own weight, to the surface upon which it reposed.   But glaciers move, and consequently the bottom of one is never completely moulded to its rock-bed.   The pressure from the weight of the ice is opposed by the motion of the glacier, and the ice is urged past depressions before it can be moulded to them.

For example, let Fig. 1 of the diagram on p. 144 represent a section of a portion of the bottom of a glacier which is beginning to work upon weathered rocks ; G, G, indicating the glacier, and the arrow the direction in which the glacier is moving.   The ice, after passing the eminences A, B, C, does not completely fill the hollows D, E, F.*

These things can be observed at the sides of most considerable glaciers, and particularly well at several places on each bank of the Gorner glacier.   At several places (such as at D in Fig. 1) one can get underneath and see the ice bridging hollows ; and notice proof of its motion, and that it is partially moulded to the

---

* The outline is a tracing from a photograph of weathered, unglaciated rocks.

rocks, in the flutings upon the bottom of the glacier leading up to
the eminences by which they have been caused.

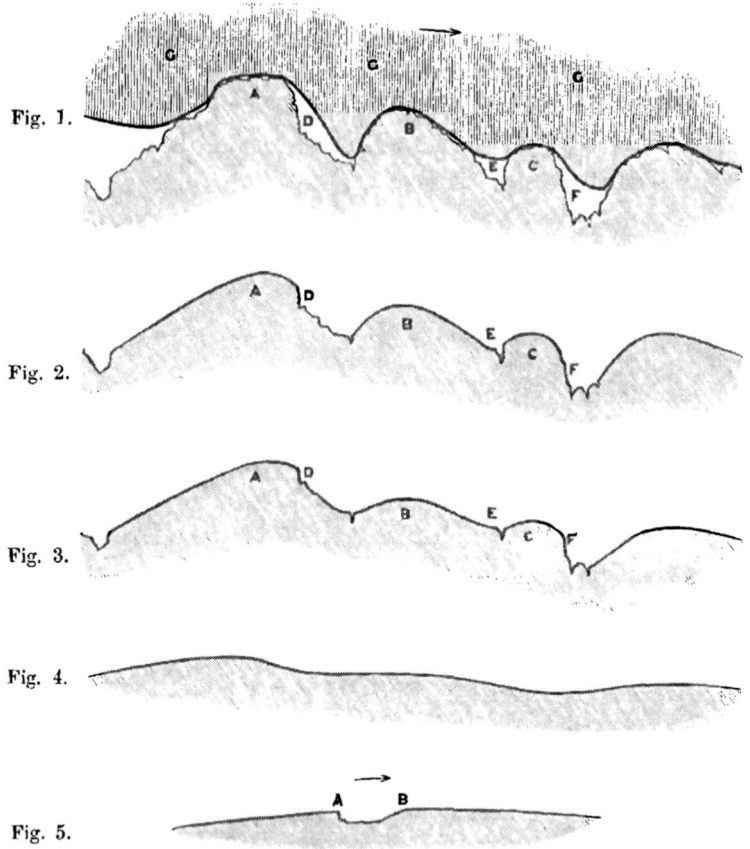

Fig. 1.

Fig. 2.

Fig. 3.

Fig. 4.

Fig. 5.

§ 3. It is, therefore, evident that when a glacier passes over
ground such as has been indicated in § 1, it is supported upon a
number of points, and bridges many hollows; that the parts of
the rock which the ice touches sustain the entire weight and
friction of the glacier, and are alone abraded, while the hollows
escape.

§ 4. But whilst the motion of the glacier is urging it onwards and *over* depressions, the weight of its ice is pressing it *into* the depressions, and hence the ice strikes the next projection at a lower level than it left the last one. For example, after passing the hollow D, the ice strikes the eminence B at a lower level than it left A (Fig. 1).

§ 5. The immediate effect is, that the minor asperities of the rock suffer, and chiefly those which are opposed to the direction of motion of the glacier. They may be actually crushed, or fragments which are already loose may be brushed or scraped away ; in any case they disappear (Fig. 2).

§ 6. In consequence of this, the glacier becomes supported upon a larger area, and its power is exerted over a greater surface. It follows, also, that the amount, in depth, of the matter which is removed constantly diminishes, if the power that is employed continues to be the same.

§ 7. A long continuance of abrasion, from the friction of the ice and by the rasping of foreign matter contained in it, lowers the level of the rock eminences ; but surfaces of fractures or depressions in the rock which are not opposed to the direction of the motion of the glacier remain unabraded, if they are perpendicular to the direction of the motion, or anything like perpendicular to it ; and they will continue to exist (although becoming less and less) until the entire bed of the glacier (that is, the surface of the rocks) has been reduced, over large areas, nearly to a plane surface.

Rocks which have been rounded by glacier action (such as in Figs. 2, 3) are termed *roches moutonnées;* and unabraded surfaces of *roches moutonnées* (such as D, F, Figs. 2, 3) are termed *lee-sides.* The *lee-sides* often afford useful indications of the directions in which extinct glaciers have moved.

§ 8. If glaciers still continue to work upon *roches moutonnées,* the effects which are produced are only an extension of those

U

described in § 7. The highest points of the rocks are most affected, while the sides of depressions escape wholly, or partially, according as they are unopposed or opposed to the direction of the motion of the glacier. Eminences are entirely removed in course of time, and their positions, and those of cracks or depressions, are only indicated by faintly-marked convexities and concavities (Fig. 4). These may at length disappear, and large areas of rock may be reduced to plane surfaces.

Such surfaces are common in Greenland, in close proximity to, and extending underneath, existing glaciers. I propose to call them *roches nivelées*, to distinguish them from *roches moutonnées.**

§ 9. Striations are frequently produced on rocks by the passage of glaciers (see illustration on p. 141). They are caused by foreign matter in the bottoms of the glaciers, fixed in the ice, or rolling or sliding between it and the rocks. This foreign matter is partly made up of fragments which have been removed from the rock-bed by the action of the glacier, and partly from rocks which have fallen on to the surface of the glacier, and which have subsequently tumbled into crevasses, or otherwise worked their way down.†

Generally speaking, striations are common upon rocks which are only '*moutonnées*,' but they are rarer, or entirely wanting, upon

---

* De Saussure was the author of the term *roches moutonnées*, and he gave (§ 1061) the following reason for its adoption :—"Farther off, behind the village of Juviana or Envionne, rocks are seen having the shape which I call *moutonnée.* . . The hillocks (montagnes) to which I apply this expression, are composed of a group of rounded prominences (têtes arrondies). . . These contiguous and frequent domes (rondeurs) give, as a whole, the impression of a well-furnished fleece, or one of those wigs which are also called *moutonnées.*"

The term was an appropriate one, applied as De Saussure used it, but it is unmeaning when applied to the more perfectly glaciated, levelled surfaces.

† "One who is familiar with the track of this mighty engine will recognise at once where the large boulders have hollowed out their deeper furrows, where small pebbles have drawn their finer marks, where the stones with angular edges have left their sharp scratches, where sand and gravel have rubbed and smoothed the rocky surface, and left it bright and polished. . . These marks are not to be mistaken by any one who has carefully observed them ; the scratches, furrows, grooves, are

roches nivelées. They indicate a comparatively early and coarse stage of glacier-action.

§ 10. More or less water is always found flowing underneath glaciers. It is produced by ablation of the surface of the glacier, and by other causes. In the earlier stages of glacier action (§§ 2-7) it finds a free course among the depressions beneath the ice ; but as the rocks become smoother and flatter it has more difficulty in discovering outlets, and must materially assist in reducing the friction of the ice upon the rocks, and in the production of highly-polished surfaces, by causing less violent and more uniform abrasion.

Such, it appears to me, are the ways in which glaciers work upon rocks, and produce surfaces *moutonnées* or *nivelées.* Before I quit this subject, I wish to make one or two remarks upon the facts which have been stated, and to draw one or two conclusions which they seem to warrant.

1. The production of the peculiar rounded rock-forms which are termed *roches moutonnées,* is to be attributed to the extremely slow rate at which the bottoms of glaciers move, not less than to the plasticity of the ice. That the rate is *very* slow may be inferred from the fact, that the smallest fractures on rocks upon which glacier has worked for any length of time, have their *weather* and their *lee sides.* That is to say, before the ice is able to move in

always rectilinear, tending in the direction in which the glacier is moving, and most distinct on that side of the surface-inequalities facing the direction of the moving mass, while the lee-side remains mostly untouched. . . .

"Here and there on the sides of the glacier it is possible to penetrate between the walls and the ice to a great depth, and even to follow such a gap to the very bottom of the valley ; and everywhere do we find the surface of the ice fretted as I have described it, with stones of every size, from the pebble to the boulder, and also with sand and gravel of all sorts, from the coarsest grain to the finest, and these materials, more or less firmly set in the ice, form the grating surface with which, on its onward movement down the Alpine valleys, it leaves everywhere unmistakeable traces of its passage."—Agassiz, in *The Atlantic Monthly.*

some cases over cavities only an eighth of an inch across, it is forced down into them, and strikes the little cliffs or slopes which are opposed to the direction of its motion at a lower level than it left those on the other side,—which latter ones remain sharp and unrounded. This can frequently be observed, even in most minute fractures, upon glaciated rocks which the ice has not long quitted.* Fig. 5, p. 144, represents an example ; the arrow points out the direction in which the glacier has moved, B the *weather*, and A the *lee side*.

This affords a means of distinguishing glacier from water action in hand specimens of rock. †

2. There is reason to believe that if glaciers were to move with rapidity, instead of with such extreme deliberation, angular surfaces would not be *rounded*, but flat surfaces would be produced from the beginning. That is to say, instead of turning out surfaces, such as are shown in the section, Fig. 3, p. 144, after many centuries of work, glaciers might produce similar ones to Fig. 4, or even flatter, in the course of a few hours. The amount of flatness which would be produced would depend upon the rate of the motion and the bulk of the ice.

Professor Steenstrup, of Copenhagen, read to me in 1867, from an unpublished MS. in his possession, a highly interesting account of some extraordinary effects which were produced in Iceland, in the year 1721, by glacier in rapid motion. It seems that in the neighbourhood of the mountain Kötlugja, in the extreme south of the island, large bodies of water formed underneath, or within, the glaciers (either on account of the interior heat of the earth, or from other causes), and at length acquired irresistible power, tore the glaciers from their moorings on the land, and swept or floated them over every obstacle into the sea. Prodigious masses of ice were thus borne for a distance of about ten miles over land in the space

---

* Glaciated rocks which have been exposed to the atmosphere for any length of time, lose, of course, all such delicate touches.

† See p. 167.

of a few hours ; and their bulk was so enormous, that they covered the sea for seven miles from the shore, and remained aground in one hundred fathoms. The denudation on the land was upon a grand scale. All superficial accumulations were swept away, and the bed-rock was exposed. It was described, in graphic language, how all irregularities and depressions were obliterated, and a smooth surface of several miles area was laid bare, and that this area had the appearance of having been *" planed by a plane."* *

Admitting the possibility of exaggeration in the narrative as

---

* The account of Professor Steenstrup was, I believe, copied many years ago, when he was travelling in Iceland, from an original Icelandic MS. Professor Paijkull, of Upsala, was favoured by Professor Steenstrup with a sight of his MS., and printed some extracts from it in his work *En Sommer i Island,* Copenhagen, 1867. The following paragraphs, which refer to this possibly unique occurrence, are taken from the English translation of that work :—

" At the commencement of the eruption a stream burst forth, consisting principally of half-melted snow and large masses of ice, which tumbled about in the sea like floating islands ; while, simultaneously, another stream issued in a south-easterly direction, and inflicted great injury on the land. The first of these two streams filled the sea with ice to such an extent that even from the highest mountains it was impossible to see open water till it was broken up by the action of the waves. It then drifted westward as far as Reykjanes, and up into the rivers along the coast, so that large icebergs were left standing in the bed of the river in the Ölfusá. The greater portion, however, of the ice that had been washed down from the glacier remained fixed aground at a distance of about seven miles from land, in a hundred fathoms water. It formed, moreover, a high ridge over the land from the sea as far as Hafrsey, a fjeld on Myrdalssandr. . . . A stream of similar terrific character broke out on the following day, and submerged the masses of ice that had been previously discharged into the sea, as far as the eye could reach. Further, it made its way through Kerlingar valley, and dammed up the stream there. The deluge, or, more properly speaking, the ice, carried, moreover, immense masses of rock with it ; and in the vicinity of Hjörleifshöfdi, a mountain on Myrdalssandr, a rock of twenty fathoms in height, entirely disappeared ; not to speak of other instances. One can form some idea of the altitude of this barrier of ice, when it is mentioned that from Höfdabrekka farm, which lies high up on a fjeld of the same name, one could not see Hjörleifshöfdi opposite, which is a fell 640 feet in height ; but in order to do so, had to clamber up a mountain slope east of Höfdabrekka, 1200 feet high. The distance between Höfdabrekka and Hjörleifshöfdi is one (Danish) geographical mile, or the fifteenth part of a degree."

quoted below, there is not, I think, any reason to doubt the literal accuracy of the particular point to which attention has just been drawn ; and hence it would appear that the effects produced on rocks by glacier ice in rapid motion may be identical with those caused by it after a great lapse of time, when it is working at its ordinary rate.

3. These results are not surprising when we remember that glaciers are always endeavouring to work in right lines. This is proved by the marks they leave, which Agassiz has well pointed out (see note to p. 146) are always more or less *rectilinear*.

This disposition to work in right lines, combined with inability to operate upon depressions (except to the limited extent already shown), points to the reason why it is that 'ultimately all angles, and almost all curves, are obliterated, and large areas of flat surfaces are produced' (p. 141).

It should be observed that glaciated rocks, of the forms termed *moutonnées*, cannot possibly have been eroded to any great depth by glaciers during the modern * glacial period.

The degree of flatness of glaciated rocks bears a direct relation to the amount of power which has been employed. In the earlier stages (§§ 2-7) the forms are round ; in the more advanced ones, they are flat. The *rotundity* of the form of *roches moutonnées* is proof that no great amount of destruction has taken place ; and their *lee-sides* are additional and equally strong evidence.

4. For, unless it can be shown to have been produced subsequently to the retreat of the ice, even a *single lee-side* to a glaciated rock informs us that we see a surface which was exposed to the atmosphere before the glaciers began to work ; while *many lee-sides*, found together, one after another, within an area of a few yards (and they are often so found in localities where enormous depth of excavation has been presumed to have taken place through glacier

---

* Geologists begin to speak of glacial periods of a much more remote date than that to which I am referring.

agency), renders it certain that the entire surface of the bed-rock has been lowered, at the most, but a few yards.

Weathered rocks, upon a small scale, do not take shapes such as are figured in this diagram, but rather such as those which are shown in Fig. 1, p. 144. We do not find deep pits or troughs produced in rocks (whatever may be their nature or composition) by weathering or through any of the ordinary operations of nature. Still less do we find a large number of such pits or troughs close to one another. Therefore, when we see *lee-sides* as at D and F, Fig. 3, p. 144 (separated, perhaps, from each other by a distance of less than a dozen feet ; and representing, as it has been already stated, the remains of hollows or fractures which existed before the glacier began to work), it is certain that the eminences B C, between them, have been lowered only a few feet ; and probable that the depth of the rock which has been removed does not exceed the length of a line drawn from D to F.

The unworn *lee-sides* to glaciated rocks have, therefore, a special value, as they afford indications (although imperfect ones), of the *amount* of excavation that has been performed by the glaciers which worked above and around them.

5. In § 6 it was stated that the amount, *in depth*, of the matter which is removed constantly diminishes, if the power that is employed continues to be the same. That is to say, if a glacier 1000 feet thick, moving down a valley at the rate of 300 feet per annum, is able to remove a depth of one inch from the whole of those portions of the surfaces that it touches, in the course of one year, the amount that it will remove in the course of the next (assuming that the depth of 1000 feet is maintained, and the rate of motion is the same) will not be one inch, but will be something less ; because the power employed will be distributed over a greater area. It does not, however, follow that the *bulk* of the matter which is removed will be less and less from the very beginning.

There cannot, however, be a doubt but that, after a certain lapse of time, the *bulk* of the matter removed becomes less and less.

For these reasons. The rock that is removed is taken away by friction. Of two kinds. The first, of the foreign matter imbedded in the bottom of the glacier (or rolling underneath it) against the bed-rock, which foreign matter it has been already stated (§ 9) is derived from two sources—viz. from the rock-bed itself, and from masses which have fallen on to the surface of the glacier, and afterwards worked their way down.

It is obvious, as the rocks which are being operated upon by the glacier become more and more smooth, that the supply from the first of these sources must constantly diminish. It is equally certain that when the rock-bed has lost many of its asperities, and the glacier—so to speak—fits more closely to it, the matter which falls from above has greater difficulty in getting between the ice and the rock-bed. Here are two ways of accounting for the fact that striations are rare or wanting upon *roches nivelées*, and it will now be perceived why it was said (§ 9) that striations "indicate a comparatively early and coarse stage of glacier action."

There remains to be considered the friction of the ice itself against the rock-bed. This, too, must diminish as the surfaces over which the glacier passes become smoother and flatter. The more thoroughly parallel the bottom of the glacier and the bed-rock are to each other, the less friction will there be, and the less abrasion.

There is therefore good reason to believe that not only is the depth of rock removed from any given place less and less year by year, but that the total amount of matter removed by the glacier constantly diminishes. Just as a smoothing-plane, that is set fine, will take shaving after shaving from a plank (each shaving being thinner than the last), and at length glides over the wood without producing any effect except a kind of rude polishing ; so a glacier, passing over rocks, takes shaving after shaving (in the form of sand or mud), and at length glides on, and puts the finishing touches, by polishing, to the surfaces which it had formerly prepared by rasping and filing.

The calculations of the effects that have been produced by glacier agency, which are based on the assumption that the amount of material removed is the same from one year to another, are necessarily fallacious. There are not, moreover, any data from which the amount of work can be calculated that glaciers perform in any given time ; but there are indications in that direction, and, so far as they go, they seem to point to the conclusion that the effects which they have produced, in the way of making hollows, are much less important than many suppose.

6. If I were asked whether the action of glacier upon rocks should be considered as chiefly destructive or conservative, I should answer, without hesitation, principally as conservative. It is destructive, certainly, to a limited extent ; but, like a mason who dresses a column that is to be afterwards polished, the glacier removes a small portion of the stone upon which it works, in order that the rest may be more effectually preserved. By obliterating the inequalities of the rock, and, consequently, by reducing the area of the surfaces which are exposed to the atmosphere to a minimum, the glacier, when it retires, leaves the rock in the best possible condition to withstand the attacks of heat, cold, and water.

It has been pointed out, times without number (even by those who are in the habit of accusing glaciers of the most frightful destructiveness), that the polished surfaces which they leave behind them seem to be imperishable. All who know are agreed that centuries, nay, *thousands* of years, pass away, and still the *roches moutonnées* retain their form.

In regard to the action of the glacier, when it is in full life and activity, all are not so agreed. But when one finds evidence that glaciers which existed through vast periods of time did nothing more than *round* pre-existing weathered forms, *dress* rough and

x

uneven surfaces, and did not even entirely destroy the destructive work of the older and greater powers : while those powers were at the same time *delving* into the rocks which the glaciers were not covering ; were *not* reducing the area of exposed surfaces, but, on the contrary, were continually increasing them, and were hurling down vast masses, of which but a small portion fell on to the glaciers (but which small portion probably equalled or exceeded in bulk all that the glaciers were removing), the conclusion can hardly be avoided that glaciers, in their life as well as after their death, either considered by themselves or in comparison with other powers, should be regarded as eminently conservative in their acts and in their intentions.

We finished up the 3d of August with a walk over the Findelen glacier, and returned to Zermatt at a later hour than we intended, both very sleepy.   This is noteworthy only on account of that which followed.   We had to cross the Col de Valpelline on the next day, and an early start was desirable.   Monsieur Seiler, excellent man, knowing this, called us himself, and when he came to my door, I answered, " All right, Seiler, I will get up," and immediately turned over to the other side, saying to myself, " First of all, ten minutes more sleep."   But Seiler waited and listened, and, suspecting the case, knocked again.   " Herr Whymper, have you got a light ?" Without thinking what the consequences might be, I answered, " No," and then the worthy man actually forced the lock off his own door to give me one.   By similar and equally friendly and disinterested acts, Monsieur Seiler has acquired his enviable reputation.

At 4 A.M. we left his Monte Rosa Hotel, and were soon pushing our way through the thickets of grey alder that skirt the path up the exquisite little valley which leads to the Z'mutt-gletscher.*

Nothing can seem or be more inaccessible than the Matterhorn

* The path on the right bank (southern side) of the valley is much more picturesque than that on the other side.   For our route, see the maps of the valley of Zermatt and the valley of Valpelline.

upon this side ; and even in cold blood one holds the breath when looking at its stupendous cliffs. There are but few equal to them in size in the Alps, and there are none which can more truly be termed *precipices.* Greatest of them all is the immense north cliff,—that which bends over towards the Z'muttgletscher. Stones which drop from the top of that amazing wall fall for about 1500 feet before they touch anything ; and those which roll down from above, and bound over it, fall to a much greater depth, and leap well nigh 1000 feet beyond its base. This side of the mountain has always seemed sombre—sad—terrible ; it is painfully suggestive of decay, ruin, and death ; and it is now, alas ! more than terrible by its associations.

"There is no aspect of destruction about the Matterhorn cliffs," says Professor Ruskin. Granted ;—when they are seen from afar. But approach, and sit down by the side of the Z'muttgletscher, and you will hear that their piecemeal destruction is proceeding ceaselessly—incessantly. You will *hear,* but, probably, you will not *see;* for even when the descending masses thunder as loudly as heavy guns, and the echoes roll back from the Ebihorn opposite, they will still be as pin-points against this grand old face, so vast is its scale !

If you would see the ' aspects of destruction,' you must come still closer, and climb its cliffs and ridges, or mount to the plateau of the Matterhorngletscher, which is cut up and ploughed up by these missiles, and strewn on the surface with their smaller fragments ; the larger masses, falling with tremendous velocity, plunge into the snow and are lost to sight.

The Matterhorngletscher, too, sends down *its* avalanches, as if in rivalry with the rocks behind. Round the whole of its northern side it does not terminate in the usual manner by gentle slopes, but comes to a sudden end at the top of the steep rocks which lie betwixt it and the Z'muttgletscher ; and seldom does an hour pass without a huge slice breaking away, and falling with dreadful uproar on to the slopes below, where it is re-compacted.

The desolate, outside pines of the Z'mutt forests, stripped of their bark, and blanched by the weather, are a fit foreground to a scene that can hardly be surpassed in solemn grandeur. It is a subject worthy of the pencil of a great painter, and one which would tax the powers of the very greatest.

Higher up the glacier the mountain is less savage in appearance, but it is not less impracticable ; and, three hours later, when we arrived at the island of rock, called the Stockje (which marks the end of the Z'muttgletscher proper, and which separates its higher feeder, the Stockgletscher, from its lower but greater one, the Tiefenmatten), Carrel himself, one of the least demonstrative of men, could not refrain from expressing wonder at the steepness of its faces, and at the audacity that had prompted us to camp upon the south-west ridge ; the profile of which is seen very well from the Stockje.* Carrel then saw the north and north-west sides of the mountain for the first time, and was more firmly persuaded than ever, that an ascent was possible *only* from the direction of Breil.

Three years afterwards I was traversing the same spot with the guide Franz Biener, when all at once a puff of wind brought to us a very bad smell ; and, on looking about, we discovered a dead chamois half-way up the southern cliffs of the Stockje. We clambered up, and found that it had been killed by a most uncommon and extraordinary accident. It had slipped on the upper rocks, had rolled over and over down a slope of débris, without being able to regain its feet, had fallen over a little patch of rocks that projected through the débris, and had caught the points of both

---

* Professor Ruskin's view of "the Cervin from the north-west" (*Modern Painters*, vol. iv.) is taken from the Stockje. The Col du Lion is the little depression on the ridge, close to the margin of the engraving, on the right hand side ; the third tent-platform was formed at the foot of the perpendicular cliff, on the ridge, exactly one-third way between the Col du Lion and the summit. The battlemented portion of the ridge, a little higher up, is called the "*crête du coq ;*" and the nearly horizontal portion of the ridge above it is "the shoulder." It is high testimony to the accuracy of Mr. Ruskin's work that it is possible to point out minutiæ such as these upon an engraving that was published fourteen years ago.

horns on a tiny ledge, not an inch broad. It had just been able to touch the débris, where it led away down from the rocks, and had pawed and scratched until it could no longer touch. It had evidently been starved to death, and we found the poor beast almost swinging in the air, with its head thrown back and tongue protruding, looking to the sky as if imploring help.

We had no such excitement as this in 1863, and crossed this easy pass to the châlets of Prerayen in a very leisurely fashion. From the summit to Prerayen let us descend in one step. The way has been described before ; and those who wish for information about it should consult the description of Mr. Jacomb, the discoverer of the pass.* Nor need we stop at Prerayen, except to remark that the owner of the châlets (who is usually taken for a common herdsman) must not be judged by appearances. He is a man of substance ; he has many flocks and herds ; and although, when approached politely, is courteous, he can (and probably will) act as the *master* of Prerayen, if his position is *not* recognised, and with all the importance of a man who pays taxes to the extent of 500 francs per annum to his government.

The hill-tops were clouded when we rose from our hay on the 5th of August. We decided not to continue the tour of our mountain immediately, and returned over our track of the pre-

---

* *Peaks, Passes, and Glaciers*—second series.

The summit of the Col de Valpelline is about 11,650 feet above the sea. The pass is the easiest one in the Alps of this height, and (if the best route is followed) it may be crossed during fine weather, and under favourable circumstances, without cutting a single step. It may be added, at the same time, that if one does not take the best route, the pass may become one of first-rate difficulty. Much time and trouble will be saved by strictly adhering to the left bank (eastern side) of the Zardesan glacier. Mr. Jacomb followed the right bank.

There is a very fine view from the point that is situated about two-thirds of a mile S. by E. of the summit of the Col. This point (marked 3813 mètres = 12,410 feet, on the map of the Valley of Zermatt) has no name. It is connected with the Col by snow-covered glacier at a very moderate angle, and from it one looks well over the Tête Blanche, which is 200 feet less in elevation. It was ascended by the author in 1866.

ceding day to the highest châlet on the left bank of the valley,* with the intention of attacking the Dent d'Erin on the next morning. We were interested in this summit, more on account of the excellent view which it commanded of the south-west ridge and the terminal peak of the Matterhorn, than from any other reason.

The Dent d'Erin had not been ascended at this time, and we had diverged from our route on the 4th, and had scrambled some distance up the base of Mont Brulé, to see how far its south-western slopes were assailable. We were divided in opinion as to the best way of approaching the peak. Carrel, true to his habit of sticking to rocks in preference to ice, counselled ascending by the long buttress of the Tête de Bella Cia (which descends towards the west, and forms the southern boundary of the last glacier that falls into the Glacier de Zardesan), and thence traversing the heads of all the tributaries of the Zardesan to the western and rocky ridge of the Dent. I, on the other hand, proposed to follow the Glacier de Zardesan itself throughout its entire length, and from the plateau at its head (where my proposed route would cross Carrel's) to make directly towards the summit, up the snow-covered glacier slope, instead of by the western ridge. The hunchback, who was accompanying us on these excursions, declared in favour of Carrel's route, and it was accordingly adopted.

The first part of the programme was successfully executed; and at 10.30 A.M. on the 6th of August, we were sitting astride the western ridge, at a height of about 12,500 feet, looking down upon the Tiefenmatten glacier. To all appearance another hour would place us on the summit; but in another hour we found

---

* See map of the Valley of Valpelline. The châlet is marked " la vielle."

The reader will probably notice the discrepancies between this part of the map of the Valley of Zermatt and that of the Valley of Valpelline. The latter one is correct. The former is after the Swiss Government map, which is extremely accurate on the Swiss side of the frontier line, but does not pretend to be so on the Italian side.

that we were not destined to succeed. The ridge (like all of the principal rocky ridges of the great peaks upon which I have stood) had been completely shattered by frost, and was nothing more than a heap of piled-up fragments. It was always narrow, and where it was narrowest it was also the most unstable and the most difficult. On neither side could we ascend it by keeping a little below its crest,—on the side of the Tiefenmatten because it was too steep, and on both sides because the dislodgment of a single block would have disturbed the equilibrium of all those which were above. Forced, therefore, to keep to the very crest of the ridge, and unable to deviate a single step either to the right or to the left, we were compelled to trust ourselves upon unsteady masses, which trembled under our tread, which sometimes settled down, grating in a hollow and ominous manner, and which seemed as if a little shake would send the whole roaring down in one awful avalanche.

I followed my leader, who said not a word, and did not rebel until we came to a place where a block had to be surmounted which lay poised across the ridge. Carrel could not climb it without assistance, or advance beyond it until I joined him above ; and as he stepped off my back on to it, I felt it quiver and bear down upon me. I doubted the possibility of another man standing upon it without bringing it down. Then I rebelled. There was no honour to be gained by persevering, or dishonour in turning from a place which was dangerous on account of its excessive difficulty. So we returned to Prerayen, for there was too little time to allow us to re-ascend by the other route, which was subsequently shown to be the right way up the mountain.

Four days afterwards a party of Englishmen (including my friends, W. E. Hall, Crauford Grove, and Reginald Macdonald), arrived in the Valpelline, and (unaware of our attempt) on the 12th, under the skilful guidance of Melchior Anderegg, made the first ascent of the Dent d'Erin by the route which I had proposed. This is the only mountain which I have essayed to ascend, that has not, sooner or later, fallen to me. Our failure was mortifying, but I am satisfied that we did wisely in returning, and that if we had persevered, by Carrel's route, another Alpine accident would have been recorded. I have not heard that another ascent has been made of the Dent d'Erin.*

On the 7th of August we crossed the Va Cornère pass,† and had a good look at the mountain named the Grand Tournalin as we descended the Val de Chignana. This mountain was seen from so many points, and was so much higher than any peak in its immediate neighbourhood, that it was bound to give a very fine view ; and (as the weather continued unfavourable for the Matterhorn) I arranged with Carrel to ascend it the next day, and despatched him direct to the village of Val Tournanche to make the necessary preparations, whilst I, with Meynet, made a short

---

* On p. 10 it is stated that there was not a pass from Prerayen to Breil in 1860, and this is correct. On July 8, 1868, my enterprising guide, Jean-Antoine Carrel, started from Breil at 2 A.M. with a well-known comrade—J. Baptiste Bic, of Val Tournanche—to endeavour to make one. They went towards the glacier which descends from the Dent d'Erin to the south-east, and on arriving at its base, ascended at first by some snow between it and the cliffs on its south, and afterwards took to the cliffs themselves. [This glacier they called the glacier of Mont Albert, after the local name of the peak which on Mr. Reilly's map of the Valpelline is called ' Les Jumeaux.' On Mr. Reilly's map the glacier is called ' Glacier d'Erin.'] They ascended the rocks to a considerable height, and then struck across the glacier, towards the north, to a small ' *rognon* ' (isolated patch of rocks) that is nearly in the centre of the glacier. They passed above this, and between it and the great *seracs*. Afterwards their route led them towards the Dent d'Erin, and they arrived at the base of its final peak by mounting a *couloir* (gully filled with snow), and the rocks at the head of the glacier. They gained the summit of their pass at 1 P.M., and, descending by the glacier of Zardesan, arrived at Prerayen at 6.30 P.M.

As their route joins that taken by Messrs. Hall, Grove, and Macdonald, on their ascent of the Dent d'Erin in 1863, it is evident that that mountain can be ascended from Breil. Carrel considers that the route taken by himself and his comrade Bic can be improved upon ; and, if so, it is possible that the ascent of the Dent d'Erin can be made from Breil in less time than from Prerayen. Breil is very much to be preferred as a starting-point.

† See p. 11. The height of this pass, according to Canon Carrel, is 10,335 feet.

cut to Breil, at the back of Mont Panquero, by a little pass locally known as the Col de Fenêtre. I rejoined Carrel the same evening at Val Tournanche, and we started from that place at a little before 5 A.M. on the 8th, to attack the Tournalin.

Meynet was left behind for that day, and most unwillingly did the hunchback part from us, and begged hard to be allowed to come. "Pay me nothing, only let me go with you;" "I shall want but a little bread and cheese, and of that I won't eat much ;" "I would much rather go with you than carry things down the valley." Such were his arguments, and I was really sorry that the rapidity of our movements obliged us to desert the good little man.

Carrel led over the meadows on the south and east of the bluff upon which the village of Val Tournanche is built, and then by a zig-zag path through a long and steep forest, making many short cuts, which showed he had a thorough knowledge of the ground. After we came again into daylight, our route took us up one of those little, concealed, lateral valleys which are so numerous on the slopes bounding the Val Tournanche.

This valley, the Combe de Ceneil, has a general easterly trend, and contains but one small cluster of houses (Ceneil). The Tournalin is situated at the head of the Combe, and nearly due east of the village of Val Tournanche, but from that place no part of the mountain is visible. After Ceneil is passed it comes into view, rising above a cirque of cliffs (streaked by several fine waterfalls), at the end of the Combe. To avoid these cliffs the path bends somewhat to the south, keeping throughout to the left bank of the valley, and at about 3500 feet above Val Tournanche, and 1500 feet above Ceneil and a mile or so to its east, arrives at the base of some moraines, which are remarkably large considering the dimensions of the glaciers which formed them. The ranges upon the western side of the Val Tournanche are seen to great advantage from this spot ; but here the path ends and the way steepens.

When we arrived at these moraines, we had a choice of two

Y

routes. One, continuing to the east, over the moraines themselves, the débris above them, and a large snow-bed still higher up, to a kind of *col* or depression to the *south* of the peak, from whence an easy ridge led towards the summit. The other, over a shrunken glacier on our north-east (now, perhaps, not in existence), which led to a well-marked *col* on the *north* of the peak, from whence a less easy ridge rose directly to the highest point. We followed the first named of these routes, and in a little more than half-an-hour stood upon the Col, which commanded a most glorious view of the southern side of Monte Rosa, and of the ranges to its east, and to the east of the Val d'Ayas.

Whilst we were resting at this point a large party of vagrant chamois arrived on the summit of the mountain from the northern side, some of whom—by their statuesque position—seemed to appreciate the grand panorama by which they were surrounded, while others amused themselves, like two-legged tourists, in rolling stones over the cliffs. The clatter of these falling fragments made us look up. The chamois were so numerous that we could not count them ; clustered around the summit, totally unaware of our presence ; and they scattered in a panic, as if a shell had burst amongst them, when saluted by the cries of my excited comrade ; plunging wildly down in several directions, with unfaltering and unerring bounds, with such speed and with such grace that we were filled with admiration and respect for their mountaineering abilities.

The ridge that led from the Col towards the summit was singularly easy, although well broken up by frost, and Carrel thought that it would not be difficult to arrange a path for mules out of the shattered blocks ; but when we arrived on the summit we found ourselves separated from the very highest point by a cleft which had been concealed up to that time : its southern side was nearly perpendicular, but it was only fourteen or fifteen feet deep. Carrel lowered me down, and afterwards descended on to the head of my axe, and subsequently on to my shoulders, with

a cleverness which was almost as far removed from my awkwardness as his own efforts were from those of the chamois. A few
easy steps then placed us on the highest
point. It had not been ascended before,
and we commemorated the event by
building a huge cairn, which was seen
for many a mile, and would have lasted
for many a year, had it not been thrown
down by the orders of Canon Carrel,
on account of its interrupting the sweep
of a camera which he took to the lower
summit in 1868, in order to photograph
the panorama. According to that well-
known mountaineer, the summit of the
Grand Tournalin is 6100 feet above the
village of Val Tournanche, and 11,155
feet above the sea. Its ascent (including
halts) occupied us only four hours.

CARREL LOWERED ME DOWN.

I recommend the ascent of the Tournalin to any person who has a day to
spare in the Val Tournanche. It should
be remembered, however (if its ascent is
made for the sake of the view), that
these southern Pennine Alps seldom re-
main unclouded after mid-day, and, indeed, frequently not later
than 10 or 11 A.M. Towards sunset the equilibrium of the atmosphere is restored, and the clouds very commonly disappear.

I advise the ascent of this mountain not on account of its
height, or from its accessibility or inaccessibility, but simply for
the wide and splendid view which may be seen from its summit.
Its position is superb, and the list of the peaks which can be seen
from it includes almost the whole of the principal mountains of the
Cottian, Dauphiné, Graian, Pennine, and Oberland groups. The
view has, in the highest perfection, those elements of picturesque-

ness which are wanting in the purely panoramic views of higher summits. There are three principal sections, each with a central or dominating point, to which the eye is naturally drawn. All three alike are pictures in themselves ; yet all are dissimilar. In the south, softened by the vapours of the Val d'Aoste, extends the long line of the Graians, with mountain after mountain 12,000 feet and upwards in height. It is not upon these, noble as some of them are, that the eye will rest, but upon the Viso, far off in the background. In the west and towards the north the range of Mont Blanc, and some of the greatest of the Central Pennine Alps (including the Grand Combin and the Dent Blanche), form the background, but they are overpowered by the grandeur of the ridges which culminate in the Matterhorn. Nor in the east and north, where pleasant grassy slopes lead downwards to the Val d'Ayas, nor upon the glaciers and snow-fields above them, nor upon the Oberland in the background, will the eye long linger, when immediately in front, several miles away, but seeming close at hand, thrown out by the pure azure sky, there are the glittering crests of Monte Rosa.

Those who would, but cannot, stand upon the highest Alps, may console themselves with the knowledge that they do not usually yield the views that make the strongest and most permanent impressions. Marvellous some of the panoramas seen from the greatest peaks undoubtedly are ; but they are necessarily without those isolated and central points which are so valuable pictorially. The eye roams over a multitude of objects (each, perhaps, grand individually), and, distracted by an embarrassment of riches, wanders from one to another, erasing by the contemplation of the next the effect that was produced by the last ; and when those happy moments are over, which always fly with too great rapidity, the summit is left with an impression that is seldom durable, because it is usually vague.

No views create such lasting impressions as those which are seen but for a moment, when a veil of mist is rent in twain, and a single spire or dome is disclosed. The peaks which are seen at these moments are not, perhaps, the greatest or the noblest, but the recollection of them outlives the memory of any panoramic view, because the picture, photographed by the eye, has time to dry, instead of being blurred, while yet wet, by contact with other impressions. The reverse is the case with the bird's-eye panoramic views from the great peaks, which sometimes embrace a hundred miles in nearly every direction. The eye is confounded by the crowd of details, and unable to distinguish the relative importance of the objects which are seen. It is almost as difficult to form a just estimate (with the eye) of the respective heights of a number of peaks from a very high summit, as it is from the bottom of a valley. I think that the grandest and the most satisfactory standpoints for viewing mountain scenery are those which are sufficiently elevated to give a feeling of depth, as well as of height, which are lofty enough to exhibit wide and varied views, but not so high as to sink everything to the level of the spectator. The view from the Grand Tournalin is a favourable example of this class of panoramic views.

We descended from the summit by the northern route, and found it tolerably stiff clambering as far as the Col ; but thence, down the glacier, the way was straightforward, and we joined the route taken on the ascent at the foot of the ridge leading towards the east. In the evening we returned to Breil.

There is an abrupt rise in the valley about two miles to the north of the village of Val Tournanche, and just above this step the torrent has eaten its way into its bed and formed an extraordinary chasm, which has long been known by the name Gouffre des Busserailles. We lingered about this spot to listen to the thunder of the concealed water, and to watch its tumultuous boiling as it issued from the gloomy cleft, but our efforts to peer into the mysteries of the place were baffled. In November 1865, the intrepid Carrel induced two trusty comrades—the Maquignaz's of Val Tournanche—to lower him by a rope into the chasm and over the cataract. The feat required iron nerves, and muscles and sinews of no ordinary kind ; and its performance alone stamps Carrel as a man of dauntless courage. One of the Maquignaz's subsequently descended in the same way, and these two men were so astonished at what they saw, that they forthwith set to work with hammer and chisel to make a way into this romantic gulf. In a few days they constructed a rough but convenient plank gallery into the centre of the *gouffre*, along its walls ; and, on payment of a toll of half-a-franc, any one can now enter the Gouffre des Busserailles.

I cannot, without a couple of sections and a plan, give an exact idea to the reader of this remarkable place. It corresponds in some of its features to the gorge figured upon page 140, but it exhibits in a much more notable manner the characteristic action and power of running water. The length of the chasm or *gouffre* is about 320 feet, and from the top of its walls to the surface of the water is about 110 feet. At no part can the entire length or depth be seen at a glance ; for, although the width at some places is 15 feet or more, the view is limited by the sinuosities of the walls. These are everywhere polished to a smooth, vitreous-in-appearance surface. In some places the torrent has wormed into the rock, and has left natural bridges. The most extraordinary features of the Gouffre des Busserailles, however, are the caverns (or *marmites* as they are termed), which the water has hollowed out of the heart of the rock. Carrel's plank path leads into one of the greatest,—a grotto that is about 28 feet across at its largest diameter, and 15 or 16 feet high ; roofed above by the living rock, and with the torrent roaring 50 feet or thereabouts below, at the bottom of a fissure. This cavern is lighted by candles, and talking in it can only be managed by signs.

I visited the interior of the *gouffre* in 1869, and my wonder at its caverns was increased by observing the hardness of the hornblende out of which they have been hollowed. Carrel chiselled off a large piece, which is now lying before me. It has a highly polished, glassy surface, and might be mistaken, for a moment, for ice-polished rock. But the water has found out the atoms which were least hard, and it is dotted all over by minute depressions, much as the face of one is who has suffered from smallpox. The edges of these little hollows are *rounded,* and the whole sur-faces of the depressions are polished nearly, or quite, as highly as the general surface of the fragment.* The water has drilled more deeply into some veins of steatite than in other places, and the presence of the steatite may possibly have had something to do with the formation of the *gouffre.*

I arrived at Breil again after an absence of six days, well satis-fied with my tour of the Matterhorn, which had been rendered very pleasant by the willingness of my guides, and by the kindliness of the natives. But it must be admitted that the inhabitants of the Val Tournanche are behind the times. Their paths are as bad as, or worse than, they were in the time of De Saussure, and their inns are much inferior to those on the Swiss side. If it were otherwise there would be nothing to prevent the valley becoming one of the most popular and frequented of all the valleys in the Alps ; but, as it is, tourists who enter it seem to think only about how soon they can get out of it, and hence it is much less known than it deserves to be on account of its natural attractions.

I believe that the great hindrance to the improvement of the paths in the Italian valleys generally is the wide-spread impression that the innkeepers would alone directly benefit by any amelioration of their condition. To a certain extent this view is correct; but inasmuch as the prosperity of the natives is connected with that of the innkeepers, the interests of both are pretty nearly identical. Until their paths are rendered less rough and swampy, I think the Italians must submit to see the golden harvest principally reaped in Switzerland and Savoy. At the same time, let the innkeepers look to the commissariat. Their supplies are not unfrequently

---

* The depressions in glaciated rocks (which are not water-worn) are more or less angular. See p. 148.

deficient in quantity, and, according to my experience, very often deplorable in quality.

I will not venture to criticise in detail the dishes which are brought to table, since I am profoundly ignorant of their constitution. It is commonly said amongst Alpine tourists that goat flesh represents mutton, and mule does service for beef and chamois. I reserve my own opinion upon this point until it has been shown what becomes of all the dead mules. But I may say, I hope, without wounding the susceptibilities of my acquaintances among the Italian innkeepers, that it would tend to smoothen their intercourse with their guests if requests for solid food were less frequently regarded as criminal. The deprecating airs with which inquiries for really substantial food are received always remind me of a Dauphiné innkeeper, who remarked that he had heard a good many tourists travel in Switzerland. " Yes," I answered, " there are a good many." " How many?" " Well," I said, " I have seen a hundred or more sit down at a table d'hôte." He lifted up his hands—" Why," said he, " they would want meat every day!" " Yes, that is not improbable." " In that case," he replied, " *I think we are better without them.*"

CHAPTER VII.

" But mighty Jove cuts short, with just disdain,
    The long, long views of poor, designing man."
                                    HOMER.

CARREL had *carte blanche* in the matter of guides, and his choice fell upon his relative Cæsar, Luc Meynet, and two others whose names I do not know. These men were now brought together, and our preparations were completed, as the weather was clearing up.

We rested on Sunday, August 9, eagerly watching the lessening of the mists around the great peak, and started just before dawn upon the 10th, on a still and cloudless morning, which seemed to promise a happy termination to our enterprise.

By going always, but gently, we arrived upon the Col du Lion before nine o'clock. Changes were apparent. Familiar ledges had vanished ; the platform, whereupon my tent had stood, looked very forlorn, its stones had been scattered by wind and frost, and had half disappeared ; and the summit of the Col itself, which in 1862 had always been respectably broad, and covered by snow, was now sharper than the ridge of any church-roof, and was hard ice. Already we had found that the bad weather of the past week had done its work. The rocks for several hundred feet below the Col were varnished with ice. Loose, incoherent snow covered the older and harder beds below, and we nearly lost our leader through its treacherousness. He stepped on some snow which seemed firm, and raised his axe to deliver a swinging blow, but, just as it was highest, the crust of

---

* A brief account of this excursion was published in the *Athenæum*, August 29, 1863.

the slope upon which he stood broke away, and poured down in serpentine streams, leaving long, bare strips, which glittered in the sun, for they were glassy ice. Carrel, with admirable readiness, flung himself back on to the rock off which he had stepped, and was at once secured. He simply remarked, "It is time we were tied up," and, after we had been tied up, he went to work again as if nothing had happened.*

We had abundant illustrations during the next two hours of the value of a rope to climbers. We were tied up rather widely apart, and advanced, generally, in pairs. Carrel, who led, was followed closely by another man, who lent him a shoulder or placed an axe-head under his feet, when there was need ; and when this couple were well placed the second pair advanced, in similar fashion,— the rope being drawn in by those above, and paid out gradually by those below. The leading men again advanced, or the third pair, and so on. This manner of progression was slow, but sure. One man only moved at a time, and if he slipped (and we frequently did slip) he could slide scarcely a foot without being checked by the others. The certainty and safety of the method gave confidence to the one who was moving, and not only nerved him to put out his powers to the utmost, but sustained nerve in really difficult situations. For these rocks (which, it has been already said, were easy enough under ordinary circumstances) were now difficult in a high degree. The snow-water which had trickled down for many days past in little streams, had taken, naturally, the very route by which we wished to ascend ; and, refrozen in the night, had glazed the slabs over which we had to pass,—sometimes with a fine film of ice as thin as a sheet of paper, and sometimes so thickly that we could

---

* This incident occurred close to the place represented in the engraving facing p. 120. The new, dry snow was very troublesome, and poured down like flour into the steps which were cut across the slopes. The front man accordingly moved ahead as far as possible, and anchored himself to rocks. A rope was sent across to him, was fixed at each end, and was held as a rail by the others as they crossed. We did not trust to this rope alone, but were tied in the usual manner. The second rope was employed as an additional security against slips.

almost cut footsteps in it. The weather was superb, the men made light of the toil, and shouted to rouse the echoes from the Dent d'Herens.

We went on gaily, passed the second tent platform, the Chimney, and the other well-remembered points, and reckoned, confidently, on sleeping that night upon the top of " the shoulder ;" but, before we had well arrived at the foot of the Great Tower, a sudden rush of cold air warned us to look out.

It was difficult to say where this air came from ; it did not blow as a wind, but descended rather as the water in shower-bath ! All was tranquil again ; the atmosphere *showed* no signs of disturbance ; there was a dead calm, and not a speck of cloud to be seen anywhere. But we did not remain very long in this state. The cold air came again, and this time it was difficult to say where it did not come from. We jammed down our hats as it beat against the ridge, and screamed amongst the crags. Before we had got to the foot of the Tower, mists had been formed above and below. They appeared at first in small, isolated patches (in several places at the same time), which danced and jerked and were torn into shreds by the wind, but grew larger under the process. They were united together, and rent again,—showing us the blue sky for a moment, and blotting it out the next ; and augmented incessantly, until the whole heavens were filled with whirling, boiling clouds. Before we could take off our packs, and get under any kind of shelter, a hurricane of snow burst upon us from the east. It fell so thickly that in a few minutes the ridge was covered by it. " What shall we do ?" I shouted to Carrel. "Monsieur," said he, " the wind is bad ; the weather has changed ; we are heavily laden. Here is a fine *gîte;* let us stop ! If we go on we shall be half-frozen. That is *my* opinion." No one differed from him ; so we fell to work to make a place for the tent, and in a couple of hours completed the platform which we had commenced in 1862. The clouds had blackened during that time, and we had hardly finished our task before a thunderstorm broke upon us with appalling fury. Forked lightning shot out at the turrets above, and at the crags below. It was so close that we quailed at its darts. It seemed to scorch us,—we were in the very focus of the storm. The thunder was simultaneous with the flashes; short and sharp, and more like the noise of a door that is violently slammed, multiplied a thousand-fold, than any noise to which I can compare it.

When I say that the thunder was *simultaneous* with the lightning, I speak as an inexact person. My meaning is that the time which elapsed between seeing the flash and hearing the report was inappreciable to me. I wish to speak with all possible precision, and there are two points in regard to this storm upon which I can speak with some accuracy. The first is in regard to the distance of the lightning from our party. We *might* have been 1100 feet from it if a second of time had elapsed between seeing the flashes and hearing the reports ; and a second of time is not appreciated by inexact persons. It was certain that we were sometimes less than that distance from the lightning, because I saw it pass in front of well-known points on the ridge, both above and below us, which were less (sometimes considerably less) than a thousand feet distant.

Secondly, in regard to the difficulty of distinguishing sounds which are merely echoes from true thunder, or the noise which occurs simultaneously with lightning. Arago entered into this subject at some length in his Meteorological Essays, and seemed to doubt if it would ever be possible to determine whether echoes are *always* the cause of the rolling sounds commonly called thunder.* I shall not attempt to show whether the rolling sounds should ever, or never, be regarded as true thunder, but only that during this storm upon the Matterhorn it was possible to distinguish the sound of the thunder itself from the sounds (rolling and otherwise) which were merely the echoes of the first, original sound.

* "There is, therefore, little hope of thus arriving at anything decisive as to the exact part which echoes take in the production of the rolling sound of thunder." P. 165, English ed., translated by Col. Sabine : Longmans, 1855.

At the place where we were camped a remarkable echo could be heard (one so remarkable that if it could be heard in this country it would draw crowds for its own sake) ; I believe it came from the cliffs of the Dent d'Herens. It was a favourite amusement with us to shout to rouse this echo, which repeated any sharp cry, in a very distinct manner, several times, after the lapse of something like a dozen seconds. The thunderstorm lasted nearly two hours, and raged at times with great fury ; and the prolonged rollings from the surrounding mountains, after one flash, had not usually ceased before another set of echoes took up the discourse, and maintained the reverberations without a break. Occasionally there was a pause, interrupted presently by a single clap, the accompaniment of a single discharge, and after such times I could recognise the echoes from the Dent d'Herens by their peculiar repetitions, and by the length of time which had passed since the reports had occurred of which they were the echoes.

If I had been unaware of the existence of this echo, I should have supposed that the resounds were original reports of explosions which had been unnoticed, since in intensity they were scarcely distinguishable from the true thunder ; which, during this storm, seemed to me, upon every occasion, to consist of a single, harsh, instantaneous sound.[*]

Or if, instead of being placed at a distance of less than a thousand feet from the points of explosion (and consequently hearing the report almost in the same moment as we saw the flash, and

---

[*] The same has seemed to me to be the case at all times when I have been close to the points of explosion. There has been always a distinct interval between the first explosion and the rolling sounds and secondary explosions which I have *believed* to be merely echoes ; but it has never been possible (except in the above-mentioned case) to *identify* them as such.

Others have observed the same. " The geologist, Professor Theobald, of Chur, who was in the Solferino storm, between the Tschiertscher and Urden Alp, in the electric clouds, says that the peals were short, like cannon shots, but of a clearer, more cracking tone, and that the rolling of the thunder was only heard further on." Berlepsch's *Alps*, English ed., p. 133.

the rollings after a considerable interval of time), we had been placed so that the original report had fallen on our ears nearly at the same moment as the echoes, we should probably have considered that the successive reports and rollings of the echoes were reports of successive explosions occurring nearly at the same moment, and that they were not echoes at all.

This is the only time (out of many storms witnessed in the Alps) I have obtained evidence that the rollings of thunder are actually echoes ; and that they are not, necessarily, the reports of a number of discharges over a long line, occurring at varying distances from the spectator, and consequently unable to arrive at his ear at the same moment, although they follow each other so swiftly as to produce a sound more or less continuous.*

The wind during all this time seemed to blow tolerably consistently from the east. It smote the tent so vehemently (notwithstanding it was partly protected by rocks) that we had grave fears our refuge might be blown away bodily, with ourselves inside ; so, during some of the lulls, we issued out and built a wall to windward. At half-past three the wind changed to the north-west, and the clouds vanished. We immediately took the opportunity to send down one of the porters (under protection of some of the others, a little beyond the Col du Lion), as the tent would accommodate only five persons. From this time to sunset the weather was variable. It was sometimes blowing and snowing hard, and sometimes a dead calm. The bad weather was evidently confined to the Mont Cervin, for when the clouds lifted we could see every-

* Mr. J. Glaisher has frequently pointed out that all sounds in balloons at some distance from the earth are notable for their brevity. " It is one sound only ; *there is no reverberation, no reflection ;* and this is characteristic of all sounds in the balloon, one clear sound, continuing during its own vibrations, then gone in a moment." (*Good Words*, 1863, p. 224.)

I learn from Mr. Glaisher that the thunder claps which have been heard by him during his ' travels in the air ' have been no exception to the general rule, and the absence of rolling has fortified his belief that the rolling sounds which accompany thunder are echoes, and echoes *only*.

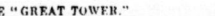

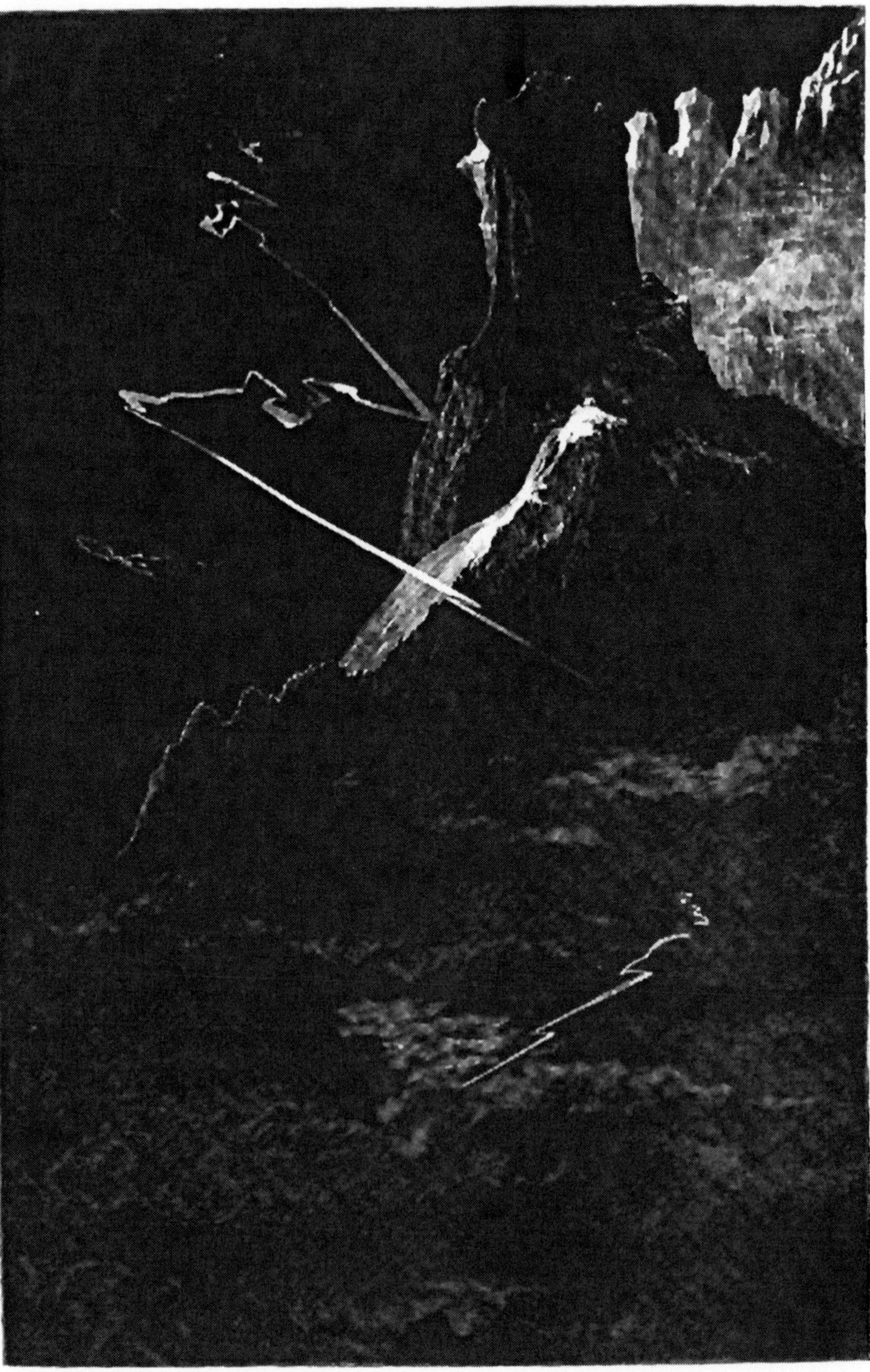

THE CRAGS OF THE MATTERHORN, DURING THE STORM, MIDNIGHT, AUGUST 10, 1863.

thing that could be seen from our gîte. Monte Viso, a hundred miles off, was clear, and the sun set gorgeously behind the range of Mont Blanc. We passed the night comfortably—even luxuriously —in our blanket-bags, but there was little chance of sleeping, between the noise of the wind, of the thunder, and of the falling rocks. I forgave the thunder for the sake of the lightning. A more splendid spectacle than its illumination of the Matterhorn crags I do not expect to see.*

The greatest rock-falls always seemed to occur in the night, between midnight and daybreak. This was noticeable on each of the seven nights which I passed upon the south-west ridge, at heights varying from 11,800 to 13,000 feet.

I may be wrong in supposing that the falls in the night are greater than those in the daytime, since sound causes much more effect during darkness than when the cause of its production is seen. Even a sigh may be terrible in the stillness of the night. In the daytime one's attention is probably divided between the sound and the motion of rocks which fall ; or it may be concentrated on other matters. But it is certain that the greatest of the falls which happened during the night took place after midnight, and this I connect with the fact that the maximum of cold during any twenty-four hours very commonly occurs between midnight and dawn.

We turned out at 3.30 A.M. on the 11th, and were dismayed to find that it still continued to snow. At 9 A.M. the snow ceased to fall, and the sun showed itself feebly, so we packed up our baggage, and set out to try to get upon " the shoulder." We struggled upwards until eleven o'clock, and then it commenced to snow again. We held a council ; the opinions expressed at it were unanimous against advancing, and I decided to retreat. For we had risen less than 300 feet in the past two hours, and had not even arrived at the rope which Tyndall's party left behind, attached to the rocks,

---

* See Appendix for the experiences of Mr. R. B. Heathcote during a thunderstorm on the Matterhorn in 1869.

in 1862. At the same rate of progression it would have taken us from four to five hours to get upon "the shoulder." Not one of us cared to attempt to do so under the existing circumstances; for besides having to move our own weight, which was sufficiently troublesome at this part of the ridge, we had to transport much heavy baggage, tent, blankets, and provisions, ladder, and 450 feet of rope, besides many other smaller matters. These, however, were not the most serious considerations. Supposing that we got upon "the shoulder," we might find ourselves detained there several days, unable either to go up or down.* I could not risk any such detention, being under obligations to appear in London at the end of the week.

We got to Breil in the course of the afternoon; it was quite fine there, and the tenants of the inn received our statements with

evident scepticism. They were astonished to learn that we had been exposed to a snow-storm of twenty-six hours' duration. "Why," said Favre, the innkeeper, "*we* have had no snow; it has been fine all the time you have been absent, and there has been only that small cloud upon the mountain." Ah! that small cloud! None except those who have had experience of

MONSIEUR FAVRE.

it can tell what a formidable obstacle it is.

Why is it that the Matterhorn is subject to these abominable variations of weather? The ready answer is, "Oh, the mountain is so isolated; it attracts the clouds." This is not a sufficient answer. Although the mountain *is* isolated, it is not so much more isolated than the neighbouring peaks that it should gather clouds when none of the others do so. It will not at all account for the

* Since then (on at least one occasion), several persons have found themselves in this predicament for five or six consecutive days!

cloud to which I refer, which is not formed by an aggregation of smaller, stray clouds drawn together from a distance (as scum collects round a log in the water), but is created against the mountain itself, and springs into existence where no clouds were seen before. It is formed and hangs chiefly against the southern sides, and particularly against the south-eastern side. It frequently does not envelop the summit, and rarely extends down to the Glacier du Lion, and to the Glacier du Mont Cervin below. It forms in the finest weather ; on cloudless and windless days.

I conceive that we should look to differences of temperature rather than to the height or isolation of the mountain for an explanation. I am inclined to attribute the disturbances which occur in the atmosphere of the southern sides of the Matterhorn on fine days,* principally to the fact that the mountain is a *rock* mountain ; that it receives a great amount of heat,† and is not only warmer itself, but is surrounded by an atmosphere of a higher temperature than such peaks as the Weisshorn and the Lyskamm, which are eminently *snow* mountains.

In certain states of the atmosphere its temperature may be tolerably uniform over wide areas and to great elevations. I have known the thermometer to show 70° in the shade at the top of an Alpine peak more than 13,000 feet high, and but a very few degrees higher 6000 or 7000 feet lower. At other times, there will be a difference of forty or fifty degrees (Faht.) between two stations, the higher not more than 6000 or 7000 feet above the lower.

Provided that the temperature was uniform, or nearly so, on all sides of the Matterhorn, and to a considerable distance above its summit, no clouds would be likely to form upon it. But if the atmosphere immediately surrounding it is warmer than the contiguous strata, a local 'courant ascendant' must necessarily be generated ; and portions of the cooler superincumbent (or circum-

---

* I am speaking exclusively of the disturbances which occur in the day-time during fine weather.

† The rocks are sometimes so hot that they are almost painful to touch.

2 A

jacent) air will naturally be attracted towards the mountain, where they will speedily condense the moisture of the warm air in contact with it. I cannot explain the downrushes of cold air which occur on it, when all the rest of the neighbourhood appears to be tranquil, in any other way. The clouds are produced by the contact of two strata of air (of widely different temperatures) charged with invisible moisture, as surely as certain colourless fluids produce a white, turbid liquid, when mixed together. The order has been—wind of a low temperature—mist—rain—snow or hail.*

This opinion is borne out to some extent by the behaviour of the neighbouring mountains. The Dom (14,935 feet) and the Dent Blanche (14,318) have both of them large cliffs of bare rock upon their southern sides, and against those cliffs clouds commonly form (during fine, still weather) at the same time as the cloud on the Matterhorn ; whilst the Weisshorn (14,804) and the Lyskamm (14,889), (mountains of about the same altitude, and which are in corresponding situations to the former pair) usually remain perfectly clear.

I arrived at Chatillon at midnight on the 11th, defeated and disconsolate ; but, like a gambler who loses each throw, only the more eager to have another try, to see if the luck would change : and returned to London ready to devise fresh combinations, and to form new plans.

* The mists are extremely deceptive to those who are on the mountain itself. Sometimes they *seem* to be created at a *considerable distance*, as if the whole of the atmosphere of the neighbourhood was undergoing a change, when in reality they are being formed in immediate proximity to the mountain.

CROSSING THE CHANNEL.

CHAPTER VIII.

FROM ST. MICHEL ON THE MONT CENIS ROAD BY THE COL DES AIGUILLES D'ARVE, COL DE MARTIGNARE, AND THE BRÈCHE DE LA MEIJE TO LA BÉRARDE.*

"The more to help the greater deed is done."

HOMER.

WHEN we arrived upon the highest summit of Mont Pelvoux, in Dauphiné, in 1861, we saw, to our surprise and disappointment, that it was not the culminating point of the district ; and that another mountain—distant about a couple of miles, and separated from us by an impassable gulf—claimed that distinction. I was troubled in spirit about this mountain, and my thoughts often reverted to the great wall-sided peak, second in apparent inaccessibility only to the Matterhorn. It had, moreover, another claim to attention—it was the highest mountain *in* France.

The year 1862 passed away without a chance of getting to it, and my holiday was too brief in 1863 even to think about it ; but in the following year it was possible, and I resolved to set my mind at rest by completing the task which had been left unfinished in 1861.

In the meantime others had turned their attention to Dauphiné. First of all (in 1862) came Mr. F. Tuckett—that mighty mountaineer, whose name is known throughout the length and breadth of the Alps—with the guides Michel Croz, Peter Perrn, and Bartolommeo Peyrotte, and great success attended his arms. But Mr. Tuckett halted before the Pointe des Ecrins, and, dismayed by its appearance, withdrew his forces to gather less dangerous laurels elsewhere.

His expedition, however, threw some light upon the Ecrins.

* For routes described in this chapter, see the General Map and the plan in the text at p. 183.

He pointed out the direction from which an attack was most likely to be successful, and Mr. William Mathews and the Rev. T. G. Bonney (to whom he communicated the result of his labours) attempted to execute the ascent, with the brothers Michel and J. B. Croz, by following his indications. But they too were defeated, as I shall relate more particularly presently.

MICHEL-AUGUSTE CROZ (1865.)

The guide Michel Croz had thus been engaged in both of these expeditions in Dauphiné, and I naturally looked to him for assistance. Mr. Mathews (to whom I applied for information) gave him a high character, and concluded his reply to me by saying, " he was only happy when upwards of 10,000 feet high."

I know what my friend meant. Croz was happiest when he was employing his powers to the utmost. Places where you and I would " toil and sweat, and yet be freezing cold," were bagatelles to

him, and it was only when he got above the range of ordinary
mortals, and was required to employ his magnificent strength,
and to draw upon his unsurpassed knowledge of ice and snow, that
he could be said to be really and truly happy.

Of all the guides with whom I travelled, Michel Croz was
the man who was most after my own heart. He did not work like
a blunt razor, and take to his toil unkindly. He did not need
urging, or to be told a second time to do anything. You had but to
say *what* was to be done, and *how* it was to be done, and the work
was done, if it was possible. Such men are not common, and when
they are known they are valued. Michel was not widely known,
but those who did know him came again and again. The inscription that is placed upon his tomb truthfully records that he was
" beloved by his comrades and esteemed by travellers."

At the time that I was planning my journey, my friends,
Messrs. A. W. Moore and Horace Walker were also drawing up their
programme ; and, as we found that our wishes were very similar,
we agreed to unite our respective parties. The excursions which are
described in this and the two following chapters are mutual ideas
which were jointly executed.

Our united programme was framed so as to avoid sleeping in
inns, and so that we should see from the highest point attained on
one day, a considerable portion of the route which was intended to
be followed on the next. This latter matter was an important
one to us, as all of our projected excursions were new ones, and led
over ground about which there was very little information in print.

My friends had happily secured Christian Almer of Grindelwald
as their guide. The combination of Croz and Almer was a perfect
one. Both men were in the prime of life ;* both were endued with
strength and activity far beyond the average ; and the courage and
the knowledge of each was alike undoubted. The temper of Almer
it was impossible to ruffle ; he was ever obliging and enduring,—

* Croz was born at the Village du Tour, in the valley of Chamounix, on April 22,
1830 ; Almer was a year or two older.

a bold but a safe man. That which he lacked in fire—in dash—was supplied by Croz, who, in his turn, was kept in place by Almer. It is pleasant to remember how they worked together, and how each one confided to you that he liked the other *so* much because he worked *so* well; but it is sad, very sad, to those who have known the men, to know that they can never work together again.

We met at St. Michel on the Mont Cenis road, at midday on June 20, 1864, and proceeded in the afternoon over the Col de Valloires to the village of the same name. The summit of this pretty little pass is about 3500 feet above St. Michel, and from it we had a fair view of the Aiguilles d'Arve, a group of three peaks of singular form, which it was our especial object to investigate.* They had been seen by ourselves and others from numerous distant points, and always looked very high and very inaccessible ; but we had been unable to obtain any information about them, except the few words in Joanne's *Itinéraire du Dauphiné*. Having made out from the summit of the Col de Valloires that they could be approached from the Valley of Valloires, we hastened down to find a place where we could pass the night, as near as possible to the entrance of the little valley leading up to them.

By nightfall we arrived at the entrance to this little valley (Vallon des Aiguilles d'Arve), and found some buildings placed just where they were wanted. The proprietress received us with civility, and placed a large barn at our disposal, on the conditions that no lights were struck or pipes smoked therein ; and when her terms were agreed to, she took us into her own chalet, made up a huge fire, heated a gallon of milk, and treated us with genuine hospitality.

In the morning we found that the Vallon des Aiguilles d'Arve led away nearly due west from the Valley of Valloires, and that the village of Bonnenuit was placed (in the latter valley) almost exactly opposite to the junction of the two.

---

* The Pointe des Écrins is also seen from the top of the Col de Valloires, rising above the Col du Galibier. This is the lowest elevation from which I have seen the actual summit of the Écrins.

At 3.55 A.M. on the 21st we set out up the Vallon, passed for a time over pasture-land, and then over a stony waste, deeply channelled by watercourses. At 5.30 the two principal Aiguilles were well seen, and as, by this time, it was evident that the authors of

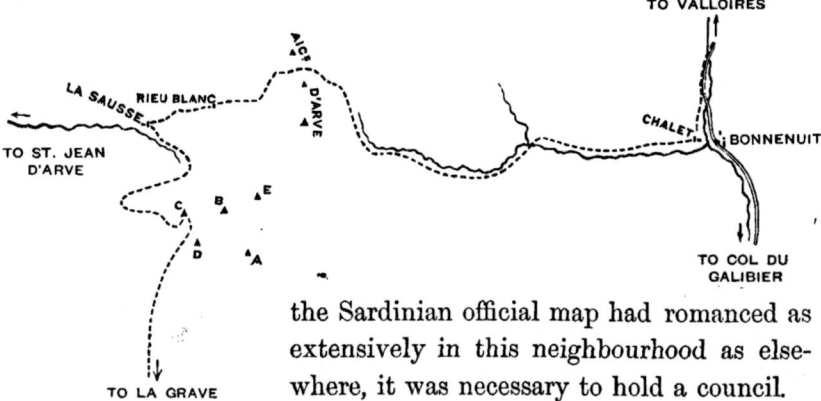

the Sardinian official map had romanced as extensively in this neighbourhood as elsewhere, it was necessary to hold a council. Three questions were submitted to it :—Firstly, Which is the highest of these Aiguilles ? Secondly, Which shall we go up ? Thirdly, How is it to be done ?

The French engineers, it was said, had determined that the two highest of them were respectively 11,513 and 11,529 feet in height ; but we were without information as to which two they had measured.* Joanne indeed said (but without specifying whether he meant all three) that the Aiguilles had been several times ascended, and particularly mentioned that the one of 11,513 feet was " relatively easy."

We therefore said, " We will go up the peak of 11,529 feet." But that determination did not settle the second question. Joanne's " relatively easy " peak, according to his description, was evidently the most northern of the three. *Our* peak then was to be one of the

---

* It should be observed that these mountains were included in the territory recently ceded to France. The Sardinian map above referred to was the old official map. The French survey alluded to afterwards is the survey in continuation of the great French official map. The sheet (No. 179) which will include the Aiguilles d'Arve is not yet published.

other two ;—but which of them ?   We were inclined to favour the central one ; but it was hard to determine, they looked so equal in height.   When, however, the council came to study the third question—" How is it to be done?" it was unanimously voted that upon the eastern and southern sides it was certainly relatively difficult, and that a move should be made round to the northern side.

The movement was duly executed, and after wading up some snow-slopes of considerable steepness (going occasionally beyond 40°), we found ourselves in a gap or nick, between the central and northernmost Aiguille, at 8.45 A.M.   We then studied the northern face of our intended peak, and finally arrived at the conclusion that it was relatively impracticable.   Croz shrugged his big shoulders, and said, " My faith ! I think you will do well to leave it to others." Almer was more explicit, and volunteered the information that a thousand francs would not tempt him to *try* it.   We then turned to the northernmost peak, but found its southern faces even more hopeless than the northern faces of the central one.   We enjoyed accordingly the unwonted luxury of a three-hours' rest on the top of our pass ; for pass we were determined it should be.

We might have done worse.   We were 10,300 or 10,400 feet above the level of the sea, and commanded a most picturesque view of the mountains of the Tarentaise ; while, somewhat east of south, we saw the monarch of the Dauphiné *massif*, whose closer acquaintance it was our intention to make.   Three sunny hours passed away, and then we turned to the descent.   We saw the distant pastures of a valley (which we supposed was the Vallon or Ravine de la Sausse), and a long snow-slope leading down to them.   But from that slope we were cut off by precipitous rocks, and our first impression was that we should have to return in our track.   Some running up and down, however, discovered two little gullies, filled with threads of snow, and down the most northern of these we decided to go.   It was a steep way but a safe one, for the cleft was so narrow that we could press the shoulder against one side whilst the feet were against the other, and the last remnant of the winter's

snow, well hardened, clung to the rift with great tenacity, and gave us a path when the rocks refused one. In half-an-hour we got to the top of the great snow-slope. Walker said—"Let us glis-sade;" the guides — "No, it is too steep." Our friend, however, started off at a standing glissade, and advanced for a time very skilfully; but after a while he lost his balance, and progressed downwards and backwards with

THE AIGUILLES D'ARVE, FROM ABOVE THE CHALETS OF RIEU BLANC.

great rapidity, in a way that seemed to us very much like tumbling head over heels. He let go his axe, and left it behind, but it overtook him and batted him heartily. He and it travelled in this fashion for some hundreds of feet, and at last subsided into

2 B

the rocks at the bottom. In a few moments we were reassured as to his safety, by hearing him ironically request us not to keep him waiting down there.

We others followed the track shown by the dotted line upon the engraving (making zigzags to avoid the little groups of rocks which jutted through the snow, by which Walker had been upset), descended by a *sitting* glissade, and rejoined our friend at the bottom. We then turned sharply to the left, and tramped down the summit ridge of an old moraine of great size. Its mud was excessively hard, and where some large erratic blocks lay perched upon its crest, we were obliged to cut steps (in the mud) with our ice-axes.

Guided by the sound of a distant 'moo,' we speedily found the highest chalets in the valley, named Rieu Blanc. They were tenanted by three old women (who seemed to belong to one of the missing links sought by naturalists), destitute of all ideas except in regard to cows, and who spoke a barbarous patois, well-nigh unintelligible to the Savoyard Croz. They would not believe that we had passed between the Aiguilles,—" It is impossible, the *cows* never go there." " Could we get to La Grave over yonder ridge ?" " Oh yes ! the *cows* often crossed !" Could they show us the way ? No ; but we could follow the *cow*-tracks.

We stayed a while near these chalets, to examine the western sides of the Aiguilles d'Arve, and, according to our united opinion, the central one was as inaccessible from this direction as from the east, north, or south. On the following day we saw them again, from a height of about 11,000 feet, in a south-easterly direction, and our opinion remained unchanged.

We saw (on June 20-22) the central Aiguille from all sides, and very nearly completely round the southernmost one. The northern one we also saw on all sides excepting from the north. (It is, however, precisely from this direction M. Joanne says that its ascent is relatively easy.) We do not, therefore, venture to express any opinion respecting its ascent, except as regards its actual summit. This is formed of two curious prongs, or pinnacles of rock, and we do not understand in what way they (or either of them) can be ascended ; nor shall we be surprised if this ascent is discovered to have been made in spirit rather than body ; in fact, in the same manner as the celebrated ascent of Mont Blanc, " not entirely to the summit, but as far as the Montanvert !"

All three of the Aiguilles *may* be accessible, but they look as inaccessible as anything I have seen.   They are the highest summits between the valleys of the Romanche and the Arc ; they are placed slightly to the north of the watershed between those two valleys, and a line drawn through them runs, pretty nearly, north and south.

We descended by a rough path from Rieu Blanc to the chalets of La Sausse, which give the name to the Vallon or Ravine de la Sausse, in which they are situated.   This is one of the numerous branches of the valley that leads to St. Jean d'Arve, and subsequently to St. Jean de Maurienne.

Two passes, more or less known, lead from this valley to the village of La Grave (on the Lautaret road) in the valley of the Romanche, viz. :—the Col de l'Infernet and the Col de Martignare. The former pass was crossed, just thirty years ago, by J. D. Forbes, and was mentioned by him in his *Norway and its Glaciers.*   The latter one lies to the north of the former, and is seldom traversed by tourists, but it was convenient for us, and we set out to cross it on the morning of the 22d, after having passed a comfortable, but not luxurious, night in the hay, at La Sausse, where, however, the simplicity of the accommodation was more than counterbalanced by the civility and hospitality of the people in charge.*

---

* While stopping in the hospice on the Col de Lautaret, in 1869, I was accosted by a middle-aged peasant, who asked if I would ride (for a consideration) in his cart towards Briançon.   He was inquisitive as to my knowledge of his district, and at last asked, " Have you been at La Sausse ?"   " Yes."   " Well, then, I tell you, *you saw there some of the first people in the world.*"   " Yes," I said, " they were primitive, certainly."   But he was serious, and went on—" Yes, real brave people ;" and, slapping his knee to give emphasis, " *but that they are first-rate for minding the cows !*"

After this he became communicative.   " You thought, probably," said he, " when I offered to take you down, that I was some poor ——, not worth a *sou ;* but

[Our object now was to cross to La Grave (on the high road from Grenoble to Briançon), and to ascend, *en route,* some point sufficiently high to give us a good view of the Dauphiné Alps in general, and of the grand chain of the Meije in particular. Before leaving England a careful study of ' Joanne' had elicited the fact that the shortest route from La Sausse to La Grave was by the Col de Martignare ; and also that from the aforesaid Col it was possible to ascend a lofty summit, called by him the Bec-du-Grenier, also called Aiguille de Goléon. On referring, however, to the Sardinian survey, we found there depicted, to the east of the Col de Martignare, not *one* peak bearing the above *two* names, but *two distinct summits;* one—just above the Col—the Bec-du-Grenier (the height of which was not stated) ; the other, still farther to the east, and somewhat to the south of the watershed—the Aiguille du Goléon (11,250 English feet in height), with a very considerable glacier—the Glacier Lombard—between the two. On the French map,* on the other hand, neither of the above names was to be found, but a peak called Aiguille de la Sausse (10,897 feet), was placed in the position assigned to the Bec-du-Grenier in the Sardinian map ; while farther to the east was a second and nameless peak (10,841), not at all in the position given to the Aiguille du Goléon, of which and of the Glacier Lombard there was not a sign. All this was very puzzling and unsatisfactory ; but as we had no doubt of being able to climb one of the points to the east of the Col de Martignare (which overhung the Ravine de la Sausse), we determined to make that col the basis of our operations.]†

I will tell you, that was my mountain ! *my* mountain ! that you saw at La Sausse ; they were *my* cows ! a hundred of them altogether." " Why, you are rich." " Passably rich. I have another mountain on the Col du Galibier, and another at Villeneuve." He (although a common peasant in outward appearance) confessed to being worth four thousand pounds.

* We had seen a tracing from the unpublished sheets of the French Government Survey.

† The bracketed paragraphs in Chaps. viii. ix. and x. are extracted from the Journal of Mr. A. W. Moore.

It would be uninteresting and unprofitable to enter into a discussion of the con-

We left the chalets at 4.15 A.M. [under a shower of good wishes from our hostesses], proceeded at first towards the upper end of the ravine, then doubled back up a long buttress which projects in an unusual way, and went towards the Col de Martignare ; but before arriving at its summit we again doubled, and resumed the original course.*   At 6 A.M. we stood on the watershed, and followed it towards the east ; keeping for some distance strictly to the ridge, and afterwards diverging a little to the south to avoid a considerable secondary aiguille, which prevented a straight track being made to the summit at which we were aiming.   At 9.15 we stood on its top, and saw at once the lay of the land.

We found that our peak was one of four which enclosed a plateau that was filled by a glacier.   Let us call these summits A, B, C, D (see plan on p. 183).   We stood upon C, which was almost exactly the same elevation as B, but was higher than D, and lower than A.   Peak A was the highest of the four, and was about 200 feet higher than B and C ; we identified it as the Aiguille de Goléon (French survey, 11,250 feet).   Peak D we considered was the Bec-du-Grenier ; and, in default of other names, we called B and C the Aiguilles de la Sausse.   The glacier flowed in a south-easterly direction, and was the Glacier Lombard.

Peaks B and C overhung the Ravine de la Sausse, and were connected with another aiguille—E —which did the same.   A continuation of the ridge out of which these three aiguilles rose joined the Aiguilles d'Arve.   The head of the Ravine de la Sausse was therefore encircled by six peaks ; three of which it was convenient to term the Aiguilles de la Sausse, and the others were the Aiguilles d'Arve.

We were very fortunate in the selection of our summit.   Not to

fusion of these names at greater length. It is sufficient to say that they were confounded in a most perplexing manner by all the authorities we were able to consult, and also by the natives on the spot.

* A great part of this morning's route led over shales, which were loose and troublesome, and were probably a continuation of the well-known beds of the Col du Galibier and the Col de Lautaret.

speak of other things, it gave a grand view of the ridge which culminates in the peak called La Meije (13,080 feet), which used to be mentioned by travellers under the name Aiguille du Midi de la Grave. The view of this mountain from the village of La Grave itself can hardly be praised too highly,—it is one of the very finest road-views in the Alps. The Ortler Spitz from the Stelvio is, in fact, its only worthy competitor ; and the opinions generally of those who have seen the two views are in favour of the former. But from La Grave one can no more appreciate the noble proportions and the towering height of the Meije, than understand the symmetry of the dome of St. Paul's by gazing upon it from the churchyard. To see it fairly, one must be placed at a greater distance and at a greater height.

I shall not try to describe the Meije. The same words, and the same phrases, have to do duty for one and another mountain ; their repetition becomes wearisome ; and 'tis a discouraging fact that any description, however true or however elaborated, seldom or never gives an idea of the reality.

Yet the Meije deserves more than a passing notice. It is the last—the only—great Alpine peak which has never known the foot of man, and one cannot speak in exaggerated terms of its jagged ridges, torrential glaciers, and tremendous precipices.* But were I

---

* The ridge called La Meije runs from E.S.E. to W.N.W., and is crowned by numerous aiguilles of tolerably equal elevation. The two highest are towards the eastern and western ends of the ridge, and are rather more than a mile apart. To the former the French surveyors assign a height of 12,730, and to the latter 13,080 feet. In our opinion the western aiguille can hardly be more than 200 feet higher than the eastern one. It is possible that its height may have diminished since it was measured.

In 1869 I carefully examined the eastern end of the ridge from the top of the Col de Lautaret, and saw that the summit at that end can be ascended by following a long glacier which descends from it towards the N.E. into the valley of Arsine. The highest summit may present difficulties, but is possibly accessible. Any attempts upon it must be made from the northern side (see p. 198).

Sheet 189 of the French map is extremely inaccurate in the neighbourhood of the Meije, and particularly so on its northern side. The ridges and glaciers which are laid down upon it can scarcely be identified on the spot.

to discourse upon these things without the aid of pictures, or to endeavour to convey in *words* a sense of the loveliness of *curves,* of the beauty of *colour,* or of the harmonies of *sound,* I should try to accomplish that which is impossible ; and, at the best, should succeed in but giving an impression that the things spoken of may have been pleasant to hear or to behold, although they are perfectly incomprehensible to read about.   Let me therefore avoid these things, not because I have no love for or thought of them, but because they cannot be translated into language ; and presently, when topographical details must, of necessity, be returned to again, I will endeavour to relieve the poverty of the pen by a free use of the pencil.

Whilst we sat upon the Aiguille de la Sausse, our attention was concentrated on a point that was immediately opposite—on a gap or cleft between the Meije and the mountain called the Rateau. It was, indeed, in order to have a good view of this place that we made the ascent of the Aiguille.   It (that is the gap itself) looked, as my companions remarked, obtrusively and offensively a pass. It had not been crossed, but it ought to have been ; and this seemed to have been recognised by the natives, who called it, very appropriately, the Brèche de la Meije.

I had seen the place in 1860, and again in 1861, but had not then thought about getting through it ; and our information in respect to it was chiefly derived from a photographic reproduction of the then unpublished sheet 189, of the great map of France, which Mr. Tuckett, with his usual liberality, had placed at our disposal. It was evident from this map that if we could succeed in passing the Brèche, we should make the most direct route between the village of La Grave and that of Bérarde in the Department of the Isère, and that the distance between these two places by this route, would be less than one-third that of the ordinary way *via* the villages of Freney and Venos.   It may occur to some of my readers, why had it not been done before ?   For the very sound reason that the valley on its southern side (Vallon des Étançons) is uninhabited, and La

Bérarde itself is a miserable village, without interest, without commerce, and almost without population. Why then did *we* wish to cross it? Because we were bound to the Pointe des Ecrins, to which La Bérarde was the nearest inhabited place.

When we sat upon the Aiguille de la Sausse, we were rather despondent about our prospects of crossing the Brèche, which seemed to present a combination of all that was formidable. There was, evidently, but one way by which it could be approached. We saw that at the top of the pass there was a steep wall of snow or ice (so steep that it was most likely ice) protected at its base by a big schrund or moat, which severed it from the snow-fields below. Then (tracking our course downwards) we saw undulating snow-fields leading down to a great glacier. The snow-fields would be easy work, but the glacier was riven and broken in every direction; huge crevasses seemed to extend entirely across it in some places, and everywhere it had that strange twisted look, which tells of the unequal motion of the ice. Where could we get on to it? At its base it came to a violent end, being cut short by a cliff, over which it poured periodical avalanches, as we saw by a great triangular bed of débris below. We could not venture there,—the glacier must be taken in flank. But on which side? Not on the west, —no one could climb those cliffs. It must, if any where, be by the rocks on the east; and *they* looked as if they were *roches moutonnées.*

So we hurried down to La Grave, to hear what Melchior Anderegg (who had just passed through the village with the family of our friend Walker) had to say on the matter. Who is Melchior Anderegg? Those who ask the question cannot have been in Alpine Switzerland, where the name of Melchior is as well known as the name of Napoleon. Melchior, too, is an Emperor in his way—a very Prince among guides. His empire is amongst the 'eternal snows,'—his sceptre is an ice-axe.

Melchior Anderegg, more familiarly, and perhaps more gene-rally known simply as Melchior, was born at Zaun, near

Meiringen, on April 6, 1828.   He was first brought into public
notice in Hinchcliff's *Summer Months in the Alps*, and was
known to very few persons at the time that little work was
published.   In 1855 he was "Boots" at the Grimsel Hotel, and
in those days, when he went
out on expeditions, it was for
the benefit of his master, the
proprietor ; Melchior himself
only got the *trinkgelt*.   In 1856
he migrated to the Schwaren-
bach Inn on the Gemmi, where
he employed his time in carving
objects for sale.   In 1858 he
made numerous expeditions with
Messrs. Hinchcliff and Stephen,
and proved to his employers that
he possessed first-rate skill, in-
domitable courage, and an admirable character.   His position
has never been doubtful since
that year, and for a long time
there has been no guide whose
services have been more in request : he is usually engaged a
year in advance.

MELCHIOR ANDEREGG IN 1864.

It would be almost an easier
task to say what he has not done than to catalogue his achievements.
Invariable success attends his arms ; he leads his followers to victory,
but not to death.   I believe that no accident has ever befallen travellers in his charge.   Like his friend Almer, he can be called a *safe*
man.   It is the highest praise that can be given to a first-rate guide.

Early in the afternoon we found ourselves in the little inn at
La Grave, on the great Lautaret road, a rickety, tumble-down
sort of place, with nothing stable about it, as Moore wittily

remarked, except the smell.* Melchior had gone, and had left behind a note which said, "I think the passage of the Brèche is possible, but that it will be very difficult." His opinion coincided with ours, and we went to sleep, expecting to be afoot about eighteen or twenty hours on the morrow.

At 2.40 the next morning we left La Grave, in a few minutes crossed the Romanche, and at 4 A.M. got to the moraine of the eastern branch of the glacier that descends from the Brèche.† The rocks by which we intended to ascend were placed between the two branches of this glacier, and still looked smooth and unbroken. But by 5 o'clock we were upon them. We had been deluded by them. No carpenter could have planned a more convenient staircase. They were *not moutonnée,* their smooth look from a distance was only owing to their singular firmness. [It was really quite a pleasure to scale such delightful rocks. We felt the stone held the boot so well, that, without making a positive effort to do so, it would be almost impossible to slip.] In an hour we had risen above the most crevassed portion of the glacier, and began to look for a way on to it. Just at the right place there was a patch of old snow at the side, and, instead of gaining the ice by desperate acrobatic feats, we passed from the rocks on to it as easily as one walks across a gangway. At half-past 6 we were on the centre of the glacier, and the inhabitants of La Grave turned out *en masse* into the road, and watched us with amazement as they witnessed the falsification of their confident predictions. Well might they stare, for our little caravan, looking to them like a train of flies on a wall, crept up and up, without

---

* The justness of the observation will be felt by those who knew La Grave in or before 1864. At that time the horses of the couriers who were passing from Grenoble to Briançon, and *vice versa,* were lodged immediately underneath the salle-à-manger and bedrooms, and a pungent, steamy odour rose from them through the cracks in the floor, and constantly pervaded the whole house. I am told that the inn has been improved since 1864.

† Our route from La Grave to La Bérarde will be seen on the accompanying map.

hesitation and without a halt—lost to their sight one minute as it dived into a crevasse, then seen again clambering up the other side. The higher we rose the easier became the work, the angles lessened, and our pace increased. The snow remained shadowed, and we walked as easily as on a high road ; and when (at 7.45) the summit of the Brèche was seen, we rushed at it as furiously as if it had been a breach in the wall of a fortress, carried the moat by a dash, with a push behind and a pull before, stormed the steep slope above, and at 8.50 stood in the little gap, 11,054 feet above the level of the sea. The Brèche was won. Well might they stare ; five hours and a quarter had sufficed for 6500 feet of ascent.* We screamed triumphantly as they turned in to breakfast.

SCALE, THREE MILES TO AN INCH.

All mountaineers know how valuable it is to study beforehand an intended route over new ground from a height at some distance. None but blunderers fail to do so, if it is possible ; and one cannot do so too thoroughly. As a rule, the closer one approaches underneath a summit, the more difficult it is to pick out a path with judgment. Inferior peaks seem unduly important, subordinate ridges are exalted, and slopes conceal points beyond ; and if one blindly undertakes an ascent, without having acquired a tolerable notion of the relative importance of the parts, and of their positions to one another, it will be miraculous if great difficulties are not encountered.

But although the examination of an intended route from a height at a distance will tell one (who knows the meaning of the

---

* Taking one kind of work with another, a thousand feet of height per hour is about as much as is usually accomplished on great Alpine ascents.

things he is looking at) a good deal, and will enable him to steer
clear of many difficulties against which he might otherwise blindly
run, it will seldom allow one to pronounce positively upon the
practicability or impracticability of the whole of the route. No
living man, for example, can pronounce positively from a distance
in regard to rocks. Those just mentioned are an illustration of this.
Three of the ablest and most experienced guides concurred in thinking that they would be found very difficult, and they proved to be
of no difficulty whatever. In truth, the sounder and less broken
up are the rocks, the more impracticable do they usually look from
a distance ; while soft and easily rent rocks, which are often
amongst the most difficult and perilous to climb, very frequently
look from afar as if they might be traversed by a child.

It is possible to decide with greater certainty in regard to the
practicability of glacier. When one is seen to have few open crevasses (and this may be told from a great distance), then we know
that it is *possible* to traverse it ; but to what extent it, or a glacier
that is much broken up by crevasses, will be troublesome, will
depend upon the width and length of the crevasses, and upon the
angles of the surface of the glacier itself. A glacier may be greatly
crevassed, but the fissures may be so narrow that there is no occasion to deviate from a straight line when passing across them ; or
a glacier may have few open crevasses, and yet may be practically
impassable on account of the steepness of the angles of its surface.
Nominally, a man with an axe can go anywhere upon a glacier, but
in practice it is found that to move freely upon ice one must have
to deal only with small angles. It is thus necessary to know approximately the angles of the surfaces of a glacier before it is possible to determine whether it will afford easy travelling, or will be
so difficult as to be (for all practical purposes) impassable. This
cannot be told by looking at glaciers in full face from a distance ;
they must be seen in profile ; and it is often desirable to examine
them both from the front and in profile,—to do the first to study
the direction of the crevasses, to note where they are most and least

numerous ; and the second to see whether its angles are moderate or great. Should they be very steep, it may be better to avoid them altogether, and to mount even by difficult rocks ; but upon glaciers of *gentle* inclination, and with few open crevasses, better progress can always be made than upon the *easiest* rocks.

So much to explain why we were deceived when looking at the Brèche de la Meije from the Aiguille de la Sausse. We took note of all the difficulties, but did not pay sufficient attention to the distance that the Brèche was south of La Grave. My meaning will be apparent from the accompanying diagram, Fig. 1 (constructed

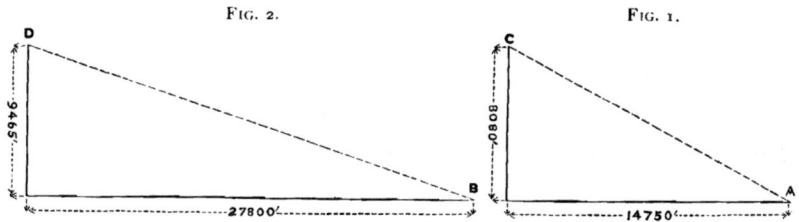

FIG. 2.   FIG. 1.

upon the data supplied by the French surveyors), which will also serve to illustrate how badly angles of elevation are judged by the unaided eye.

The village of La Grave is just 5000 feet, and the highest summit of the Meije is 13,080 feet above the level of the sea. There is therefore a difference in their levels of 8080 feet. But the summit of the Meije is south of La Grave about 14,750 feet, and, consequently, a line drawn from La Grave to the summit of the Meije is no steeper than the dotted line drawn from A to C, Fig. 1 ; or, in other words, if one could go in a direct line from La Grave to the summit of the Meije the ascent would be at an angle of less than 30°. Nine persons out of ten would probably estimate the angle on the spot at double this amount.*

The Brèche is 2000 feet below the summit of the Meije, and only 6000 feet above La Grave. A direct ascent from the village

---

* Fig. 2 represents in a similar manner the distance and elevation of the Matterhorn from and above Zermatt. See p. 83.

to the Brèche would consequently be at an angle of not much more than 20°. But it is not possible to make the ascent as the crow flies ; it has to be made by an indirect and much longer route. Our track was probably double the length of a direct line between the two places. Doubling the length halves the angles, and we therefore arrive at the somewhat amazing conclusion, that upon this, one of the steepest passes in the Alps, the mean of all the angles upon the ascent could not have been greater than 11° or 12°. Of course, in some places, the angles were much steeper, and in others less, but the *mean* of the whole could not have passed the angle above indicated.

We did not trouble ourselves much with these matters when we sat on the top of the Brèche. Our day's work was as good as over (for we knew from Messrs. Mathews and Bonney that there was no difficulty upon the other side), and we abandoned ourselves to ease and luxury ; wondering, alternately, as we gazed upon the Rateau and the Ecrins, how the one mountain could possibly hold itself together, and whether the other would hold out against us. The former looked [so rotten that it seemed as if a puff of wind or a clap of thunder might dash the whole fabric to pieces] ; while the latter asserted itself the monarch of the group, and towered head and shoulders above all the rest of the peaks which form the great horse-shoe of Dauphiné. At length a cruel rush of cold air made us shiver, and shift our quarters to a little grassy plot, 3000 feet below—an oasis in a desert—where we lay nearly four hours admiring the splendid wall which protects the summit of the Meije from assault upon this side.* Then we tramped down the Vallon des Etançons, a howling wilderness, the abomination of desolation ; destitute alike of animal or vegetable life ; pathless, of course ;

---

* This wall may be described as an exaggerated Gemmi, as seen from Leukerbad. From the highest summit of La Meije right down to the Glacier des Etançons (a depth of about 3200 feet), the cliff is all but perpendicular, and appears to be completely unassailable. The dimensions of these pages are insufficient to do justice to this magnificent wall, which is the most imposing of its kind that I have seen ; otherwise it would have been engraved.

suggestive of chaos, but of little else ; covered almost throughout its entire length with débris from the size of a walnut up to that of a house ; in a word, it looked as if half-a-dozen moraines of first-rate dimensions had been carted and shot into it. Our tempers were soured by constant pitfalls [it was impossible to take the eyes

THE VALLON DES ETANÇONS (LOOKING TOWARDS LA BERARDE).*

from the feet, and if an unlucky individual so much as blew his nose, without standing still to perform the operation, the result was either an instantaneous tumble, or a barked shin, or a half-twisted ankle. There was no end to it, and we became more savage at every step, unanimously agreeing that no power on earth would ever induce us to walk up or down this particular valley again]. It was not just to the valley, which was enclosed by noble mountains,—unknown, it is true, but worthy of a great reputation, and

* The drawing was inadvertently made the right way on the wood, and the view is now *reversed* in consequence.

which, if placed in other districts, would be sought after, and cited as types of daring form and graceful outline.

Not so very long ago, perhaps, the Vallon des Etançons wore a more cheerful aspect. It is well known that many of the French Alpine valleys have rapidly deteriorated in quite modern times. Blanqui pointed out, a few years ago, some of the causes which have brought this about, in an address to the Academy of Sciences ; and although his remarks are not entirely applicable to this very valley, the chapter may be properly closed with some of his vigorous sentences. He said, " The abuse of the right of pasturage, and the felling of the woods, have stripped the soil of all its grass and all its trees, and the scorching sun bakes it to the consistence of porphyry. When moistened by the rain, as it has neither support nor cohesion, it rolls down into the valleys, sometimes in floods resembling black, yellow, or reddish lava, and sometimes in streams of pebbles, and even huge blocks of stone, which pour down with a frightful roar. . . . Vast deposits of flinty pebbles, many feet in thickness, which have rolled down and spread far over the plain, surround large trees, bury even their tops, and rise above them. . . . The gorges, under the influence of the sun which cracks and shivers to fragments the very rocks, and of the rain which sweeps them down, penetrate deeper and deeper into the heart of the mountain, while the beds of the torrents issuing from them are sometimes raised several feet in a single year by the débris. . . . An indirect proof of the increase of the evil is to be found in the depopulation of the country. . . . Unless prompt and energetic measures are taken, it is easy to fix the epoch when the French Alps will be but a desert. . . . Every year will aggravate the evil, and in half-a-century France will count more ruins, and a department the less."*

* Quoted from Marsh's *Man and Nature.*

CHAPTER IX.

THE ASCENT OF THE POINTE DES ECRINS.

" Filled with high mountains, rearing their heads as if to reach to heaven, crowned with glaciers, and fissured with immense chasms, where lie the eternal snows guarded by bare and rugged cliffs ; offering the most varied sights, and enjoying all tempera- tures ; and containing everything that is most curious and interesting, the most simple and the most sublime, the most smiling and the most severe, the most beau- tiful and the most awful ; such is the department of the High Alps."

LADOUCETTE.

BEFORE 5 o'clock on the afternoon of June 23, we were trotting down the steep path that leads into La Bérarde. We put up, of course, with the chasseur-guide Rodier (who, as usual, was smooth and smiling), and, after congratulations were over, we returned to the exterior to watch for the arrival of one Alexander Pic, who had been sent overnight with our baggage viâ Freney and Venos. But when the night fell, and no Pic appeared, we saw that our plans must be modified ; for he was necessary to our very existence—he carried our food, our tobacco, our all. So, after some discussion, it was agreed that a portion of our programme should be abandoned, that the night of the 24th should be passed at the head of the Glacier de la Bonne Pierre, and that, on the 25th, a push should be made for the summit of the Ecrins. We then went to straw.

Our porter Pic strolled in next morning with his usual jaunty air, and we seized upon our tooth-brushes ; but, upon looking for the cigars, we found starvation staring us in the face. " Hullo ! Monsieur Pic, where are our cigars ?" " Gentlemen," he began, " I am desolated !" and then, quite pat, he told a long rigmarole about a fit on the road, of brigands, thieves, of their ransacking the knap-

2 D

sacks when he was insensible, and of finding them gone when he revived! "Ah! Monsieur Pic, we see what it is, you have smoked them yourself!" "Gentlemen, I never smoke, *never!*" Whereupon we inquired secretly if he was known to smoke, and found that he was. However, he said that he had never spoken truer words, and perhaps he had not, for he is reported to be the greatest liar in Dauphiné!

We were now able to start, and set out at 1.15 P.M. to bivouac

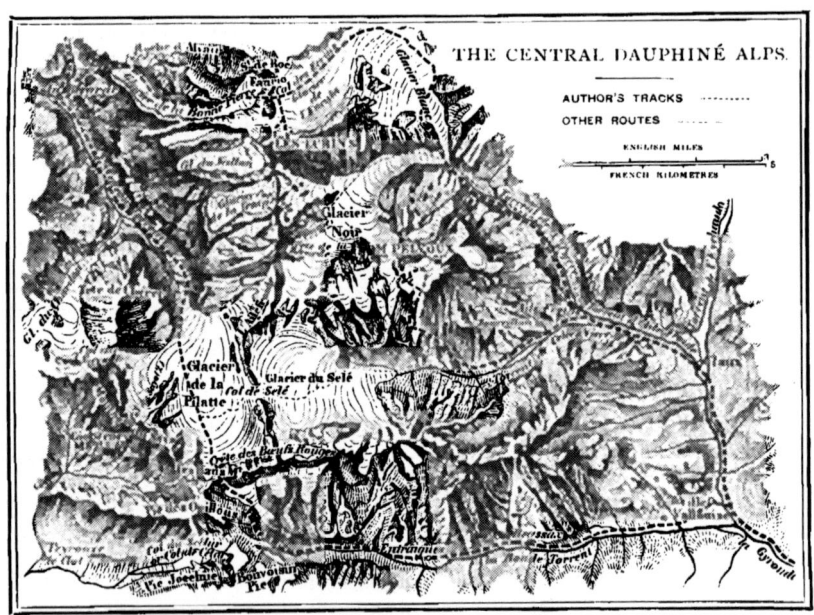

upon the Glacier de la Bonne Pierre, accompanied by Rodier, who staggered under a load of blankets. Many slopes had to be mounted, and many torrents to be crossed, all of which has been described by Mr. Tuckett.* We, however, avoided the difficulties he experienced with the latter by crossing them high up, where they were subdivided. But when we got on to the moraine on the right bank of the glacier (or, properly speaking, on to one of the moraines, for there are several), mists descended, to our great hindrance; and

* *Alpine Journal*, December 1863.

it was 5.30 before we arrived on the spot at which it was intended to camp.

Each one selected his nook, and we then joined round a grand fire made by our men. Fortnum and Mason's portable soup was sliced up and brewed, and was excellent; but it should be said that before it *was* excellent, three times the quantity named in the directions had to be used. Art is required in drinking as in making this soup, and one point is this—always let your friends drink first; not only because it is more polite, but because the soup has a tendency to burn the mouth if taken too hot, and one drink of the bottom is worth two of the top, as all the goodness settles.

[While engaged in these operations, the mist that enveloped the glacier and surrounding peaks was becoming thinner; little bits of blue sky appeared here and there, until suddenly, when we were looking towards the head of the glacier, far, far above us, at an almost inconceivable height, in a tiny patch of blue, appeared a wonderful rocky pinnacle, bathed in the beams of the fast-sinking sun. We were so electrified by the glory of the sight that it was some seconds before we realised what we saw, and understood that that astounding point, removed apparently miles from the earth, was one of the highest summits of Les Ecrins; and that we hoped, before another sun had set, to have stood upon an even loftier pinnacle. The mists rose and fell, presenting us with a series of dissolving views of ravishing grandeur, and finally died away, leaving the glacier and its mighty bounding precipices under an exquisite pale blue sky, free from a single speck of cloud.]

The night passed over without anything worth mention, but we had had occasion to observe in the morning an instance of the curious evaporation that is frequently noticeable in the High Alps. On the previous night we had hung up on a knob of rock our mackintosh bag containing five bottles of Rodier's bad wine. In the morning, although the stopper appeared to have been in all night, about four-fifths had evaporated. It was strange; my friends had not taken any, neither had I, and the guides each declared that they had not seen any one touch it. In fact it was clear that there was no explanation of the phenomenon, but in the dryness of the air. Still it is remarkable that the dryness of the air (or the evaporation of wine) is always greatest when a stranger is in one's party—the dryness caused by the presence of even a single Chamounix porter is sometimes so great, that not four-fifths but the entire quantity disappears. For a time I found difficulty in combating this phenomenon, but at last discovered that if I used the wine-flask as a pillow during the night, the evaporation was completely stopped.

At 4 A.M. we moved off across the glacier in single file towards the foot of a great gully, which led from the upper slopes of the glacier de la Bonne Pierre, to the lowest point in the ridge that runs from the Ecrins to the mountain called Roche Faurio,— cheered by Rodier, who now returned with his wraps to La Bérarde. This gully (or *couloir*) was discovered and descended by Mr. Tuckett, and we will now return for a minute to the explorations of that accomplished mountaineer.

In the year 1862 he had the good fortune to obtain from the *Dépôt de la Guerre* at Paris, a MS. copy of the then unpublished sheet 189 of the map of France, and with it in hand, he swept backwards and forwards across the central Dauphiné Alps, untroubled by the doubts as to the identity of peaks, which had perplexed Mr. Macdonald and myself in 1861 ; and, enlightened by it, he was able to point out (which he did in the fairest manner) that we had confounded the Ecrins with another mountain—the Pic Sans Nom. We made this blunder through imperfect knowledge of the district and inaccurate reports of the natives ;—but it was not an extraordinary one (the two mountains are not unlike each other), considering the difficulty that there is in obtaining from any except the very highest summits a complete view of this intricate group.

The situations of the principal summits can be perceived at a glance on the accompanying map, which is a reproduction of a portion of sheet 189. The main ridge of the chain runs, at this part, nearly north and south. Roche Faurio, at the northern extreme, is

3716 mètres, or 12,192 feet, above the level of the sea. The lowest point between that mountain and the Ecrins (the Col des Ecrins) is 11,000 feet. The ridge again rises, and passes 13,000 feet in the neighbourhood of the Ecrins. The highest summit of that mountain (13,462 feet) is, however, placed a little to the east of and off the main ridge. It then again falls, and in the vicinity of the Col de la Tempe it is, perhaps, below 11,000 feet ; but immediately to the south of the summit of that pass, there is upon the ridge a point which has been determined by the French surveyors to be 12,323 feet. This peak is without a name. The ridge continues to gain height as we come to the south, and culminates in the mountain which the French surveyors have called Sommet de l'Aile Froide. On the spot it is called, very commonly, the Aléfroide.

There is some uncertainty respecting the elevation of this mountain.* The Frenchmen give 3925 mètres (12,878) as its highest point, but Mr. Tuckett, who took a good theodolite to the top of Mont Pelvoux (which he agreed with his predecessors had an elevation of 12,973 feet), found that the summit of the Aléfroide was elevated above his station 4' ; and as the distance between the two points was 12,467 feet, this would represent a difference in altitude of 5 mètres in favour of the Aléfroide. I saw this mountain from the summit of Mont Pelvoux in 1861, and was in doubt as to which of the two was the higher, and in 1864, from the summit of the Pointe des Ecrins (as will presently be related), it looked actually higher than Mont Pelvoux. I have therefore little doubt but that Mr. Tuckett is right in believing the Aléfroide to have an elevation of about 13,000 feet, instead of 12,878, as determined by the French surveyors.

Mont Pelvoux is to the east of the Aléfroide and off the main ridge, and the Pic Sans Nom (12,845 feet) is placed between these two mountains. The latter is one of the grandest of the Dauphiné

---

* It is shown in the engraving facing p. 35. It has several points nearly equally elevated, all of which seem to be accessible. I am informed that it was ascended this year (1870), but details of the ascent have not reached me.

peaks, but it is so shut in by the other mountains, that it is seldom seen except from a distance, and then is usually confounded with the neighbouring summits. Its name has been accidentally omitted on the map, but its situation is represented by the large patch of rocks, nearly surrounded by glaciers, that is seen between the words Ailefroide and Mt. Pelvoux.

The lowest depression on the main ridge to the south of the Aléfroide is the Col du Selé, and this, according to Mr. Tuckett, is 10,834 feet. The ridge soon rises again, and, a little farther to the south, joins another ridge running nearly east and west. To a mountain at the junction of these two ridges the Frenchmen have given the singular name Crête des Bœufs Rouges! The highest point hereabouts is 11,332 feet; but a little to the west there is another peak (Mont Bans) of 11,979 feet. The main ridge runs from this last-named point, in a north-westerly direction, to the Cols de Says, both of which exceed 10,000 feet.

It will thus be seen that the general elevation of this main ridge is almost equal to that of the range of Mont Blanc, or of the central Pennine Alps; and if we were to follow it out more completely, or to follow the other ridges surrounding or radiating from it, we should find that there is a remarkable absence, throughout the entire district, of low gaps and depressions, and that there are an extraordinary number of peaks of medium elevation.[*] The difficulty which explorers have experienced in Dauphiné in identifying peaks, has very much arisen from the elevation of the ridges generally being more uniform than is commonly found in the Alps, and the consequent facile concealment of one point by another. The difficulty has been enhanced by the narrowness and erratic courses of the valleys.

The possession of the 'advanced copy' of sheet 189 of the French map, enabled Mr. Tuckett to grasp most of what I have just

---

[*] There are more than twenty peaks exceeding 12,000 feet, and thirty others exceeding 11,000 feet, within the district bounded by the rivers Romanche, Drac, and Durance.

said, and much more ; and he added, in 1862, three interesting passes across this part of the chain to those already known. The first, from Ville Vallouise to La Bérarde, *viâ* the village of Claux, and the glaciers du Selé and de la Pilatte,—this he called the Col du Selé ; the second, between Ville Vallouise and Villar d'Arène (on the Lautaret road) *viâ* Claux and the glaciers Blanc and d'Arsine,—the Col du Glacier Blanc ; and the third, from Vallouise to La Bérarde, *viâ* the Glacier Blanc, the Glacier de l'Encula, and the Glacier de la Bonne Pierre, the Col des Ecrins.

This last pass was discovered accidentally. Mr. Tuckett set out intending to endeavour to ascend the Pointe des Ecrins, but circumstances were against him, as he relates in the following words :— "Arrived on the plateau" (of the Glacier de l'Encula), "a most striking view of the Ecrins burst upon us, and a hasty inspection encouraged us to hope that its ascent would be practicable. On the sides of La Bérarde and the Glacier Noir it presents, as has been already stated, the most precipitous and inaccessible faces that can well be conceived ; but in the direction of the Glacier de l'Encula, as the upper plateau of the Glacier Blanc is named on the French map, the slopes are less rapid, and immense mases of *névé* and *séracs* cover it nearly to the summit."

"The snow was in very bad order, and as we sank at each step above the knee, it soon became evident that our prospects of success were extremely doubtful. A nearer approach, too, disclosed traces of fresh avalanches, and after much deliberation and a careful examination through the telescope, it was decided that the chances in our favour were too small to render it desirable to waste time in the attempt. . . .   I examined the map, from which I perceived that the glacier seen through the gap" (in the ridge running from Roche Faurio to the Ecrins) " to the west, at a great depth below, must be that of La Bonne Pierre ; and if a descent to its head was practicable, a passage might probably be effected to La Bérarde. On suggesting to Croz and Perrn that, though baffled by the state of the snow on the Ecrins, we might still achieve something of interest and importance by discovering a new col, they both heartily assented, and in a few minutes Perrn was over the edge, and cutting his way down the rather formidable *couloir*," etc. etc.*

This was the couloir at the foot of which we found ourselves at daybreak on the 25th of June 1864 ; but before commencing the relation of our doings upon that eventful day, I must recount the experiences of Messrs. Mathews and Bonney in 1862.

These gentlemen, with the two Croz's, attempted the ascent of the Ecrins a few weeks after Mr. Tuckett had inspected the mountain. On August 26, says Mr. Bonney, "we pushed on, and our hopes each moment rose higher and higher ; even the cautious Michel committed himself so far as to cry, 'Ah, malheureux Ecrins, vous serez bientôt morts,' as we addressed ourselves to the last slope leading up to the foot of the final cone. The old proverb about 'many a slip' was, however, to prove true on this occasion. Arrived at the top of this slope, we found that we were cut off from the peak by a formidable bergschrund, crossed by the rottenest of snow-bridges. We looked to the right and to the left, to see whether it would be possible to get on either arête at its extremity ; but instead of rising directly from the snow as they appeared to do from below, they were terminated by a wall of rock some forty feet high. There was but one place where the bergschrund was narrow enough to admit of crossing, and there a cliff of ice had to be climbed, and then a path to be cut up a steep slope of snow, before the arête could be reached. At last, after searching in vain for some time, Michel bade us wait a little, and started off to explore the gap separating the highest peak from the snow-dome on the right, and see if it were possible to ascend the rocky wall. Presently he appeared, evidently climbing with difficulty, and at last stood on the arête itself. Again we thought the victory was won, and started off to follow him. Suddenly he called to us to halt, and turned to descend. In a few minutes he

* *Alpine Journal,* Dec. 1863.

stopped.   After a long pause he shouted to his brother, saying that he was not able to return by the way he had ascended.   Jean was evidently uneasy about him, and for some time we watched him with much anxiety.   At length he began to hew out steps in the snow along the face of the peak towards us.   Jean now left us, and, making for the ice-cliff mentioned above, chopped away until, after about a quarter of an hour's labour, he contrived, somehow or other, to worm himself up it, and began to cut steps to meet his brother.   Almost every step appeared to be cut right through the snowy crust into the hard ice below, and an incipient stream of snow came hissing down the sides of the peak as they dug it away with their axes.   Michel could not have been much more than 100 yards from us, and yet it was full three quarters of an hour before the brothers met.   This done, they descended carefully, burying their axe-heads deep in the snow at every step.

Michel's account was that he had reached the arête with great difficulty, and saw that it was practicable for some distance, in fact, as far as he could see ; but that the snow was in a most dangerous condition, being very incoherent and resting on hard ice ; that when he began to descend in order to tell us this, he found the rocks so smooth and slippery that return was impossible ; and that for some little time he feared that he should not be able to extricate himself, and was in considerable danger.   Of course the arête could have been reached by the way our guides had descended, but it was so evident that their judgment was against proceeding, that we did not feel justified in urging them on.   We had seen so much of them that we felt sure they would never hang back unless there was real danger, and so we gave the word for retreating."*

On both of these expeditions there was fine weather and plenty of time.   On each occasion the parties slept out at, and started from, a considerable elevation, and arrived at the base of the final peak of the Ecrins early in the day, and with plenty of

* *Alpine Journal*, June 1863.

superfluous energy. Guides and travellers alike, on each occasion, were exceptional men, experienced mountaineers, who had proved their skill and courage on numerous antecedent occasions, and who were not accustomed to turn away from a thing merely because it was difficult to do. On each occasion the attempts were abandoned because the state of the snow on and below the final peak was such that avalanches were anticipated ; and, according to the judgment of those who were concerned, there was such an amount of *positive danger* from this condition of things, that it was unjustifiable to persevere.

We learnt privately, from Messrs. Mathews, Bonney, and Tuckett, that unless the snow was in a good state upon the final peak (that is to say, coherent and stable), we should probably be of the same opinion as themselves ; and that although the face of the mountain fronting the Glacier de l'Encula was much less steep than its other faces, and was apparently the *only* side upon which an attempt was at all likely to be successful, it was, nevertheless, so steep, that for several days, at least, after a fall of snow upon it, the chances in favour of avalanches would be considerable.

The reader need scarcely be told, after all that has been said about the variableness of weather in the High Alps, the chance was small indeed that we should find upon the 25th of June, or any other set day, the precise condition of affairs that was deemed indispensable for success. We had such confidence in the judgment of our friends, that it was understood amongst us the ascent should be abandoned, unless the conditions were manifestly favourable.

By five minutes to six we were at the top of the gully (a first-rate couloir, about 1000 feet high), and within sight of our work. Hard, thin, and wedge-like as the Ecrins had looked from afar, it had never looked so hard and so thin as it did when we emerged from the top of the couloir through the gap in the ridge ; no tender shadows spoke of broad and rounded ridges, but sharp and shadowless its serrated edges stood out against the clear

sky.*
It had been
said that the
route must be
taken by one
of the ridges of the final peak,
but both were alike repellent, hacked
and notched in numberless places. They reminded me of my
failure on the Dent d'Hérens in 1863, and of a place on a similar
ridge, from which advance or retreat was alike difficult. But,
presuming one or other of these ridges or arêtes was practicable, there remained the task of getting to them, for completely round the base of the final peak swept an enormous
bergschrund, almost separating it from the slopes which lay
beneath. It was evident thus early that the ascent would not
be accomplished without exertion, and that it would demand
all our faculties and all our time. In more than one respect
we were favoured. The mists were gone, the day was bright
and perfectly calm ; there had been a long stretch of fine weather
beforehand, and the snow was in excellent order ; and, most
important of all, the last new snow which had fallen on the
final peak, unable to support itself, had broken away and rolled
in a mighty avalanche, over schrund, névé, séracs, over hills and

* The above view of the Ecrins was taken from the summit of the Col du Galibier.

valleys in the glacier (levelling one and filling the other), completely down to the col, where it lay in huge jammed masses,
powerless to harm us ; and had made a broad track, almost a road,
over which, for part of the way at least, we might advance with
rapidity.

We took in all this in a few minutes, and seeing there was no
time to be lost, despatched a hasty meal, left knapsacks, provisions,
and all incumbrances by the col, started again at half-past six, and
made direct for the left side of the schrund, for it was there alone
that a passage was practicable. We crossed it at 8.10. Our route
can now be followed upon the annexed outline. The arrow marked D

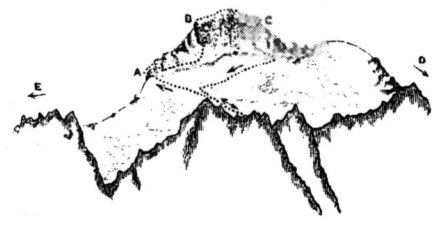

points out the direction of the
Glacier de la Bonne Pierre. The
ridge in front, that extends
right across, is the ridge that
is partially shown on the top
of the map at p. 202, leading
from Roche Faurio towards
the W.N.W. We arrived upon the plateau of the Glacier de
l'Encula, behind this ridge, from the direction of D, and then made
a nearly straight track to the left hand of the bergschrund at A.

Thus far there was no trouble, but the nature of the work
changed immediately. If we regard the upper 700 feet alone of
the final peak of the Ecrins, it may be described as a three-sided
pyramid. One face is towards the Glacier Noir, and forms one of
the sheerest precipices in the Alps. Another is towards the
Glacier du Vallon, and is less steep, and less uniform in angle than
the first. The third is towards the Glacier de l'Encula, and it was
by this one we approached the summit. Imagine a triangular
plane, 700 or 800 feet high, set at an angle exceeding 50° ;
let it be smooth, glassy ; let the uppermost edges be cut into spikes
and teeth, and let them be bent, some one way, some another.
Let the glassy face be covered with minute fragments of rock,
scarcely attached, but varnished with ice ; imagine this, and then

you will have a very faint idea of the face of the Ecrins on which we stood. It was not possible to avoid detaching stones, which, as they fell, caused words unmentionable to rise. The greatest friends would have reviled each other in such a situation. We gained the eastern arête, and endeavoured for half-an-hour to work upwards towards the summit ; but it was useless (each yard of progress cost an incredible time) ; and having no desire to form the acquaintance of the Glacier Noir in a precipitate manner, we beat a retreat, and returned to the schrund. We again held a council, and it was unanimously decided that we should be beaten if we could not cut along the upper edge of the schrund, and, when nearly beneath the summit, work up to it. So Croz took off his coat and went to work ;—on ice,—not that black ice so often mentioned and so seldom seen, but on ice as hard as ice could be. Weary work for the guides. Croz cut for more than half-an-hour, and we did not seem to have advanced at all. Some one behind, seeing how great the labour was, and how slow the progress, suggested that after all we might do better on the arête. Croz's blood was up, and indignant at this slight on his powers, he ceased working, turned in his steps, and rushed towards me with a haste that made me shudder : " By all means let us go there, the sooner the better." No slight was intended, and he resumed his work, after a time being relieved by Almer. Half-past ten came ; an hour had passed ; they were still cutting. Dreary work for us, for there was no capering about to be done here ; hand as well as foot-holes were necessary ; the fingers and toes got very cold ; the ice, as it boomed in bounding down the bergschrund, was very suggestive ; conversation was very restricted, separated as we were by our tether of 20 feet apiece. Another hour passed. We were now almost immediately below the summit, and we stopped to look up. We were nearly as far off it (vertically) as we had been more than three hours before. The day seemed going against us. The only rocks near at hand were scattered ; no bigger than tea-cups, and most of these, we found afterwards, were glazed with ice. Time forbade cutting right up to the summit, even had it been possible, which it was not. We decided to go up to the ridge again by means of the rocks ; but had we not had a certain confidence in each other, it unquestionably would not have been done ; for this, it must be understood, was a situation where not only *might* a slip have been fatal to every one, but it would have been so beyond doubt : nothing, moreover, was easier than to make one. It was a place where all had to work in unison, where there must be no slackening of the rope, and no unnecessary tension. For another hour we were in this trying situation, and at 12.30 we gained the arête again, but at a much higher point (B), close to the summit. Our men were, I am afraid, well-nigh worn out ; cutting up a couloir 1000 feet high was not the right sort of preparation for work of this kind. Be it so or not, we were all glad to rest for a short time, for we had not sat down a minute since leaving the col six hours before. Almer, however, was restless, knowing that midday was past, and that much remained to be accomplished, and untied himself, and commenced working towards the summit. Connecting the teeth of rock were beds of snow, and Almer, but a few feet from me, was crossing the top of one of these, when suddenly, without a moment's warning, it broke away under him, and plunged down on to the glacier. As he staggered for a second, one foot in the act of stepping, and the other on the falling mass, I thought him lost ; but he happily fell on to the right side and stopped himself. Had he taken the step with his right instead of the left foot, he would, in all probability, have fallen several hundred feet without touching anything, and would not have been arrested before reaching the glacier, a vertical distance of at least 3000 feet.

Small, ridiculously small, as the distance was to the summit, we were occupied nearly another hour before it was gained. Almer was a few feet in front, and he, with characteristic modesty, hesitated to step on the highest point, and drew back to allow us to pass. A cry was raised for Croz, who had done the chief part of the work, but he declined the honour, and we marched on to the top simultaneously ; that is to say, clustered round it, a yard or two below, for it was much too small to get upon.

According to my custom, I bagged a piece from off the highest rock (chlorite slate), and I found afterwards that it had a striking similarity to the final peak of the Ecrins. I have noticed the same thing on other occasions,* and it is worthy of remark that not only do fragments of such rock as limestone often present the character-istic forms of the cliffs from which they have been broken, but that morsels of mica slate will represent, in a wonder-ful manner, the identical shape of the peaks of which they have formed part. Why should it not be so, if the mountain's mass is more or less homogeneous? The same causes which produce the small forms fashion the large ones ; the same influences are at work ; the same frost and rain give shape to the mass as well as to its parts.

FRAGMENT FROM THE SUMMIT OF THE POINTE DES ECRINS.

Did space permit me, I could give but a sorry idea of the view, but it will be readily imagined that a panorama extending over as much ground as the whole of England is one worth taking some trouble to see, and one which is not often to be seen even in the Alps. No clouds obscured it, and a list of the summits that we saw would include nearly all the highest peaks of the chain. I saw the Pelvoux now—as I had seen the Ecrins from it three years before—across the basin of the Glacier Noir. It is a splendid mountain, although in height it is equalled, if not surpassed, by its neighbour the Aléfroide.

* The most striking example which has come under my notice is referred to in Chapter xx.

We could stay on the summit but a short time, and at a quarter to two prepared for the descent. Now, as we looked down, and thought of what we had passed over in coming up, we one and all hesitated about returning the same way. Moore said, no. Walker said the same, and I too; the guides were both of the same mind: this, be it remarked, although we had considered that there was no chance whatever of getting up any other way. But those 'last rocks' were not to be forgotten. Had they but protruded to a moderate extent, or had they been merely glazed, we should doubtless still have tried: but they were not reasonable rocks,—they would neither allow us to hold, nor would do it themselves. So we turned to the western arête, trusting to luck that we should find a way down to the schrund, and some means of getting over it afterwards. Our faces were a tolerable index to our thoughts, and apparently the thoughts of the party were not happy ones. Had any one then said to me, " You are a great fool for coming here," I should have answered with humility, " It is too true." And had my monitor gone on to say, " Swear you will never ascend another mountain if you get down safely," I am inclined to think I should have taken the oath. In fact, the game here was not worth the risk. The guides felt it as well as ourselves, and as Almer led off, he remarked, with more piety than logic, " The good God has brought us up, and he will take us down in safety," which showed pretty well what he was thinking about.

The ridge down which we now endeavoured to make our way was not inferior in difficulty to the other. Both were serrated to an extent that made it impossible to keep strictly to them, and obliged us to descend occasionally for some distance on the northern face and then mount again. Both were so rotten that the most experienced of our party, as well as the least, continually upset blocks large and small. Both arêtes were so narrow, so thin, that it was often a matter for speculation on which side an unstable block would fall.

At one point it seemed that we should be obliged to return to

DESCENDING THE WESTERN ARÊTE OF THE POINTE DES ÉCRINS.

the summit and try the other way down. We were on the very
edge of the arête ; on one side was the enormous precipice facing
the Pelvoux, which is not far from perpendicular ; on the other a
slope exceeding 50°. A deep notch brought us to an abrupt halt.
Almer, who was leading, advanced cautiously to the edge on hands
and knees, and peered over; his care was by no means unnecessary,
for the rocks had broken away from under us unexpectedly several
times. In this position he looked down for some moments, and
then, without a word, turned his head and looked at us. His face
may have expressed apprehension or alarm, but it certainly did not
show hope or joy. We learned that there was no means of getting
down, and that we must, if we wanted to pass it, jump across on
to an unstable block on the other side. It was decided that it should
be done, and Almer, with a larger extent of rope than usual, jumped ;
the rock swayed as he came down upon it, but he clutched a large
mass with both arms and brought himself to anchor. That which
was both difficult and dangerous for the first man was easy enough
for the others, and we got across with less trouble than I expected ;
stimulated by Croz's perfectly just observation, that if we couldn't
get across there we were not likely to get down the other way.

We had now arrived at C, and could no longer continue on
the arête, so we commenced descending the face again. Before
long we were close to the schrund, but unable to see what it was
like at this part, as the upper edge bent over. Two hours had
already passed since leaving the summit, and it began to be highly
probable that we should have to spend a night on the Glacier
Blanc. Almer, who yet led, cut steps right down to the edge, but
still he could not see below ; therefore, warning us to hold tight, he
made his whole body rigid, and (standing in the large step which
he had cut for the purpose), had the upper part of his person
lowered out until he saw what he wanted. He shouted that our
work was finished, made me come close to the edge and untie myself, advanced the others until he had rope enough, and then with
a loud *jödel* jumped down on to soft snow. Partly by skill and

2 F

partly by luck he had hit the crevasse at its easiest point, and we had only to make a downward jump of eight or ten feet.

It is now 4.45 P.M.; we had been more than eight hours and a half accomplishing the ascent of the final peak, which, according to an observation by Mr. Bonney in 1862, is only 525 feet high.* During this period we had not stopped for more than half-an-hour, and our nerves and muscles had been kept at the highest degree of tension the whole time. It may be imagined that we accepted the ordinary conditions of glacier travelling as an agreeable relief, and that that which at another time might have seemed formidable we treated as the veriest bagatelle. Late in the day as it was, and soft as was the snow, we put on such pace that we reached the Col des Ecrins in less than forty minutes. We lost no time in arranging our baggage, for we had still to traverse a long glacier, and to get clear of two ice-falls before it was dark; so, at 5.35 we resumed the march, adjourning eating and drinking, and put on a spurt which took us clear of the Glacier Blanc by 7.45 P.M.† We got clear of the moraine of the Glacier Noir at 8.45, just as the last remnant of daylight vanished. Croz and myself were a trifle in advance of the others, and fortunately so for us; for as they were about to commence the descent of the snout of the glacier, the whole of the moraine that rested on its face peeled off, and came down with a tremendous roar.

We had now the pleasure of walking over a plain that is known by the name of the Pré de Madame Carle, covered with pebbles of all sizes, and intersected by numerous small streams or torrents. Every hole looked like a stone, every stone like a hole, and we tumbled about from side to side until our limbs and our tempers became thoroughly jaded. My companions, being both short-sighted, found the travelling especially disagreeable; so

* See vol. i., p. 73, of *Alpine Journal*. We considered the height assigned to the final peak by Mr. Bonney was too small, and thought it should have been 200 feet more.

† The Glacier Blanc is in the direction indicated by the arrow below the letter **E** on the outline on p. 212.

there was little wonder that when we came upon a huge mass of rock as big as a house, which had fallen from the flanks of Pelvoux, a regular cube that offered no shelter whatever, Moore cried out in ecstasy, " Oh, how delightful ! the very thing I have been longing for. Let us have a perfectly extemporaneous bivouac." This, it should be said, was when the night threatened thunder and lightning, rain, and all other delights.

The pleasures of a perfectly extemporaneous bivouac under these circumstances not being novelties to Croz and myself, we thought we would try for the miseries of a roof, but Walker and Almer, with their usual good nature, declared it was the very thing that they, too, were longing for ; so the trio resolved to stop. We generously left them all the provisions (a dozen cubic inches or thereabouts of bacon fat, and half a candle), and pushed on for the chalets of Alé-froide, or at least we thought we did, but could not be certain. In the course of half-an-hour we got uncommonly close to the main torrent, and Croz all at once disappeared. I stepped cautiously forward to peer down into the place where I thought he was, and quietly tumbled head over heels into a big rhododendron bush. Extricating myself with some trouble, I fell backwards over some rocks, and got wedged in a cleft so close to the torrent that it splashed all over me.

The colloquy which then ensued amid the thundering of the stream was as follows :—

" Hullo, Croz !" " Eh, Monsieur." " Where are you ?" " Here, Monsieur." " Where *is* here ?" " I don't know ; where are you?" " Here, Croz ;" and so on.

The fact was, from the intense darkness, and the noise of the torrent, we had no idea of each other's situation ; in the course of ten minutes, however, we joined together again, agreed we had quite enough of that kind of thing, and adjourned to a most eligible rock at 10.15.

How well I remember the night at that rock, and the jolly way in which Croz came out ! We were both very wet about the legs, and both uncommonly hungry, but the time passed pleasantly enough round our fire of juniper, and until long past midnight we sat up recounting, over our pipes, wonderful stories of the most incredible description, in which, I must admit, my companion beat me hollow.   Then, throwing ourselves on our beds of rhododendron,

A NIGHT WITH CROZ.

we slept an untroubled sleep, and rose on a bright Sunday morning as fresh as might be, intending to enjoy a day's rest and luxury with our friends at La Ville de Val Louise.

I have failed to give the impression I wish if it has not been made evident that the ascent of the Pointe des Ecrins was not an ordinary piece of work.   There is an increasing disposition now-a-days amongst those who write on the Alps, to underrate the difficulties and dangers which are met with, and this disposition is, I think, not less mischievous than the old-fashioned style of making everything terrible.   Difficult as we found the peak, I believe we took it at the best, perhaps the only possible, time of the year. The great slope on which we spent so much time was, from being denuded by the avalanche of which I have spoken, deprived of its greatest danger. Had it had the snow still resting upon it, and had we persevered with the expedition, we should almost without doubt have ended with calamity instead of success. The ice of that slope is always below, its angle is severe, and the rocks do not project sufficiently to afford the support that snow requires, to be stable, when at a great angle. So far am I from desiring to tempt any one to repeat the expedition, that I put it on record as my belief, however sad and however miserable a man may have been, if he is found on the summit of the Pointe des Ecrins after a fall of new snow, he is likely to experience misery far deeper than anything with which he has hitherto been acquainted.*

* The ascent of the Pointe des Ecrins has been made once since 1864, by a French gentleman, named Vincent, with the Chamounix guides Jean Carrier and Alexandre Tournier. They followed our route, but reversed it ; that is to say, ascended by the western, and descended by the eastern arête.

The best course to adopt in future attacks on the mountain, would be to bring a ladder, or some other means of passing the bergschrund, in its centre, immediately under the summit. One could then proceed directly upwards, and so avoid the labour and difficulties which are inevitable upon any ascent by way of the arêtes.

CHAPTER X.

FROM VAL LOUISE TO LA BÉRARDE BY THE COL DE PILATTE.*

" How pleasant it is for him who is saved to remember his danger."

EURIPIDES.

FROM Ailefroide to Claux, but for the path, travel would be scarcely more easy than over the Pré de Madame Carle.* The valley is strewn with immense masses of gneiss, from the size of a large house downwards, and it is only occasionally that rock *in situ* is seen, so covered up is it up by the débris, which seems to have been derived almost entirely from the neighbouring cliffs.†

It was Sunday, a " day most calm and bright." Golden sunlight had dispersed the clouds, and was glorifying the heights, and we forgot hunger through the brilliancy of the morning and beauty of the mountains.

We meant the 26th to be a day of rest, but it was little that we found in the *cabaret* of Claude Giraud, and we fled before the babel of sound which rose in intensity as men descended to a depth which is unattainable by the beasts of the field, and found at the chalets of Entraigues ‡ the peace that had been denied to us at Val Louise.

---

* For route, see map in chap. ix.

† About half-a-mile above Claux there is a precipitous fall in the valley, and there (where the bed rock is too steep to allow débris to accumulate) *roches moutonnées* can be seen. At the same place the torrent of Aile Froide falls by some steep rapids through a wall-sided gorge, and the former eddyings of the water can be traced high up upon the cliffs.

‡ The path from Ville de Val Louise to Entraigues is good and well shaded by luxuriant foliage. The valley (d'Entraigues) is narrow ; bordered by fine cliffs ; and closed at its western end by a noble block of mountains, which looks much higher

Again we were received with the most cordial hospitality. Everything that was eatable or drinkable was brought out and pressed upon us ; every little curiosity was exhibited ; every information that could be afforded was given ; and when we retired to our clean straw, we again congratulated each other that we had escaped from the foul den which is where a good inn should be, and had cast in our lot with those who dwell in chalets. Very luxurious that straw seemed after two nights upon quartz pebbles and glacier mud, and I felt quite aggrieved (expecting it was the summons for departure) when, about midnight, the heavy wooden door creaked on its hinges, and a man hem'd and ha'd to attract attention ; but when it whispered, " Monsieur Edvard," I perceived my mistake,—it was our Pelvoux companion, Monsieur Reynaud, the excellent *agent-voyer* of La Bessée.

Monsieur Reynaud had been invited to accompany us on the excursion that is described in this chapter, but had arrived at Val Louise after we had left, and had energetically pursued us during the night. Our idea was that a pass might be made over the high ridge called (on the French map) Crête de Bœufs Rouges,* near to the peak named Les Bans, which might be the shortest route in time (as it certainly would be in distance) from Val Louise, across the Central Dauphiné Alps. We had seen the northern (or Pilatte) side from the Brèche de la Meije, and it seemed to be practicable at one place near the above-mentioned mountain. More than that could not be told at a distance of

than it is. The highest point (the Pic de Bonvoisin) is 11,500 feet. Potatoes, peas, and other vegetables, are grown at Entraigues (5284 feet), although the situation of the chalets is bleak, and cut off from the sun.

The Combe (or Vallon) de la Selle joins the main valley at Entraigues, and one can pass from the former by the little-known Col de Loup (immediately to the south of the Pic de Bonvoisin) into the Val Godemar. Two other passes, both of considerable height, lead from the head of the Vallon de la Selle into the valleys of Champoléon and Argentière.

* This, like many other names given to mountains and glaciers on sheet 189, is not a local name, or, at least, is not one that is in common use.

eleven miles.   We intended to try to hit a point on the ridge immediately above the part where it seemed to be easiest.

We left Entraigues at 3.30 on the morning of June 27, and proceeded, over very gently-inclined ground, towards the foot of the Pic de Bonvoisin (following in fact the route of the Col de Sellar, which leads from the Val Louise into the Val Godemar) ;* and at 5 A.M., finding that there was no chance of obtaining a view from the bottom of the valley of the ridge over which our route was to be taken, sent Almer up the lower slopes of the Bonvoisin to reconnoitre.   He telegraphed that we might proceed ; and at 5.45 we quitted the snow-beds at the bottom of the valley for the slopes which rose towards the north.

The course was N.N.W., and was prodigiously steep. *In less than two miles' difference of latitude we rose one mile of absolute height.* But the route was so far from being an exceptionally difficult one, that at 10.45 we stood on the summit of the pass, having made an ascent of more than 5000 feet in five hours, inclusive of halts.

Upon sheet 189 of the French map a glacier is laid down on the south of the Crête des Bœufs Rouges, extending along the entire length of the ridge, at its foot, from east to west.   In 1864 this glacier did not exist as *one* glacier, but in the place where it should have been there were several small ones, all of which were, I believe, separated from each other.†

We commenced the ascent from the Val d'Entraigues, to the west of the most western of these small glaciers, and quitted the valley by the first great gap in its cliffs after that glacier was passed.   We did not take to the ice until it afforded an easier route than the rocks ; then (8.30) Croz went to the front, and led with

---

* The height of Col de Sellar (or de Celar) is 10,073 feet (Forbes).   I was told by peasants at Entraigues that sheep and goats can be easily taken across it.

† See map on p. 202.   It is perhaps just possible, although improbable, that these little glaciers were united together at the time that the survey was made. Since then the glaciers of Dauphiné (as throughout the Alps generally) have shrunk very considerably.   A notable diminution took place in their size in 1869, which was attributed by the natives to the very heavy rains of that year.

admirable skill through a maze of crevasses up to the foot of a great snow *couloir*, that rose from the head of the glacier to the summit of the ridge over which we had to pass.

We had settled beforehand in London, without knowing anything whatever about the place, that such a couloir as this should be in this angle ; but when we got into the Val d'Entraigues, and found that it was not possible to see into the corner, our faith in its existence became less and less, until the telegraphing of Almer, who was sent up the opposite slopes to search for it, assured us that we were true prophets.

Snow *couloirs* are nothing more or less than

A SNOW COULOIR.

gullies partly filled by snow. They are most useful institutions, and may be considered as natural highways placed, by a kind Providence, in convenient situations for getting over places which would otherwise be inaccessible. They are a joy to the mountaineer, and, from afar, assure him of a path when all beside is uncertain ; but they are grief to novices, who, when upon steep snow, are usually seized with two notions—first, that the snow will slip, and secondly, that those who are upon it must slip too.

Nothing, perhaps, could look much more unpromising to those who do not know the virtues of couloirs than such a place as the engraving represents,* and if persons inexperienced in mountain craft had occasion to cross a ridge or to climb rocks, in which there were such couloirs, they would instinctively avoid them. But practised mountaineers would naturally look to them for a path, and would follow them almost as a matter of course, unless they turned out to be filled with ice, or too much swept by falling stones, or the rock at the sides proved to be of such an exceptional character as to afford an easier path than the snow.

Couloirs look prodigiously steep when seen from the front, and, so viewed, it is impossible to be certain of their inclination within many degrees. Snow, however, does actually lie at steeper angles in couloirs than in any other situations ;—45° to 50° degrees is not an uncommon inclination. Even at such angles, two men with proper axes can mount on snow at the rate of 700 to 800 feet per hour. The same amount can only be accomplished in the same time on steep rocks when they are of the very easiest character, and four or five hours may be readily spent upon an equal height of difficult rocks. Snow couloirs are therefore to be commended because they economise time.

Of course, in all gullies, one is liable to be encountered by falling stones. Most of those which fall from the rocks of a couloir,

---

* This drawing was made to illustrate the remarks which follow. It does not represent any particular couloir, but it would serve, tolerably well, as a portrait of the one which we ascended when crossing the Col de Pilatte.

sooner or later spin down the snow which fills the trough ; and, as their course and pace are more clearly apparent when falling over snow than when jumping from ledge to ledge, persons with lively imaginations are readily impressed by them. The grooves which are usually seen wandering down the length of snow couloirs are deepened (and, perhaps, occasionally originated) by falling stones, and they are sometimes pointed out by cautious men as reasons why couloirs should not be followed. I think they are very frequently only gutters, caused by water trickling off the rocks. Whether this is so or not, one should always consider the possibility of being struck by falling stones, and, in order to lessen the risk as far as possible, should mount upon the sides of the snow, and not up its centre. Stones that come off the rocks then fly over one's head, or bound down the middle of the trough at a safe distance.

At 9.30 A.M. we commenced the ascent of the couloir leading from the nameless glacier to a point in the ridge, just to the east of Mont Bans.* So far the route had been nothing more than a steep grind in an angle where little could be seen, but now views opened out in several directions, and the way began to be interesting. It was more so, perhaps, to us than to our companion M. Reynaud, who had no rest in the last night. He was, moreover, heavily laden. Science was to be regarded—his pockets were stuffed with books; heights and angles were to be observed—his knapsack was filled with instruments ; hunger was to be guarded against—his shoulders were ornamented with a huge nimbus of bread, and a leg of mutton swung behind from his knapsack, looking like an overgrown tail. Like a good-hearted fellow, he had brought this food, thinking we might be in need of it. As it happened, we were well provided for, and having our own packs to carry, could not relieve him of his superfluous burdens, which, naturally, he did not like to throw away. As the angles steepened,

---

* The upper part of the southern side of the Col de Pilatte, and the small glaciers spoken of on p. 224, can be seen from the high road leading from Briançon to Mont Dauphin, between the 12th and 13th kilomètre stones (from Briançon).

the strain on his strength became more and more apparent. At last he began to groan. At first a most gentle and mellow groan ; but as we rose so did his groans, till at last the cliffs were groaning in echo, and we were moved to laughter.

Croz cut the way with unflagging energy throughout the whole of the ascent, and at 10.45 we stood on the summit of our pass, intending to refresh ourselves with a good halt ; but just at that moment a mist, which had been playing about the ridge, swooped down and blotted out the whole of the view on the northern side. Croz was the only one who caught a glimpse of the descent, and it was deemed advisable to push on immediately while its recollection was fresh in his memory. We are consequently unable to tell anything about the summit of the pass, except that it lies imme-diately to the east of Mont Bans, and is elevated about 11,300 feet above the level of the sea. It is the highest pass in Dauphiné. We called it the Col de Pilatte.

We commenced to descend towards the Glacier de Pilatte by a slope of smooth ice, the face of which, according to the measure-ment of Mr. Moore, had an inclination of 54°! Croz still led, and the others followed at intervals of about 15 feet, all being tied together, and Almer occupying the responsible position of last man : the two guides were therefore about 70 feet apart. They were quite invisible to each other from the mist, and looked spectral even to us. But the strong man could be heard by all hewing out the steps below, while every now and then the voice of the steady man pierced the cloud,—" Slip not, dear sirs ; place well your feet : stir not until you are certain."

For three quarters of an hour we progressed in this fashion. The axe of Croz all at once stopped. " What is the matter, Croz ?" " Bergschrund, gentlemen." " Can we get over ?" " Upon my word, I don't know ; I think we must jump." The clouds rolled away right and left as he spoke. The effect was dramatic ! It was a *coup de théâtre*, preparatory to the ' great sensation leap ' which was about to be executed by the entire company.

"WE SAW A TOE - IT SEEMED TO BELONG TO MOORE - WE SAW REYNAUD A FLYING BODY.".

Some unseen cause, some cliff or obstruction in the rocks underneath, had caused our wall of ice to split into two portions, and the huge fissure which had thus been formed extended, on each hand, as far as could be seen. We, on the slope above, were separated from the slope below by a mighty crevasse. No running up and down to look for an easier place to cross could be done on an ice-slope of 54° ; the chasm had to be passed then and there.

A downward jump of 15 or 16 feet, and a forward leap of 7 or 8 feet had to be made at the same time. That is not much, you will say. It was not much ; it was not the quantity, but it was the quality of the jump which gave to it its particular flavour. You had to hit a narrow ridge of ice. If that was passed, it seemed as if you might roll down for ever and ever. If it was not attained, you dropped into the crevasse below, which, although partly choked by icicles and snow that had fallen from above, was still gaping in many places, ready to receive an erratic body.

Croz untied Walker in order to get rope enough, and warning us to hold fast, sprang over the chasm. He alighted cleverly on his feet ; untied himself and sent up the rope to Walker, who followed his example. It was then my turn, and I advanced to the edge of the ice. The second which followed was what is called a supreme moment. That is to say, I felt supremely ridiculous. The world seemed to revolve at a frightful pace, and my stomach to fly away. The next moment I found myself sprawling in the snow, and then, of course, vowed that it was nothing, and prepared to encourage my friend Reynaud.

He came to the edge and made declarations. I do not believe that he was a whit more reluctant to pass the place than we others, but he was infinitely more demonstrative,—in a word, he was French. He wrung his hands, "Oh! what a *diable* of a place!" "It is nothing, Reynaud," I said, "it is nothing." "Jump," cried the others, "jump." But he turned round, as far as one can do such a thing in an ice-step, and covered his face with his hands, ejaculating, "Upon my word, it is not possible. No! no!! no!!! it is not possible."

How he came over I do not know. We saw a toe—it seemed to belong to Moore ; we saw Reynaud a flying body, coming down as if taking a header into water ; with arms and legs all abroad, his leg of mutton flying in the air, his bâton escaped from his grasp ; and then we heard a thud as if a bundle of carpets had been pitched out of a window. When set upon his feet he was a sorry spectacle ; his head was a great snowball ; brandy was trickling out of one side of the knapsack, chartreuse out of the other—we bemoaned its loss, but we roared with laughter.

This chapter has already passed the limits within which it should have been confined, but I cannot close it without paying tribute to the ability with which Croz led us, through a dense mist, down the remainder of the Glacier de Pilatte. As an exhibition of strength and skill, it has probably never been surpassed in the Alps or elsewhere. On this almost unknown and very steep glacier, he was perfectly at home, even in the mists. Never able to see fifty feet ahead, he still went on with the utmost certainty, and without having to retrace a single step ; and displayed from first to last consummate knowledge of the materials with which he was dealing. Now he cut steps down one side of a *sérac*, went with a dash at the other side, and hauled us up after him ; then cut away along a ridge until a point was gained from which we could jump on to another ridge ; then, doubling back, found a snow-bridge, across which he crawled on hands and knees, towed us across by the legs, ridiculing our apprehensions, mimicking our awkwardness, declining all help, bidding us only to follow him.

About 1 P.M. we emerged from the mist and found ourselves just arrived upon the level portion of the glacier, having, as Reynaud properly remarked, come down as quickly as if there had not been any mist at all. Then we attacked the leg of mutton which my friend had so thoughtfully brought with him, and afterwards raced down, with renewed energy, to La Bérarde.

Reynaud and I walked together to St. Christophe, where we

parted. Since then we have talked over the doings of this moment-
ous day; and I know that he would not, for a good deal, have
missed the passage of the Col de Pilatte, although we failed to make
it an easier or a shorter route than the Col du Selé. I rejoined
Moore and Walker, the same evening, at Venos, and on the next
day went with them over the Lautaret road to the hospice on its
summit, where we slept.

So our little campaign in Dauphiné came to an end. It was remarkable for the absence of failures, and for the ease and precision
with which all our plans were carried out. This was due very
much to the spirit of my companions; but it was also owing to the
fine weather which we were fortunate enough to enjoy, and to our
making a very early start every morning. By beginning our work
at or before the break of day, on the longest days in the year, we
were not only able to avoid hurrying when deliberation was desirable, but could afford to spend several hours in delightful ease
whenever the fancy seized us.

I cannot too strongly recommend to tourists in search of
amusement to avoid the inns of Dauphiné. Sleep in the chalets.
Get what food you can from the inns, but by no means attempt to
pass a night in them.* *Sleep* in them you cannot. M. Joanne says
that the inventor of the insecticide powder was a native of Dauphiné. I can well believe it. He must have often felt the
necessity of such an invention in his infancy and childhood.

On June 29 I crossed the Col du Galibier to St. Michel;
on the 30th, the Col des Encombres to Moutiers; on July 1, the
Col du Bonhomme to Contamines; and on the 2d, by the Pavillon
de Bellevue to Chamounix, where I joined Mr. Adams-Reilly
to take part in some expeditions which had been planned long
before.

---

* A pound of Liebig's extract and a few pounds of chocolate are all that need be
taken in the way of food; the rest can be obtained on the spot.

CHAPTER XI.

" Nothing binds men so closely together as agreement in plans and desires."

CICERO.

TEN years ago very few persons knew from personal knowledge how extremely inaccurately the chain of Mont Blanc was delineated. During the previous half-century thousands had made the tour of the chain, and in that time at least *one* thousand individuals had stood upon its highest summit; but out of all this number there was not one capable, willing, or able, to map the mountain which, until recently, was regarded the highest in Europe.

Many persons knew that great blunders had been perpetrated, and it was notorious that even Mont Blanc itself was represented in a ludicrously incorrect manner on all sides excepting the north; but there was not, perhaps, a single individual who knew, at the time to which I refer, that errors of no less than 1000 feet had been committed in the determination of heights at each end of the chain; that some glaciers were represented of double their real dimensions; and that ridges and mountains were laid down which actually had no existence.

One portion alone of the entire chain had been surveyed at the time of which I speak with anything like accuracy. It was not done (as one would have expected) by a Government, but by a private individual,—by the British De Saussure,—the late J. D. Forbes. In the year 1842, he "made a special survey of the

Mer de Glace of Chamounix and its tributaries, which, in some of the following years, he extended by further observations, so as to include the Glacier des Bossons." The map produced from this survey was worthy of its author; and subsequent explorers of the region he investigated have been able to detect only trivial inaccuracies in his work.

The district surveyed by Forbes remained a solitary bright spot in a region where all besides was darkness until the year 1861. Praiseworthy attempts were made by different hands to throw light upon the gloom, but the efforts were ineffectual, and showed how labour may be thrown away by a number of observers working independently, without the direction of a single head.

In 1861, Sheet xxii. of Dufour's Map of Switzerland appeared. It included the section of the chain of Mont Blanc that belonged to Switzerland, and this portion of the sheet was executed with the admirable fidelity and thoroughness which characterise the whole of Dufour's unique map. The remainder of the chain (amounting to about four-fifths of the whole) was laid down after the work of previous topographers, and its wretchedness was made more apparent by contrast with the finished work of the Swiss surveyors.

Strong hands were needed to complete the survey, and it was not long before the right men appeared.

In 1863, Mr. Adams-Reilly, who had been travelling in the Alps during several years, resolved to attempt a survey of the unsurveyed portions of the chain of Mont Blanc. He provided himself with a good theodolite, and starting from a base-line measured by Forbes in the Valley of Chamounix, determined the positions of no less than 200 points. The accuracy of his work may be judged from the fact that, after having turned many corners and carried his observations over a distance of fifty miles, his Col Ferret " fell within 200 yards of the position assigned to it by General Dufour !"

In the winter of 1863 and the spring of 1864, Mr. Reilly constructed an entirely original map from his newly-acquired data. The spaces between his trigonometrically-determined points he

2 H

filled in after photographs, and a series of panoramic sketches which he made from his different stations. The map so produced was an immense advance upon those already in existence, and it was the first which exhibited the great peaks in their proper positions.

This extraordinary piece of work revealed Mr. Reilly to me as a man of wonderful determination and perseverance. With very small hope that my proposal would be accepted, I invited him to take part in renewed attacks on the Matterhorn. He entered heartily into my plans, and met me with a counter-proposition, namely, that I should accompany him on some expeditions which he had projected in the chain of Mont Blanc. The unwritten contract took this form :—I will help you to carry out your desires, and you shall assist me to carry out mine. I eagerly closed with an arrangement in which all the advantages were upon my side.

At the time that Mr. Reilly was carrying on his survey, Captain Mieulet was executing another in continuation of the great map of France ; for about one-half of the chain of Mont Blanc (including the whole of the Valley of Chamounix) had recently become French once more. Captain Mieulet was directed to survey up to his frontier only, and the sheet which was destined to include his work was to be engraved, of course, upon the scale of the rest of the map, viz., $\frac{1}{80000}$ of nature. But upon representations being made at head-quarters that it would be of great advantage to extend the survey as far as Cormayeur, Captain Mieulet was directed to continue his observations into the south (or Italian) side of the chain. A special sheet on the scale of $\frac{1}{40000}$ was promptly engraved from the materials he accumulated, and was published in 1865, by order of the late Minister of War, Marshal Randon.* This sheet was admirably executed, but it included the central portion of the chain only, and a complete map was still wanting.

Mr. Reilly presented his MS. map to the English Alpine Club. It was resolved that it should be published ; but before it passed

* Under the title of *Massif du Mont Blanc, extrait des minutes de la Carte de France, levé par M. Mieulet, Capitaine d'Etat Major.*

into the engraver's hands its author undertook to revise it carefully. To this end he planned a number of expeditions to high points which up to that time had been regarded inaccessible, and it was upon some of these ascents he invited me to accompany him.*

Before I pass on to these expeditions (which will be described very briefly, as I hope that Mr. Reilly himself will publish an account of his remarkable explorations), it will be convenient to devote a few paragraphs to the topography of the chain of Mont Blanc.†

At the present time the chain is divided betwixt France, Switzerland, and Italy. France has the lion's share, Switzerland the most fertile portion, and Italy the steepest side. It has acquired a reputation which is not extraordinary, but which is not wholly merited. It has neither the beauty of the Oberland, nor the sublimity of Dauphiné. But it attracts the vulgar by the possession of the highest summit in the Alps. If that is removed, the elevation of the chain is in nowise remarkable. In fact, excluding Mont Blanc itself, the mountains of which the chain is made up are *less* important than those of the Oberland and the central Pennine groups. The following table will afford a ready means of comparison.‡

---

* Mr. Reilly's map was published on a scale of $\frac{1}{80000}$ in 1865, at the cost of the Alpine Club, under the title *The Chain of Mont Blanc*.

† See the map of the chain of Mont Blanc at the end of the volume.

This map has been drawn after the surveys of Mieulet, Dufour, and Reilly. To assist in its production, the Dépôt de la Guerre at Paris most liberally furnished me with special copies of Captain Mieulet's map. These were reduced, by photography, to the scale of $\frac{1}{100000}$, which is the same as that of Dufour's map. The Swiss portion of the chain was then fitted on to the reduction. Photographic reductions of the basin of the Glacier du Tour and of the whole of that portion of the chain which lies to the west of the southern Glacier de Miage and to the south of the Glacier de Trélatête were then added from Mr. Reilly's map. The nomenclature of these authorities has been strictly followed. It may be remarked, however, that Captain Mieulet has departed, in many instances, from the spelling in common use.

‡ The heights (in mètres) are after Captain Mieulet.

			Mètres.		Eng. feet.*
1.	Mont Blanc	. . .	4810	=	15,781
2.	Grandes Jorasses	. . .	4206	.	13,800
3.	Aiguille Verte	. . .	4127	.	13,540
4.	„ de Bionnassay	. .	4061	.	13,324
5.	Les Droites	. . .	4030	.	13,222
6.	Aiguille du Géant . .	4010	.	13,157
7.	„ de Trélatête, No. 1	.	3932	.	12,900
	„ „ „ 2		3904	.	12,809
	„ „ „ 3		3896	.	12,782
8.	„ d'Argentière	. .	3901	.	12,799
9.	„ de Triolet	. .	3879	.	12,726
10.	„ du Midi	. . .	3843	.	12,608
11.	„ du Glacier	. .	3834	.	12,579
12.	Mont Dolent	. . .	3830	.	12,566
13.	Aiguille du Chardonnet	.	3823	.	12,543
14.	„ du Dru	. . .	3815	.	12,517
15.	„ de Miage .	. .	3680	.	12,074
16.	„ du Plan .	. .	3673	.	12,051
17.	„ de Blaitière	. .	3533	.	11,591
18.	„ des Charmoz	. .	3442	.	11,293

The frontier-line follows the main ridge. Very little of it can
be seen from the Valley of Chamounix, and from the village itself
two small strips only are visible (amounting to scarcely three miles
in length), viz. from the summit of Mont Blanc to the Dôme du
Goûter, and in the neighbourhood of the Col de Balme. All the
rest is concealed by outlying ridges and by mountains of secondary
importance.

Mont Blanc itself is bounded by the two glaciers of Miage, the
glaciers de la Brenva and du Géant, the Val Véni and the Valley
of Chamounix. A long ridge runs out towards the N.N.E. from
the summit, through Mont Maudit, to the Aiguille du Midi.
Another ridge proceeds towards the N.W., through the Bosse du
Dromadaire to the Dôme du Goûter ; this then divides into two,
of which one continues N.W. to the Aiguille du Goûter, the other

* Some of these heights have no business to figure in a list of the principal peaks
of the chain, being nothing more than teeth or pinnacles in ridges, or portions of
higher mountains. Such, for example, are the Aiguilles du Géant, du Dru, and de
Bionnassay.

(which is a part of the main ridge of the chain) towards the W. to the Aiguille de Bionnassay. The two routes which are commonly followed for the ascent of Mont Blanc lie between these two principal ridges—one leading from Chamounix, *viâ* the Grands Mulets, the other from the village of Bionnassay, *viâ* the Aiguille and Dôme du Goûter.*

The ascent of Mont Blanc has been made from several directions besides these, and perhaps there is no single point of the compass from which the mountain cannot be ascended. But there is not the least probability that any one will discover easier ways to the summit than those already known.

I believe it is correct to say that the Aiguille du Midi and the Aiguille de Miage were the only two summits in the chain of Mont Blanc which had been ascended at the beginning of 1864.† The latter of these two is a perfectly insignificant point ; and the former is only a portion of one of the ridges just now mentioned, and can hardly be regarded as a mountain separate and distinct from Mont Blanc. The really great peaks of the chain were considered inaccessible, and, I think, with the exception of the Aiguille Verte, had never been assailed.

The finest, as well as the highest peak in the chain (after Mont Blanc itself), is the Grandes Jorasses. The next, without a doubt, is the Aiguille Verte. The Aiguille de Bionnassay, which in actual height follows the Verte, should be considered as a part of Mont Blanc ; and in the same way the summit called Les Droites is only a part of the ridge which culminates in the Verte. The Aiguille de Trélatête is the next on the list that is entitled to be considered a separate mountain, and is by far the most important peak (as well as the highest) at the south-west end of the chain. Then comes the Aiguille d'Argentière, which occupies the same rank at the north-east end as the last-mentioned mountain does in the south-west. The rest of the aiguilles are comparatively insignificant ; and although some of them (such as the Mont

* These routes are laid down on the Map.   † Besides Mont Blanc itself.

Dolent) look well from low elevations, and seem to possess a certain importance, they sink into their proper places directly one arrives at a considerable altitude.

The summit of the Aiguille Verte would have been one of the best stations out of all these mountains for the purposes of my friend. Its great height, and its isolated and commanding position, make it a most admirable point for viewing the intricacies of the chain ; but he exercised a wise discretion in passing it by, and in selecting as our first excursion the passage of the Col de Triolet.*

We slept under some big rocks on the Couvercle on the night of July 7, with the thermometer at 26·5 Faht., and at 4·30 on the 8th made a straight track to the north of the Jardin, and thence went in zigzags, to break the ascent, over the upper slopes of the Glacier de Talèfre towards the foot of the Aiguille de Triolet. Croz was still my guide, Reilly was accompanied by one of the Michel Payots of Chamounix, and Henri Charlet, of the same place, was our porter.

The way was over an undulating plain of glacier of moderate inclination until the corner leading to the Col, from whence a steep secondary glacier led down into the basin of the Talèfre. We experienced no difficulty in making the ascent of this secondary glacier with such ice-men as Croz and Payot, and at 7.50 A.M. arrived on the top of the so-called pass, at a height, according to Mieulet, of 12,162 feet, and 4530 above our camp on the Couvercle.

The descent was commenced by very steep, but firm, rocks, and then by a branch of the Glacier de Triolet. Schrunds† were abundant ; there were no less than five extending completely across the glacier, all of which had to be jumped. Not one was equal in dimensions to the extraordinary chasm on the Col de Pilatte, but

---

* Previous to this we made an attempt to ascend the Aiguille d'Argentière, and were defeated by a violent wind when within a hundred feet of the summit. It is more convenient to refer to this expedition at the end of the chapter.

† Great crevasses. A bergschrund is a schrund, but something more. (See Chap. xiv.)

in the aggregate they far surpassed it. " Our lives," so Reilly expressed it, " were made a burden to us with schrunds."

Several spurs run out towards the south-east from the ridge at the head of the Glacier de Triolet, and divide it into a number of bays. We descended the most northern of these, and when we emerged from it on to the open glacier, just at the junction of our bay with the next one, there we came across a most beautiful ice-arch, festooned with icicles, the decaying remnant of an old sérac, which stood, isolated, full 30 feet above the surface of the glacier ! It was an accident, and I have not seen its like elsewhere.   When I passed the spot in 1865 no vestige of it remained.

We flattered ourselves that we should arrive at the chalets of Prè du Bar very early in the day ; but, owing to much time being lost on the slopes of Mont Rouge, it was nearly 4 P.M. before we got to them.   There were no bridges across the torrent nearer than Gruetta, and rather than descend so far, we preferred to round the base of Mont Rouge, and to cross the snout of the Glacier du Mont Dolent.*

We occupied the 9th with the ascent of the Mont Dolent. This was a miniature ascent.   It contained a little of everything. First we went up to the Col Ferret (No. 1), and had a little grind over shaly banks ; then there was a little walk over grass ; then a little tramp over a moraine (which, strange to say, gave a pleasant path) ; then a little zigzagging over the snow-covered glacier of Mont Dolent.   Then there was a little bergschrund ; then a little wall of snow,—which we mounted by the side of a little buttress ; and when we struck the ridge descending S.E. from the summit, we found a little arête of snow leading to the highest point.   The summit itself was little,—very small indeed ; it was the loveliest little cone of snow that was ever piled up on mountain-top ; so

---

* The passage of the Col de Triolet from the Couvercle to Prè du Bar occupied 8½ hours of actual walking.   If it had been taken in the contrary direction it would have consumed a much longer time.   It gave a route shorter than any known at the time between Chamounix and the St. Bernard.   As a pass I cannot conscientiously recommend it to any one (see Chap. xix.), nor am I desirous to go again over the moraine on the left bank of the Glacier de Triolet, or the rocks of Mont Rouge.

soft, so pure ; it seemed a crime to defile it ; it was a miniature Jungfrau, a toy summit, you could cover it with the hand.*

But there was nothing little about the *view* from the Mont Dolent. [Situated at the junction of three mountain ridges, it rises in a positive steeple far above anything in its immediate neighbourhood ; and certain gaps in the surrounding ridges, which seem contrived for that especial purpose, extend the view in almost every direction. The precipices which descend to the Glacier d'Argentière I can only compare to those of the Jungfrau, and the ridges on both sides of that glacier, especially the steep rocks of Les Droites and Les Courtes, surmounted by the sharp snow-peak of the Aig. Verte, have almost the effect of the Grandes Jorasses. Then, framed, as it were, between the massive tower of the Aig. de Triolet and the more distant Jorasses, lies, without exception, the most delicately beautiful picture I have ever seen—the whole *massif* of Mont Blanc, raising its great head of snow far above the tangled series of flying buttresses which uphold the Monts Maudits, supported on the left by Mont Peuteret and by the mass of ragged aiguilles which overhang the Brenva. This aspect of Mont Blanc is not new, but from this point its *pose* is unrivalled, and it has all the superiority of a picture grouped by the hand of a master. . . . The view is as extensive, and far more lovely than that from Mont Blanc itself.]†

We went down to Cormayeur, and on the afternoon of July 10 started from that place to camp on Mont Suc, for the ascent of the Aiguille de Trélatête ; hopeful that the mists which were hanging about would clear away. They did not, so we deposited ourselves, and a vast load of straw, on the moraine of the Miage Glacier, just above the Lac de Combal, in a charming little hole which some solitary shepherd had excavated beneath a great slab of rock. We spent the night there, and the whole of the next day, unwilling

---

* The ascent of Mont Dolent and return to Prè du Bar (inclusive of halts) occupied less than 11 hours.

† The bracketed paragraphs in this chapter are extracted from the notes of Mr. Reilly.

to run away, and equally so to get into difficulties by venturing into the mist. It was a dull time, and I grew restless. Reilly read to me a lecture on the excellence of patience, and composed himself in an easy attitude, to pore over the pages of a yellow-covered book. "Patience," I said to him viciously, " comes very easily to fellows who have shilling novels ; but I have not got one ; I have picked all the mud out of the nails of

my boots, and have skinned my face ; what shall I do ?" " Go and study the moraine of the Miage," said he. I went, and came back after an hour. " What news ? " cried Reilly, raising himself on his elbow. "Very little ; it's a big moraine, bigger than I

thought, with ridge outside ridge, like a fortified camp ; and there are walls upon it which have been built and loop-holed, as if for defence. " Try again," he said, as he threw himself on his back. But I went to Croz, who was asleep, and tickled his nose with a straw until

he awoke ; and then, as that amusement was played out, watched Reilly, who was getting numbed, and shifted uneasily from side to side, and threw himself on his stomach, and rested his head on his elbows, and lighted his pipe and puffed at it savagely. When I looked again, how was Reilly? An indistinguishable heap ; arms, legs, head, stones, and straw, all mixed together, his hat flung on one side, his novel tossed far away ! Then I went to him, and read him a lecture on the excellence of patience.

Bah ! it was a dull time. Our mountain, like a beautiful coquette, sometimes unveiled herself for a moment, and looked charming above, although

very mysterious below.   It was not until eventide she allowed
us to approach her ; then, as darkness came on, the curtains were
withdrawn, the light drapery was lifted, and we stole up on tiptoe
through the grand portal framed by Mont Suc.   But night advanced
rapidly, and we found ourselves left out in the cold, without a hole
to creep into or shelter from overhanging rock.   We might have
fared badly, except for our good plaids.   But when they were

OUR CAMP ON MONT SUC.*

sewn together down their long edges, and one end tossed over our
rope (which was passed round some rocks), and the other secured
by stones, there was sufficient protection ; and we slept on this
exposed ridge, 9700 feet above the level of the sea, more soundly,
perhaps, than if we had been lying on feather beds.

We left our bivouac at 4.45 A.M., and at 9.40 arrived upon the

---

* From a sketch by Mr. Adams-Reilly.   This camp was immediately at the foot
of the snow seen upon the map to the N.W. of the words Mont Suc.

highest of the three summits of the Trélatête, by passing over the lowest one. It was well above everything at this end of the chain, and the view from it was extraordinarily magnificent. The whole of the western face of Mont Blanc was spread out before us ; we were the first by whom it had been ever seen. I cede the description of this view to my comrade, to whom it rightfully belongs.

[For four years I had felt great interest in the geography of the chain ; the year before I had mapped, more or less successfully, all but this spot, and this spot had always eluded my grasp. The praises, undeserved as they were, which my map had received, were as gall and wormwood to me when I thought of that great slope which I had been obliged to leave a blank, speckled over with unmeaning dots of rock, gathered from previous maps—for I had consulted them all without meeting an intelligible representation of it. From the surface of the Miage glacier I had gained nothing, for I could only see the feet of magnificent ice-streams, but no more ; but now, from the top of the dead wall of rock which had so long closed my view, I saw those fine glaciers from top to bottom, pouring down their streams, nearly as large as the Bossons, from Mont Blanc, from the Bosse, and from the Dôme.

The head of Mont Blanc is supported on this side by two buttresses, between which vast glaciers descend. Of these the most southern* takes its rise at the foot of the precipices which fall steeply down from the Calotte,† and its stream, as it joins that of the Miage, is cut in two by an enormous *rognon* of rock. Next, to the left, comes the largest of the buttresses of which I have spoken, almost forming an aiguille in itself. The next glacier‡ descends from a large basin which receives the snows of the summit-ridge between the Bosse and the Dôme, and it is divided from the third and last glacier§ by another buttress, which joins the summit-ridge at a point between the Dôme and the Aig. de Bionnassay.]

---

* This glacier is named on the map Glacier du Mont Blanc.

† The Calotte is the name given to the dome of snow at the summit of Mont Blanc.   ‡ Glacier du Dôme.   § This is without a name.

The great buttresses betwixt these magnificent ice-streams have supplied a large portion of the enormous masses of débris which are disposed in ridges round about, and are strewn over, the termination of the Glacier de Miage in the Val Véni. These moraines* used to be classed amongst the wonders of the world. They are very large for a glacier of the size of the Miage.

The dimensions of moraines are not ruled by those of glaciers. *Many* small glaciers have large moraines,† and many large ones have small moraines. The size of the moraines of any glacier depends mainly upon the area of rock surface that is exposed to atmospheric influences within the basin drained by the glacier ; upon the nature of such rock,—whether it is friable or resistant ; and upon the dip of strata. Moraines most likely will be small if little rock surface is exposed ; but when large ones are seen, then, in all probability, large areas of rock, uncovered by snow or ice, will be found in immediate contiguity to the glacier. The Miage glacier has large ones, because it receives detritus from many great cliffs and ridges. But if this glacier, instead of lying, as it does, at the bottom of a trough, were to fill that trough, if it were to completely envelope the Aiguille de Trélatête, and the other mountains which border it, and were to descend from Mont Blanc unbroken by rock or ridge, it would be as destitute of morainic matter as the great *Mer de Glace* of Greenland. For if a country or district is *completely* covered up by glacier, the moraines may be of the very smallest dimensions.‡

The contributions that are supplied to moraines by glaciers themselves, from the abrasion of the rocks over which their ice

* I do not know the origin of the term *moraine*. De Saussure says (vol. i. p. 380, § 536), "the peasants of Chamounix call these heaps of débris *the moraine* of the glacier." It may be inferred from this that the term was a local one, peculiar to Chamounix.

† An example is referred to on p. 161. Much more remarkable cases might be instanced.

‡ It is not usual to find small moraines to large glaciers fed by many branches draining many different basins. That is, if the branches are draining basins which

passes, are minute compared with the accumulations which are furnished from other sources. These great rubbish-heaps are formed, one may say almost entirely, from débris which falls, or is washed down the flanks of mountains, or from cliffs bordering glaciers ; and are composed, to a very limited extent only, of matter that is ground, rasped, or filed off by the friction of the ice.

If the contrary view were to be adopted, if it could be maintained that " glaciers, *by their motion, break off masses of rock from the sides and bottoms of their valley courses,* and crowd along every thing that is movable, so as to form large accumulations of débris in front, and along their sides,"* the conclusion could not be resisted, the greater the glacier, the greater should be the moraine.

This doctrine does not find much favour with those who have personal knowledge of what glaciers do at the present time. From De Saussure † downwards it has been pointed out, time after time, that moraines are chiefly formed from débris coming from rocks or soil *above* the ice, not from the bed over which it passes. But amongst the writings of modern speculators upon glaciers and glacier-action in bygone times, it is not uncommon to find the notions entertained, that moraines represent the amount of *excavation* (such is the term employed) performed by glaciers, or at least are comprised of matter which has been excavated by glaciers ; that vast moraines have necessarily been produced by vast glaciers ; and that a great extension of glaciers—a glacial period—necessarily causes the production of vast moraines. It is needless to cite more

---

are separated by mountain ridges, or which, at least, have islands of rock protruding through the ice. The small moraines contributed by one affluent are balanced, probably, by great ones brought by another feeder.

* *Atlas of Physical Geography,* by Augustus Petermann and the Rev. T. Milner. The italics are not in the original.

† " The stones that are found upon the upper extremities of glaciers are of the same nature as the mountains which rise above ; but, as the ice carries them down into the valleys, they arrive between rocks of a totally different nature from their own."—De Saussure, § 536.

than one or two examples to show that such generalisations cannot be sustained. Innumerable illustrations might be quoted.

In the chain of Mont Blanc one may compare the moraines of the Miage with those of the Glacier d'Argentière. The latter glacier drains a basin equal to or exceeding that of the former ; but its moraines are small compared with those of the former. More notable still is the disparity of the moraines of the Gorner glacier (that which receives so many branches from the neighbourhood of Monte Rosa*), and of the Z'Muttgletscher. The area drained by the Gorner greatly exceeds the basin of the Z'Mutt, yet the moraines of the Z'Mutt are incomparably larger than those of the Gorner. No one is likely to say that the Z'Mutt and Miage glaciers have existed for a far greater length of time than the other pair ; an explanation must be sought amongst the causes to which reference has been made.

More striking still is it to see the great interior *Mer de Glace* of Greenland almost without moraines. This vast ice-plateau, although smaller than it was in former times, is still so extensive that the whole of the glaciers of the Alps might be merged into it without its bulk being perceptibly increased. If the size of moraines bore any sort of relation to the size of glaciers, the moraines of Greenland should be far greater than those of the Alps.

This interior ice-reservoir of Greenland, enormous as it is, must be considered as but the remnant of a mass which was incalculably greater, and which is unparalleled at the present time outside the Antarctic Circle. With the exception of localities where the rocks are easy of disintegration, and the traces of glacier-action have been to a great extent destroyed, the whole country bears the marks of the grinding and polishing of ice ; and, judging by the flatness of the curves of the *roches moutonnées*, and by the perfection of the polish which still remains upon the rocks after they have sustained

---

* The Unter Theodul, Klein Matterhorn, Breithorn, Schwarze, Zwillinge, Grenz, and Monte Rosa glaciers, are all feeders of the Gorner. The Z'Mutt receives the Tiefenmatten, Stock, and Schönbühl glaciers only.

(through many centuries) extreme variations of temperature, the period during which such effects were produced must have widely exceeded in duration the 'glacial period' of Europe. If moraines were built from matter excavated by glaciers, the moraines of Greenland should be the greatest in the world !

The absence of moraines upon and at the termination of this great *Mer de Glace* is due to the want of rocks rising above the ice.* On two occasions, in 1867, I saw, at a glance, at least 600 square miles of it, from the summits of small mountains on its outskirts. Not a single peak or ridge was to be seen rising above, nor a single rock reposing upon the ice. The country was *completely* covered up by glacier ; all was ice, as far as the eye could see.†

There is evidence, then, that considerable areas of exposed rock surface are essential to the production of large moraines, and that glacial periods do not necessarily produce vast moraines. That moraines are not built up of matter which is excavated by glaciers, but simply illustrate the powers of glaciers for transportation and arrangement.‡

* I refer to those portions of it which I have seen in the neighbourhood of Disco Bay. There are moraines in this district, but they were formed when the great *Mer de Glace* stretched nearer to the sea,—when it sent arms down through the valleys in the belt of land which now intervenes between sea and glacier.

† The interior of Greenland appears to be absolutely covered by glacier between 68° 30′—70° N. Lat. Others speak of peaks peeping through the ice to the N. and S. of this district ; but I suspect that these peaks are upon the outskirts of the great *Mer de Glace.*

‡ The striations which are found upon rocks over which glaciers have worked, are universally held by the ablest writers to be caused by foreign matter held in the grip of the ice, or rolling between it and the rock-bed (§ 9, p. 146). If the principal source of the tools which make these marks is cut off, the marks should, of course, be less numerous.

The rarity of striations in the neighbourhood of the great *Mer de Glace* of Greenland was very noticeable. There was perfection of glaciation ; but, over large areas, striations, flutings, and groovings were entirely wanting. Weathering, subsequently to the retreat of the ice, had not taken place, to any perceptible extent, in the localities to which I refer.

Striations, groovings, and flutings, are seen on the outskirt land ; but they are less common in Greenland than in the Alps.

We descended in our track to the Lac de Combal,* and from thence went over the Col de la Seigne to les Motets, where we slept ; on July 13, crossed the Col du Mont Tondu to Contamines (in a sharp thunderstorm), and the Col de Voza to Chamounix. Two days only remained for excursions in this neighbourhood, and we resolved to employ them in another attempt to ascend the Aiguille d'Argentière, upon which mountain we had been cruelly defeated just eight days before.

It happened in this way.—Reilly had a notion that the ascent of the Aiguille could be accomplished by following the ridge leading to its summit from the Col du Chardonnet. At half-past six, on the morning of the 6th, we found ourselves accordingly on the top of that pass.† The party consisted of our friend Moore and his guide Almer, Reilly and his guide François Couttet, myself and Michel Croz. So far the weather had been calm, and the way easy ; but immediately we arrived on the summit of the pass, we got into a furious wind. Five minutes earlier we were warm,—now we were frozen. Fine snow, whirled up into the air, penetrated every crack in our harness, and assailed our skins as painfully as if it had been red hot instead of freezing cold. The teeth chattered involuntarily—talking was laborious ; the breath froze instantaneously ; eating was disagreeable ; sitting was impossible !

* The ascent of the Aiguille de Trélatête from our camp on Mont Suc (2½ hours above the Lac de Combal) and its descent to les Motets, occupied 9½ hours. After quitting the lake, the route led up the largest of the ravines on the S. E. side of Mont Suc, and then along the top of the gently-inclined snow-ridge which was at the summit of that buttress of the Trélatête. It then descended on to a branch of the Glacier d'Allée Blanche, through a gap in one of the minor ridges of Mont Suc. The course was then straight up this glacier (a little W. of N.), until the ridge was struck that descends from the summit of the Trélatête in the direction of Mont Blanc. This was followed, and the highest (central) peak (12,900 feet) was arrived at by passing over the peak No. 3 (12,782). It is possible to descend from the highest point of this mountain on to the Glacier de Trélatête. I wished to adopt this course in 1864, but was outvoted.

Mont Suc is a famous locality for crystals. We discovered several sparkling, fairy caves, encrusted with magnificent specimens, smoky and clear ; but, as usual, the best were injured before they could be detached.

† The Col du Chardonnet is about 11,000 or 11,100 feet above the level of the sea.

We looked towards our mountain. Its aspect was not encouraging. The ridge that led upwards had a spiked arête, palisaded with miniature aiguilles, banked up at their bases by heavy snowbeds, which led down, at considerable angles, on one side towards the Glacier de Saleinoz, on the other towards the Glacier du Chardonnet. Under any circumstances, it would have been a stiff piece of work to clamber up that way. Prudence and comfort counselled, " Give it up." Discretion overruled valour. Moore and Almer crossed the Col du Chardonnet to go to Orsières, and we others returned towards Chamounix.

But when we got some distance down, the evil spirit which prompts men to ascend mountains tempted us to stop, and to look back at the Aiguille d'Argentière. The sky was cloudless ; no wind could be felt, nor sign of it perceived ; it was only eight o'clock in the morning ; and there, right before us, we saw another branch of the glacier leading high up into the mountain— far above the Col du Chardonnet—and a little couloir rising from its head almost to the top of the peak. This was clearly the right route to take. We turned back, and went at it.

The glacier was steep, and the snow gully rising out of it was steeper. Seven hundred steps were cut. Then the couloir became *too* steep. We took to the rocks on its left, and at last gained the ridge, at a point about 1500 feet above the Col. We faced about to the right, and went along the ridge ; keeping on some snow a little below its crest, on the Saleinoz side. Then we got the wind again ; but no one thought of turning, for we were within 250 feet of the summit.

The axes of Croz and Couttet went to work once more, for the slope was about as steep as snow could be. Its surface was covered with a loose, granular crust ; dry and utterly incoherent ; which slipped away in streaks directly it was meddled with. The men had to cut through this into the old beds underneath, and to pause incessantly to rake away the powdery stuff, which poured down in hissing streams over the hard substratum. Ugh ! how cold it was! How the wind blew! Couttet's hat was torn from its fastenings, and went on a tour in Switzerland. The flour-like snow, swept off the ridge above, was tossed spirally upwards, eddying in *tourmentes ;* then, dropt in lulls, or caught by other gusts, was flung far and wide to feed the Saleinoz.

"My feet are getting suspiciously numbed," cried Reilly: "how about frost-bites?" "Kick hard, sir," shouted the men; "it's the only way." *Their* fingers were kept alive by their work ; but it was cold for the feet, and they kicked and hewed simultaneously. I followed their example, but was too violent, and made a hole clean through my footing. A clatter followed as if crockery had been thrown down a well.

I went down a step or two, and discovered in a second that all were standing over a cavern (not a crevasse, speaking properly) that was bridged over by a thin vault of ice, from which great icicles hung in groves. Almost in the same minute Reilly pushed one of his hands right through the roof. The whole party might have tumbled through at any moment. "Go ahead, Croz, we are over a chasm!" "We know it," he answered, "and we can't find a firm place."

In the blandest manner, my comrade inquired if to persevere would not be to do that which is called "tempting Providence." My reply being in the affirmative, he further observed, "Suppose we go down?" "Very willingly." "Ask the guides." They had not the least objection ; so we went down, and slept that night at the Montanvert.

Off the ridge we were out of the wind. In fact, a hundred feet down *to windward*, on the slope fronting the Glacier du Chardonnet, we were broiling hot ; there was not a suspicion of a breeze. Upon that side there was nothing to tell that a hurricane was raging a hundred feet higher,—the cloudless sky looked tranquillity itself : whilst to leeward the only sign of a disturbed atmosphere was the friskiness of the snow upon the crests of the ridges.

We set out on the 14th, with Croz, Payot, and Charlet, to finish off the work which had been cut short so abruptly, and slept, as before, at the Chalets de Lognan. On the 15th, about midday, we arrived upon the summit of the aiguille, and found that we had actually been within one hundred feet of it when we turned back upon the first attempt.

It was a triumph to Reilly. In this neighbourhood he had performed the feat (in 1863) of joining together " two mountains, each about 13,000 feet high, standing on the map about a mile and a half apart." Long before we made the ascent he had procured evidence which could not be impugned, that the Pointe des Plines, a fictitious summit which had figured on other maps as a distinct mountain, could be no other than the Aiguille d'Argentière, and he had accordingly obliterated it from the preliminary draft of his map. We saw that it was right to do so. The Pointe des Plines did not exist. We had ocular demonstration of the accuracy of his previous observations.

I do not know which to admire most, the fidelity of Mr. Reilly's map, or the indefatigable industry by which the materials were accumulated from which it was constructed. To men who are sound in limb it may be amusing to arrive on a summit (as we did upon the top of Mont Dolent), sitting astride a ridge too narrow to stand upon ; or to do battle with a ferocious wind (as we did on the top of the Aiguille de Trélatête) ; or to feel half-frozen in midsummer (as we did on the Aiguille d'Argentière). But there is extremely little amusement in making sketches and notes under such conditions. Yet upon all these expeditions, under the most adverse circumstances, and in the most trying situations, Mr. Reilly's brain and fingers were always at work. Throughout all he was ever alike ; the same genial, equable-tempered companion, whether victorious or whether defeated ; always ready to sacrifice his own desires to suit our comfort and convenience. By a happy union of audacity and prudence, combined with untiring perseverance, he eventually completed his self-imposed task—a work which would have been intolerable except as a labour of love—and which, for a single individual, may well-nigh be termed Herculean.

We separated upon the level part of the Glacier d'Argentière, Reilly going with Payot and Charlet *viâ* the chalets of Lognan and de la Pendant, whilst I, with Croz, followed the right bank of the glacier to the village of Argentière.* At 7 P.M. we entered the humble inn, and ten minutes afterwards heard the echoes of the cannon which were fired upon the arrival of our comrades at Chamounix.†

---

* One cannot do worse than follow that path.

† The lower chalet de Lognan is 2½ hours' walking from Chamounix. From thence to the summit of the Aiguille d'Argentière, and down to the village of the same name, occupied 12½ hours.

CHAPTER XII.

" A daring leader is a dangerous thing."

EURIPIDES.

On July 10, Croz and I went to Sierre, in the Valais, *viâ* the Col de Balme, the Col de la Forclaz, and Martigny. The Swiss side of the Forclaz is not creditable to Switzerland. The path from Martigny to the summit has undergone successive improvements in these latter years ; but mendicants permanently disfigure it.

We passed many tired pedestrians toiling up this oven, persecuted by trains of parasitic children. These children swarm there like maggots in a rotten cheese. They carry baskets of fruit with which to plague the weary tourist. They flit around him like flies ; they thrust the fruit in his face ; they pester him with their pertinacity. Beware of them !—taste, touch not their fruit. In the eyes of these children, each peach, each grape, is worth a prince's ransom. It is to no purpose to be angry ; it is like flapping wasps—they only buzz the more. Whatever you do, or whatever you say, the end will be the same. " Give me something," is the alpha and omega of all their addresses. They learn the phrase, it is said, before they are taught the alphabet. It is in all their mouths. From the tiny toddler up to the maiden of sixteen, there is nothing heard but one universal chorus of—" Give me something ; will you have the goodness to give me something ?"

From Sierre we went up the Val d'Anniviers to Zinal, to join our former companions, Moore and Almer. Moore was ambitious to discover a shorter way from Zinal to Zermatt than the two passes which were known.* He had shown to me, upon Dufour's map, that a direct line, connecting the two places, passed exactly over the depression between the Zinal-Rothhorn and the Schall-horn. He was confident that a passage could be effected over this depression, and was sanguine that it would (in consequence of its directness) prove to be a quicker route than the circuitous ones over the Triftjoch and the Col Durand.

He was awaiting us, and we immediately proceeded up the valley, and across the foot of the Zinal glacier to the Arpitetta Alp, where a chalet was supposed to exist in which we might pass the night. We found it at length,† but it was not equal to our expect-ations. It was not one of those fine timbered chalets, with huge overhanging eaves, covered with pious sentences carved in unin-telligible characters. It was a hovel, growing, as it were, out of the hill-side; roofed with rough slabs of slaty stone; without a door or window ; surrounded by quagmires of ordure, and dirt of every description.

A foul native invited us to enter. The interior was dark ; but, when our eyes became accustomed to the gloom, we saw that our palace was in plan about 15 by 20 feet ; on one side it was scarcely five feet high, but on the other was nearly seven. On this side there was a raised platform, about six feet wide, littered with dirty straw and still dirtier sheepskins. This was the bedroom. The remainder of the width of the apartment was the parlour. The rest was the factory. Cheese was the article which was being fabricated, and the foul native was engaged in its manufacture. He was garnished behind with a regular cowherd's one-legged stool, which gave him a queer, uncanny look when it was elevated in the air as he bent over into his tub ; for the making of his cheese required him to blow into a tub for ten minutes at a time. He

---

* The Col de Zinal or Triftjoch, between the Trifthorn and the Ober Gabelhorn ; and the Col Durand between the last-mentioned mountain and the Dent Blanche. For our route from Zinal to Zermatt, see the map of the valley of Zermatt.

† High above the Glacier de Moming at the foot of the Crête de Milton.

then squatted on his stool to gain breath, and took a few whiffs at a short pipe ; after which he blew away more vigorously than before. We were told that this procedure was necessary. It appeared to us to be nasty. It accounts, perhaps, for the flavour possessed by certain Swiss cheeses.

Big, black, and leaden-coloured clouds rolled up from Zinal, and met in combat on the Moming glacier with others which descended from the Rothhorn. Down came the rain in torrents, and crash went the thunder. The herd-boys hurried under shelter, for the frightened cattle needed no driving, and tore spontaneously down the Alp as if running a steeple-chase. Men, cows, pigs, sheep, and goats forgot their mutual animosities, and rushed to the only refuge on the mountain. The spell was broken which had bound the elements for some weeks past, and the *cirque* from the Weisshorn to Lo Besso was the theatre in which they spent their fury.

A sullen morning succeeded an angry night. We were undecided in our council whether to advance or to return down the valley. Good seemed likely to overpower bad ; so, at 5.40, we left the chalet *en route* for our pass [amidst the most encouraging assurances from all the people on the Alp that we need not distress ourselves about the weather, as it was not possible to get to the point at which we were aiming]. *

Our course led us at first over ordinary mountain slopes, and then over a flat expanse of glacier. Before this was quitted, it was needful to determine the exact line which was to be taken. We were divided betwixt two opinions. I advocated that a course should be steered due south, and that the upper plateau of the Moming glacier should be attained by making a great detour to our right. This was negatived without a division. Almer declared in favour of making for some rocks to the south-west of the Schallhorn, and attaining the upper plateau of the glacier by mounting them. Croz advised a middle course, up some very

* Moore's Journal.

steep and broken glacier. Croz's route seemed likely to turn out to be impracticable, because much step-cutting would be required upon it. Almer's rocks did not look good ; they were, possibly, unassailable. I thought both routes were bad, and declined to vote for either of them. Moore hesitated, Almer gave way, and Croz's route was adopted.

He did not go very far, however, before he found that he had undertaken too much, and after [glancing occasionally round at us, to see what we thought about it, suggested that it might, after all, be wiser to take to the rocks of the Schallhorn]. That is to say, he suggested the abandonment of his own and the adoption of Almer's route. No one opposed the change of plan, and, in the absence of instructions to the contrary, he proceeded to cut steps across an ice-slope towards the rocks.

Let the reader now cast his eye upon the map of the valley of Zermatt, and he will see that when we quitted the slopes of the Arpitetta Alp, we took a south-easterly course over the Moming glacier. We halted to settle the plan of attack shortly after we got upon the ice. The rocks of the Schallhorn, whose ascent Almer recommended, were then to our south-east. Croz's proposed route was to the south-west of the rocks, and led up the southern side of a very steep and broken glacier.* The part he intended to traverse was, in a sense, undoubtedly practicable. He gave it up because it would have involved too much step-cutting. But the part of this glacier which intervened between his route and Almer's rocks was, in the most complete sense of the word, impracticable. It passed over a continuation of the rocks, and was broken in half by them. The upper portion was separated from the lower portion by a long slope of ice that had been built up from the débris of the glacier which had fallen from above. The foot of this slope was surrounded by immense quantities of the larger avalanche blocks. These we cautiously skirted, and when Croz halted they had been left far below, and we were half-way up

* Through what is technically called an "ice-fall."

the side of the great slope which led to the base of the ice-wall above.

Across this ice-slope Croz now proceeded to cut. It was executing a flank movement in the face of an enemy by whom we might be attacked at any moment. The peril was obvious. It was a monstrous folly. It was foolhardiness. A retreat should have been sounded.*

" I am not ashamed to confess," wrote Moore in his Journal, " that during the whole time we were crossing this slope my heart was in my mouth, and I never felt relieved from such a load of care as when, after, I suppose, a passage of about twenty minutes, we got on to the rocks and were in safety. . . . I have never heard a positive oath come from Almer's mouth, but the language in which he kept up a running commentary, more to himself than to me, as we went along, was stronger than I should have given him credit for using. His prominent feeling seemed to be one of *indignation* that we should be in such a position, and self-reproach at being a party to the proceeding ; while the emphatic way in which, at intervals, he exclaimed, ' Quick ; be quick,' sufficiently betokened his alarm."

It was not necessary to admonish Croz to be quick. He was fully as alive to the risk as any of the others. He told me afterwards, that this place was not only the most dangerous he had ever crossed, but that no consideration whatever would tempt him to cross it again. Manfully did he exert himself to escape from the impending destruction. His head, bent down to his work, never turned to the right or to the left. One, two, three, went his axe, and then he stepped on to the spot where he had been cutting. How painfully insecure should we have considered those steps at any other time ! But now, we thought of nothing but the rocks in front, and of the hideous *séracs*, lurching over above us, apparently in the act of falling.

* The responsibility did not rest with Croz. His part was to advise, but not to direct.

2 L

We got to the rocks in safety, and if they had been doubly as difficult as they were, we should still have been well content. We sat down and refreshed the inner man ; keeping our eyes on the towering pinnacles of ice under which we had passed ; but which, now, were almost beneath us. Without a preliminary warning sound, one of the largest—as high as the Monument at London Bridge—fell upon the slope below. The stately mass heeled over as if upon a hinge (holding together until it bent thirty degrees forwards), then it crushed out its base, and, rent into a thousand fragments, plunged vertically down upon the slope that we had crossed ! Every atom

ICE-AVALANCHE ON THE MOMING PASS.

of our track, that was in its course, was obliterated ; all the new snow was swept away, and a broad sheet of smooth, glassy ice showed the resistless force with which it had fallen.

It was inexcusable to follow such a perilous path, but it is easy

THE SUMMIT OF THE MOMING PASS IN 1864.

to understand why it was taken.   To have retreated from the place where Croz suggested a change of plan, to have descended below the reach of danger, and to have mounted again by the route which Almer suggested, would have been equivalent to abandoning the excursion ; for no one would have passed another night in the chalet on the Arpitetta Alp.   " Many," says Thucydides, " though seeing well the perils ahead, are forced along by fear of dishonour —as the world calls it—so that, vanquished by a mere word, they fall into irremediable calamities."   Such was nearly the case here. No one could say a word in justification of the course which was adopted ; all were alive to the danger that was being encountered ; yet a grave risk was deliberately—although unwillingly—incurred, in preference to admitting, by withdrawal from an untenable posi- tion, that an error of judgment had been committed.

After a laborious trudge over many species of snow, and through many varieties of vapour—from the quality of a Scotch mist to that of a London fog—we at length stood on the depression between the Rothhorn and the Schallhorn.*   A steep wall of snow was upon the Zinal side of the summit ; but what the descent was like on the other side we could not tell, for a billow of snow tossed over its crest by the western winds, suspended o'er Zermatt with motion arrested, resembling an ocean-wave frozen in the act of breaking, cut off the view.†

Croz—held hard in by the others, who kept down the Zinal side—opened his shoulders, flogged down the foam, and cut away the cornice to its junction with the summit ; then boldly leaped down, and called on us to follow him.

* The summit of the pass has been marked on Dufour's map 3793 mètres, or 12,444 feet.

† These snow-cornices are common on the crests of high mountain ridges, and it is always prudent (just before arriving upon the summit of a mountain or ridge) to *sound* with the alpenstock, that is to say, drive it in, to discover whether there is one or not.   Men have often narrowly escaped losing their lives from neglecting this precaution.

These cornices are frequently rolled round in a volute, and sometimes take most extravagant forms.   See page 34.

It was well for us now that we had such a man as leader. An
inferior, or less daring guide, would have hesitated to enter upon the
descent in a dense mist ; and Croz himself would have done right
to pause had he been less magnificent in *physique.* He acted,
rather than said, " Where snow lies fast, there man can go ; where
ice exists, a way may be cut ; it is a question of power ; I have
the power,—all you have to do is to follow me." Truly, he did not
spare himself, and could he have performed the feats upon the
boards of a theatre that he did upon this occasion, he would have
brought down the house with thunders of applause. Here is what
Moore wrote in *his* Journal.

[The descent bore a strong resemblance to the Col de Pilatte,
but was very much steeper and altogether more difficult, which is
saying a good deal. Croz was in his element, and selected his way
with marvellous sagacity, while Almer had an equally honourable
and, perhaps, more responsible post in the rear, which he kept with
his usual steadiness. . . . One particular passage has impressed
itself on my mind as one of the most nervous I have ever made.
We had to pass along a crest of ice, a mere knife-edge,—on our
left a broad crevasse, whose bottom was lost in blue haze, and on
our right, at an angle of 70°, or more, a slope falling to a similar
gulf below. Croz, as he went along the edge, chipped small
notches in the ice, in which we placed our feet, with the toes well
turned out, doing all we knew to preserve our balance. While
stepping from one of these precarious footholds to another, I
staggered for a moment. I had not really lost my footing ; but
the agonised tone in which Almer, who was behind me, on seeing
me waver, exclaimed, " Slip not, sir ! " gave us an even livelier
impression than we already had of the insecurity of the position.
. . . One huge chasm, whose upper edge was far above the lower
one, could neither be leaped nor turned, and threatened to prove
an insuperable barrier. But Croz showed himself equal to the
emergency. Held up by the rest of the party, he cut a series of
holes for the hands and feet, down and along the almost perpen-

dicular wall of ice forming the upper side of the *schrund*. Down
this slippery staircase we crept, with our faces to the wall, until a
point was reached where the width of the chasm was not too great
for us to drop across. Before we had done, we got quite accustomed to taking flying leaps over the *schrunds*. . . . To make a
long story short ; after a most desperate and exciting struggle, and
as bad a piece of ice-work as it is possible to imagine, we emerged
on to the upper plateau of the Hohlicht glacier.]

The glimpses which had been caught of the lower part of the
Hohlicht glacier were discouraging, so it was now determined to
cross over the ridge between it and the Rothhorn glacier. This
was not done without great trouble. Again we rose to a height
exceeding 12,000 feet. Eventually we took to the track of the
despised Triftjoch, and descended by the well-known, but rough,
path which leads to that pass ; arriving at the Monte Rosa hotel
at Zermatt at 7.20 P.M. We occupied nearly twelve hours of actual
walking in coming from the chalet on the Arpitetta Alp (which was
2½ hours above Zinal), and we consequently found that the Moming pass was not the shortest route from Zinal to Zermatt, although
it was the most direct.

Two dozen guides—good, bad, and indifferent ; French, Swiss,
and Italian—can commonly be seen sitting on the wall on the front
of the Monte Rosa hotel : waiting on their employers, and looking
for employers ; watching new arrivals, and speculating on the
number of francs which may be extracted from their pockets. The
Messieurs—sometimes strangely and wonderfully dressed—stand
about in groups, or lean back in chairs, or lounge on the benches
which are placed by the door. They wear extraordinary boots, and
still more remarkable head-dresses. Their peeled, blistered, and
swollen faces are worth studying. Some, by the exercise of watch-
fulness and unremitting care, have been fortunate enough to acquire
a fine raw sienna complexion. But most of them have not been so
happy. They have been scorched on rocks, and roasted on glaciers.
Their cheeks—first puffed, then cracked—have exuded a turpentine-

like matter, which has coursed down their faces, and has dried in patches like the resin on the trunks of pines. They have removed it, and at the same time have pulled off large flakes of their skin. They have gone from bad to worse—their case has become hopeless—knives and scissors have been called into play ; tenderly, and daintily, they have endeavoured to reduce their cheeks to one, uniform hue. It is not to be done. But they have gone on, fascinated, and at last have brought their unhappy countenances to a state of helpless and complete ruin. Their lips are cracked ; their cheeks are swollen ; their eyes are blood-shot ; their noses are peeled and indescribable.

Such are the pleasures of the mountaineer ! Scornfully and derisively the last comer compares the sight with his own flaccid face and dainty hands ; unconscious that he too, perhaps, will be numbered with those whom he now ridicules.

There is a frankness of manner about these strangely-apparelled and queer-faced men, which does not remind one of drawing-room, or city life ; and it is good to see—in this club-room of Zermatt—those cold bodies, our too-frigid countrymen, regele together when brought into contact ; and it is pleasant to witness the hearty welcome given to the new-comers by the host and his excellent wife.*

I left this agreeable society to seek letters at the post. They yielded disastrous intelligence. My holiday was brought to an abrupt termination, and I awaited the arrival of Reilly (who was convoying the stores for the attack on the Matterhorn) only to inform him that our arrangements were upset ; then travelled home, day and night, as fast as express trains would carry me.

---

* This opportunity has been taken to introduce to the reader some of the most expert amateur mountaineers of the time ; and a few of the guides who have been, or will be, mentioned in the course of the book.

Peter Perrn is on the extreme right. Then come young Peter Taugwalder (upon the bench) ; and J. J. Maquignaz (leaning against the door-post). Franz Andermatten occupies the steps, and Ulrich Lauener towers in the background.

THE CLUB-ROOM OF ZERMATT, IN 1864.

CHAPTER XIII.

THE ASCENT OF THE GRAND CORNIER.

"Ye crags and peaks, I'm with you once again !
.   .   .   Methinks I hear
A spirit in your echoes answer me,
And bid your tenant welcome to his home
Again !"   .   .   .   .

S. KNOWLES.

OUR career in 1864 had been one of unbroken success, but the great ascent upon which I had set my heart was not attempted, and, until it was accomplished, I was unsatisfied. Other things, too, influenced me to visit the Alps once more. I wished to travel elsewhere, in places where the responsibility of direction would rest with myself alone. It was well to know how far my judgment in the choice of routes could be relied upon.

The journey of 1865 was chiefly undertaken, then, to find out to what extent I was capable to select paths over mountainous country. The programme which was drawn up for this journey was rather ambitious, since it included almost all of the great peaks which had not then been ascended ; but it was neither lightly undertaken nor hastily executed. All pains were taken to secure success. Information was sought from those who could give it, and the defeats of others were studied, that their errors might be avoided. The results which followed came not so much, perhaps, from luck, as from forethought and careful calculation.

For success does not, as a rule, come by chance, and when one fails there is a reason for it. But when any notable, or so-called brilliant thing is done, we are too apt to look upon the success alone, without considering how it was accomplished. Whilst, when men fail, we inquire why they have not succeeded. So failures are oftentimes more instructive than successes, and the disappointments of some become profitable to others.

Up to a certain point, the programme was completely and happily carried out. Nothing but success attended our efforts so long as the excursions were executed as they had been planned. Most of them were made upon the very days which had been fixed for them months beforehand; and all were accomplished, comparatively speaking, so easily, that their descriptions must be, in the absence of difficulty and danger, less interesting to the general reader than they would have been if our course had been marked by blunders and want of judgment. Before proceeding to speak of these excursions, it will not be entirely useless to explain the reasons which influenced the selection of the routes which were adopted upon them.

In the course of the past five seasons my early practices were revolutionised. My antipathy to snow was overcome, and my predilection for rocks was modified. Like all those who are not mountaineers born, I was, at the first, extremely nervous upon steep snow. The snow seemed bound to slip, and all those who were upon it to go along with it. Snow of a certain quality is undoubtedly liable to slip when it is at a certain inclination.* The exact states which are dangerous, or safe, it is not possible to describe in writing. That is only learnt by experience, and confidence upon snow is not really felt until one has gained experience. Confidence gradually came to me, and as it came so did my partiality for rocks diminish. For it was evident, to use a common expression, that it paid better to travel upon snow than upon rocks. This applies to snow-beds pure and simple, or to snow which is lying over glacier; and in the selection of routes it has, latterly, always been my practice to look for the places where snow slopes, or snow-covered glaciers, reach highest into mountains.†

* See pp. 116, 170, and 249.   † See p. 197.

It is comparatively seldom, however, that an ascent of a great mountain can be executed exclusively upon snow and glacier. Ridges peep through which have to be surmounted. In my earlier scramblings I usually took to, or was taken upon, the summits (or arêtes) of the ridges, and a good many mountaineers habitually take to them on principle, as the natural and proper way. According to my experience, it is seldom well to do so when any other course is open. As I have already said, and presently shall repeat more particularly, the crests of all the main ridges of the great peaks of the Alps are shattered and cleft by frost ; and it not unfrequently happens that a notch in a ridge, which appears perfectly insignificant from a distance, is found to be an insuperable barrier to further progress ; and a great detour, or a long descent, has to be made to avoid the obstacle. When committed to an arête one is tied, almost always, to a particular course, from which it is difficult to deviate. Much loss of time must result if any serious obstruction occurs ; and total defeat is not at all improbable.

But it seldom happens that a great alpine peak is seen that is cut off abruptly, in all directions, from the snows and glaciers which surround it. In its gullies snow will cling, although its faces may be too steep for the formation of permanent snow-beds. The merits of these snow-gullies (or *couloirs*) have been already pointed out,* and it is hardly necessary to observe, after that which was just now said about snow, that ascents of snow-gullies (with proper precautions) are very much to be preferred to ascents of rocky arêtes.

By following the glaciers, the snow-slopes above, and the couloirs rising out of them, it is usually possible to get very close to the summits of the great peaks in the Alps. The final climb will, perhaps, necessarily be by an arête. The less of it the better.

It occasionally occurs that considerable mountain slopes, or faces, are destitute of snow-gullies. In that case it will, very likely, be best to adhere to the faces (or to the gullies or minor ridges upon them) rather than take to the great ridges. Upon a

* See pp. 225-7.

2 M

face one can move to the right or to the left with more facility than upon the crest of a ridge ; and when a difficulty is arrived at, it is, consequently, less troublesome to circumvent.

In selecting the routes which were taken in 1865, I looked, first, for places where glaciers and snow extended highest up into the mountains which were to be ascended, or the ridges which were to be crossed. Next, for gullies filled with snow leading still higher ; and finally, from the heads of the gullies we completed the ascents, whenever it was practicable, by faces instead of by arêtes. The ascent of the Grand Cornier (13,022), of the Dent Blanche (14,318), Grandes Jorasses (13,700), Aiguille Verte (13,540), Rui-nette (12,727), and the Matterhorn (14,780), were all accomplished in this way ; besides the other excursions which will be referred to by and by. The route selected, before the start was made, was in every case strictly followed out.

We inspected all of these mountains from neighbouring heights before entering upon their ascents. I explained to the guides the routes I proposed to be taken, and (when the courses were at all complicated) sketched them out on paper to prevent misunderstanding. In some few cases they suggested variations, and in every case the route was well discussed. The *execution* of the work was done by the guides, and 1 seldom interfered with, or attempted to assist in it.

The 13th of June 1865 I spent in the valley of Lauterbrunnen with the Rev. W. H. Hawker and the guides Christian and Ulrich Lauener ; and on the 14th crossed the Petersgrat with Christian Almer and Johann Tännler to Turtman (Tourtemagne) in the Valais. Tännler was then paid off, as Michel Croz and Franz Biener were awaiting me.

It was not possible to find two leading guides who worked together more harmoniously than Croz and Almer. Biener's part was subordinate to theirs, and he was added as a convenience rather than as a necessity. Croz spoke French alone ; Almer little else than German. Biener spoke both languages, and was useful on that account ; but he seldom went to the front, excepting during the early part of the day, when the work was easy, and he acted throughout more as a porter than as a guide.

The importance of having a reserve of power on mountain expeditions cannot be too strongly insisted upon. We always had some in hand, and were never pressed, or overworked, so long as we were together. Come what might, we were ready for it. But by a series of chances, which I shall never cease to regret, I was first obliged to part with Croz, and then to dismiss the others ;* and so, deviating from the course that I had deliberately adopted, which was successful in practice because it was sound in principle, became fortuitously a member of an expedition that ended with the catastrophe which brings this book, and brought my scrambles amongst the Alps, to a close.†

* See Chapter xx.

† I engaged Croz for 1865 before I parted from him in 1864 ; but upon writing to him in the month of April to fix the dates of his engagement, I found that he had supposed he was free (in consequence of not having heard from me earlier), and had engaged himself to a Mr. B—— from the 27th of June. I endeavoured to hold him to his promise, but he considered himself unable to withdraw from his later obligation. His letters were honourable to him. The following extract from the last one he wrote to me is given as an interesting souvenir of a brave and upright man :—

On June 15 we went from Turtman to Z'meiden, and thence over the Forcletta pass to Zinal. We diverged from the summit of the pass up some neighbouring heights to inspect the Grand Cornier, and I decided to have nothing to do with its northern side. The mountain was more than seven miles away, but it was quite safe to pronounce it inaccessible from our direction.

On the 16th we left Zinal at 2.5 A.M., having been for a moment greatly surprised by an entry in the hotel-book,[*] and ascending by the Zinal glacier, and giving the base of our mountain a wide berth in order that it might the better be examined, passed gradually right round to its south, before a way up it was seen.[†] At 8.30 we arrived upon the plateau of the glacier that descends towards the east, between the Grand Cornier and the Dent Blanche, and from this place a route was readily traced. We steered to the north (as shown upon the map) over the glacier, towards the ridge that descends to the east ; gained it by mounting snow-slopes, and followed it to the summit, which was arrived at before half-past twelve. From first to last the route was almost entirely over snow.

The ridges leading to the north and to the south from the summit of the Grand Cornier, exhibited in a most striking manner the extraordinary effects that may be produced by violent alternations of heat and cold. The southern one was hacked and split into the wildest forms ; and the northern one was not less cleft and impracticable, and offered the droll piece of rock-carving which is represented upon page 270. Some small blocks actually

---

[*] It was an entry describing an ascent of the Grand Cornier (which we supposed had never been ascended) from the very direction which we had just pronounced to be hopeless ! It was especially startling, because Franz Biener was spoken of in it as having been concerned in the ascent. On examining Biener it was found that he had made the excursion, and had supposed at the time he was upon his summit that it was the Grand Cornier. He saw afterwards that they had only ascended one of the several points upon the ridge running northwards from the Grand Cornier—I believe, the Pigne de l'Allée (11,168 feet) !

[†] For route, see the map of the Valley of Zermatt.

tottered and fell before our eyes, and, starting others in their down-ward course, grew into a perfect avalanche, which descended with a solemn roar on to the glaciers beneath.

It is natural that the great ridges should present the wildest forms—not on account of their dimensions, but by reason of their

PART OF THE SOUTHERN RIDGE OF THE GRAND CORNIER.

positions. They are exposed to the fiercest heat of the sun, and are seldom in shadow as long as it is above the horizon. They are entirely unprotected, and are attacked by the strongest blasts and by the most intense cold. The most durable rocks are not proof against such assaults. These grand, apparently solid—eternal—mountains, seeming so firm, so immutable, are yet ever changing and crumbling into dust. These shattered ridges are evidence of their sufferings. Let me repeat that every principal ridge of every great peak in the Alps amongst those I have seen has been shattered in this way ; and that every summit, amongst the rock-summits upon which I have stood, has been nothing but a piled-up heap of fragments.

The minor ridges do not usually present such extraordinary forms as the principal ones. They are less exposed, and they are less broken up ; and it is reasonable to assume that their annual degradation is less than that of the summit-ridges.

The wear and tear does not cease even in winter, for these great ridges are never completely covered up by snow,* and the sun has still power. The destruction is incessant, and increases as time goes on ; for the greater the surfaces which are exposed to the practically inexhaustible powers of sun and frost, the greater ruin will be effected.

PART OF THE NORTHERN RIDGE OF THE GRAND CORNIER.

The rock-falls which are continually occurring upon all rock

---

* I wrote in the *Athenæum*, August 29, 1863, to the same effect. "This action of the frost does not cease in winter, inasmuch as it is impossible for the Matterhorn to be entirely covered by snow. Less precipitous mountains may be entirely covered up during winter, and if they do not then actually gain height, the wear and tear is, at least, suspended. . . . We arrive, therefore, at the conclusion that, although such snow-peaks as Mont Blanc *may* in the course of ages grow higher, the Matterhorn must decrease in height." These remarks have received confirmation.

The men who were left by M. Dollfus-Ausset in his observatory upon the summit of the Col Theodule, during the winter of 1865, remarked that the snow was partially melted upon the rocks in their vicinity upon 19th, 20th, 21st, 22d, 23d, 26th, 27th December of that year, and upon the 22d of December they entered in their Journal, " *Nous avons vu au Matterhorn que la neige se fondait sur roches et qu'il s'en écoulait de l'eau.*"—*Matériaux pour l'étude des Glaciers*, vol. viii. part i. p. 246, 1868 ; and vol. viii. part ii. p. 77, 1869.

mountains (such as are referred to upon pp. 32, 92-3) are, of course, caused by these powers. No one doubts it ; but one never believes it so thoroughly as when the quarries are seen from which their materials have been hewn ; and when the germs, so to speak, of these avalanches have been seen actually starting from above.

These falls of rock take place from two causes. First, from the heat of the sun detaching small stones or rocks which have been arrested on ledges or slopes and bound together by snow or ice. I have seen such released many times when the sun has risen high ; fall gently at first, gather strength, grow in volume, and at last rush down with a cloud trailing behind, like the dust after an express train. Secondly, from the freezing of the water which trickles, during the day, into the clefts, fissures, and crannies. This agency is naturally most active in the night, and then, or during very cold weather, the greatest falls take place.*

When one has continually seen and heard these falls, it is easily understood why the glaciers are laden with moraines. The wonder is, not that they are sometimes so great, but that they are not always greater. Irrespective of lithological considerations, one knows that this débris cannot have been excavated by the glaciers. The moraines are *borne* by glaciers, but they are *born* from the ridges. They are generated by the sun, and delivered by the frost. " Fire," it is well said in Plutarch's life of Camillus, " is the most active thing in nature, and all generation is motion, or at least, with motion; all other parts of matter without warmth lie sluggish and dead, and crave the influence of heat as their life, and when that comes upon them, they immediately acquire some active or passive qualities."†

---

* In each of the seven nights I passed upon the south-west ridge of the Matter-horn in 1861-3 (at heights varying from 11,844 to 12,992 feet above the level of the sea), the rocks fell incessantly in showers and avalanches. See p. 175.

† Tonson's Ed. of 1758. Bacon may have had this passage in mind when he wrote, " It must not be thought that heat generates motion, or motion heat (though in some respects this be true), but that the very essence of heat, or the substantial self of heat, is motion and nothing else."—*Novum Organum*, book ii. Devey's Translation.

If the Alps were granted a perfectly invariable temperature, if they were no longer subjected, alternately, to freezing blasts and to scorching heat, they might more correctly be termed 'eternal.' They might still continue to decay, but their abasement would be much less rapid.

When rocks are covered up by a sheet of glacier they do enjoy an almost invariable temperature. The extremes of summer and winter are unknown to rocks which are so covered up,—a range of a very few degrees is the most that is possible underneath the ice.* There is, *then*, little or no disintegration from unequal expansion and contraction. Frost, *then*, does not penetrate into the heart of the rock, and cleave off vast masses. The rocks, *then*, sustain grinding instead of cleaving. Atoms, *then*, come away instead of masses. Fissures and overhanging surfaces are bridged, for the ice cannot get at them;† and after many centuries of grinding have been sustained, we still find numberless angular surfaces (in the *lee-sides*) which were fashioned before the ice began to work.

The points of difference which are so evident between the operations of heat, cold, and water, and the action of glaciers upon rocks, are as follow. The former take advantage of cracks, fissures, joints, and soft places ; the latter does not. The former can work *underneath* overhanging masses ; the latter cannot. The effects produced by the former continually increase, because they continually expose fresh surfaces by forming new cracks, fissures, and holes. The effects which the latter produces constantly diminish, because the area of the surfaces operated upon becomes less and less, as they become smoother and flatter.

What can one conclude, then, but that sun, frost, and water, have

---

* Doubtless, *at the sides* of glacier-beds, the range of temperature is greater. But there is evidence that the winter cold does not penetrate to the innermost recesses of glacier-beds in the fact that streams continue to flow underneath the ice all the year round, winter as well as summer, in the Alps and (I was informed in Greenland) in Greenland. Experimental proof can be readily obtained that even in midsummer the bottom temperature is close to 32° Faht.

† See pp. 143-4.

had infinitely more to do than glaciers with the fashioning of mountain-forms and valley-slopes ? Who can refuse to believe that powers which are at work everywhere, which have been at work always, which are so incomparably active, capable, and enduring, must have produced greater effects than a solitary power which is always local in its influence, which has worked, *comparatively*, but for a short time, which is always slow and feeble in its operations, and which constantly diminishes in intensity ?

Yet there are some who refuse to believe that sun, frost, and water have played an important part in modelling the Alps, and hold it as an article of their faith that the Alpine region " owes its present conformation mainly to the action of its ancient glaciers "!*

My reverie was interrupted by Croz observing that it was time to be off. Less than two hours sufficed to take us to the glacier plateau below (where we had left our baggage) ; three quarters of an hour more placed us upon the depression between the Grand Cornier and the Dent Blanche (Col du Grand Cornier †), and at 6 P.M. we arrived at Abricolla. Croz and Biener hankered after milk, and descended to a village lower down the valley ; but Almer and I stayed where we were, and passed a chilly night on some planks in a half-burnt chalet.‡

---

* Professor Tyndall " On the Conformation of the Alps," *Phil. Mag.*, Sept. 1862.

† This had been crossed, for the first time, a few months before.

‡ The following details may interest mountain-climbers. Left Zinal (5505 feet) 2.5 A.M. Thence to plateau S.E. of summit of Grand Cornier, 5 h. 25 min. Plateau to summit of mountain, 2½ hours. The last 300 feet of the ridge followed were exceedingly sharp and narrow, with a great cornice, from which huge icicles depended. We were obliged to go *underneath* the cornice, and to cut a way through the icicles. Descent from summit to plateau, 1 h. 40 min. Sharp snowstorm, with thunder. Plateau to summit of Col du Grand Cornier (rocks easy), 45 min. From the summit of the Col to the end of glacier leading to the west, 55 min. Thence to Abricolla (7959), 15 min.

CHAPTER XIV.

THE ASCENT OF THE DENT BLANCHE.

"God help thee, Trav'ller, on thy journey far ;
The wind is bitter keen,—the snow o'erlays
The hidden pits, and dang'rous hollow-ways,
And darkness will involve thee.—No kind star
To-night will guide thee." . . .

H. KIRKE WHITE.

CROZ and Biener did not return until past 5 A.M. on June 17, and we then set out at once for Zermatt, intending to cross the Col d'Hérens. But we did not proceed far before the attractions of the Dent Blanche were felt to be irresistible, and we turned aside up the steep lateral glacier which descends along its south-western face.

The Dent Blanche is a mountain that is little known except to the climbing fraternity. It was, and is, reputed to be one of the most difficult mountains in the Alps. Many attempts were made to scale it before its ascent was accomplished. Even Leslie Stephen himself, fleetest of foot of the whole Alpine brotherhood, once upon a time returned discomfited from it.

LESLIE STEPHEN.

It was not climbed until 1862 ; but in that year Mr. T. S. Kennedy, with Mr. Wigram, and the guides Jean B. Croz* and Kronig, managed to conquer it. They had a hard fight though before they gained

* The brother of my guide Michel Croz.

the victory ; a furious wind and driving snow, added to the natural difficulties, nearly turned the scale against them.*

Mr. Kennedy started from Abricolla between 2 and 3 A.M. on July 18, 1862, and ascending the glacier that is mentioned in the opening paragraph, went towards the point marked 3912 mètres upon the map ;† then turned to the left (that is, to the north), and completed the ascent by the southern ridge,—that which overhangs the western side of the Schönbühl glacier.

Mr. Kennedy described his expedition in a very interesting paper in the *Alpine Journal.* His account bore the impress of truth ; but unbelievers said that it was impossible to have told (in weather such as was experienced) whether the summit had actually been attained, and sometimes roundly asserted that the mountain, as the saying is, yet remained virgin.

I did not share these doubts, although they influenced me to make the ascent. I thought it might be possible to find an easier route than that taken by Mr. Kennedy, and that if we succeeded in discovering one we should be able at once to refute his traducers, and to vaunt our superior wisdom. Actuated by these elevated motives, I halted my little army at the foot of the glacier, and inquired, " Which is best for us to do ?—to ascend the Dent Blanche, or to cross to Zermatt ?" They answered, with befitting solemnity, " We think Dent Blanche is best."

From the chalets of Abricolla the south-west face of the Dent Blanche is regarded almost exactly in profile. From thence it is seen that the angle of the face scarcely exceeds thirty degrees, and after observing this I concluded that the face would, in all probability, give an easier path to the summit than the crest of the very jagged ridge which was followed by Mr. Kennedy.

We zigzagged up the glacier along the foot of the face, and looked for a way on to it. We looked for some time in vain, for a mighty *bergschrund* effectually prevented approach, and, like a fortress' moat, protected the wall from assault. We went up and

* See note to p. 108. † See map of the Valley of Zermatt.

up, until, I suppose, we were not more than a thousand feet below the point marked 3912 mètres ; then a bridge was discovered, and we dropped down on hands and knees to cross it.

A bergschrund, it was said on p. 238, is a schrund, and something more than a schrund. A schrund is simply a big crevasse. A bergschrund is frequently, but not always, a big crevasse. The term is applied to the last of the crevasses that one finds, in ascending, before quitting the glacier, and taking to the rocks which bound it. It is the mountains' schrund. Sometimes it is *very* large, but early in the season (that is to say in the month of June, or before) bergschrunds are usually snowed up, or well bridged over, and do not give much trouble. Later in the year, say in August, they are frequently very great hindrances, and occasionally are completely impassable.

They are lines of rupture consequent upon unequal motion. The glaciers below move quicker than the snow or ice which clings immediately to the mountains ; hence these fissures result. The slower motion of that which is above can only be attributed to its having to sustain greater friction ; for the rule is that the upper portion is set at a steeper angle than the lower. As that is the case, we should expect that the upper portion would move *quicker* than the lower, and it would do so, doubtless, but for the retardation of the rocks over which, and through which, it passes.*

We crossed the bergschrund of the Dent Blanche, I suppose, at a height of about 12,000 feet above the level of the sea. Our work may be said to have commenced at that point. The face, although not steep in its general inclination, was so cut up by little ridges and cliffs, and so seamed with incipient couloirs, that it had all the difficulty of a much more precipitous slope. The difficulties were never great, but they were numerous, and made a very respectable total when put together. We passed the

---

* Couloirs are invariably protected at their bases by bergschrunds. An example of a couloir with a double bergschrund is given on p. 225.

THE BERGSCHRUND ON THE DENT BLANCHE IN 1865.

bergschrund soon after nine in the morning, and during the next eleven hours halted only five-and-forty minutes. The whole of the remainder of the time was occupied in ascending and descending the 2400 feet which compose this south-western face ; and inasmuch as 1000 feet per hour (taking the mean of ascent and descent) is an ordinary rate of progression, it is tolerably certain that the Dent Blanche is a mountain of exceptional difficulty.

The hindrances opposed to us by the mountain itself were, however, as nothing compared with the atmospheric obstructions. It is true there was plenty of, "Are you fast, Almer?" "Yes." "Go ahead, Biener." Biener, made secure, cried, "Come on, sir," and *Monsieur* endeavoured. "No, no," said Almer, "not there,— *here*,"—pointing with his bâton to the right place to clutch. Then 'twas Croz's turn, and we all drew in the rope as the great man followed. "Forwards" once more—and so on.

Five hundred feet of this kind of work had been accomplished when we were saluted (not entirely unexpectedly) by the first gust of a hurricane which was raging above. The day was a lovely one for dwellers in the valleys, but we had, long ago, noted some light, gossamer clouds, that were hovering round our summit, being drawn out in a suspicious manner into long, silky threads. Croz, indeed, prophesied before we had crossed the schrund, that we should be beaten by the wind, and had advised that we should return. But I had retorted, "No, my good Croz, you said just now 'Dent Blanche is best;' we must go up the Dent Blanche."

I have a very lively and disagreeable recollection of this wind. Upon the outskirts of the disturbed region it was only felt occasionally. It then seemed to make rushes at one particular man, and when it had discomfited him, it whisked itself away to some far-off spot, only to return, presently, in greater force than before.

My old enemy—the Matterhorn—seen across the basin of the Z'Muttgletscher, looked totally unassailable. "Do you think," the men asked, "that you, or any one else, will ever get up *that* mountain?" And when, undismayed by their ridicule, I stoutly answered, "Yes, but not upon that side," they burst into derisive chuckles. I must confess that my hopes sank; for nothing can look, or be, more completely inaccessible than the Matterhorn on its northern and north-west sides.

"Forwards" once again. We overtopped the Dent d'Herens. "Not a thousand feet more; in three hours we shall be on the summit." "You mean *ten*," echoed Croz, so slow had been the progress. But I was not far wrong in the estimate. At 3.15 we struck the great ridge followed by Mr. Kennedy, close to the top of the mountain. The wind and cold were terrible there. Progress was oftentimes impossible, and we waited, crouching under the lee of rocks, listening to 'the shrieking of the mindless wind,' while the blasts swept across, tearing off the upper snow and blowing it away in streamers over the Schönbühl glacier—"nothing seen except an indescribable writhing in the air, like the wind made visible."

Our goal was concealed by mist, although it was only a few yards away, and Croz's prophecy, that we should stay all night upon the summit, seemed likely to come true. The men rose with the occasion, although even their fingers had nearly lost sensation. There were no murmurings, nor suggestions of return, and they pressed on for the little white cone which they knew must be near at hand. Stopped again; a big mass perched loosely on the ridge barred the way; we could not crawl over, and scarcely dared creep round it. The wine went round for the last time. The liquor was half-frozen,—still we would more of it. It was all gone; the bottle was left behind, and we pushed on, for there was a lull.

The end came almost before it was expected. The clouds opened, and I saw that we were all but upon the highest point, and that, between us and it, about twenty yards off, there was a little artificial pile of stones. Kennedy was a true man,—it was a cairn which he had erected. "What is that, Croz?" "*Homme des pierres*," he bawled. It was needless to proceed further; I jerked the rope from Biener, and motioned that we would go back. He did the same to Almer, and we turned immediately. *They* did not see the stones (they were cutting footsteps), and misinterpreted the reason of the retreat. Voices were inaudible, and explanations impossible.*

We commenced the descent of the face. It was hideous work. The men looked like impersonations of Winter, with their hair all frosted, and their beards matted with ice. My hands were numbed —dead. I begged the others to stop. " *We cannot afford to stop ; we must continue to move,*" was their reply. They were right ; to stop was to be entirely frozen. So we went down ; gripping rocks varnished with ice, which pulled the skin from the fingers. Gloves were useless ; they became iced too, and the bâtons slid through them as slippery as eels. The iron of the axes stuck to the fingers —it felt red-hot ; but it was useless to shrink, the rocks and the axes had to be firmly grasped—no faltering would do here.

We turned back at 4.12 P.M., and at 8.15 crossed the bergschrund again, not having halted for a minute upon the entire descent. During the last two hours it was windless, but time was of such vital importance that we pressed on incessantly, and did not stop until we were fairly upon the glacier. Then we took stock of what remained of the tips of our fingers ; there was not much skin left ; they were perfectly raw, and for weeks afterwards I was reminded of the ascent of the Dent Blanche by the twinges which I felt when I pulled on my boots. The others escaped with some slight frost-bites ; and, altogether, we had reason to congratulate ourselves that we got off so lightly. The men complimented me upon the descent, and I could do the same honestly to them. If they had worked less vigorously, or harmoniously, we should have been benighted upon the face, where there was not a single spot upon which it was possible to sit ; and if that had happened, I do not think that one would have survived to tell the tale.

* The summit of the Dent Blanche is a ridge, perhaps one hundred yards in length. The highest point is usually at its north-eastern end.

We made the descent of the glacier in a mist, and of the moraine at its base, and of the slopes below, in total darkness, and regained the chalets of Abricolla at 11.45 P.M. We had been absent eighteen and a half hours, and out of that time had been going not less than seventeen.   That night we slept the sleep of those who are thoroughly tired.*

Two days afterwards, when walking into Zermatt, whom should we meet but Mr. Kennedy. " Hullo!" we said, " we have just seen

T. S. KENNEDY.

your cairn on the top of the Dent - Blanche." " No, you haven't," he answered, very positively. " What do you mean?" " Why, that you cannot have seen my cairn, because I didn't make one !" " Well, but we saw *a* cairn." " No doubt ; it was made by a man who went up the mountain last year with Lauener and Zurfluh." " O-o-h," we said, rather disgusted at hearing news when we expected to communicate some, " O-o-h! good morning, Kennedy." Before this happened, we managed to lose our way upon the Col d'Hérens ; but an account of that must be reserved for the next chapter.

---

* The ascent of the Dent Blanche is the hardest that I have made.   There was nothing upon it so difficult as the last 500 feet of the Pointe des Ecrins ; but, on the other hand, there was hardly a step upon it which was positively easy.   The whole of the face required actual climbing.   There was, probably, very little difference in difficulty between the route we took in 1865, and that followed by Mr. Kennedy in 1862.

CHAPTER XV.

LOST ON THE COL D'HÉRENS.—MY SEVENTH ATTEMPT
TO ASCEND THE MATTERHORN.

"Oh ! ye immortal gods, where in the world are we ?"
CICERO.

WE should have started for Zermatt about 7 A.M. on the 18th, had
not Biener asked to be allowed to go to mass at Evolène, a village
about two and a half hours from Abricolla. He received permission,
on the condition that he returned not later than mid-day, but he
did not come back until 2.30 P.M., and we thereby got into a pretty
little mess.

The pass which we were about to traverse to Zermatt—the Col
d'Hérens—is one of the few glacier-passes in this district which
have been known almost from time immemorial. It is frequently
crossed in the summer season, and is a very easy route, notwithstanding that the summit of the pass is 11,417 feet above the level
of the sea.*

From Abricolla to the summit the way lies chiefly over the flat
Glacier de Ferpècle. The walk is of the most straightforward kind.
The glacier rises in gentle undulations ; its crevasses are small and
easily avoided ; and all you have to do, after once getting upon the
ice, is to proceed due south, in the most direct manner possible.
If you do so, in two hours you should be upon the summit of the
pass.

We tied ourselves in line, of course, when we entered upon the

* See map of the Valley of Zermatt. The route taken upon June 19 is alone
marked.

glacier ; and placed Biener to lead, as he had frequently crossed the pass ; supposing that his local knowledge might save us some time upon the other side. We had proceeded, I suppose, about half-way up, when a little, thin cloud dropped down upon us from above ; but it was so light, so gauzy, that we did not for a moment suppose that it would become embarrassing, and hence I neglected to note at the proper moment the course which we should steer,— that is to say, to observe our precise situation, in regard to the summit of the pass.

For some little time Biener progressed steadily, making a tolerably straight track ; but at length he wavered, and deviated sometimes to the right, and sometimes to the left. Croz rushed forward directly he saw this, and taking the poor young man by his shoulders gave him a good shaking, told him that he was an imbecile, to untie himself at once, and go to the rear. Biener looked half-frightened, and obeyed without a murmur. Croz led off briskly, and made a good straight track for a few minutes ; but then, it seemed to me, began to move steadily round to the left. I looked back, but the mist was now too thick to see our traces, and so we continued to follow our leader. At last the others (who were behind, and in a better position to judge) thought the same as I did, and we pulled up Croz to deliver our opinion. He took our criticism in good part, but when Biener opened his mouth that was too much for him to stand, and he told the young man again, " You are imbecile ; I bet you twenty francs to one that *my* track is better than *yours;* twenty francs, now then, imbecile !"

Almer went to the front. He commenced by returning in the track for a hundred yards or so, and then started off at a tangent from Croz's curve. We kept this course for half-an-hour, and then were certain that we were not on the right route, because the snow became decidedly steep. We bore away more and more to the right, to avoid this steep bank, but at last I rebelled, as we had for some time been going almost south-west, which was altogether the wrong direction. After a long discussion we returned some distance in our track, and then steered a little east of south, but we continually met steep snow-slopes, and to avoid them went right or left as the case might require.

We were greatly puzzled, and could not in the least tell whether we were too near the Dent Blanche or too close to the Tête Blanche. The mists had thickened, and were now as dense as a moderate London fog. There were no rocks or echoes to direct us, and the guidance of the compass brought us invariably against these steep snow-banks. The men were fairly beaten ; they had all had a try, or more than one, and at last gave it up as a bad job, and asked what was to be done. It was 7.30 P.M. and only an hour of daylight was left. We were beginning to feel used up, for we had wandered about at tip-top speed for the last three hours and a half, so I said, " This is my advice ; let us turn in our track, and go back as hard as ever we can, not quitting the track for an instant." They were well content, but just as we were starting off, the clouds lifted a little, and we thought we saw the Col. It was then to our right, and we went at it with a dash, but before we had gone a hundred paces down came the mist again. We kept on nevertheless for twenty minutes, and then, as darkness was perceptibly coming on, and the snow was yet rising in front, we turned back, and by running down the entire distance managed to get clear of the Ferpècle glacier just as it became pitch dark. We arrived at our cheerless chalet in due course, and went to bed supperless, for our food was gone ; all very sulky—not to say savage—agreeing in nothing except in bullying Biener.

At 7 A.M. on the 19th, we set out, for the third time, for the Col d'Hérens. It was a fine day, and we gradually recovered our tempers as we saw the follies which had been committed on the previous evening. Biener's wavering track was not so bad ; but Croz had swerved from the right route from the first, and had traced a complete semicircle, so that when we stopped him we were facing Abricolla—whence we had started. Almer had commenced with great discretion ; but he kept on too long, and crossed the proper route. When I stopped them (because we were going south-west), we were a long way up the Tête Blanche! Our last attempt was in the right direction; we were actually upon the summit of the pass, and in another ten yards we should have commenced to go down hill! It is needless to point out that if the compass had been looked to at the proper moment—that is, immediately the mist came down—we should have avoided all our troubles. It was little use afterwards, except to tell us when we were going *wrong*.

We arrived at Zermatt in six and a half hours' walking from Abricolla, and Seiler's hospitable reception set us all right again. On the 20th we crossed the Theodule pass, and diverged from its summit up the Theodulhorn (11,391) to examine a route which 1 suggested for the ascent of the Matterhorn; but before continuing an account of our proceedings, I must stop for a minute to explain why this new route was proposed, in place of that up the south-western ridge.

The Matterhorn may be divided into three sections.* The first, facing the Z'Muttgletscher, which looks, and is, completely unassailable; the second, facing the east, which seems inaccessibility itself; the third, facing Breil, which does not look entirely hopeless. It was from this last direction that all my previous attempts were made. It was by the south-western ridge, it will be remembered, that not only I, but Mr. Hawkins, Professor Tyndall, and the chasseurs of Val Tournanche, essayed to climb the mountain. Why then abandon a route which had been shown to be feasible up to a certain point?

I gave it up for four reasons. 1. On account of my growing disinclination for arêtes, and preference for snow and rock faces (see Chap. xiii.) 2. Because I was persuaded that meteorological disturbances (by which we had been baffled several times) might be expected to occur again and again † (see Chaps. v. and

---

* See Chap. iv. pp. 82-4.

† Subsequent experiences of others have strengthened this opinion.

CAMI

THE MATTERHORN FROM THE RIFFELBERG.

vii.)   3. Because I found that the east face was a gross imposition —it looked not far from perpendicular, while its angle was, in fact, scarcely more than 40°.   4. Because I observed for myself that the strata of the mountain dipped to the west-south-west.   It is not necessary to say anything more than has been already said upon the first two of these four points, but upon the latter two a few words are indispensable.   Let us consider, first, why most persons receive such an exaggerated impression of the steepness of the eastern face.

When one looks at the Matterhorn from Zermatt, the mountain is regarded (nearly) from the north-east.   The face that fronts the east is consequently neither seen in profile nor in full front, but almost half-way between the two ; it looks, therefore, more steep than it really is.   The majority of those who visit Zermatt go up to the Riffelberg, or to the Gornergrat, and from these places the mountain naturally looks still more precipitous, because its eastern face (which is almost all that is seen of it) is viewed more directly in front.   From the Riffel hotel the slope seems to be set at an angle of 70°.   If the tourist continues to go southwards, and crosses the Theodule pass, he gets, at one point, immediately in front of the eastern face, which then seems to be absolutely perpendicular.   Comparatively few persons correct the erroneous impressions they receive in these quarters by studying the face in profile, and most go away with a very incorrect and exaggerated idea of the precipitousness of this side of the mountain, because they have considered the question from one point of view alone.

Several years passed away before I shook myself clear of my early and false impressions regarding the steepness of this side of the Matterhorn.   First of all, I noticed that there were places on this eastern face where snow remained permanently all the year round.   I do not speak of snow in gullies, but of the considerable slopes which are seen upon the accompanying engraving, about half-way up the face.   Such beds as these could not continue to remain throughout the summer, unless the snow had been able to accumulate in the winter in large masses ; and snow cannot accumulate and remain in large masses, in a situation such as this, at angles much exceeding 45°.* Hence I was bound to conclude that the eastern face was many degrees removed from perpendicularity ; and, to be sure on this point, I went to the slopes between the Z'Muttgletscher and the Matterhorngletscher, above the chalets of Staffel, whence the face could be seen in profile. Its appearance from this direction would be amazing to one who had seen it only from the east. It looks so totally different from the apparently sheer and perfectly unclimbable cliff one sees from the Riffelberg, that it is hard to believe the two slopes are one and the same thing. Its angle scarcely exceeds 40°.

A great step was made when this was learnt. This knowledge alone would not, however, have caused me to try an ascent by the eastern face instead of by the south-west ridge. Forty degrees may not seem a formidable inclination to the reader, nor is it for only a small cliff. But it is very unusual to find so steep a gradient maintained continuously as the general angle of a great mountain-slope, and very few instances can be quoted from the High Alps of such an angle being preserved over a rise of 3000 feet.

I do not think that the steepness or the height of this cliff would have deterred climbers from attempting to ascend it, if it had not, in addition, looked so repulsively smooth. Men despaired of finding anything to grasp. Now, some of the difficulties of the south-west ridge came from the smoothness of the rocks, although that ridge, even from a distance, seemed to be well broken up. How much greater, then, might not have been the difficulty of climbing a face which looked smooth and unbroken close at hand?

A more serious hindrance to mounting the south-west ridge is found in the dip of its rocks to the west-south-west. The great mass of the Matterhorn, it is now well ascertained, is composed of

---

* I prefer to be on the safe side. My impression is that snow cannot accumulate in large masses at 45°.

regularly stratified rocks,* which rise towards the east. It has been mentioned in the text, more than once, that the rocks on some portions of the ridge leading from the Col du Lion to the summit dip outwards, and that fractured edges overhang.† This is shown in the illustrations facing pp. 119 and 127; and the annexed diagram, Fig. 1, exhibits the same thing still more clearly. It will be readily understood that such an arrangement is not favourable for climbers, and that the degree of facility with which rocks can be ascended that are so disposed, must depend very much upon the frequency or paucity of fissures and joints. The rocks of the south-west ridge are sufficiently provided with cracks, but if it were otherwise, their texture and arrangement would render them unassailable.‡

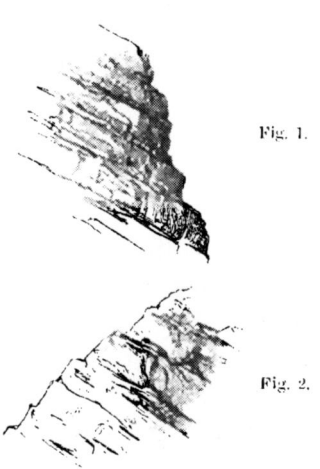

Fig. 1.

Fig. 2.

It is not possible to go a single time upon the rocks of the south-west ridge, from the Col du Lion to the foot of the Great Tower, without observing the prevalence of their outward dip, and that their fractured edges have a tendency to overhang ; nor can one fail to notice that it is upon this account the débris, which is rent off by frost, does not remain *in situ*, but pours down in showers over the surrounding cliffs. Each day's work, so to speak, is cleared away ; the ridge is swept clean ; there is scarcely anything seen but firm rock.§

* Upon this subject I beg to refer the reader to the valuable note furnished by Signor F. Giordano in the Appendix.

† See pp. 94 and 111.

‡ Weathered granite is an admirable rock to climb ; its gritty texture giving excellent hold to the nails in one's boots. But upon such metamorphic schists as compose the mass of the great peak of the Matterhorn, the texture of the rock itself is of no value.

§ I refer here only to that portion of the ridge which is between the Col du Lion

The fact that the mountain is composed of a series of stratified beds was pointed out long ago. De Saussure remarked it, and recorded explicitly, in his *Travels* (§ 2243), that they " rose to the north-east at an angle of about 45°." Forbes noticed it also ; but gave it as his opinion that the beds were " less inclined, or nearly horizontal." He added, " De Saussure is no doubt correct."* The truth, I think, lies between the two.

I was acquainted with both of the above-quoted passages, but did not turn the knowledge to any practical account until I re-observed the same fact for myself. It was not until after my repulse in 1863, that I referred the peculiar difficulties of the south-west ridge to the dip of the strata ; but when once persuaded that structure and not texture was the real impediment, it was reasonable to infer that the opposite side, that is to say the eastern face, might be comparatively easy. In brief, that an arrangement should be found like Fig. 2, instead of like Fig. 1. This trivial deduction was the key to the ascent of the Matterhorn.

The point was, Did the strata continue with a similar dip throughout the mountain ? If they did, then this great eastern face, instead of being hopelessly impracticable, should be quite the reverse. In fact, it should be a great natural staircase, with steps inclining inwards ; and, if it were so, its smooth aspect might be of no account, for the smallest steps, inclined in this fashion, would afford good footing.

They did so, as far as one could judge from a distance. When snow fell in the summer time, it brought out long terraced lines upon the mountain ; rudely parallel to each other ; inclined in the direction shown (approximately) upon the figures in the accompanying plate : and the eastern face, on those occasions, was often whitened almost completely over ; while the other sides, with the

and the Great Tower. The remarks would not apply to the rocks higher up (see p. 118) ; higher still the rocks are firm again ; yet higher (upon the " Shoulder ") they are much disintegrated ; and then, upon the final peak, they are again firm.

* *Travels through the Alps,* 2d ed. p. 317.

THE MATTERHORN FROM THE SUMMIT OF THE THEODULE PASS.

THE MATTERHORN FROM THE NORTH-EAST.

THE SPACES BETWEEN THE PARALLEL RED LINES REPRESENT, ON AN AVERAGE, A VERTICAL HEIGHT OF ABOUT
60 FEET; BUT, ON ACCOUNT OF FORESHORTENING, THE HEIGHT BETWEEN THE UPPERMOST LINES IS SOMEWHAT
MORE THAN THIS AMOUNT.

exception of the powdered terraces, remained black—for the snow could not rest upon them.

The very outline of the mountain, too, confirmed the conjecture that its structure would assist an ascent on the eastern face, although it opposed one on all other sides. Look at any photograph of the peak from the north-east (or, failing one, the outline facing page 288, which is carefully traced from one), and you will see that upon the right-hand side (that facing the Z'Muttgletscher) there is an incessant repetition of overhanging cliffs, and of slopes all trending downwards ; in short, that the character of the whole of that side is similar to Fig. 1, p. 287 ; and that upon the left hand (or south-east) ridge, the forms, as far as they go, are suggestive of the structure of Fig. 2. There is no doubt that the contours of the mountain, seen from this direction, have been largely influenced by the direction of its beds.

It was not, therefore, from a freak, that I invited Mr. Reilly to join in an attack upon the eastern face, but from a gradually-acquired conviction that it would prove to give the easiest path to the summit ; and, if we had not been obliged to part, the mountain would, doubtless, have been ascended in 1864.

My guides readily admitted that they had been greatly deceived as to the steepness of the eastern face, when they were halted to look at it in profile, as we came down the Z'Muttgletscher, on our way to Zermatt ; but they were far from being satisfied that it would turn out to be easy to climb, and Almer and Biener expressed themselves decidedly averse to making an attempt upon it. I gave way temporarily before their evident reluctance, and we made the ascent of the Theodulhorn to examine an alternative route, which I expected would commend itself to them in preference to the other, as a great part of it led over snow.

There is an immense gully in the Matterhorn, which leads up from the Glacier du Mont Cervin to a point high up on the

south-eastern ridge.*   I proposed to ascend this to its head, and to
cross over the south-east ridge on to the eastern face.   This would
have brought us on a level with the bottom of the great snow-slope
shown upon the centre of the eastern face in the engraving facing
p. 285.   This snow-slope was to be crossed diagonally, with the
view of arriving at the snow upon the north-east ridge, which is
shown upon the same engraving, about half-an-inch from the
summit.   The remainder of the ascent was to be made by the
broken rocks, mixed with snow, upon the north side of the mountain.   Croz caught the idea immediately, and thought the plan
feasible ; details were settled, and we descended to Breil.   Luc
Meynet, the hunchback, was summoned, and expressed himself
delighted to resume his old vocation of tent-bearer ; and Favre's
kitchen was soon in commotion preparing three days' rations, for I
intended to take that amount of time over the affair—to sleep on
the first night upon the rocks at the top of the gully ; to make a
push for the summit, and to return to the tent on the second day ;
and upon the third to come back to Breil.

We started at 5.45 A.M. on June 21, and followed the route of the
Breuiljoch† for three hours.   We were then in full view of our gully,
and turned off at right angles for it.   The closer we approached,
the more favourable did it look.   There was a good deal of snow in
it, which was evidently at a small angle, and it seemed as if one-
third of the ascent, at least, would be a very simple matter.   Some
suspicious marks in the snow at its base suggested that it was not
free from falling stones, and, as a measure of precaution, we turned
off on one side, worked up under cover of the cliffs, and waited to
see if anything should descend.   Nothing fell, so we proceeded up
its right or northern side, sometimes cutting steps up the snow
and sometimes mounting by the rocks.   Shortly before 10 A.M. we
arrived at a convenient place for a halt, and stopped to rest upon

* Its position is shown by the letter F, on the right of the outline, on p. 128.
See also map of the Matterhorn and its glaciers.

† See p. 137.

some rocks, immediately close to the snow, which commanded an excellent view of the gully.

While the men were unpacking the food I went to a little promontory to examine our proposed route more narrowly, and to admire our noble couloir, which led straight up into the heart of the mountain for fully one thousand feet. It then bent towards the north, and ran up to the crest of the south-eastern ridge. My curiosity was piqued to know what was round this corner, and whilst I was gazing up at it, and following with the eye the exquisitely drawn curves which wandered down the snow in the gully, all converging to a large rut in its centre, I saw a few little stones skidding down. I consoled myself with thinking that they would not interfere with us if we adhered to the side. But then a larger one came down, a solitary fellow, rushing at the rate of sixty miles an hour—and another—and another. I was unwilling to raise the fears of the men unnecessarily, and said nothing to them. They did not hear the stones. Almer was seated on a rock, carving large slices from a leg of mutton, the others were chatting, and the first intimation they had of danger was from a crash—a sudden roar—which reverberated awfully amongst the cliffs, and, looking up, they saw masses of rocks, boulders and stones, big and little, dart round the corner eight hundred feet or so above us, fly with fearful fury against the opposite cliffs, rebound from them against the walls on our side, and descend; some ricochetting from side to side in a frantic manner; some bounding down in leaps of a hundred feet or more over the snow; and more trailing down in a jumbled, confused mass, mixed with snow and ice, deepening the grooves which, a moment before, had excited my admiration.

The men looked wildly around for protection, and, dropping the food, dashed under cover in all directions. The precious mutton was pitched on one side, the wine-bag was let fall, and its contents gushed out from the unclosed neck, while all four cowered under defending rocks, endeavouring to make themselves as small as possible. Let it not be supposed that their fright was unreasonable, or that I was free from it. I took good care to make myself safe, and went and cringed in a cleft until the storm had passed. But their scramble to get under shelter was indescribably ludicrous. Such a panic I have never witnessed, before or since, upon a mountain-side.

This ricochet practice was a novelty to me. It arose, of course, from the couloir being bent, and from the falling rocks having acquired great pace before they passed the angle. In straight gullies it will, probably, never be experienced. The rule is, as I have already remarked (p. 225), that falling stones keep down the centres of gullies, and they are out of harm's way if one follows the sides.

MY TENT-BEARER—THE HUNCHBACK.

There would have been singularly little amusement, and very great risk, in mounting this gully, and we turned our backs upon it with perfect unanimity. The question then arose, "What is to be done?" I suggested climbing the rocks above us, but this was voted impossible. I thought the men were right, but would not give in without being assured of the fact, and clambered up to settle the question. In a few minutes I was brought to a halt. My forces were scattered ; the little hunchback alone was closely following me—with a broad grin upon his face, and the tent upon his shoulder ; Croz, more behind, was still keeping an eye upon his *Monsieur ;* Almer, a hundred feet below, sat on a rock with his face buried in his hands ; Biener was nowhere, out of sight. " Come down, come down," shouted Croz ; " it is useless," and I turned at length, convinced that it was even as he said. Thus my little plan was knocked on the head, and we were thrown back upon the original scheme.

We at once made a straight track for Mr. Morshead's Breuiljoch,* (which was the most direct route to take in order to get to the Hornli, where we intended to sleep, preparatory to attacking the eastern face), and arrived upon its summit at 12.30 P.M. We were then unexpectedly checked. The pass, as one, had vanished ! and we found ourselves cut off from the Furggengletscher by a small but precipitous wall of rock ;—the glacier had shrunk so much that descent was impracticable. During the last hour clouds had been coming up from the south ; they now surrounded us, and it began to blow hard. The men clustered together, and advocated leaving the mountain alone. Almer asked, with more point than politeness, " Why don't you try to go up a mountain which *can* be ascended?" "It is impossible," chimed in Biener. "Sir," said Croz, " if we cross to the other side we shall lose three days, and very likely shall not succeed. You want to make ascents in the chain of Mont Blanc, and I believe they can be made. But I shall not be able to make them with you if I spend these days here, for I must be at Chamounix on the 27th." There was force in what he said, and his words made me hesitate. I relied upon his strong arms for some work which it was expected would be unusually difficult. Snow began to fall ; that settled the matter, and I gave the word to retreat. We went back to Breil, and on to the village of Val Tournanche, where we slept ; and the next day pro-

* See note to p. 138.

ceeded to Chatillon, and thence up the valley of Aosta to Cormayeur.

I cannot but regret that the counsels of the guides prevailed. If Croz had not uttered his well-intentioned words, he might still have been living. He parted from us at Chamounix at the appointed time, but by a strange chance we met again at Zermatt three weeks later, and two days afterwards he perished before my eyes on the very mountain from which we turned away, at his advice, on the 21st of June.

CHAPTER XVI.

VALLEY OF AOSTA, AND ASCENT OF THE GRANDES JORASSES.

> *   *   *   " When we were boys,
> Who would believe that there were mountaineers
> Dew-lapp'd like bulls, whose throats had hanging at them
> Wallets of flesh ? "   .   .   .   .   .   .
>
> SHAKESPEARE.

THE valley of Aosta is famous for its Bouquetins, and infamous for its Crétins. The Bouquetin, Steinbock, or Ibex, was formerly widely distributed throughout the Alps. It is now confined almost entirely, or absolutely, to a small district on the south of the valley of Aosta, and fears have been repeatedly expressed in late years that it will speedily become extinct.

But the most sanguine person does not imagine that crétinism will be eradicated for many generations. It is widely spread throughout the Alps ; it is by no means peculiar to the valley of Aosta ; but nowhere does it thrust itself more frequently upon the attention of the traveller, and in no valley where " every prospect pleases," is one so often and so painfully reminded that " only man is vile."

It seems premature to fear that the bouquetin will soon become extinct. It is not easy to take a census of them, for, although they have local habitations, it is extremely difficult to find them at home. But there is good reason to believe that there are at least 600 still roaming over the mountains in the neighbourhood of the valleys of Grisanche, Rhèmes, Savaranche, and Cogne.

It would be a pity if it were otherwise. They appeal to the sympathies of all as the remnants of a diminishing race, and no mountaineer or athletic person could witness without sorrow the extinction of an animal possessing such noble qualities ;—which a few months after birth can jump over a man's head at a bound, without taking a run ; which passes its whole life in a constant fight for existence ; which has such a keen appreciation of the beauties of nature, and such disregard of pain that it will "stand for hours like a statue, in the midst of the bitterest storm, until the tips of its ears are frozen"! and which, when its last hour arrives, "climbs to the highest mountain-peaks, hangs on a rock with its horns, twists itself round and round upon them until they are worn off, and then falls down and expires "!!* Even Tschudi himself calls this story wonderful. He may well do so. I disclaim belief in it, —the bouquetin is too fine a beast to indulge in such antics.

Forty-five keepers, selected from the most able chasseurs of the district, guard its haunts. Their task is not a light one, although they are, naturally, acquainted with those who are most likely to attempt poaching. If they were withdrawn, it would not be long before the ibex would be an extinct wild animal, so far as the Alps are concerned. The passion for killing something, and the present value of the beast itself, would soon lead to its extermination. For as meat alone the bouquetin is valuable ; the gross weight of one that is full grown amounting from 160 to 200 lbs ; while its skin and horns are worth £10 and upwards, according to condition and dimensions.

In spite of the keepers, and of the severe penalties which may be inflicted for killing a bouquetin, poaching occurs constantly. Knowing that this was the case, I inquired at Aosta, upon my last visit, if any skins or horns were for sale, and in ten minutes was taken into a garret where the remains of a splendid beast were concealed,—a magnificent male, presumed to be more than twenty years old, as its massive horns had twenty-two more or less strongly marked knobby rings. The extreme length of the skin, from the tip of the nose to the end of the tail, was 1 mètre 69 centimètres

* Tschudi's *Sketches of Nature in the Alps.*

(about 5 feet 7 inches),* and from the ground to the top of its back had been, apparently, about 77 centimètres. It is rare to meet with a bouquetin of these dimensions, and the owner of this skin might have been visited with several years' imprisonment if it had been known that it was in his possession.

THE BOUQUETIN.

The chase of the bouquetin is properly considered a sport fit for a king, and his Majesty Victor-Emmanuel, for whom it is reserved, is too good a sportsman to slaughter indiscriminately an animal which is an ornament to his dominions. Last year (1869)

* Probably stretched in skinning.

2 Q

seventeen fell to his gun at one hundred yards and upwards. In 1868 his Majesty presented a fine specimen to the Italian Alpine Club. The members banqueted, I believe, upon its flesh, and they have had the skin stuffed, and set up in their rooms at Aosta. It is said by connoisseurs to be badly stuffed,—that it is not broad enough in the chest, and is too large behind. Still it looks well proportioned, although it seems made for hard work rather than for feats of agility. From this specimen the accompanying engraving has been made.

It is a full-grown male, about twelve years old, and if it stood upright would measure 3 feet 3½ inches from the ground to the base of its horns. Its extreme length is 4 feet 7 inches. Its horns have eleven well-marked rings, besides one or two faintly-marked ones, and are (measured round their curvature) 54½ centimètres in length. The horns of the specimen referred to on p. 296 (measured in the same way) had a length of only 53½ centimètres, although they were ornamented with nearly double the number of rings, and were presumably of double the age of the former.*

The keepers, and the chasseurs of this district, not only say that the rings upon the horns of the ibex tell its age (each one reckoning as a year), but that the half-developed ones, which sometimes are very feebly marked indeed, show that the animal has suffered from hunger during the winter. Naturalists are sceptical upon this point ; but inasmuch as they offer no better reason against the reputed fact than the natives do in its favour (one saying that it is not so, and the other saying that it is so), we may, perhaps, be permitted to consider it an open question. I can only say that if the faintly-marked rings do denote years of famine, the times for the bouquetin are very hard indeed ; since, in most of the horns which I have seen, the lesser rings have been very numerous, and sometimes more plentiful than the prominent ones.

* Mr. King, in his *Italian Valleys of the Alps*, says, " In the pair (of horns) I possess, which are *two feet* long, there are eight of these yearly rings." It would seem, therefore (if the rings are annual ones), that the maximum length of horn is attained at a comparatively early age.

The Chef of the keepers (who judges by the above-mentioned indications) tells me that the ibex not unfrequently arrives at the age of thirty years, and sometimes to forty or forty-five. He says, too, that it is not fond of traversing steep snow, and in descending a couloir that is filled with it, will zig-zag down, by springing from one side to the other, in leaps of fifty feet at a time ! Jean Tairraz,* the worthy landlord of the Hotel du Mont Blanc at Aosta (who has had opportunities of observing the animal closely), assures me that at the age of four or five months it can easily clear a height of nine or ten feet at a bound !

Long live the bouquetin ! and long may its chase preserve the health of the mountaineering king, Victor-Emmanuel. Long life to the bouquetin ! but down with the crétin !

The peculiar form of idiocy which is called Crétinism† is so highly developed in the Valley of Aosta, and the natives are so familiarised with it, that they are almost indignant when the surprised traveller remarks its frequency. One is continually reminded that it is not peculiar to the valley, and that there are crétins elsewhere. It is too true that this terrible scourge is wide-spread throughout the Alps and over the world, and that there are places where the proportion of crétins to population is, or has been, even greater than in the Valley of Aosta ; but I have never seen, or heard of, a valley so fertile and so charming, of one which—apart from crétinism—leaves so agreeable an impression upon the wayfarer, where equal numbers are reduced to a condition which any respectable ape might despise.

The whole subject of crétinism is surrounded with difficulty. The number of those who are afflicted by it is unknown ; its cure is doubtful ; and its origin is mysterious. It has puzzled the most

---

* Jean Tairraz was the leading guide of the late Albert Smith on his celebrated ascent of Mont Blanc.

† " Crétinism may be looked upon as being the highest stage of Idiocy, although it differs from it, in having a vitiated state of the body, in conjunction with the loss of the faculties of the mind. Thus it is composed of two distinct elements, the one, Idiocy, the other, bad habit of body."—Blackie, *On Crétinism*, p. 6.

acute observers, and every general statement in regard to it must be fenced by qualifications.

It is tolerably certain, however, that the centre of its distribution in the valley of Aosta is about the centre of the valley. The city of Aosta itself may be regarded as its head-quarters. It is there, and in the neighbouring towns of Gignod, Villeneuve, St. Vincent, and Verrex, and in the villages and upon the high-road between those places, that these distorted, mindless beings, more like brutes than men, commonly excite one's disgust by their hideous, loathsome, and uncouth appearance, by their obscene gestures, and by their senseless gabbling.

The accompanying portrait of one is by no means over-drawn—some are too frightful for representation.

How can we account for this particular intensity towards the middle of the valley? Why is it that crétins become more and more numerous after Ivrea is passed, attain their highest ratio and lowest degradation at or about the chief town of the valley, and then diminish in numbers as its upper termination is approached? This maximum of intensity

A CRÉTIN OF AOSTA.

must certainly point to a cause, or to a combination of causes, operating about Aosta, which are less powerful at the two extremities of the valley ; and if the reason for it could be determined, the springs of crétinism would be exposed.

The disease would be even more puzzling than it is if it were confined to this single locality, and the inquirer were to find not merely that it was almost unknown upon the plains to the east and in the districts to the west, but that the valleys radiating north and south from the main valley were practically unaffected by it. For it is a remarkable circumstance, which has attracted the notice of all who have paid attention to crétinism, that the natives of the tributary valleys are almost free from the malady ; —that people of the same race, speaking the same language, breathing the same air, eating the same food, and living the same life, enjoy almost entire immunity from it, while, at the distance of a very few miles, thousands of others are completely in its power.

A parallel case is found, however, on the other side of the Pennine Alps. The Rhone valley is almost equally disfigured by crétinism, and in it, too, the extremities of the valley are slightly affected compared with the intermediate districts—particularly those between Brieg and St. Maurice.* This second example strengthens the conviction that the great development of crétinism in the middle of the valley of Aosta is not the result of accidental circumstances.

It was formerly supposed that crétinism arose from the habitual drinking of snow and glacier-water. De Saussure opposed to this conjecture the facts, that the disease was entirely unknown precisely in those places where the inhabitants were most dependent upon these kinds of water, and that it was most common where such was not the case ;—that the high valleys were untainted, while the low ones were infected.† The notion seems to have proceeded from crétins being confounded with persons who were merely goîtred ; or, at least, from the supposition that goître was an incipient stage of crétinism.

Goître, it is now well ascertained, is induced by the use of

---

* It was stated a few years ago that one in twenty-five of the natives of the Canton Valais (which is chiefly occupied by the valley of the upper Rhone) were crétins. This would give about 3500 to the canton. At the same time the valley of Aosta contained about 2000 crétins.

† *Voyages dans les Alpes*, § 1033.

chemically impure water, and especially hard water ; and the investigations of various observers have discovered that goître has an intimate connection with certain geological formations.* In harmony with these facts, it is found that infants are seldom born with goîtres, but that they develop as the child grows up ; that they will sometimes appear and disappear from mere change of locality ;† and that it is possible to produce them intentionally.

It is not so certain that the causes which produce goître should be regarded as causes of the production or maintenance of crétinism. It is true that crétins are very generally goîtrous, but it is also true that there are tens of thousands of goîtrous persons who are entirely free from all traces of crétinism. Not only so, but that there are districts in the Alps, and outside of them (even in our own country), where goître is not rare, but where the crétin is unknown. Still, regarding the evil state of body which leads to goître as being, possibly, in alliance with crétinism, it will not be irrelevant to give the former disease a little more attention before continuing the consideration of the main subject.

In this country the possession of a goître is considered a misfortune rather than otherwise, and individuals who are afflicted with these appendages attempt to conceal their shame. In the Alps it is quite the reverse. In France, Italy, and Switzerland, it is a positive advantage to be goîtred, as it secures exemption from military service. A goître is a thing to be prized, exhibited, preserved—it is worth so much hard cash ; and it is an unquestionable fact that the perpetuation of the great goîtrous family is assisted by this very circumstance.

When Savoy was annexed to France, the administration took stock of the resources of its new territory, and soon discovered

* Dr. Moffat communicated a paper on this subject at the last (1870) meeting of the British Association at Liverpool, in which he stated he had ascertained that in a Carboniferous district goître was prevalent, and that it was absent on New Red Sandstone.

† Goître is endemic at Briançon, and frequently affects, temporarily, the soldiers who are stationed in that fortress. Chabrand (a doctor of Briançon) says that no less

that, although the acres were many, the conscripts would be few. The government bestirred itself to amend this state of affairs, and after arriving at the conclusion that goître was produced by drinking bad water (and that its production was promoted by sottish and bestial habits), took measures to cleanse the villages, to analyse the waters (in order to point out those which should not be drank), and to give to children who came to school lozenges containing small doses of iodine. It is said that out of 5000 goîtrous children who were so treated in the course of eight years, 2000 were cured, and the condition of 2000 others was improved; and that the number of cures would have been greater if the parents " had not opposed the care of the government, *in order to preserve the privilege of exemption from military service.*" * These benighted creatures refused the Marshal's bâton and preferred their " wallets of flesh !"†

No wonder that the Préfet for Haute-Savoie proposes that goîtrous persons shall no longer be privileged. Let him go farther, and obtain a decree that all of them capable of bearing arms shall

than one in twenty-five of the men of the 34th regiment of infantry, who were in garrison in 1857, became goîtrous during their stay. This regiment came from Perpignan, where the disease is not common.—*Goître et Crétinisme endemique,* Paris, 1864, p. 56.

* The substance of this paragraph is taken from the *Bullettino del Club Alpino Italiano,* No. 13, 1869.

† Blackie says that " Dr. Mottard mentions the case of a so-called goître well near St. Julien in Maurienne, the water of which encrusted the trees in the vicinity with lime, and the use of which produced goître in a couple of months ; and he mentions five young men who had voluntarily drunk its water, and produced goître, in order to be free from military service."

Chabrand, in the pamphlet already quoted, says, " It is deplorable that young people who have a swelling of the thyröid gland (in the Briançonnais), far from endeavouring to get rid of it, occupy themselves only with making it bigger, in order to escape military service. Especially as the time of drawing for the conscription approaches, do they use every means supposed to be capable of producing goître ; drink much water, take '*courses*' with burdens " (on their heads ?) " and tighten the cravat above the swelling. . . . From 1842 to 1847 inclusive, 91 in 1000 obtained exemption on account of goître in the Department of the High Alps." The same writer places the number of goîtrous persons in France at 450,000, and of crétins at 35,000 to 40,000.

be immediately drafted into the army. Let them be formed into regiments by themselves, brigaded together, and commanded by crétins. Think what *esprit de corps* they would have! Who could stand against them? Who would understand their tactics? He would save his iodine, and would render an act of justice to the non-goîtred population. The subject is worthy of serious attention. If goître is really an ally of crétinism, the sooner it is eradicated the better.*

De Saussure substituted heat and stagnation of air as the cause of crétinism in the place of badness of water. But this was only giving up one unsatisfactory explanation for another equally untenable ; and since there are places far hotter and with pernicious atmospheres where the disease is unknown, while, on the other hand, there are situations in which it is common where the heat is not excessive, and which enjoy a freely circulating atmosphere, his assumption may be set aside as insufficient to account for the crétinism of the Valley of Aosta. And in regard to its particular case, it may be questioned whether there is anything more than an imaginary stagnation of air. For my own part, I attribute the oppression which strangers say they feel, in the middle of the valley, not to stagnation of air but to absence of shadow, in consequence of the valley's course being east to west ; and believe, that if the force of the wind were observed and estimated according to the methods in common use, it would be found that there is no deficiency of motion in the air throughout the entire year. Several towns and villages, moreover, where crétins are most numerous, are placed at the entrances of valleys and upon elevated slopes, with abundant natural facilities for drainage—free from malaria, which

* " Goîtrous persons, exempt from military service, remain in their native districts, marry, and thus cause the disease to become hereditary. If, on the contrary, they were drawn, and were sent into untainted departments (particularly those upon the sea-coast), they would return perfectly cured at the expiration of their term of service. Further, if goîtrous persons were not exempt, a greater number of healthy individuals would remain at home, would marry, and would become parents of sound and vigorous children."—Guy and Dagand.

has been suggested as accounting for the crétinism of the Rhone valley.

Others have imagined that intemperance,* poor living, foul habits, and personal uncleanliness, sow the seeds of crétinism, and this opinion is entitled to full consideration. Intemperance of divers kinds is fruitful in the production of insanity,† and herding together in filthy dwellings, with little or no ventilation, may possibly deteriorate *physique*, as much as extreme indulgence may the mind. These ideas are popularly entertained because crétins are more numerous amongst the lower orders than amongst the well-to-do classes. Yet they must, each and all, be regarded as inadequate to account for the disease, still less to explain its excess in the centre of the valley. For in these respects there is little or no distinction between it, the two extremities, and the neighbouring districts.

A conjecture remains to be considered regarding the origin of crétinism, which is floating in the minds of many persons (although it is seldom expressed), which carries with it an air of probability that is wanting in the other explanations, and which is supported by admitted facts.

The fertility of the Valley of Aosta is proverbial. It is covered with vineyards and corn-fields; flocks and herds abound in it ; and its mineral resources are great. There is enough and to spare both for man and beast. There are poor in the valley, as there are everywhere, but life is so far easy that they are not driven to seek for subsistence in other places, and remain from generation to

---

* An instance was mentioned to me, in 1869, of a small proprietor in the Valley of Aosta, who had a wife and several healthy children, having, successively, two good years with his vines. He ate and drank the proceeds up, instead of husbanding his resources, and in the two following years two crétin children were born to him. Several indifferently-good years have succeeded since then, he has been obliged to live frugally, and has had several more children, all of whom are healthy. The parents are apparently free from all taint of crétinism.

† See Dr. Robert Christison *On some of the Medico-legal Relations of the Habit of Intemperance*, 1861 ; Dr. Edward Jarvis *On the Causes of Insanity*, 1851 ; and Reports of the Commissioners in Lunacy.

generation rooted to their native soil.   The large numbers of persons who are found in this valley having the same surnames is a proof of the well-known fact that there is little or no emigration from the valley, and that there is an indefinite amount of intermarriage between the natives.   It is conjectured that the continuance of these conditions through a long period has rendered the population more or less consanguineous, and that we see in crétinism an example, upon a large scale, of the evil effects of alliances of kindred.

This explanation commends itself by reason of its general applicability to crétinism.   The disease is commonly found in valleys, on islands,* or in other circumscribed areas, in which circulation is restricted, or the inhabitants are non-migratory ; and it is rare on plains, where communications are free.   It will at once be asked, " Why, then, are not the tributary valleys of the valley of Aosta full of crétins ?"   The answer is, that these lateral valleys are comparatively sterile, and are unable to support their population from their internal resources.   Large numbers annually leave, and do not return,—some come back, having formed alliances elsewhere.   There is a constant circulation and introduction of new blood.   I am not aware that there are returns to show the extent to which this goes on, but the fact is notorious.†

* Dr. Blackie gives the remarkable instance of "the island of Medwörth (Niederwörth ?), near Coblence, where the inhabitants hold no connection with those on shore, and consequently intermarry constantly with one another."   This island, according to Dr. Blackie, had no less than 40 crétins out of a population of 750.

† The case of the Val Sesia is not strictly in point, since it is not a tributary of the Val d'Aoste, but it may be quoted to show the extent to which this migration goes on.   Mr. King says, " The population of the whole Val Sesia being estimated at 35,000, it is evidently utterly unable to maintain a tithe˳of that number from its own resources.   The necessary result is, a regular periodical migration of all the able-bodied and active males, for varying lengths of time, into different parts of Europe. . . . A large number of the towns of Italy and France, as Genoa, Milan, Turin, and even Paris, are supplied with an immense influx of skilled labourers and artificers from these Vals.   Some idea of the extent of this migration may be formed from the fact, that 8000 Val Sesians leave their homes annually, many of them for years."— *Italian Valleys of the Alps,* p. 373.

This conjecture explains, far better than the other guesses, why it is that crétinism has so strong a hold upon the lower classes, while it leaves the upper ones almost untouched ; for the former are most likely to intermarry with people of their own district, whilst the latter are under no sort of compulsion in this respect. It gives a clue, too, to the reason of the particular intensity in the centre of the valley.   The inhabitants of the lower extremity communicate and mix with the untainted dwellers on the plains, whilst the conditions at the upper extremity approximate to those of the lateral valleys.   Before this explanation will be generally received, a closer connection will have to be established between the assumed cause and the presumed effect.*   Accepting it, nevertheless, as a probable and reasonable one, let us now consider what prospect there is of checking the progress of the disease.

It is, of course, impossible to change the habits of the natives of the valley of Aosta suddenly, and it would, probably, be very difficult to cause any large amount of emigration or immigration. In the present embarrassed condition of Italian finances there is very small chance of any measure of the sort being undertaken if it would involve a considerable expenditure.   The opening of a railway from Ivrea to Aosta might possibly bring about, in a natural way, more movement than would be promoted by any legislation, and by this means the happiest effects might be produced.†

There is little hope of practical results from attempts to cure

* It may be mentioned, as a link in the evidence, that the Department of the Hautes Alpes (which contains a prodigious number of crétins) has, according to Chipault, a larger proportion of deaf and dumb persons to its population than any other department of France, viz. 1 in 419.   The Department of the Basses Pyrénées comes next, with 1 in 677.

† "M. Rambuteau (Préfet of the Department of the Simplon, under the first Napoleon) and M. Fodéré assure us, that at the close of last century the number of crétins in the Canton Valais diminished to a very great degree.   The former attributed this amelioration to the embankment of the Rhone, and the draining of the marshes ; to the clearing of the land ; and the consequent changes in the character of the inhabitants, who became more industrious and active, and less given to gluttony and drunkenness.   The latter author rather imputed it to the opening of the great

crétins. Once a crétin, you are always one.* The experiments of the late Dr. Guggenbühl demonstrated that some *half*-crétins may even become useful members of society, if they are taken in hand early in life ; but they did not show that the nature of the true or complete crétin could be altered.† He essayed to modify some of the mildest forms of crétinism, but did not strike at the root of the evil. If fifty Guggenbühls were at work in the single valley of Aosta, they would take several generations to produce an appreciable effect, and they would never extirpate the disease so long as its sources were unassailed.

Nor will the house which has been built at Aosta‡ to contain 200 crétin beggars do much, unless the inmates are restrained from perpetuating their own degradation. Even the lowest types of crétins may be procreative, and it is said that the unlimited liberty which is allowed to them has caused infinite mischief. A large proportion of the crétins who will be born in the next generation will undoubtedly be offspring of crétin parents. It is strange that self-interest does not lead the natives of Aosta to place their crétins under such restrictions as would prevent their illicit intercourse ; and it is still more surprising to find the Catholic Church actually legalising their marriage. There is something horribly grotesque in the idea of *solemnising* the union of a brace of idiots ;

pass of the Simplon, and consequent more easy communication with other countries, the people being thus more incited to bestir themselves," etc. ; Blackie, p. 53. This testimony, from authors who held totally different opinions as to the origin of crétinism, is strongly confirmatory of the conjecture last advanced.

* " Le crétinisme achevé est incurable ; l'état physique et intellectuel des crétineux et des demi-crétins est susceptible d'amélioration par un traitement convenable, des soins et l'éducation ; mais jamais on ne pourra faire d'eux des hommes complets sous le rapport physique, moral, et intellectuel."—Guy and Dagand on *Crétinisme dans le Département de la Haute-Savoie.*

† Great expectations were raised some years ago by the reports of Dr. Guggenbühl, and by those of visitors to his establishment on the Abendberg, at Interlachen ; but they have been disappointed, and the institution itself has been closed.

‡ At the expense of some unknown charitable person. Besides this establishment, there is an hospital at Aosta, belonging to the order of St. Maurice et Lazare, containing twelve beds for crétin children.

and since it is well known that the disease is hereditary, and develops in successive generations, the fact that such marriages are sanctioned is scandalous and infamous.*

The supply, therefore, is kept up from two sources. The first contingent is derived from apparently healthy parents ; the second, by inheritance from diseased persons. The origin of the first is obscure ; and before its quota can be cut off, or even diminished, the mystery which envelopes it must be dissipated. The remedy for the second is obvious, and is in the hands of the authorities— particularly in those of the clergy. Marriage must be prohibited to all who are affected ; the most extreme cases must be placed under restraint ; and crétins whose origin is illegitimate must be subject to disabilities. Nothing short of the adoption of these measures will meet the case. Useless it will be, so long as the primary sources of the disease are untouched, to build hospitals, to cleanse dwellings, to widen streets, or to attempt small ameliorations of the social circumstances of the natives. All of these things are good enough in themselves, but they are wholly impotent to effect a radical change.

No satisfactory conclusion will be arrived at regarding the origin of crétinism until the pedigrees of a large number of examples have been traced. The numerical test is the only one which is likely to discover the reality. The necessary inquiries are beyond the powers of private persons, and their pursuit will be found suf-

---

* It should be stated, that some of the clergy, at least, refuse to unite the worst kinds of crétins. I have heard it said, however, that all are not so particular ; and, again, others have told me that crétins are *never* legally married in the valley of Aosta. I imagine the truth to be, that some of the priests are scrupulous, and that others are not. The evidence of the natives upon this subject was so conflicting, that I applied to the Canon Carrel (of Aosta) for information. His answer was sufficiently explicit as to the *general* custom :—" ll y a des crétins qui parlent avec une certaine intelligence, et qui sont capables d'apprendre quelques vérités et quelques notions nécessaires aux devoirs sociaux. Ceux-ci contractent quelquefois mariage. Quant à ceux qui ont l'intelligence très obtuse, on ne leur permet pas le mariage, quoiqu'ils puissent encore engendrer ce qui tient plus de la loi naturelle que de la loi civile."

ficiently difficult by official investigators. Great reluctance will be exhibited to disclose the information which should be sought, and the common cry will certainly be raised, that such scrutiny is without general advantage, and is painful to private feelings. But, in matters which affect mankind in general, individual feelings must always be subordinated to the public interest; and if the truth is to be arrived at in regard to crétinism, the protests of the ignorant will have to be overridden.

Hitherto, those who have written upon the disease have confined themselves, almost exclusively, to guessing at its origin; and accurate data, from which sound deductions can be made, are, I believe, entirely wanting.* *We*, however, are not in a position to taunt others with neglect of inquiry. Only a few months ago the House of Commons rejected, by a considerable majority, a proposition that was designed to throw light upon the causes of idiocy; and the opponents of the words which it was sought to introduce, although strictly parliamentary in their arguments and language, afforded a deplorable proof that crétinism is not unknown in our own country.†

Crétinism is the least agreeable feature of the valley of Aosta, but it is, at the same time, the most striking. It has been touched upon for the sake of its human interest, and on account of those unhappy beings who—punished by the errors of their fathers—are powerless to help themselves;—the first sight of whom produced such an impression upon the most earnest of all Alpine writers, that he declared, in a twice-repeated expression, its recollection would never be effaced from his memory.‡

At some very remote period the valley of Aosta was occupied

---

* For further information upon crétinism, see the works of Ferrus, Niepce, Fabre, Séguin, Nystrom, Morel, etc.

† Debate on the Census Bill, on the motion by Sir John Lubbock to insert the words "whether married to a first cousin." The opponents of Sir J. Lubbock's motion should read Chipault *Sur les Mariages Consanguines* : Paris, 1863.

‡ De Saussure, §§ 954, 1030.

by a vast glacier, which flowed down its entire length from Mont Blanc to the plain of Piedmont, remained stationary, or nearly so, at its mouth for many centuries, and deposited there enormous masses of débris. The length of this glacier exceeded 80 miles, and it drained a basin 25 to 35 miles across, bounded by the highest mountains in the Alps. It did not fill this basin. Neither the main stream nor its tributaries completely covered up the valleys down which they flowed. The great peaks still rose several thousand feet above the glaciers, and then, as now, shattered by sun and frost, poured down their showers of rocks and stones, in witness of which there are the immense piles of angular fragments that constitute the moraines of Ivrea.* The wine which is drunk in that town is produced from soil that was borne by this great glacier from the slopes of Monte Rosa; and boulders from Mont Blanc are spread over the country between that town and the Po, supplying excellent materials for building purposes, which were known to the Romans, who employed them in some of their erections at Santhia.†

The moraines around Ivrea are of extraordinary dimensions. That which was the lateral moraine of the left bank of the glacier is about *thirteen miles* long, and, in some places, rises to a height of 2130 feet above the floor of the valley ! Professor Martins terms it " la plus elevée, la plus régulière, et la mieux caractérisée des Alpes." ‡ It is locally called *la Serra*. The lateral moraine of the right bank also rises to a height of 1000 feet, and would be deemed enormous but for the proximity of its greater comrade ; while the terminal moraines cover something like twenty square miles of country.

The erratic nature of the materials of these great rubbish-heaps was distinctly pointed out by De Saussure (*Voyages*, §§ 974-978); their true origin was subsequently indicated by Messrs. Studer (1844) and Guyot (1847); and the excellent account of

---

* See General Map.   † I am indebted for this fact to Professor Gastaldi.

‡ *Revue des Deux Mondes.*

them which has recently been published by Professors Martins and Gastaldi leaves nothing to be desired either in accuracy or completeness.* It is not my purpose, therefore, to enter into a description of them, but only to discuss some considerations arising out of the facts which have been already mentioned.

It has been proved beyond doubt that these gigantic mounds around Ivrea are actually the moraines of a glacier (now extinct) which occupied the valley of Aosta ; and it is indisputable that there are boulders from Mont Blanc amongst them. The former facts certify that the glacier was of enormous size, and the latter that it must have existed for a prodigious length of time.

The height of *la Serra* indicates the *depth* of the glacier. It does not fix the depth absolutely, inasmuch as its crest must have been degraded during the thousands of years which have elapsed since the retreat of the ice ; and, further, it is possible that some portions of the surface of the glacier may have been considerably elevated above the moraine when it was at its maximum altitude. Anyhow, at the mouth of the valley of Aosta, the thickness of the glacier must have been at least 2000 feet, and its width, at that part, five miles and a quarter.

The boulders from Mont Blanc, upon the plain below Ivrea, assure us that the glacier which transported them existed for a prodigious length of time. Their present distance from the cliffs from which they were derived is about 420,000 feet, and if we assume that they travelled at the rate of 400 feet per annum, their journey must have occupied them no less than 1055 years ! In all probability they did not travel so fast. But even if they were to be credited with a quicker rate of motion, the length of time which their journey must have taken will be sufficient for my purposes.†

* *Essai sur les terrains superficiels de la Vallée du Po*, extrait du Bulletin de la Société Géologique de France, 1850.

† See Forbes' *Occasional Papers on the Theory of Glaciers*, pp. 193-95, and *Travels through the Alps of Savoy*, 2d ed. pp. 86-7, for information bearing upon the mean annual motion of existing Alpine glaciers. In the former work an account is given of the discovery of the remains of a knapsack ten years after it had been

The space of 1055 years, however, by no means represents the duration of the life of the glacier of Aosta. It may have existed for immense periods both anterior and posterior to the journeys of the Mont Blanc boulders. The frontal terminal moraines, which stretch from Caluso to Viverone (a distance of more than ten miles), are evidence that the snout of the glacier remained stationary, or nearly so, for a length of time which must at least be estimated by centuries, and probably extended over thousands of years. These moraines constitute important chains of hills whose bases are several miles across, and which attain a height of more than a thousand feet ; and, as they were formed by the gradual and slow spreading out of the medial and lateral moraines, it is evident that they were not built up in a day.

Moreover, when the glacier of Aosta shrank away from Ivrea, its retrogression may have been comparatively rapid, or it may have been conducted with extreme deliberation. But, under any circumstances, the extinction of such a tremendous body of ice must have extended over many years, and for a portion of that time a large part of the mass must have been advancing down the valley, although the snout of the glacier was retreating, and although the entire mass was diminishing in volume. If the time is

dropped in a crevasse, at a horizontal distance of 4300 feet from the place at which it had been lost, showing an average annual motion of 430 feet. In the latter work there is a relation of the recovery of the remains of a ladder used by De Saussure, which had travelled about 13,000 feet in 44 years, or 295 feet per annum. Forbes says that the first of these two examples is better ascertained in all its particulars than the other. It should be observed that the knapsack in question made the descent of the well-known " ice-fall " of the Glacier de Talèfre, and that there was a difference of level between the place at which it was lost and that at which it was found of 1145 feet ; that is to say, it descended one foot in every four that it advanced. This rapid descent undoubtedly accelerates the motion of the Glacier de Talèfre. The town of Ivrea, on the other hand, is 768 feet (Ball) above the level of the sea, while Entrèves (at the foot of Mont Blanc) is 4216 feet (Mieulet). So that the glacier which once spread over the sites of these two places (which are about 65 miles apart) descended by an average gradient of almost exactly 1 in 100. This moderate rate of inclination would as certainly tend to retard the motion of the glacier.

2 s

considered which was consumed during this phase of its life, and the time which elapsed during its prolonged sojourn at Ivrea, and the time which passed before it attained its maximum dimensions, it must be conceded that the period of 1055 years was, in all probability, only a *small* portion of the epoch during which the Valley of Aosta sustained the grinding of this enormous mass of ice.

Let us confine ourselves to certainties. Here, then, was a glacier which flowed down the Valley of Aosta for more than a thousand years, having a thickness of 2000 feet,* a width of several miles, and a length of eighty miles. The existing glaciers of the Alps do not approach these dimensions, and even in the period when the ice-streams of Europe had so great an extension there were very few which surpassed them. Still fewer, perhaps, existed for so long a period, and there are probably only one or two—such as the ancient glacier of the Rhone—which have received as much attention and have been as carefully studied. For these reasons it seems to me to be more advantageous to refer to it than to instances more imperfectly known and more open to doubt; and I have selected it, on account of these reasons, as a valley which should afford strong testimony in support of the theories which assert that the valleys and many of the lake-basins of the Alps have been excavated by glaciers.

The latter of these two theories was communicated to the Geological Society, by Professor Ramsay, on March 5, 1862.† It received much attention, and excited much criticism. I am not aware that Professor Ramsay replied to any of his critics, excepting Sir Roderick Murchison and Sir Charles Lyell. But in answer to the objections which were raised against the reception of his theory

---

* This is understating the case. The thickness of the glacier exceeded 2000 feet at the *mouth* of the valley, where it had a width of 5¼ miles. In the valley itself, where the width was less, the thickness appears to have been considerably more than 2000 feet.

† Professor Ramsay's paper was printed in the *Quarterly Journal Geol. Soc.*, August 1862. The germs of the Professor's theory are to be found in his *Old Glaciers of Switzerland and North Wales*, 1860, pp. 86, 107, 109, 110.

by these distinguished geologists, he published two papers in the *Philosophical Magazine ;* * and, in endeavouring to present my reader with a *résumé* of the Professor's views, I shall draw from these papers as freely as from his original memoir, for they afford amplification and elucidation of his argument. †

Professor Ramsay said, in opening his case, " There is no point in physical geography more difficult to account for than the origin of most lakes. When thought about at all, it is easy to see that lakes are the result of the formation of hollows, a great proportion of which are true *rock-basins*, that is to say, in hollows entirely surrounded by solid rocks, the waters not being retained by loose detritus." ‡ It is in reference to such ones alone that his theory is propounded. He then went on to state, in especial reference to lakes of this class in the Alps—

§ 1. "That the theory of an area of *special subsidence* for each lake is untenable.

§ 2. That none of them lie in lines of *gaping fracture* (rents and fissures).

§ 3. That none of them occupy simple synclinal basins formed by the mere disturbance of the strata after the close of the Miocene epoch."§

And he therefore argued that they must have been produced by erosion ; but

§ 4. They do not lie in hollows of common watery erosion, nor can they be effects of marine denudation.

He consequently concluded, "If we have disposed of these hypotheses for the formation of such hollows, what is left ?

§ 5. The only remaining agent is the denuding power of ice." ‖

He then proved that, in the Alps and elsewhere,

* October 1864, and April 1865.

† I shall also occasionally refer to his *Physical Geology and Geography of Great Britain*, and to *Old Glaciers of Switzerland*, etc.

‡ *Physical Geology and Geography of Great Britain*, p. 86.

§ *Proc. Geol. Soc.*, Aug. 1862, p. 200.   ‖ *Physical Geology and Geography*, p. 88.

§ 6. "Each of the lakes lies in an area once covered by a vast glacier."*

And went on to reason—

§ 7. "If a glacier can round, polish, and cover with striations the rocks over which it passes—if, flowing from its caverns, it can charge rivers thickly with the finest mud, then it can wear away its rocky floor and sides." †

§ 8. He assumed that glaciers are competent to produce lake-basins, and that they have done so by scooping out softer parts of the country, leaving hollows surrounded by a framework of harder rocks ; "but perhaps more generally they (the rock-basins) were formed by the greater thickness and weight, and consequently proportionally greater grinding pressure of glacier-ice in particular areas,"‡ "the situations of which may have been determined by accidental circumstances, the clue to which is lost, from our inability perfectly to reconstruct the original forms of the glaciers."§

The particular manner in which he supposed the great lake-basins of the Alps were formed was as follows :—

§ 9. "It will be evident that when the general inclination of a valley was comparatively steep, a glacier could have had no opportunity of cutting for itself any special basin-shaped hollows. Its course, with a difference, is like that of a torrent. But in a flat-bottomed part of a valley, or in a comparative plain that lies at the base of a mountain range, the case is not the same. For instance, to take an extreme case, if a glacier tumble over a slope of 45°, no one would dream of the ice-flow producing any special effect, except that in the long run, the upper edge of the rock that forms the cataract being worn away, its average angle would be lowered. And so of minor slopes ; if the ice flowing fast (for a glacier) rendered the rocky surface underneath unequal, such inequalities could not become great and permanent ; for the rapidly-flowing ice

---

* *Proc. Geol. Soc.*, p. 199.　　† *Phil. Mag.*, October 1864, p. 303.
‡ *Proc. Geol. Soc.*, 1862, p. 188.　　§ *Ibid.* p. 200.

would attack the projecting parts with greater power and effect than the minor hollows, and so preserve an approximate uniformity, or an average angle of moderate inclination.   But when a monstrous glacier descended into a comparative plain, or into a low flat valley, the case was different.   There, to use homely phrases, the ice had time to select soft places for excavation, and there, if from the confluence of large glaciers, or for other reasons, the downward pressure of the ice was of extra amount, the excavating effect, I contend, must have been unusually great in special areas, and have resulted in the formation of rock-bound hollows."*

He accounted for the deep parts of the lakes by supposing that—

§ 10. "The grinding action lasted after a glacier had retired above the position of the present lake-barrier, so that the waste of the rocky floor being long continued, by degrees the glacier wore out a depression deeper and deeper, till, on its final retirement, the space once occupied by ice became filled with the water drainage of the valley."†

The shallowness at their mouths was thus explained :—

§ 11. As the glaciers "progressed and melted, the ice must have been thinner, and must have exercised less erosive power than where it was thick, whence the gradual slope of the bottom of these lakes towards their outflows."‡

§ 12. "Therefore I have been forced to the conclusion, from a critical examination of many of the lakes in and around the Alps, that their basins were scooped out by the great glaciers of the glacial period."§

The astonishment which Professor Ramsay's theory created had not subsided when Professor Tyndall brought forward opinions of an even bolder character,|| and avowed his belief that the *valleys* of

---

* *Phil. Mag.*, October 1864, p. 305.   ‡ *Phil. Mag.*, April 1865, p. 298.
† *Old Glaciers*, pp. 104-5.   § *Phys. Geol. and Geog.* p. 90.
|| *Phil. Mag.* Sept. 1862.

the Alps had been (entirely?) excavated by glaciers !   His summing up was as follows :—

"That such an agent was competent to plough out the Alpine valleys cannot, I think, be doubted ; while the fact that during the ages which have elapsed since its disappearance the ordinary denuding action of the atmosphere has been unable, in most cases, to obliterate even the superficial traces of the glaciers, suggests the incompetence of that action to produce the same effect.   That the glaciers have been the real excavators seems to me far more probable than the supposition that they merely filled valleys which had been previously formed by water denudation.   Indeed the choice lies between these two suppositions : shall we assume that glaciers filled valleys which were previously formed by what would undoubtedly be a weaker agent ? or shall we conclude that they have been the excavators which have furrowed the uplifted land with the valleys which now intersect it ?   I do not hesitate to accept the latter view."—*Phil. Mag.*, Sept. 1862, p. 172.

Except for the character of the magazine in which Dr. Tyndall's paper appeared, it might have been supposed that he was poking fun at his readers and at Professor Ramsay.   For although to some persons he might have seemed to be supporting the views of the Professor, he was, in reality, advancing opinions which were directly opposed to them.   Professor Ramsay promptly repudiated this doubtful extension of his theory.   Indeed, he could hardly do otherwise, after having spoken of "the well-ascertained fact, that *previous to the Tertiary glacial epoch,* most of the grander contours of hill and valley were in Britain (and elsewhere in Europe and America), *nearly the same as now.*"* He now repeated the same statement in slightly different words.   "The evidence is imperfect ; but such as it is, it gives much more than a hint that the large valleys were in their main features approximately as deep as now, before they were filled with ice;"† and, further, he produced in evidence a potent reason for declining to believe that the Valley of Aosta had been excavated by glaciers.   This latter passage will presently be quoted at length, on account of its importance.‡

For a time Dr. Tyndall made no sign in reply, but, in October

* *Old Glaciers of Wales,* p. 94.   † *Phil. Mag.* Nov. 1862, p. 379.
‡ See pp. 341-2.

1864, he communicated another paper to the *Philosophical Magazine,* in which he modified his views to a certain extent (and made the important admission that it was perhaps impossible to say whether water or ice had produced the greatest amount of erosion), although upon the whole he adhered to his former assertions. This paper contained one remarkable passage; remarkable, because it partly showed the workings of its author's mind, and because it was, apparently, intended to controvert Professor Ramsay's theory. It was as follows :—

" On the higher slopes and plateaus—in the region of cols—the power (of glaciers) is not fully developed ; but lower down tributaries unite, erosion is carried on with increased vigour, and the excavation gradually reaches a maximum. Lower still the elevations diminish and the slopes become more gentle ; the cutting power gradually relaxes, and *finally the eroding agent quits the mountains altogether, and the grand effects which it produced in the earlier portions of its course entirely disappear.*" *—Phil. Mag.*, Oct. 1864, p. 264.

That is to say, precisely in the situations where Professor Ramsay required glaciers to produce the greatest effects, Dr. Tyndall asserted they produced none whatever ! Professor Ramsay did not allow much time to elapse before he contradicted these statements categorically.

" Every physicist," said he, " knows that when such a body as glacier-ice descends a slope, the direct vertical pressure of the ice will be proportional to its thickness and weight and the angle of the slope over which it flows. If the angle be 5°, the weight and erosive power of a given thickness of ice will be so much, if 10° so much less, if 20° less still, till at length, if we may imagine the fall to be over a vertical wall of rock, the pressure against the wall (except accidentally) will be *nil. But when the same vast body of ice has reached the plain,* then motion and erosion would cease, were it not for pressure from behind (excepting what little motion forward and sideways might be due to its own weight). This pressure, however, must have been constant as long as supplies of snow fell on the mountains, and therefore the inert mass in the plain was constantly urged onwards ; and because of its vertical pressure *its direct erosive power would necessarily be proportional to its thickness, and greater than when it lay on a slope ;* for it would grate across the rocks, as

_____

* The italics are not in the original.

it were, unwillingly and by compulsion, instead of finding its way onwards more or less by virtue of gravity. *Indeed the idea is forced on the mind, that the sluggish ice would have a tendency to heap itself up just outside the mouth of the valley, and there attain an unusual thickness, thus exercising, after its descent, an extra erosive power."* *—*Phil. Mag.*, April 1865, p. 287.

Professor Tyndall does not appear to have found the reply convincing. He is reported to have said at the last Birmingham meeting of the British Association, "that he was convinced that the glaciers of the Alps were competent to scoop out the valleys of the Alps," † and I am unaware that his opinions have undergone any alteration since that time. In 1869 he gave a hard side-blow to Professor Ramsay, in *Macmillan's Magazine*, by proving that some existing Alpine glaciers exercise little or no erosion upon their beds near and at their terminations (snouts), because at such places they are *almost stationary.*‡

It is impossible to criticise these two theories at the same moment. Both of them agree in attributing enormous powers of excavation to glaciers, but they disagree totally and completely as to the *modus operandi* by which the effects were produced. They differ even in their general conclusions. One asserts that the greatest effects were produced upon the plains, and that very little was done amongst the mountains ; whilst the other declares that the mountains owe their actual forms to the carving of glaciers, and that the plains did not suffer at all ! There is no wonder that the unenlightened public enquired, " Who shall decide between the disagreements of these doctors ?" But it *is* surprising to find numerous persons accepting as gospel truth the contradictory *dicta* of these eminent men, and speaking and writing as if it were

* Comparison of the sentences placed in italics, with the preceding one from Dr. Tyndall, will show how irreconcilable were the opinions of these two writers.

† *Birmingham Daily Post*, September 13, 1865.

‡ It must not be understood that anything of the nature of a controversy was carried on, in the magazines cited, by the two Professors. They did not refer to each other by name ; but it was impossible to read the passages which have been quoted, without feeling that they were intended to be replies to objections on the other side.

established that lake-basins and mountain-valleys have been excavated by glaciers.

It is not requisite to decide between all the differences contained in these two theories, in order to arrive at a tolerably correct judgment upon the general conclusions. Professor Ramsay, for example, attributes the production of the greatest effects to the *weight* of glaciers. Professor Tyndall, on the other hand, assigns most power to the *motion.* I shall ignore these points, because I have no data from which to arrive at a satisfactory decision, and because it is not necessary for them to be mixed up with a discussion of the question, Were the valleys of the Alps excavated by glaciers? For the consideration of this subject, let us now return to the Valley of Aosta.

The town of Ivrea is placed at the mouth of, but not actually within the valley, and several miles of flat, dusty road have to be traversed before it is entered. Upon this portion of the country civilisation is doing its best to efface the traces of the glacial period. Cultivation of the soil disturbs all deposits, and the hammers of the masons destroy the erratics. After quitting Ivrea, almost the first object of interest is the castle of Montalto, perched on a commanding crag, nearly in the centre of the valley. Thence, from Settimo Vittone up to the foot of the existing glaciers of the range of Mont Blanc, there are traces of glacier-action upon each hand. The road need not be quitted to seek for them ;—they are *everywhere.* I refer especially to the rocks *in situ.* The rock-forms called *roches moutonnées* are universally distributed, and it is needless, at the present moment, to point to any in particular. Although of varying degrees of resistancy, they have, upon the whole, stood the weathering remarkably well of the thousands of years which have elapsed since the glacier covered them. The floor of the valley, generally speaking, has not been lowered since that time, by the combined agencies of sun, frost, and water, to any appreciable extent. The forms which the *roches moutonnées* present to-day, are the forms which they presented, perhaps, ten thousand

2 T

years ago. Many of those which are *freely* exposed to the atmosphere retain a high polish and fine striations. If the soil were to be removed that covers the flatter portions of the valley we, should doubtless find *higher* polish, and still *finer* striations. Nevertheless, those which are visible remain so perfect, that it is certain weathering has done exceedingly little to alter their contours, and we may argue regarding them as if their icy covering had been but just removed. This point is of no small importance ; and, it seems to me, it may be demonstrated from the very contours of these glaciated rocks, that the valley was *not* excavated by glaciers, and indeed, that it was eroded by glaciers only to a very limited extent.

For the forms which are called *moutonnées* preponderate very largely. The rocks which I have ventured to term *roches nivelées*, are comparatively rare,* although they are sufficiently numerous to show that the valley was subjected to severe grinding for a great length of time. They are found upon the floor of the valley, or in places where it narrows, or upon the lower sides of little ravines (now watercourses) which the glacier had to cross, into which it was forced down when in the act of crossing, and out of which it escaped by mounting the opposite bank. In brief, they are found precisely where they should be found. In those places where the thickness of the ice was greatest, and where the motion was (probably) quickest ; where the glacier was compressed laterally, so that its power was distributed over a smaller area of rock-surface ; and where erosion had produced ruts into which the glacier was pressed down, and out of which it could only extricate itself by a severe struggle.

Throughout the valley, in conjunction with the *roches moutonnées*, there are innumerable *angular rock-surfaces* which seem never to have been abraded by glacier. These *lee-sides†* are found right up to the bases of the existing glaciers. That is to say, they are found in spots which were not only covered by ice during the whole of the period in which the ancient glacier of Aosta

* See p. 146.   † See p. 145.

extended to Ivrea, but have been covered by it in quite recent times. Glacier moved over them, probably, ages before the great glacier filled the valley; and, for aught we know to the contrary, it has done the same almost ever since. Yet, to all appearance, ice has never *touched* the *lee-sides*, or, if it has done so, it has been done so tenderly, that the marks have been subsequently obliterated.

Now, whilst it may readily be admitted that atmospheric action is capable of completely effacing feeble traces of glacier-erosion,* we cannot in the present instances admit any more. The contiguous surfaces to the *lee-sides* which are highly polished and bearing fine striations, show that sun, frost, and water, have done very little upon them since the ice departed. It would be absurd to suppose that these powers have been able to rub out *all* traces of ice-action (if the traces were other than very feeble) in one square yard, when in the next, upon the same rock, they have been unable even to roughen the surface, or get rid of fine scratches. It is doubly impossible to suppose that the rock-surfaces were uniformly ground down by ice, and that all the inequalities seen at the present time are the result of subsequent decomposition. I do not think any one will have the hardihood to assert the contrary.

It is stated, therefore—1. That the glacier-eroded rocks in the Valley of Aosta are chiefly characterised by *convexity*, and principally belong to the class termed *moutonnées*. 2. That there are examples of *roches nivelées* in the valley; that they are rare in comparison with the *roches moutonnées*; and that they are mostly found upon the floor of the valley, or in places where it is narrowest, or where unusual obstructions have occurred. 3. That there are innumerable angular rock-surfaces (intermingled with these glaciated surfaces upon the floor and on the sides of the valley) which cannot have been produced since glacier covered the rocks. For the bearing of these facts upon Dr. Tyndall's theory, I must now recapitulate from Chapter VI.

In the preliminary remarks at pp. 142-3, after appealing to

* Or, given sufficient time, of destroying highly-glaciated surfaces.

Studer's observation that glacier-erosion was distinguished by the production of convex forms, I proceeded to show that such forms naturally resulted from glacier working upon surfaces which had been antecedently broken up by diverse actions ; and pointed out that when glacier-action was long continued, the obliteration of all angular surfaces, and of almost all curves, was inevitable. I concluded, therefore (and am prepared to accept all the responsibility which attaches to the conclusion), that the convexity of *roches moutonnées* was to be regarded as a proof that no great amount of glacier-erosion had occurred ; that rock-surfaces with a *small* degree of convexity, which had obviously been glaciated, indicated a *greater* erosion ; and that the degree of flatness bore a direct relation to the amount of power which had been employed. And further, that when unworn, angular rock-surfaces were found in the immediate vicinity of glaciated rocks, they were to be regarded as additional and confirmatory evidence that the depth of matter taken away by the glacier could not have been important, unless it could be shown that the angularity was due to subsequent operations.

Applying these conclusions to the case of the Valley of Aosta, we find—1. That as recent denudation has been unequal, throughout the valley, to obliterate polish and fine striations on the rocks, we are unable to believe that the vast number of angular surfaces which are found in contiguity to the abraded ones can possibly have been produced subsequently to the retreat of the glacier. 2. Their existence in connection with innumerable convex glaciated surfaces, throughout the valley, is irrefutable evidence that the valley was not excavated by glaciers. 3. The comparative scarcity of *roches nivelées*, combined with the other evidence, affords a strong presumption that the so-called *excavation* has not amounted, throughout the valley, to more than a very few feet of depth.

Hitherto, I have chiefly appealed to the bed (or floor) of the valley. Almost equally stubborn facts are obtainable from the slopes of its bounding mountains. If the valley had been excavated by glaciers, very emphatic traces would have been left behind *every-*

where,—above as well as *below.* I contend that if the entire valley had been excavated by glaciers, the surface of the rocks would have been as smooth as glass, from one end to the other, when the ice retired.* Now, I have frankly admitted (note to p. 323) that, given sufficient time, sun, frost, and water, are capable of destroying highly glaciated surfaces ; but I will not admit the possibility of such perfection of glaciation as I have just indicated being completely effaced (say, at heights exceeding 9000 feet), while a few yards lower down ice-marks are seen, and seen everywhere. For it is well known to all who have scrambled amongst the Alps, that those mountains are not glaciated from summit to base. The marks of the great glaciers of the olden time extend up to a certain height, and then they cease. This is the case throughout the Alps generally. The limit of glaciation is usually placed at about 9000 feet. Above this limit the mountains are more or less rugged and angular. Below it, the traces of the glacial period are more or less apparent. Above it, you seek in vain for glacier-eroded rocks.† Below it, they are found almost everywhere. Here is the evidence of Agassiz upon this point :—

" Every mountain-side in the Alps is inscribed with these ancient characters, recording the level of the ice in past times. . . . Thousands of feet above the present level of the glacier, far up towards their summits, we find the sides of the mountains furrowed, scratched, and polished, in exactly the same manner as the surfaces over which the glaciers pass at present. These marks are as legible and clear to one who is familiar with glacial traces as are hieroglyphics to the Egyptian scholar ; indeed, more so,—for he not only recognizes their presence, but reads their meaning at a glance. *Above the line at which these indications cease, the edges of the rocks are sharp and angular, the surface of the mountain rough, unpolished, and absolutely devoid of*

---

* See p. 152.

† It is not, of course, meant that there are no traces of glacier-action above 9000 feet, upon rocks bounding, or surrounded by, the *existing* glaciers. There are, for example, many islands of rock in the Alps, surrounded by glacier, at elevations considerably exceeding 9000 feet, which are highly glaciated. I refer to those mountains which are away from the existing glaciers, and which have never been influenced by them.

*all those marks resulting from glacial action.** On the Alps these traces are visible to a height of nine thousand feet."—*Atlantic Monthly*, Feb. 1864.

If these facts mean anything, they mean that the great glaciers of the glacial period did not extend above this limit. For I cannot suppose that Dr. Tyndall is a believer in the childish notion of the late Dollfus-Ausset, that glaciers are, and were, permanently frozen to the rocks at heights exceeding 9000 feet, and therefore do not, and did not, erode them !† If that idea is correct, why are there any crevasses at heights exceeding 9000 feet? In what manner is the continuity of the glaciers maintained, if their lower portions move down, whilst their upper ones are immovable? Dr. Tyndall is far too well acquainted with glaciers to believe any such absurdity. I maintain that this evidence (although scarcely so conclusive as that which has preceded it) affords strong grounds for believing that the valleys of the Alps were never completely filled by glaciers, and therefore that the valleys were not excavated by glaciers.

The evidence from the *mouths* of the valleys of the Alps is not less hostile to Dr. Tyndall's theory. For, observe, 1. The glaciers existed for a briefer period at the mouths of the valleys than at their upper portions. 2. The glaciers must have moved there, as a rule, at a slower rate than at the upper portions ; because, as a rule, the gradients at the mouths were more moderate, and frequently (as in the case of the Valley of Aosta), there was a dead level. 3. The glaciers had usually received, before arriving at the mouths of the valleys, the whole of their most important affluents, and must have been rapidly diminishing in volume. The conclusion which is inevitable from these considerations is, that the glaciers must have exercised less erosion at the mouths of the valleys than at their upper portions ; and this conclusion agrees very well with that arrived at by Dr. Tyndall himself, namely—" Lower still the elevations diminish and the slopes become more gentle ; the cutting

---

* The italics are not in the original.

† See *Matériaux pour l'étude des Glaciers*, vol. i. part iii. p. 11. The same idea is repeated in many other places in the same work.

power gradually relaxes, and finally the eroding agent quits the mountains altogether, and the grand effects which it produced in the earlier portion of its course entirely disappear."* But does this conclusion agree with the fact that the valleys are usually wider —much wider—at their mouths than elsewhere, and that the beds of the valleys at their mouths are at a lower level than at the upper extremities? If the glaciers had flowed *up* the valleys, these facts might be explicable ; but they are unintelligible if the valleys were excavated by glaciers which flowed *down* them.

The mouths, the beds, the walls, and the terminations of the valleys, and the slopes of the mountains which bound them, proclaim alike that the present modelling of the Alps has been only slightly modified by glaciers. It would, however, be unreasonable to conclude, because such is the case, that glaciers are incompetent to excavate valleys under *any* circumstances; and, before taking leave of Professor Tyndall, it is only due to him to examine his opinions upon the subject. He is, like Professor Ramsay, a great believer in soft places. He believes that glaciers not only erode soft rocks more rapidly than hard ones (which is a reasonable belief), but he considers that all the chief inequalities which are now seen in valleys that have been eroded by glaciers are due to the greater or less resistancy of the rocks to the action of *the ice.* " Were its bed uniform in the first instance, the glacier would, in my opinion, *produce* the inequalities."† Now, I could not differ greatly from Dr. Tyndall, if he were to say that glaciers must erode soft rocks more rapidly than hard ones, and that they might, in consequence, ultimately produce inequalities, if set to work upon a smooth surface containing both hard and soft places. But he goes far beyond this. It is necessary for him to explain how it comes to pass that such masses are left behind as that at Montalto, at the entrance of the Valley of Aosta, or those upon which the castles of Sion stand. The valleys of Aosta and of the Rhone, he says, have been excavated by glaciers, yet here are these obstinate crags stand-

* *Phil. Mag.*, Oct. 1864, p. 264.   † *Phil. Mag.*, Oct. 1864, p. 266.

ing in the very centres of the valleys. They must have been exposed to the full force of the glaciers ; nay, the ice-streams were evidently split by them, and had to flow upon either side and over them. " Assuredly," says Dr. Tyndall, " a glacier *is* competent to remove such barriers, and they probably have been ground down in some cases thousands of feet. But being of a more resisting material than the adjacent rock, they were not ground down to the level of that rock."* Examination of such masses has led me to form a very different opinion. The contours of their rocks, upon the sides opposed to the direction of the flow of the glaciers, are frequently flatter, and suggestive of a greater degree of abrasion, than the adjacent and lower rocks. They have been lowered *more*, not less, than their surroundings. Yet the indications are, as a rule, that these obtrusive crags have only been lowered to a trifling extent, and, most certainly, not thousands of feet. Still, let us suppose, for the sake of argument, that the adjacent rocks were actually softer, and *were* ground down a hundred or more feet upon each side of the hard crags, which, in consequence, became that amount above the level of their surroundings. The adjacent rocks would then, according to my opinion, have been prodigiously eroded ; all their angles would have been obliterated ; they would have become exceeding flat, and such forms as they would present would be characteristic of a high degree of glaciation. Yet we find that such is *not* the case. The rocks adjacent to the crags are frequently *less* flat, *less* abraded than the crags,† and, to all appearance, their surfaces have not been lowered more than a very few feet. The conclusions are inevitable in such cases that the adjacent rocks have suffered *less* than the obtrusive crags, and that any real or imaginary softness of rock has not assisted glacier-erosion to the extent assumed by Dr. Tyndall.

The enormous amount of excavation assumed by Dr. Tyndall is further accounted for by him upon the supposition that glaciers

* *Phil. Mag.*, Oct. 1864, p. 266.
† I do not know an instance where the reverse is the case.

are competent to "root masses (of rock) bodily away."*   He seems to feel that mere grinding, rasping, and polishing would not be equal to the production of valleys, thousands of feet in depth, in any reasonable length of time, and so invokes this quicker process to get himself out of the difficulty.   When and how Dr. Tyndall became possessed of this extraordinary idea I have no means of telling.   Comparison of the following passages would lead one to suppose that it was acquired posterior to the publication of his *Glaciers of the Alps* :—

"The lighter débris is scattered by the winds far and wide over the glacier, sullying the purity of its surface.   Loose shingle rattles at intervals down the sides of the mountains, and falls upon the ice where it touches the rocks.   Large rocks are continually let loose, which come jumping from ledge to ledge, the cohesion of some being proof against the shocks which they experience ; while others, when they hit the rocks, burst like bomb-shells, and shower their fragments upon the ice.   Thus the glacier is incessantly loaded along its borders with the ruins of the mountains which limit it."— *Glaciers of the Alps*, Chapter on Moraines, p. 263 (1860).

"In the vast quantities of moraine-matter which cumbers many of the valleys we have also suggestions as to the magnitude of the erosion which has taken place.   This moraine-matter, moreover, *is only in part* derived from the falling of rocks from the eminences upon the glacier ; it is also *in great part derived from the grinding and ploughing-out of the glacier itself.*   This accounts for the magnitude of many of these ancient moraines, which date from a period when almost all the mountains were covered with ice and snow, and when consequently the quantity of moraine-matter derived from the naked crests cannot have been considerable." †— *Phil. Mag.*, Oct. 1864, p. 271.

It has been already shown (pp. 325-6) that the notion that the mountains were completely covered by glaciers (or anything like completely covered) is erroneous, and the evidence which leads to that conclusion is clearly supported by the fact that a great proportion (I think it may be said *the* great proportion) of the materials are *angular* which compose the moraines of the past, as well as of

---

* *Phil. Mag.*, Oct. 1864, p. 265.   † See p. 245.

the existing glaciers of the Alps.* Their angularity is a certain proof that they were borne *upon* the glaciers, and were not transported *under* them. For, if they had been forced along underneath the ice, they would most certainly have become, at the least, subangular, or rounded or scratched. It is well known that this is what takes place at the present time in regard to débris underneath glaciers, and that the pebbles and boulders which are moved along in such a way acquire a character of their own which is unmistakable. The moraines, then, do not support, but clearly reject, Dr. Tyndall's notion. Nor is the evidence of the rocks from which he supposes that masses have been "rooted away" less distinctly against him. How could these masses be broken away without angular surfaces being left behind? and how is it that in those places where glacier-action has been *most* powerful angular surfaces are *most wanting?* Dr. Tyndall appeals to the *magnitude* of the old glaciers, and to the enormous *pressure* which they exerted upon their beds, to explain his " rooting-away," as confidently as if his case was completely proved thereby. Yet, in those places where glaciers are and have been the greatest, and where their pressure has been the most tremendous, and exerted for the greatest length of time, we find the rocks which have been worked upon are the most highly polished, the most flat in contour, and the most devoid of all angularity whatsoever!

It is clear, therefore, that the theory of " soft places," as applied by Dr. Tyndall, cannot be sustained, and does not in the least assist us to determine how far glaciers are competent to excavate valleys. The idea is plausible that soft rocks must suffer under the grinding of glaciers more rapidly than hard ones, and may be admitted ; but it will be shown presently that there are things to be said upon the other side. The notion that glaciers root away

---

* I am, of course, aware that there are glacial deposits in Great Britain, and elsewhere, in which sub-angular and scratched stones are largely in excess of those which are simply angular. The manner in which such deposits were formed is not yet clearly understood.

masses of rock incessantly, or to any great extent, must be unhesi-
tatingly rejected as being opposed to reason and to facts.* However, " confining the action of glaciers to the simple rubbing away
of the rocks, and allowing them sufficient time to act, it is not a
matter of opinion, but a physical certainty, that they" would produce cavities or depressions of one sort or another.   Given *eternity*,
glaciers might even grind out valleys of a peculiar kind.   Such
valleys would bear remarkably little resemblance to the valleys of
the Alps.   They might be interesting, but they would be miserably
unpicturesque. The hob-nailed boots of the Alpine tourists would be
useless in them ; we should have to employ felt slippers or skates.

I have advanced only a few of the more obvious objections to
Dr. Tyndall's theory.   Many others might be urged, for the position taken up by the Doctor has been from the first an essentially false one, and has permitted him to be attacked from nearly
every direction.   Had he confined himself to stating that glaciers
were competent to excavate valleys, without offering examples, and
without attempting to show how they would do it, many persons
might have differed from him, but would have done so chiefly *in
degree*.   The declaration that the valleys of the Alps had been so
excavated was a statement of a much more advanced and of a
much graver nature, and I cannot but think that in making it Dr.
Tyndall has materially retarded the progress of knowledge.   There
are many persons, I am convinced, who would learn with satisfaction
that he repudiates a doctrine which can be disproved in a multitude of ways, and which is flatly contradicted by a host of facts.

Whatever may be the popular opinion about Professor Ramsay's theory regarding the formation of rock-basins, its author is
entitled to credit for having attempted to grapple with an acknow-
ledged difficulty, and to be congratulated upon the number of valu-

---

* It has been already admitted (§ 5, p. 145) that the minor asperities of rocks
suffer, and may be actually crushed or scraped away. That this happens cannot be
doubted, but this (comparatively) speedily comes to an end.   It is mere brushing of
the surface preparatory to polishing.

able facts which he has elicited. Exceptions can be taken to it, of course. It may be asked, at the very outset, Is it absolutely necessary to accept this dogma that the *only* remaining agent is the denuding power of ice ? Have we arrived at the end of all knowledge ? And the cogency of the reasoning may be doubted by which the conclusion is derived, that rock-basins have necessarily been excavated by ice, because they are commonly found in districts which were formerly covered by glacier. It may be said that the connection which has been shown between the two* may be nothing more than an accidental coincidence, and that, taken by itself, it is scarcely more convincing than that icebergs have made the Arctic seas, because those seas are full of icebergs. Such objections, however, do not touch Professor Ramsay's main arguments ; and I think that any one who honestly endeavours to master them will feel that they are very ingenious, and that they are by no means easy to refute.

It is impossible to deny a certain limited power of erosion to glaciers ; and it is difficult to see why a great glacier should not make a hollow (a shallow one) if it were to come down upon a plain, and work there for a long time. For example, let A C B D, in the accompanying diagram, be a transverse section of a glacier which is moving over level ground, A G D F B. The glacier would naturally be thickest towards the centre, and its motion would probably be greatest in the same neighbourhood. It should therefore erode its bed to a greater extent at or about the point D than anywhere else ; and as the motion and weight of the ice would be greater at or about F and G than at points between F B or G A, so also would the erosion be greater thereabouts. In short, it is reasonable to conclude that in course of time the glacier might form a hollow in its previously level bed, such as is represented by the dotted

* Professor Ramsay claims to be the first who has pointed out this connection. Professor Dana extends the statement still further :—" Another great fact that belongs to the Drift latitudes on all the continents, and may have the same origin, is the occurrence, on the coasts, of fiord valleys,—deep, narrow channels, occupied by the sea, and extending inward often 50 or 100 miles."-- *Manual of Geology*, 1867, p. 541.

line A E B. This would account for the hollowing out of rock-basins across their shorter axes. I do not merely think that this

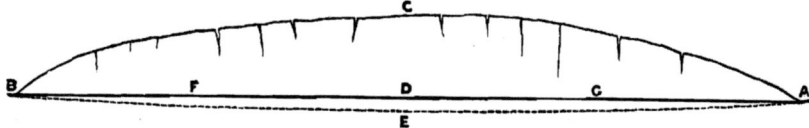

is what *might* happen, but that it is what *must* happen in course of time ; and saying as much is practically admitting the power of glaciers to produce concavities in large areas of rock. It may seem now as if all were conceded that is required by Professor Ramsay. It is not so. His principle appears to me to be sound, but his conclusions entirely unwarrantable. There is not the least doubt that rocks underneath the thicker parts of the existing glaciers are being eroded to a greater extent than those which are covered by a small amount of ice. The same must have happened during the glacial period. But these differences in the depth of the erosion may, I think, be disregarded, because the difference between the maximum and the minimum in any given area would not amount to more than a very few feet ; as the evidence which has already been recounted tends to show that glacier-erosion has been insignificant at any and every part of the valleys; and the valleys, it must always be remembered, were occupied by the glaciers for more time than the plains out of which Professor Ramsay would have us believe that his great lake-basins were excavated.

To the foregoing remarks the Professor has two answers. First, he has the idea that the retardation which a glacier would experience upon its arrival on a plain would tend to "heap-up" the ice (see p. 320). This is no doubt correct. He considers that the glacier would in consequence "attain an unusual thickness, thus exercising, after its descent, an extra erosive power." Here we get into the region of surmises. To this we may demur. For he overlooks, or, at least, does not notice, that the glacier would be melting at a rapid rate, at or near its end, and that, in all probability, the extra ablation would counterbalance whatever thickening might arise from the tendency to " heap-up." The " unusual thickness " by which he gets his " extra erosive power," is entirely conjectural, and, judging by the glaciers of the present time, it is very doubtful if it had any existence whatever. If the Professor could point to a single glacier which is doubled in thickness through retardation, he would materially fortify his argument ; but, in the absence of any such evidence, we may be permitted to doubt if there is much force in his idea.*

Secondly, the great basins which Professor Ramsay believes were excavated by glaciers,† are assumed to have been scooped out of areas filled by especially soft strata, which were removed with comparative facility, and at a rapid rate. Very eminent geologists disbelieve in the existence of these especially soft areas. ‡ Others, again, offer evidence which leads us to believe that some of the great Alpine lake-basins existed *before* the glacial period.§ But let us suppose that they are all wrong, and that the Professor is right. Let us suppose, too, that retardation actually *doubled* the thickness of the glaciers. Taking all this for granted, it is still incomprehensible how the ancient glacier of the Rhone managed to excavate the bed of the Lake of Geneva to the depth of 984 feet (opposite to Evian), when it was unable to remove a tenth part of that amount from the valley of the Rhone (say between Sion and Sierre) ; for it was working for a greater

---

* No one can consult the excellent map which accompanies Martins' and Gastaldi's *Terrains Superficiels* without seeing in a moment, from the disposition of the moraines, that the great glacier of Aosta *spread itself out directly it arrived upon the plain.* Hence, any material thickening through retardation was impossible. It can readily be shown that this *spreading-out* frequently occurs to the glaciers of the present time, when they pass from confined places on to open spaces (places where the valleys widen).

† The basins of the lakes of Geneva, Neuchâtel, Thun, Zug, Lucerne, Zurich, Constance, etc. etc.

‡ For example, see the remarks of Prof. Favre upon the Lake of Geneva, in *Phil. Mag.*, March 1865.

§ Sir Charles Lyell, for example. In regard to the lakes of Zurich, etc., see his *Antiquity of Man*, 3d ed., pp. 314-16.

length of time in the valley, and no doubt with a *higher* rate of motion, than it was upon the bed of the Lake of Geneva.

I have often wondered, considering the extent to which Professors Ramsay and Tyndall lean upon soft places, that they, or some of their adherents, have not thought it worth while to point out examples, upon a small and upon a large scale, of soft rocks which have been eroded by glaciers to a greater extent than harder rocks in their immediate vicinity. If Professor Ramsay is correct in supposing that glaciers wear away soft rocks with *much* greater rapidity than hard ones, it ought to be a very easy thing to produce examples. Yet, as far as I know, not one of the principal writers upon the subject has ever attempted to *prove* that glacier-erosion proceeds at an accelerated rate upon soft rocks, and is retarded by hard ones. It has been repeatedly asserted, or assumed, that such is the case, but proofs have been very rarely advanced.

Whilst this is the case, it has been continually remarked by writers upon glacier-action (who have not, however, attached any particular importance to the fact), that quartz-veins are cut down, by the passage of ice over them, to the level of the rocks in which they are found. Quartz, one of the very hardest of commonly diffused minerals, is unable to resist the grinding of glacier. Its hardness does not prevent its being polished down to the same extent as the much less resistant rocks which enclose it. If it suffered less than its surroundings, it would, of course, protrude. It does not, because it is eroded *equally* with the much softer rock. No distinction is made by the glacier, and the presence of the quartz is not sensible to the touch from any elevation or depression.

If glacier-eroded rocks containing veins of quartz are exposed to the influences of sun, frost, and water, it is not long before the quartz begins to assert its superior resistancy. If it is in gneiss, the gneiss in contact with it speedily suffers. Minute cracks radiate from the junction of the two substances over the surface of the weaker material. Water enters the tiny fissures, and, ex-

panding under the influence of cold, rends away grain by grain,
until at length, as in the accompanying
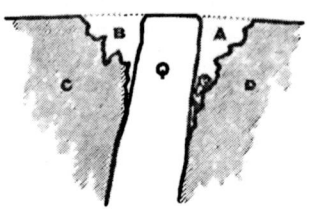
diagram at A and B, little ravines are
formed upon each side of the quartz-
vein Q.*

If, on the other hand, the eroded
rocks continue to experience the grinding of glacier, nothing of this kind
results. The tendency of the quartz to protrude is incessantly
checked, because, at the slightest suspicion of protrusion, it is attacked by the ice with increased power. If by any chance it
becomes elevated above the surrounding rock, it *bears off* the
weight of the ice from the surrounding rock, and this condition
of affairs continues until both quartz and gneiss are brought to the
same level.

There is little difference of opinion about these matters. It is
perfectly well known that projections in the bed of a glacier are
attacked by the ice, and that depressions escape abrasion through the
protection afforded by the eminences.† Hence it is that ultimately
all angles and almost all curves are obliterated from the surfaces of
rocks upon which glaciers work. Hence it is that in a district which
has been severely eroded by glacier we find the rocks more flat—
that is, less convex—than in one which has been less eroded.

It is evident, then, that glacier does not and cannot dig away
into soft places occupying *limited areas*. This is not a matter of
opinion, but a certainty ; and it seems to me to be entirely un-

---

* In Greenland I have seen gneiss cracked away from quartz-veins in glacier-
eroded rocks, in this manner, to a depth of two inches and more. Where the same
veins had been protected from the atmosphere, they were without the little trenches
on each side. To the same effect see Geikie *On Modern Denudation*, Trans. Geol.
Soc. Glasgow, 1868.

† "In descending from the summit of the Weisshorn on the 19th of August last
I found, near the flanks of one of its glaciers, *a portion of the ice completely roofing a
hollow, over which it had been urged without being squeezed into it.*"—Tyndall's *Mountaineering in 1861*, p. 73. Dr. Tyndall's testimony is especially valuable, because he
is by no means prejudiced in favour of the views which I am supporting.

warrantable to assert, in the face of a well-ascertained fact like this, that the pools and small tarns lying in rock-basins (which are numerous in almost all mountainous countries) owe their existence to the excavating power of glacier, merely because glacier has passed over the spots which they occupy ; and, to say the least, to be in-judicious to apply terms like " scooping out" to the rounding and polishing-up of the beds of such pools, because those terms convey an impression that is entirely erroneous. The hollows in which such pools are found would necessarily have been obliterated, not deepened, if the glaciers had worked for a greater length of time.*

Professor Ramsay holds the directly contrary opinion. Unless I am entirely mistaken in regard to his ideas, he supposes that the beds of almost all pools, tarns, and lakes, which lie in true rock-basins, have been scooped out or excavated by glaciers. As a rule he does not consider that these lakes occupy hollows which were formed either entirely or in part through upheaval or subsidence, (either or both), or antecedent erosion, but that the lake-basins are simply holes which glaciers have dug out. How or in what way the glaciers did the work, I have not the most remote idea. I turn the Professor's pages over and over without gaining the slightest clue.† But I gather from the *Proceedings of the Geological Society,*

* Sir Charles Lyell remarks with much force, in the 6th ed. of his *Elements,* p. 170, "Where opportunities are enjoyed of seeing part of a valley from which a glacier has retreated in historical times, no basin-shaped hollows are conspicuous. Dome-shaped protuberances, the *roches moutonnées* before described, are frequent ; but the converse of them, or cup-and-saucer-shaped cavities, are wanting." The justness of these ob-servations is undeniable. The perusal of Professor Ramsay's papers would lead any one personally unacquainted with glacier-eroded rocks to conclude that the reverse was the case—that saucer-shaped hollows were abundant, or, in other words, that concavities predominated.

† I cannot find anything more explicit than this :—"The greater number lie in *rock-basins* formed by the grinding of glacier-ice." This is simple assertion ; now for the proof. "Sometimes in the convolutions of the strata (conjoined with preglacial denudation subsequent to the contortion of the beds) softer parts of the country *may* have been scooped out ; but *perhaps* more generally they were formed by the greater thickness and weight of glacier-ice on *particular areas,* due to *accidents* to which it is now often difficult or impossible to find the clue."—*Proc. Geol. Soc.,* 1862, p. 188.

that it was from the examination of the small pools he first came to
the conclusion that glaciers scooped out basins in rock ; that he
was at first " too timid to include the larger lakes ;" and that becoming convinced the larger lakes occupied true rock-basins, he included them in the category of lakes which had been formed by the
agency of glacier, because glacier alone, in his opinion, is capable of
excavating true rock-basins !

The smaller idea has been shown to be fallacious, and it might
be said that the larger one, which is built upon it, necessarily falls
through. This is scarcely the case. The former deals with square
yards, and the latter with square miles. A glacier we know, as a
matter of fact, polishes down a quartz-vein in the same way as it
does a bed of soft limestone. A plane which is adapted for plan-
ing wood may cut through a nail in a plank whilst taking off a
shaving. But the plane is unable to take a shaving off a solid mass
of iron, and it might be said, with some plausibility, that a glacier
might be equally impotent if it had to work over square miles of
quartz instead of square feet. To form a just idea of the probability
of a glacier producing a lake-basin in one place (in soft strata), when
during the same, or a longer, period, it only slightly erodes the surface at another place (hard strata), we ought to find out the effects
which are actually produced by glaciers when working over a series
of strata of unequal hardness, where the strike of the beds coincides
with the direction of the motion of the ice. The idea, indeed, has
often occurred to me, that insignificant quartz-veins might resist the
grinding of glacier if they were worked upon longitudinally. It
is not, of course, an easy thing to find a vein of quartz which has
been worked upon longitudinally for a considerable distance ; and
I have never observed a better example than that which is described
in the following paragraph.

In 1867, upon the shores of a fiord, about nine miles to the east
of the settlement of Claushavn in North Greenland, I had the good
fortune to discover the finest examples of *roches nivelées* which I have
seen anywhere. The great interior *mer de glace* was near at hand,
and a branch of it closed the inlet with an unbroken wall of ice,

which was nearly a mile across. This branch had formerly filled the fiord, and had apparently covered the place to which I refer at no very remote date. Tremendous evidences of its power had been left behind. The gneiss upon the shores was literally levelled, and extended for hundreds of yards in continuous sheets, with polished surfaces destitute of all detritus, difficult to walk upon, for there was nothing to arrest the feet when they slipped. In these rocks there were two great veins of quartz, each three to four feet thick, which attracted notice at a considerable distance by their excessive brilliancy when the sun fell upon them. These ran roughly parallel to each other for about eighty yards, and throughout that distance their direction had nearly coincided with that in which the glacier had moved. The glacier had passed over them at an angle of about 10°. Upon this quartz my hammer danced and rang, and made scarcely any impression. I chipped away the gneiss without difficulty. The glacier had worked upon two substances of unequal resistancy. Yet, if a line had been stretched between the highest points across any hundred feet of these sheets of rock, I do not think that any part of the rock would have been depressed one foot below the cord. The quartz, instead of standing up in ridges, as I thought it might have done, was cut down to the same level as the gneiss ; the keenest scrutiny could not detect the least difference.

It was evident, from the entire obliteration of form, that these rocks had had enormous power exerted upon them, and that a not inconsiderable depth of rock had been removed. It is immaterial whether the effects had been produced by comparatively limited force spread over an enormous length of time, or whether by greater force in a less time. The same effects would have been produced if the same amount of abrading power had been exerted over an equal area of similar rock in the Alps. But it is doubtful, perhaps, if there is in the Alps an equal area of rock which can be compared for perfection of glaciation to that of which I have spoken. I think it may certainly be asserted that there is not either in the Valley of the Rhone or in the Valley of Aosta. The glacier-eroded rocks of those valleys, and of the Alps generally, are notable for their convexity, and this affords evidence that the Alps have been subjected to less abrading power than the district in Greenland to the east of Claushavn. Now, if there is any truth in the assumption that glaciers dig away into soft rocks with much greater rapidity than into hard ones, there is, of course, greater opportunity for the exercise of this discriminative excavation when great power is exerted and when great erosion occurs, than when less power is exercised and less matter is removed. In Greenland, although enormous power has been exerted, and a considerable depth of rock has been undoubtedly removed, we find no appreciable distinction made in the treatment of two materials of very different degrees of hardness. How, then, is it possible to suppose that the prodigious amount of distinction could have been made which is assumed by Professor Ramsay in the less eroded Alps?

These are by no means the only obstacles which stand in the way of acceptance of his theory.* The difficulty is great of explaining how the glaciers excavated the rock-basins which exist, but it is still more troublesome to account for the non-existence of those which ought to have been made. The Professor explained at considerable length why they would not be formed upon steep ground (§ 9, p. 316), and I cordially agree with the first part of his remarks ; but he went on to say that when a glacier descended into a "flat valley the case was different. There, to use homely phrases, the ice had time to select soft places for excavation." "Why, then," asked several eminent persons—Mr. John Ball and Professor Favre amongst the number—"are there not lakes in the Valley of Aosta?" The valley is precisely the kind of one in which they should have been formed. Its inclination, as I have shown (p. 313), is very moderate, and several parts of it (the site of the city of Aosta, for example) are almost plains. The glacier which occupied it, one would have thought, was thick enough to have ground out basins in

---

* For some of the more important objections, see Sir R. Murchison's Address to the Royal Geog. Soc. 1864 ; Sir C. Lyell's *Antiquity of Man* and *Elements of Geology;* Prof. Studer's *Origine des Lacs Suisses;* Prof. Favre in *Phil. Mag.* March 1865 ; and Mr. John Ball in *Phil. Mag.* Feb. 1863.

the rock at any part, and *retardation* thickened it still more, occasionally.* Are there no *soft places* throughout this great valley? Were there no *accidents*, which caused exceptional grinding on *particular areas*, throughout the whole of that long period during which the valley was occupied by glacier? Apparently there were not; anyhow, there are no lakes in the valley worthy of mention, nor are there, as far as can be told, any places where basins were excavated in the rock. The Professor evidently feels that the great glacier of Aosta did not behave as it should have done, and seems to be nettled by the references which have been made to its unaccountable remissness. " I have attempted," said he, " to explain why the rock-basins are present, and not why they are absent."† He had, in fact, already accounted for their non-formation. He had shown that the great valleys of the Alps were approximately the same in their general features before they were filled with ice as they are at the present time. He had brought forward proof that this was the case with the Valley of Aosta, had shown that the great glacier which issued on to the plain at Ivrea had been unable to remove loose river-gravel, and had declared explicitly that the reason was that *time* was wanting. The entire passage is as follows :—

" When lately south of the Alps, it was proved to me by Mr. Gastaldi,‡ that at the mouths of the great Alpine valleys opening on the plain of the Po, there were ancient alluvial fan-shaped masses of gravel quite analogous to those that by the agency of existing torrents have issued from the gorges on either side (for instance) of the valleys of the Rhone or the Dora, or of those that still issue at their mouths. These were deposited on a plain rather lower than the existing one, above Pliocene marine deposits, at a time when the true mountain valleys—at all events near their mouths—were just about as deep as they are

---

* Professor Guyot has remarked striations ascending towards the mouth of the valley in places where the valley narrows. See Gastaldi's *Terrains Superficiels.*

† *Phil. Mag.*, Oct. 1864, pp. 305-6.

‡ Professor Gastaldi had published the same fact more than twelve years before. "On voit au ravin du torrent de Boriana, qui descend de la tourbière de San-Giovanni, que le terrain glaciare eparpillé supporte la moraine superficielle, et se confond lui-même avec le diluvium Alpin qui repose inférieurement sur le pliocène marin."—*Terrains Superficiels*, 1850.

now; for the great glaciers that filled the larger valleys issued out upon and overflowed these low-lying river-gravels, and deposited their moraines *above* them, only in part scooping them away, apparently because the glaciers did not endure long enough of sufficient size to complete their destruction. No better proof could be required that in great part the valleys of the Alps were approximately as deep before the glacial epoch as they are at present; and I believe, with the Italian geologists, that all that the glaciers as a whole effected was only slightly to deepen these valleys."—*Phil. Mag.*, Nov. 1862, p. 379.

This passage was, I presume, intended to upset the doctrines of Dr. Tyndall, and it did so, conclusively, as far as the mouth of the Valley of Aosta was concerned. It struck almost as severely at the opinions of its author. Indeed, there is scarcely anything more damaging to be found in the whole of the remarks which the publication of his original memoir called forth. At the mouth of the Valley of Aosta, during the glacial epoch, the whole of the conditions were found which Professor Ramsay requires for the formation of lake-basins. There was a *vast glacier* that issued out upon a plain, and which, in consequence of *retardation*, worked with unusual effect (?). It is demonstrable that it existed upon the plain for an *enormous length of time*; it is certain that it was *extraordinarily thick*; and the *particular area* upon which it worked was undoubtedly *favourable for excavation*. Yet the Professor is obliged to confess that the ice was unable to remove loose river-gravel lying upon the surface (indeed, that the glacier actually left another stratum of drift upon the gravel), and that the solid rock beneath did not experience any excavation whatever! There are many other places at which the same thing is known to have occurred, and so far from there being any especial tendency to excavate towards the snouts of glaciers, well-established facts lead rather to the opposite conclusion. A glacier which is bearing moraines always has those moraines brought together, jumbled together, towards its snout. Much of this moraine-matter falls down the sides of the glacier, and gets wedged between the ice and the bed-rock; much more falls over the terminal face of ice, and forms a stratum over which the glacier has to pass. This continually happens as the glacier progresses; and until this stratum, interposed by the glacier itself, is ground away, the bed-rock (or whatever may happen to be over the bed-rock) is not assailed.   The evidence is that the stratum of glacial drift which was deposited in this way at the mouth of the Valley of Aosta was able to resist the grinding of the glacier during the whole of its prolonged operations around Ivrea, and this fact gives, perhaps, a clearer idea of the extremely limited power of glaciers for excavation than any other which can be brought forward.

The weight of evidence seems to me to bear heavily against Professor Ramsay's theory.   In support of it, he has literally nothing more than the facts that glaciers abrade rocks over which they pass, and that there are numerous rock-basins (occupied or not occupied by lakes) lying within areas which were formerly covered by glacier.   Here certainty ends.   There are nothing but conjectures left, most of which have not even probability on their side.   The idea that all petty pools and small tarns (which lie in rock-basins) occupy areas which have been subjected to special grinding, seems to me to be fully as absurd as the notion that each one lies in an area of special subsidence ; and if all the geologists in the world were to swear that it was a solemn verity, I could not believe it, after what I have seen of the behaviour of glaciers upon rocks.   The notion that the great lake-basins occupy areas that were filled with especially soft strata, which were subjected to exceptional grinding, seems to me not to be warranted.   It is doubtful if the soft strata had any existence ; it is doubtful if there was exceptional grinding ; and it is highly improbable that the glaciers would have worked upon those basins at a rate ten, fifty, or a hundred times faster than they did in other places, even if the basins were filled with soft strata.   More evidence is wanted upon this head ; but it will be surprising if fresh facts upset those which have been already observed.   Looking at all this doubt and conjecture on one side, and the numerous facts upon the other which prove that very small glacier-erosion has occurred throughout the Alps generally, and the extremely limited capacity of glaciers for excavation under any circumstances, it seems less probable that Professor Ramsay's theory will work its way to popular acceptance, than that it will quietly take its place amongst the exploded dogmas which are left behind in the progress of scientific inquiry.

Our thoughts were more than usually set upon *roches mouton-nées*, and rocks of that *genus*, upon the 23d of June 1865. My guides and I were reposing upon the top of Mont Saxe, scanning the Grandes Jorasses, with a view to ascending it. Five thousand feet of glacier-covered precipices rose above us, and up all that height we tracked a way to our satisfaction. Three thousand feet more of glacier and forest-covered slopes lay beneath, and *there*, there was only one point at which it was doubtful if we should find a path. The glaciers were shrinking, and were surrounded by bastions of rounded rock, far too polished to please the rough mountaineer. We could not track a way across them. However, at 4 A.M. the next day,* under the dexterous leading of Michel Croz, we passed the doubtful spot. Thence it was all plain sailing, and at 1 P.M. we gained the summit. The weather was boisterous in the upper regions, and storm-clouds driven before the wind, and wrecked against our heights, enveloped us in misty spray, which danced around and fled away, which cut us off from the material universe, and caused us to be, as it were, suspended betwixt heaven and earth, seeing both occasionally, but seeming to belong to neither.

The mists lasted longer than my patience, and we descended without having attained the object for which the ascent was made. At first we followed the little ridge shown upon the accompanying engraving, leading from our summit† towards the spectator, and

* For route, see map of the chain of Mont Blanc.

† The ascent of the Grandes Jorasses was made to obtain a view of the upper part of the Aig. Verte, and upon that account the westernmost summit was selected in preference to the highest one. Both summits are shown upon the accompanying engraving. That on the right is (as it appears to be) the highest. That upon its left is the one which we ascended, and is about 100 feet lower than the other. A couple of days after our ascent, Henri Grati, Julien Grange, Jos. Mar. Perrod, Alexis Clusaz, and Daniel Gex (all of Courmayeur), followed our traces to the summit in order to

THE GRANDES JORASSES AND THE DOIRE TORRENT, VAL FERRET (D'ITALIE).

then took to the head of the corridor of glacier on its left, which in the view is left perfectly white. The slopes were steep and covered with new-fallen snow, flour-like and evil to tread upon. On the ascent we had reviled it, and had made our staircase with much caution, knowing full well that the disturbance of its base would bring down all that was above. In descending, the bolder spirits counselled trusting to luck and a glissade ; the cautious ones advocated avoiding the slopes and crossing to the rocks on their farther side. The advice of the latter prevailed, and we had half-traversed the snow, to gain the ridge, when the crust slipped and we went along with it. " Halt !" broke from all four, unanimously. The axe-heads flew round as we started on this involuntary glissade. It was useless, they slid over the underlying ice fruitlessly. " Halt !" thundered Croz, as he dashed his weapon in again with superhuman energy. No halt could be made, and we slid down slowly, but with accelerating motion, driving up waves of snow in front, with streams of the nasty stuff hissing all around. Luckily, the slope eased off at one place, the leading men cleverly jumped aside out of the moving snow, we others followed, and the young avalanche which we had started, continuing to pour down, fell into a yawning crevasse, and showed us where our grave would have been if we had remained in its company five seconds longer. The whole affair did not occupy half-a-minute. It was the solitary incident of a long day, and at nightfall we re-entered the excellent house kept by the courteous Bertolini, well satisfied that we had not met with more incidents of a similar description.

learn the way. As far as my observation extends, such things are seldom done by money-grasping or spiritless guides, and I have much pleasure in being able to mention their names. The highest point (13,799) was ascended on June 29-30, 1868, by Mr. Horace Walker, with the guides Melchior Anderegg, J. Jaun, and Julien Grange.

CHAPTER XVII.

THE COL DOLENT.

"Men willingly believe what they wish."—Cæsar.

FREETHINKING mountaineers have been latterly in the habit of going up one side of an Alp and coming down the other, and calling the route a pass. In this confusion of ideas may be recognised the result of the looseness of thought which arises from the absence of technical education. The true believer abhors such heresies, and observes with satisfaction that Providence oftentimes punishes the offenders for their greediness by causing them to be benighted. The faithful know that passes must be made between mountains, and not over their tops. Their creed declares that between any two mountains there *must* be a pass, and they believe that the end for which big peaks were created—the office they are especially designed to fulfil—is to point out the way one should go. This is the true faith, and there is no other.

We set out upon the 26th of June to endeavour to add one more to the passes which are strictly orthodox. We hoped, rather than expected, to discover a quicker route from Courmayeur to Chamounix than the Col du Géant, which was the easiest, quickest, and most direct pass known at the time across the main chain of Mont Blanc.* The misgivings which I had as to the result caused us to start at the unusual hour of 12.40 A.M. At 4.30 we passed the chalets of Prè du Bar, and thence, for some distance, followed the track which we had made upon the ascent of Mont Dolent, over the

---

* The view of Mont Blanc from a gorge on the south of the Italian Val Ferret, mid-way between the villages of La Vachey-and Praz Sec, and about 3000 feet above them, is, in my opinion, the finest which can be obtained of that mountain range anywhere upon the Italian side.

THE SUMMIT OF THE COL DOLENT.

glacier of the same name (p. 239). At a quarter past 8 we arrived at the head of the glacier, and at the foot of the only steep gradient upon the whole of the ascent.

It was the beau-ideal of a pass. There was a gap in the mountains, with a big peak on each side (Mont Dolent and the Aig. de Triolet). A narrow thread of snow led up to the lowest point between those mountains, and the blue sky beyond said, Directly you arrive here you will begin to go down. We addressed ourselves to our task, and at 10.15 A.M. arrived at the top of the pass.

Had things gone as they ought, within six hours more we should have been at Chamounix. Upon the other side we knew that there was a couloir in correspondence with that up which we had just come. If it had been filled with snow all would have been well. It turned out to be filled with ice. Croz, who led, passed over to the other side, and reported that we should get down somehow, but I knew from the sound of his axe how the somehow would be, and settled myself to sketch, well assured that *I* should not be wanted for an hour to come. What I saw is shown in the engraving. A sharp aiguille (nameless), perhaps the sharpest in the whole range, backed on the left by the Aig. de Triolet ; queer blocks of (probably) protogine sticking out awkwardly through the snow ; and a huge cornice from which big icicles depended, that broke away occasionally and went skiddling down the slope up which we had come. Of the Argentière side I could not see anything.

Croz was tied up with our good Manilla rope, and the whole 200 feet were payed out gradually by Almer and Biener before he ceased working. After two hours' incessant toil, he was able to anchor himself to the rock on his right. He then untied himself, the rope was drawn in, Biener was attached to the end and went down to join his comrade. There was then room enough for me to stand by the side of Almer, and I got my first view of the other side. For the first and only time in my life I looked down a slope more than a thousand feet long, set at an angle of about 50°, which was a sheet of ice from top to bottom. It was unbroken by rock or crag, and anything thrown down it sped away unarrested until the level of the Glacier d'Argentière was reached. The entire basin of that noble glacier* was spread out at our feet, and the ridge beyond, culminating in the Aig. d'Argentière, was seen to the greatest advantage. I confess, however, that I paid very little attention to the view, for there was no time to indulge in such luxuries. I descended the icy staircase and joined the others, and then we three drew in the rope tenderly as Almer came down. His was not an enviable position, but he descended with as much steadiness as if his whole life had been passed on ice-slopes of 50°. The process was repeated; Croz again going to the front, and availing himself very skilfully of the rocks which projected from the cliff on our right. Our 200 feet of rope again came to an end, and we again descended one by one. From this point we were able to clamber down by the rocks alone for about 300 feet. They then became sheer cliff, and we stopped for dinner, about 2.30 P.M., at the last place upon which we could sit. Four hours' incessant work had brought us rather more than half-way down the gully. We were now approaching, although we were still high above, the schrunds at its base, and the guides made out, in some way unknown to me, that Nature had perversely placed the only snow-bridge across the topmost one towards the centre of the gully. It was decided to cut diagonally across the gully to the point where the snow-bridge was supposed to be. Almer and Biener undertook the work, leaving Croz and myself firmly planted on the rocks to pay out the rope to them as they advanced.

It is generally admitted that veritable ice-slopes (understanding by *ice* something more than a crust of hard snow over soft snow) are only rarely met with in the Alps. They are frequently spoken of, but such as that to which I refer are *very* rarely seen, and still more seldom traversed. It is, however, always possible that they may be encountered, and on this account, if for no other, it is

---

* The next generation may witness its extinction. The portion of it seen from the village of Argentière is (1869) at least one quarter less in width than it was ten years ago.

necessary for men who go mountaineering to be armed with ice-axes, and with good ones. The form is of more importance than might be supposed. Of course, if you intend to act as a simple amateur, and let others do the work, and only follow in their steps, it is not of much importance what kind of ice-axe you carry, so long as its head does not fall off, or otherwise behave itself improperly.* There is no better weapon for cutting steps in ice than a common pick-axe, and the form of ice-axe which is now usually employed by the best guides is very like a miniature pick. My own axe is copied from Melchior Anderegg's. It is of wrought iron, with point and edge steeled. Its weight, including spiked handle, is four pounds. For cutting steps in ice, the pointed end of the head is almost exclusively employed ; the adze-end is handy for polishing them up, but is principally used for cutting in hard snow. Apart from its value as a cutting weapon, it is invaluable as a grapnel. It is natu-

MY ICE-AXE.

rally a rather awkward implement when it is not being employed for its legitimate purpose, and is likely to give rise to much strong

* This observation is not made without reason. I have seen the head of one tumble off at a slight tap, in consequence of its handle having been perforated by an ingenious but useless arrangement of nails.

language in crushes at railway termini, unless its head is protected with a leathern cap, or in some other way. Many attempts have been made, for the sake of convenience, to fashion an ice-axe with a movable head, but it seems difficult or impossible to produce one except at the expense of cutting qualities, and by increasing the weight.

Mr. T. S. Kennedy (of the firm of Fairbairn & Co.), whose practical acquaintance with mountaineering, and with the use and manufacture of tools, makes his opinion particularly valuable, has contrived the best that I have seen ; but even it seems to me to be deficient in rigidity, and not to be so powerful a weapon as the more common kind with the fixed head. The simple instrument which is

KENNEDY ICE-AXE.

shown in the annexed diagram is the invention of Mr. Leslie Stephen, and it answers the purposes for which he devised it, namely, for giving better hold upon snow

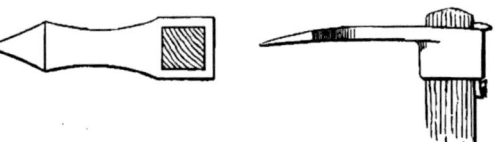

and ice than can be obtained from the common alpenstock, and for cutting an occasional step. The amateur scarcely requires anything more imposing, but for serious ice-work a heavier weapon is indispensable.

To persons armed with the proper tools, ice-slopes are not so dangerous as many places which appeal less to the imagination. Their ascent or descent is necessarily laborious (to those who do the work), and they may therefore be termed difficult. They *ought* not to be dangerous. Yet they always seem dangerous, for one is profoundly convinced that if he slips he will certainly go to the bottom.

Hence, any man, who is not a fool, takes particular care to preserve his balance, and, in consequence, we have the noteworthy fact
that accidents have seldom or never taken place upon ice-slopes.

The same slopes covered with snow are much less impressive,
and *may* be much more dangerous. They may be less slippery, the
balance may be more easily preserved, and if one man slips he may
be stopped by his own personal efforts, provided the snow which
over-lies the ice is consolidated and of a reasonable depth. But if, as
is more likely to be the case upon an angle of 50° (or anything approaching that angle), there is only a thin stratum of snow which is
not consolidated, the occurrence of a slip will most likely take the
entire party as low as possible, and in addition to the chance of
broken necks, there will be a strong probability that some, at least,
will be smothered by the dislodged snow. Such accidents are far too
common, and their occurrence, as a rule, may be traced to the want
of caution which is induced by the apparent absence of danger.

I do not believe that the use of the rope, in the ordinary way,
affords the least *real* security upon ice-slopes. Nor do I think that
any benefit is derived from the employment of crampons. Mr.
Kennedy was good enough to present me with a pair some time
ago, and one of these has been
engraved. They are the best
variety I have seen of the
species, but I only feel comfortable with them on my feet
in places where they are not
of the slightest use, that is in
situations where there is no

possibility of slipping, and would not wear them upon an ice-slope for
any consideration whatever. All such adventitious aids are useless
if you have not a good step in the ice to stand upon, and if you have
got that, nothing more is wanted except a few nails in the boots.

Almer and Biener got to the end of their tether ; the rope no
longer assured their safety, and they stopped work as we advanced

and coiled it up. Shortly afterwards they struck a streak of snow that proved to be just above the bridge of which they were in search. The slope steepened, and for thirty feet or so we descended face to the wall, making steps by kicking with the toes, and thrusting the arms well into the holes above, just as if they had been rounds in a ladder. At this time we were crossing the uppermost of the schrunds. Needless to say that the snow was of an admirable quality ; this performance would otherwise have been impossible. It was soon over, and we then found ourselves upon a huge rhomboidal mass of ice, and still separated from the Argentière glacier by a gigantic crevasse. The only bridge over this lower schrund was at its eastern end, and we were obliged to double back to get to it. Cutting continued for half-an-hour after it was passed, and it was 5.35 P.M. before the axes stopped work, and we could at last turn back and look comfortably at the formidable slope upon which seven hours had been spent.†

The Col Dolent is not likely to compete with the Col du Géant, and I would recommend any person who starts to cross it to allow himself plenty of time, plenty of rope, and ample guide-power. There is no difficulty whatever upon any part of the route, excepting upon the steep slopes immediately below the summit on each side. When we arrived upon the Glacier d'Argentière, our work was as good as over. We drove a straight track to the chalets of Lognan, and thence the way led over familiar ground. Soon after dusk we got into the high road at les Tines, and at 10 P.M. arrived at Chamounix. Our labours were duly rewarded. Houris brought us champagne and the other drinks which are reserved for the faithful, but before my share was consumed I fell asleep in an arm-chair. I slept soundly until daybreak, and then turned into bed and went to sleep again.

* It occupies about one-sixth of an inch upon the map. I estimate its height at 1200 feet. The triangulation of Capt. Mieulet places the summit of the pass 11,624 feet above the sea. This, I think, is rather too high.

CHAPTER XVIII.

" Few have the fortitude of soul to honour
A friend's success, without a touch of envy."

ÆSCHYLUS.

MICHEL CROZ now parted from us. His new employer had not arrived at Chamounix, but Croz considered that he was bound by honour to wait for him, and thus Christian Almer, of Grindelwald, became my leading guide.

Almer displayed aptitude for mountaineering at an early age. Whilst still a very young man he was known as a crack chamois-hunter, and he soon developed into an accomplished guide. Those who have read Mr. Wills' graphic account of the first ascent of the Wetterhorn * will remember that, when his party was approaching the top of the mountain, two stranger men were seen climbing by a slightly different route, one of whom carried upon his back a young fir-tree, branches, leaves, and all. Mr. Wills' guides were extremely indignant with these two strangers (who were evidently determined to be the first at the summit), and talked of giving them blows. Eventually they gave them a cake of chocolate instead, and declared that they were good fellows. " Thus the pipe of peace was smoked, and tranquillity reigned between the rival forces." Christian Almer was one of these two men.

This was in 1854. In 1858-9 he made the first ascents of the Eigher and the Mönch, the former with a Mr. Harrington (?), and the latter with Dr. Porges. Since then he has wandered far and

Wanderings among the High Alps, 1858.

near, from Dauphiné to the Tyrol.* With the exception of Melchior Anderegg, there is not, perhaps, another guide of such wide experience, or one who has been so invariably successful ; and his numerous employers concur in saying that there is not a truer heart or a surer foot to be found amongst the Alps.

CHRISTIAN ALMER.†

Before recrossing the chain to Courmayeur, we ascended the Aiguille Verte. In company with Mr. Reilly I inspected this mountain from every direction in 1864, and came to the conclusion that an ascent could more easily be made from the south than upon any other side. We set out upon the 28th from Chamounix to attack it, minus Croz, and plus a porter (of whom I will speak more particularly presently), leaving our comrade very downcast at having to kick his heels in idleness, whilst we were about to scale the most celebrated of his native Aiguilles.

Our course led us over the old Mer de Glace—the glacier made famous by De Saussure and Forbes. The heat of the day was

* Most of his principal exploits are recorded in the publications of the Alpine Club.

† Engraved, by permission, from a photograph by Mr. E. Edwards.

over, but the little rills and rivulets were still flowing along the surface of the ice ; cutting deep troughs where the gradients were small ; leaving ripple-marks where the water was with more difficulty confined to one channel ; and falling over the precipitous walls of the great crevasses, sometimes in bounding cascades, and sometimes in diffused streams, which marked the perpendicular

ON THE MER DE GLACE.

faces with graceful sinuosities.* As night came on, their music died away, the rivulets dwindled down to rills ; the rills ceased to murmur, and the sparkling drops, caught by the hand of frost, were bound to the ice, coating it with an enamelled film which lasted until the sun struck the glacier once more.

* Admirably rendered in the accompanying drawing by Mr. Cyrus Johnson. The " ripple-marks " are seen in the engraving upon p. 356.

The weathering of the walls of crevasses, which *obscures* the internal structure of the glacier, has led some to conclude that the stratification which is seen in the higher glacier-regions is *obliterated* in the lower ones.   Others, Agassiz and Mr. John Ball for example, have disputed this opinion,* and my own experiences accord with those of these accurate observers.   It is, undoubtedly, very difficult to trace stratification in the lower ends of the Alpine glaciers ; but

ON THE MER DE GLACE.

we are not, upon that account, entitled to conclude that the original structure of the ice has been obliterated.   There are thousands of crevasses in the upper regions upon whose walls no traces of bedding are apparent, and we might say, with equal unreasonableness, that it was obliterated there also.   Take an axe, and clear away the ice which has formed from water trickling down

* See Agassiz in *Atlantic Monthly*, Dec. 1863 ; and Mr. J. Ball in *Phil. Mag.* Dec. 1857 (supplementary number), and April 1859.

the faces, and the weathered ice beneath, and you will expose sections of the mingled strata of pure and of imperfect ice, and see clearly enough that the primitive structure of the glacier has not been effaced, although it has been obscured.

Notwithstanding all that has been written to the contrary by very eminent authorities, I believe that the strata of ice which are formed by weathering, upon the beds of snow that are deposited in the higher regions, exist (unless they are originally of very small thickness) to the ends of the glaciers, and that many of the veins of blue ice which are seen on the surfaces of the lower parts of Alpine glaciers are nothing more than the outcropping of the primarily horizontal strata.

Some of those who have maintained the contrary opinion, have evidently had a very insufficient idea of the extent to which the upper snows are pervaded by the strata of blue ice, and of their thickness. In the Appendix it is shown that there were in the upper 22 feet of snow at the summit of the Col de Valpelline, in 1866, no less than 75 layers of ice, one of which was more than 6 inches in thickness, whilst numerous others ranged from half-an-inch to one inch. The total depth of these 75 layers amounted to 25⅝ inches, or nearly one-tenth of the mass which we were able to penetrate. As far as I am aware, it has not been proved experimentally that it is possible (by compression, or in any other way) to obliterate a plate of ice, even an inch in thickness, placed between snow, or between ice of inferior density, except by liquefaction of the entire mass.

Others who have pronounced against the possibility of the horizontal strata of blue ice contributing any of the veins of blue ice which constitute the *veined structure** of glaciers, have done so

* The late Principal J. D. Forbes was the first to attach any importance to the veined structure of glaciers. I gather the following definitions of it from different pages of his *Occasional Papers.* " I cannot more accurately describe it, than by calling it a *ribboned structure,* formed by thin and delicate blue and bluish-white bands or strata, which appear to traverse the ice in a vertical direction, or rather which, by their apposition, formed the entire mass of the ice. The direction of these bands was

upon the ground that all traces of stratification are obliterated before the appearance of the veined structure. It is, however, now well known that the primitive structure has been detected *after* the appearance of the veins on the surfaces of glaciers—the veins, indeed, have been observed in the walls of crevasses cutting the original structure.* It is proved thereby that the original structure remains in existence down to a low point, and that, so far at least, it is not obliterated.†

It has also been urged that "the blue veins of glaciers are not always, nor even generally, such as we should *expect* to result from stratification. The latter would furnish us with distinct planes extending parallel to each other for considerable distances through the glacier; but this, though sometimes the case, is by no means the general character of the structure." With this observation I agree. It amounts, however, only to saying, that it is impossible to con-

parallel to the length of the glacier" (p. 3.) "In some parts of the glacier it appears more developed than in others. . . It penetrates the *thickness* of the glacier to great depths. It is an integral part of its inmost structure" (p. 5.) "The breadth of these (bands) varies from a small fraction of an inch to several inches" (p. 8). "This structure consists in the alternation of more or less perfectly crystallised ice in parallel layers, often thinning out altogether like veins in marble" (p. 19).

Forbes' "veined structure" is frequently cut, both horizontally and vertically, by other veins, which latter seem to me to have clearly a different origin from the former. Proper discrimination has not hitherto been made between the two. Observers sometimes call one, sometimes the other, and sometimes both, the "veined structure." It would, I think, be convenient and appropriate to term Forbes' structure "the laminated structure of glacier." In 1867, upon the surface of a glacier in the Jakobshavn district, North Greenland, I saw three series of veins crossing each other in three different directions, forming a cross-bar or net-work pattern upon the ice. This was certainly not Forbes' structure.

* This of course proves that the origin of all the veins is not found in stratification, but it does not prove (as some appear to think) that *all* of the veins have a different origin.

† I believe that I have seen the planes of the original bedding still remaining parallel to the surface in some icebergs floating into Disco Bay, which had come from a glacier at least 20 miles long. If I am not mistaken, this is a most important and significant fact.

sider that all of the blue veins have their origin in the stratified beds of snow and ice from which glaciers are born.   Any person who has been close to an " ice-fall " on one of the principal Alpine glaciers, and observed the great *séracs* lurching forward, with the primitive beds remaining parallel, or nearly so, to the surface of the glacier, must feel that it is extremely improbable that the masses will be so re-compacted lower down as to " furnish us with distinct planes extending parallel to each other for *considerable distances.*" It will be felt that some of the *séracs* will be so smashed up that the original structure will be got rid of ; that others, which descend more gently, will remain intact, but will settle down with their beds more or less inclined to the horizon ; and that it will be a very extraordinary chance if the *dip* of the strata of any two of the masses coincides within many degrees.

Upon these grounds I believe that many of the veins of the veined structure of glaciers are nothing more than the upturned layers of blue ice which are formed upon and between the beds of snow that are deposited in the higher regions.*   I am far from thinking that the occurrence of the whole of the veins of blue ice which are found in glaciers should be accounted for in this way.   I do not believe that the combinations of different varieties of ice that are found in glaciers, which have been referred to by various authors as the *veined structure,* can be accounted for in two or even in three ways.   Avoiding disputed points, I will observe that there are at least two other modes by which many veins of blue ice are undoubtedly produced in glaciers.

First, by water freezing into crevasses.   I have seen hundreds of crevasses in Greenland nearly full of water ; never *quite* full : the water seldom came within two or three feet of the surface of the glacier.   I have seen the entire surface of the water in such crevasses frozen and freezing.   I have seen the water sometimes frozen solid at one end and remaining liquid at the other end ; and in the walls of icebergs I have seen sections of crevasses that have been

* Sometimes, probably thickened by pressure.

nearly filled with water, in which the water has been frozen solid.* These veins in icebergs are frequently one to three feet thick, and can be seen at several miles' distance. If veins of blue ice are not formed in the Alpine glaciers in the same manner, it is only because there are outlets from the crevasses by which the water escapes. It is rare to see a crevasse even partly filled with water in the Alps.†

Secondly, by the closing together of crevasses. The unequal motion of the parts of a glacier causes crevasses continually to open and to close up ; and the walls of these crevasses, whether 12,000 feet or more above the level of the sea, or whether only 5000, all become weathered and more or less coated with pure ice. Even narrow crevasses in the high regions, well bridged with snow, are not exempt. The warm air of midsummer penetrates the chasms, and, assisted by the percolation of snow water, glazes the walls from top to bottom. The superficial coatings of ice which are thus formed upon the sides of crevasses vary greatly in thickness according to circumstances—in a single crevasse they may range from a thickness of less than an inch to more than a foot.‡ The crevasses close up ; the surfaces of their icy walls are brought into contact ; they regele, and the coalesced films will then appear as veins of pure ice in the generally whitish mass of the glacier. When one considers the myriads of crevasses which there are in any glacier, and the incessant opening and closing up that goes forward, it is easy to see that a large proportion of the veins of pure ice which constitute the veined structure of glaciers must be considered as the *scars of healed crevasses.*

* These veins in icebergs are frequently seen intersecting each other. Dr. Rink has shown this in an illustration in his *Grönland Geographisk og Statistisk*, vol. i. 1852.

† Charpentier long ago advanced the opinion that the motion of glaciers was promoted by freezing of water in crevasses. His notion is commonly regarded as exploded, but there may be something in it after all.

‡ The same thing is to be noticed in regard to the blue veins of the veined structure. The veins frequently thin out and are lost, or swell into lenticular masses. This is best seen when the veins are regarded in vertical sections of the glacier.

We camped on the Couvercle (7800) under a great rock, and at 3.15 the next morning started for our aiguille, leaving the porter in charge of the tent and of the food.   Two hours' walking over crisp snow brought us up more than 4000 feet, and within about 1600 feet of the summit.*   From no other direction can it be approached so closely with equal facility.   Thence the mountain steepens.   After his late severe piece of ice-work, Almer had a natural inclination for rocks ; but the lower rocks of the final peak of the Verte were not inviting, and he went on and on, looking for a way up them, until we arrived in front of a great snow couloir that led from the Glacier de Talèfre right up to the crest of the ridge connecting the summit of the Verte with the mountain called Les Droites.   This was the route which I intended to be taken ; but Almer pointed out that the gully narrowed at the lower part, and that, if stones fell, we should stand some chance of getting our heads broken ; and so we went on still more to the east of the summit, to another and smaller couloir which ran up side by side with the great one.   At 5.30 we crossed the schrund which protected the final peak, and, a few minutes afterwards, saw the summit and the whole of the intervening route.   "Oh ! Aiguille Verte," said my guide, stopping as he said it, "you are dead, you are dead ;" which, being translated into plain English, meant that he was cock-sure we should make its ascent.

Almer is a quiet man at all times.   When climbing he is taciturn—and this is one of his great merits.   A garrulous man is always a nuisance, and upon the mountain-side he may be a danger, for actual climbing requires a man's whole attention.   Added to this, talkative men are hindrances ; they are usually thirsty, and a thirsty man is a drag.

Guide-books recommend mountain-walkers to suck pebbles, to prevent their throats from becoming parched.   There is not much goodness to be got out of the pebbles ; but you cannot suck them

---

* Or, upon the map of the chain of Mont Blanc, to within a third of an inch of the black triangle which marks the summit.

and keep the mouth open at the same time, and hence the throat does not become dry. It answers just as well to keep the mouth shut, without any pebbles inside,—indeed, I think, better ; for if you have occasion to open your mouth, you can do so without swallowing any pebbles.* As a rule, amateurs, and particularly novices, *will not* keep their mouths shut. They attempt to " force the pace," they go faster than they can go without being compelled to open their mouths to breathe, they pant, their throats and tongues become parched, they drink and perspire copiously, and, becoming exhausted, declare that the dryness of the air, or the rarefaction of the air (everything is laid upon the air), is in fault. On several accounts, therefore, a mountain-climber does well to hold his tongue when he is at his work.

At the top of the small gully we crossed over the intervening rocks into the large one, and followed it so long as it was filled with snow. At last ice replaced snow, and we turned over to the rocks upon its left. Charming rocks they were ; granitic in texture,† gritty, holding the nails well. At 9.45 we parted from them, and completed the ascent by a little ridge of snow which descended in the direction of the Aiguille du Moine. At 10.15 we stood on the summit (13,540), and devoured our bread and cheese with a good appetite.

I have already spoken of the disappointing nature of purely panoramic views. That seen from Mont Blanc itself is notoriously unsatisfactory. When you are upon that summit you look down upon all the rest of Europe. There is nothing to look up to ; all is below ; there is no one point for the eye to rest upon. The man who is there is somewhat in the position of one who has attained all that he desires,—he has nothing to aspire to ; his

* I heard lately of two well-known mountaineers who, under the influence of sudden alarm, *swallowed their crystals.* I am happy to say that they were able to cough them up again.

† Hand specimens of the highest rocks of the Aiguille Verte cannot be distinguished from granite. The rock is almost identical in quality with that at the summit of Mont Dolent, and is probably a granitöid gneiss.

position must needs be unsatisfactory. Upon the summit of the Verte there is not this objection. You see valleys, villages, fields ; you see mountains interminable rolling away, lakes resting in their hollows ; you hear the tinkling of the sheep-bells as it rises through the clear mountain air, and the roar of the avalanches as they descend to the valleys : but above all there is the great white dome, with its shining crest high above ; with its sparkling glaciers that descend between buttresses which support them; with its brilliant snows, purer and yet purer the farther they are removed from this unclean world.*

Even upon this mountain-top it was impossible to forget the world, for some vile wretch came to the Jardin and made hideous sounds by blowing upon a horn. Whilst we were denouncing him a change came over the weather; cumulous clouds gathered in all directions, and we started off in hot haste. Snow began to fall heavily before we were off the summit-rocks, our track was obscured and frequently lost, and everything became so sloppy and slippery that the descent took as long as the ascent. The schrund was re-crossed at 3.15 P.M., and thence we raced down to the Couvercle, intending to have a carouse there ; but as we rounded our rock a howl broke simultaneously from all three of us, for the porter had taken down the tent, and was in the act of moving off with it. "Stop, there! what are you doing?" He observed that he had thought we were killed, or at least lost, and was going to Chamounix to communicate his ideas to the *guide chef.* "Unfasten the tent, and get out the food." But instead of doing so the porter fumbled in his pockets. "Get out the food," we roared, losing all patience. "Here it is," said our worthy friend, producing a dirty piece of bread about as big as a halfpenny roll. We three looked solemnly at the fluff-covered morsel. It was past a joke,—he had devoured everything. Mutton, loaves, cheese, wine, eggs, sausages—all was

---

* The summit of the Aiguille Verte was a snowy dome, large enough for a quadrille. I was surprised to see the great height of Les Droites. Captain Mieulet places its summit at 13,222 feet, but I think it must be very slightly lower than the Verte itself.

gone—past recovery.   It was idle to grumble, and useless to wait.
We were light, and could move quickly,—the porter was laden
inside and out.   We went our hardest,—he had to shuffle and trot.
He streamed with perspiration ; the mutton and cheese oozed out
in big drops,—he larded the glacier.   We had our revenge, and
dried our clothes at the same time, but when we arrived at the Montanvert the porter was as wet as we had been upon our arrival at
the Couvercle.   We halted at the inn to get a little food, and at
a quarter past eight re-entered Chamounix, amidst firing of cannon
and other demonstrations of satisfaction on the part of the hotel-
keepers.

One would have thought that the ascent of this mountain,
which had been frequently assailed before without success, would
have afforded some gratification to a population whose chief
support is derived from tourists, and that the prospect of the
perennial flow of francs which might be expected to result from
it would have stifled the jealousy consequent on the success of
foreigners.*

It was not so.   Chamounix stood on its rights.   A stranger
had ignored their regulations, had imported two foreign guides,
and, furthermore, he had added injury to that insult—he had not
taken a single Chamounix guide.   Chamounix would be revenged !
It would bully the foreign guides ; it would tell them they had
lied,—they had not made the ascent !   Where were their proofs ?
Where was the flag upon the summit ?

Poor Almer and Biener were accordingly chivied from pillar to
post, from one inn to another, and at length complained to me.
Peter Perrn, the Zermatt guide, said on the night that we returned
that this was to happen, but the story seemed too absurd to be
true.   I now bade my men go out again, and followed them
myself to see the sport.   Chamounix was greatly excited.   The
bureau of the *guide chef* was thronged with clamouring men.

---

* The Chamounix tariff price for the ascent of the Aiguille is now placed at £4
per guide.

Their ringleader—one Zacharie Cachat—a well-known guide, of no particular merit, but not a bad fellow, was haranguing the multitude. He met with more than his match. My friend Kennedy, who was on the spot, heard of the disturbance and rushed into the fray, confronted the burly guide, and thrust back his absurdities into his teeth.

There were the materials for a very pretty riot ; but they manage these things better in France than we do, and the gensdarmes—three strong—came down and dispersed the crowd. The guides quailed before the cocked hats, and retired to cabarets to take little glasses of absinthe and other liquors more or less injurious to the human frame. Under the influence of these stimulants, they conceived an idea which combined revenge with profit. " You have ascended the Aiguille Verte, you say. *We* say we don't believe it. *We* say, do it again ! Take three of us with you, and we will bet you two thousand francs to one thousand, that you won't make the ascent ! "

This proposition was formally notified to me, but I declined it, with thanks, and recommended Kennedy to go in and win. I accepted, however, a hundred franc share in the bet, and calculated upon getting two hundred per cent on my investment. Alas ! how vain are human expectations ! Zacharie Cachat was put into confinement, and although Kennedy actually ascended the Aiguille a week later, with two Chamounix guides and Peter Perrn, the bet came to nothing.*

The weather arranged itself just as this storm in a teapot blew over, and we left at once for the Montanvert, in order to show the Chamouniards the easiest way over the chain of Mont Blanc, in return for the civilities which we had received from them during the past three days.

---

* It should be said that we received the most polite apologies for this affair from the chief of the gensdarmes, and an invitation to lodge a complaint against the ringleaders. We accepted his apologies, and declined his invitation. Needless to add, Michel Croz took no part in the demonstration.

CHAPTER XIX.

THE COL DE TALÈFRE.

" 'Tis more by art than force of numerous strokes."

HOMER.

THE person who discovered the Col du Géant must have been a shrewd mountaineer. The pass was in use before any other was known across the main chain of Mont Blanc, and down to the present time it remains the easiest and quickest route from Chamounix to Courmayeur, with the single exception of the pass that we crossed upon the 3d of July, for the first time, which lies about mid-way between the Aiguille de Triolet and the Aiguille de Talèfre, and which, for want of a better name, I have called the Col de Talèfre.

When one looks toward the upper end of the Glacier de Talèfre from the direction of the Jardin or of the Couvercle, the ridge that bounds the view seems to be of little elevation. It is overpowered by the colossal Grandes Jorasses, and by the almost equally magnificent Aiguille Verte. The ridge, notwithstanding, is by no means despicable. At no point is its elevation less than 11,600 feet. It does not look anything like this height. The Glacier de Talèfre mounts with a steady incline, and the eye is completely deceived.

In 1864, when prowling about with Mr. Reilly, I instinctively fixed upon a bent couloir* which led up from the glacier to the lowest part of the ridge ; and when, after crossing the Col de Triolet, I saw that the other side presented no particular difficulty, it seemed to me that this was the *one* point in the whole of the range which would afford an easier passage than the Col du Géant.

We set out from the Montanvert at 4 A.M. upon July 3, to see whether this opinion was correct, and it fortunately happened that the Rev. A. G. Girdlestone and a friend, with two Chamounix guides, left the inn at the same hour as ourselves, to cross the Col du Géant. We kept in company as far as our routes lay together, and at 9.35 we arrived at the top of our pass, having taken the route to the south of the Jardin. Description is unnecessary, as our track is laid down very clearly on the engraving at the head of this chapter, and upon the map.

Much snow had fallen during the late bad weather, and as we reposed upon the top of our pass (which was about 11,650 feet above the level of the sea, and 600 feet above the Col du Géant), we saw that the descent of the rocks which intervened between us and the Glacier de Triolet would require some caution, for the sun's rays poured down directly upon them, and the snow slipped away every now and then from ledge to ledge just as if it had been water,—in cascades not large enough to be imposing, but sufficient to knock us over if we got in their way. This little bit of cliff consequently took a longer time than it should have done, for when we heard the indescribable swishing, hissing sound which announced a coming fall, we of necessity huddled under the lee of the rocks until the snow ceased to shoot over us.

We got to the level of the Glacier de Triolet without misad-

* This couloir is narrow and not steeply inclined. As a general rule, broad couloirs should be avoided, as they are usually of ice, if at all steep. Narrow couloirs are almost always snowy.

venture, then steered for its left bank to avoid the upper of its two formidable ice-falls, and after descending the requisite distance by some old snow lying between the glacier and the cliffs which border it, crossed directly to the right bank over the level ice between the two ice-falls.* The right bank was gained without any trouble, and we found there numerous beds of hard snow (avalanche débris) down which we could run or glissade as fast as we liked.

Glissading is a very pleasant employment when it is accomplished successfully, and I have never seen a place where it can be  more safely indulged in than the snowy valley on the right bank of the glacier de Triolet. In my dreams I glissade delightfully, but in practice I find that somehow the snow will not behave properly, and that my alpenstock *will* get between my legs. Then my legs go where my head should be, and I see the sky revolving at a rapid pace ; the snow rises up and smites me, and runs away ; and when it is at last overtaken it suddenly stops, and we come into violent collision. Those who are with me say that I tumble head over heels, and there may be some truth in what they say. Streaks of ice are apt to make the heels shoot away, and stray stones cause one to pitch headlong down. Somehow these things always seem to come in the way, so it is as well to glissade only when there is something soft to tumble into.†

* Below the second ice-fall the glacier is completely covered up with moraine matter, and if the *left* bank is followed, one is compelled either to traverse this howling waste or to lose much time upon the tedious and somewhat difficult rocks of Mont Rouge.

† In glissading an erect position should be maintained, and the point of the alpenstock allowed to trail over the snow. If it is necessary to stop, or to slacken speed, the point is pressed against the slope, as shown in the illustration.

Near the termination of the glacier we could not avoid traversing a portion of its abominable moraine, but at 1.30 P.M. we were clear of it, and threw ourselves upon some springy turf conscious that our day's work was over. An hour afterwards we resumed the march, crossed the Doire torrent by a bridge a little below Gruetta, and at five o'clock entered Courmayeur, having occupied somewhat less than ten hours on the way. Mr. Girdlestone's party came in, I believe, about four hours afterwards, so there was no doubt that we made a shorter pass than the Col du Géant ; and I believe we discovered a quicker way of getting from Chamounix to Courmayeur, or *vice versa,* than will be found elsewhere, so long as the chain of Mont Blanc remains in its present condition.*

* Comparison of the Col de Triolet with the Col de Talèfre will show what a great difference in ease there may be between tracks which are nearly identical. For a distance of several miles these routes are scarcely more than half-a-mile apart. Nearly every step of the former is difficult, whilst the latter has no difficulty whatever. The route we adopted over the Col de Talèfre may perhaps be improved. It may be possible to go directly from the head of the Glacier de Triolet to its right bank, and, if so, at least thirty minutes might be saved.

The following is a complete list of the so-called passes across the main ridge of the range of Mont Blanc, with the years in which the first passages were effected, as far as I know them :—1. Col de Trélatête (1864), between Aig. du Glacier and Aig. de Trélatête. 2. Col de Miage, between Aig. de Miage and Aig. de Bionnassay. 3. Col du Dôme (1865), over the Dôme du Goûter. 4. Col du Mont Blanc (1868), over Mont Blanc. 5. Col de la Brenva (1865), between Mont Blanc and Mont Maudit. 6. Col de la Tour Ronde (1867), over la Tour Ronde. 7. Col du Géant, between la Tour Ronde and Aigs. Marbrées. 8. Col Pierre Joseph (1866), over Aig. de l'Eboulement. 9. Col de Talèfre (1865), between Aigs. Talèfre and Triolet. 10. Col de Triolet (1864), between Aigs. Talèfre and Triolet. 11. Col Dolent (1865), between Aig. de Triolet and Mont Dolent. 12. Col d'Argentière (1861), between Mont Dolent and le Tour Noir. 13. Col du Chardonnet (1863), between Aigs. d'Argentière and Chardonnet. 14. Col du Tour, between Aigs. du Chardonnet and Tour.

CHAPTER XX.

" In almost every art, experience is worth more than precepts."

QUINTILIAN.

ALL of the excursions that were set down in my programme had been carried out, with the exception of the ascent of the Matterhorn, and we now turned our faces in its direction, but instead of returning *via* the Val Tournanche, we took a route across country, and bagged upon our way the summit of the Ruinette.

We passed the night of July 4, at Aosta, under the roof of the genial Tairraz, and on the 5th went by the Val d'Ollomont and the Col de la Fenêtre (9140) to Chermontane.* We slept that night at the chalets of Chanrion (a foul spot, which should be avoided), left them at 3.50 the next morning, and after a short scramble over the slope above, and a half-mile tramp on the glacier de Breney, we crossed directly to the Ruinette, and went almost straight up it. There is not, I suppose, another mountain in the Alps of the same height that can be ascended so easily. You have only to go ahead : upon its southern side one can walk about almost anywhere.

Though I speak thus slightingly of a very respectable peak, I will not do anything of the kind in regard to the view which it gives. It is happily placed in respect to the rest of the Pennine Alps, and as a stand-point it has not many superiors. You see mountains, and nothing but mountains. It is a solemn—some would say a dreary—view, but it is very grand. The great Combin

---

* For routes, see Map of the Valley of Valpelline, etc.

(14,164), with its noble background of the whole range of Mont Blanc, never looks so big as it does from here. In the contrary direction, the Matterhorn overpowers all besides. The Dent d'Herens, although closer, looks a mere outlier of its great neighbour, and the snows of Monte Rosa, behind, seem intended for no other purpose than to give relief to the crags in front. To the south there is an endless array of Bec's and Becca's, backed by the great Italian peaks, whilst to the north Mont Pleureur (12,159) holds its own against the more distant Wildstrubel.

We gained the summit at 9.15,* and stayed there an hour and a half. My faithful guides then admonished me that Prerayen, whither we were bound, was still far away, and that we had yet to cross two lofty ridges. So we resumed our harness and departed ; not, however, before a huge cairn had been built out of the blocks of gneiss with which the summit is bestrewn. Then we trotted down the slopes of the Ruinette, over the glacier de Breney, and across a pass which (if it deserves a name) may be called the Col des Portons, after the neighbouring peaks. From thence we proceeded across the great Otemma glacier towards the Col d'Olen.

The part of the glacier that we traversed was overspread with snow which completely concealed its numerous pitfalls. We marched across it in single file, and, of course, roped together. All at once Almer dropped into a crevasse up to his shoulders. I pulled in the rope immediately, but the snow gave way as it was being done, and I had to spread out my arms to stop my descent. Biener held fast, but said afterwards, that his feet went through as well, so, for a moment, all three were in the jaws of the crevasse. We now altered our course, so as to take the fissures transversely, and after the centre of the glacier was passed changed it again and made directly for the summit of the Col d'Olen.

* After crossing the glacier de Breney, we ascended by some débris, and then by some cliffy ground, to the glacier which surrounds the peak upon the south ; bore to the left (that is to the west) and went up the edge of the glacier ; and lastly took to the arête of the ridge which descends towards the south-west, and followed it to the summit (12,727).

It is scarcely necessary to observe, after what was said upon p. 116, that it is my invariable practice to employ a rope when traversing a snow-covered glacier. Many guides, even the best ones, object to be roped, more especially early in the morning when the snow is hard. They object sometimes, because they think it is unnecessary. Crevasses that are bridged by snow are almost always more or less perceptible by undulations on the surface ; the snow droops down, and hollows mark the courses of the chasms beneath. An experienced guide usually notices these almost imperceptible wrinkles, steps one side or the other, as the case may require, and rarely breaks through unawares. Guides think there is no occasion to employ a rope because they think that they will *not* be taken by surprise. Michel Croz used to be of this opinion. He used to say that only imbeciles and children required to be tied up in the morning. I told him that in this particular matter I was a child to him. "You see these things, my good Croz, and avoid them. I do not, except you point them out to me, and so that which is not a danger to you, *is* a danger to me." The sharper one's eyes get by use, the less is a rope required as a protective against these hidden pitfalls ; but, according to my experience, the sight never becomes so keen that they can be avoided with unvarying certainty, and I mentioned what occurred upon the Otemma glacier to show that this is so.

I well remember my first passage of the Col Theodule—the easiest of the higher Alpine glacier passes. We had a rope, but my guide said it was not necessary, he knew all the crevasses. However, we did not go a quarter of a mile before he dropped through the snow into a crevasse up to his neck. He was a heavy man, and would scarcely have extricated himself alone ; anyhow, he was very glad of my assistance. When he got on to his legs again, he said, "Well, I had no idea that there was a crevasse there !" He no longer objected to use the rope, and we proceeded ; upon my part, with greater peace of mind than before. I have crossed the pass thirteen times since then, and have invariably insisted upon being tied together.

Guides object to the use of the rope upon snow-covered glacier, because they are afraid of being laughed at by their comrades ; and this, perhaps, is the more common reason.   To illustrate this, here is another Theodule experience.   We arrived at the edge of the ice, and I required to be tied.   My guide (a Zermatt man of repute) said that no one used a rope going across that pass.   I declined to argue the matter, and we put on the rope ; though very much against the wish of my man, who protested that he should have to submit to perpetual ridicule if we met any of his acquaintances.   We had not gone very far before we saw a train coming in the contrary direction.   " Ah !" cried my man, " there is R— (mentioning a guide who used to be kept at the Riffel Hotel for the ascent of Monte Rosa) ; it will be as I said, I shall never hear the end of this."   The guide we met was followed by a string of tom-fools, none of whom were tied together, and had his face covered by a mask to prevent it becoming blistered.   After we had passed, I said, " Now, should R— make any observations to you, ask him why he takes such extraordinary care to preserve the skin of his face, which will grow again in a week, when he neglects such an obvious precaution in regard to his life, which he can only lose once."   This was quite a new idea to my guide, and he said nothing more against the use of the rope so long as we were together.

I believe that the unwillingness to use a rope upon snow-covered glacier which born mountaineers not unfrequently exhibit, arises—First, on the part of expert men, from the consciousness that they themselves incur little risk ; secondly, on the part of inferior men, from fear of ridicule, and from aping the ways of their superiors ; and, thirdly, from pure ignorance or laziness. Whatever may be the reason, I raise up my voice against the neglect of a precaution so simple and so effectual.   In my opinion, the very first thing a glacier traveller requires is plenty of good rope.

A committee of the English Alpine Club was appointed in

1864 to test, and to report upon, the most suitable ropes for mountaineering purposes, and those which were approved are probably as good as can be found. One is made of Manilla and another of Italian hemp. The former is the heavier, and weighs a little more than an ounce per foot (103 ozs. to 100 feet). The latter weighs 79 ozs. per 100 feet ; but I prefer the Manilla rope, because it is more handy to handle. Both of these ropes will sustain 168 lbs. falling 10 feet, or 196 lbs. falling 8 feet, and they break with a dead weight of two tons.* In 1865 we carried two 100 feet lengths of the Manilla rope, and the inconvenience arising from its weight was more than made up for by the security which it afforded. Upon several occasions it was worth more than an extra guide.

Now, touching the *use* of the rope. There is a right way, and there are wrong ways of using it. I often meet, upon glacier-passes, elegantly got-up persons, who are clearly out of their element, with a guide stalking along in front, who pays no attention to the inno-

cents in his charge. They are tied to-gether as a matter of form, but they evidently have no idea *why* they are tied up, for they walk side by side, or close together, with the rope trailing on the snow. If one tumbles into a crevasse, the rest stare, and say, " La ! what is the matter with Smith ?" unless, as is more likely, they all tumble in together. This is the wrong way to use a rope. It is abuse of the rope.

It is of the first importance to keep the rope taut from man to man. There is no real security if this is not done, and your risks may be considerably magnified. There is little or no difficulty in

* Manufactured and sold by Messrs. Buckingham, Broad Street, Bloomsbury.

extricating one man who breaks through a bridged crevasse if the rope is taut; but the case may be very awkward if two break through at the same moment, close together, and there are only two others to aid, or perhaps only one other. Further, the rope ought not upon any account to graze over snow, ice, or rocks, otherwise the strands suffer, and the lives of the whole party may be endangered. Apart from this, it is extremely annoying to have a rope knocking about one's heels. If circumstances render it impossible for the rope to be kept taut by itself, the men behind should gather it up round their hands,* and not allow it to incommode those in advance. A man must either be incompetent,

THE RIGHT WAY TO USE THE ROPE.

careless, or selfish, if he permits the rope to dangle about the heels of the person in front of him.

The distance from man to man must neither be too great nor too small. About 12 feet between each is sufficient. If there are only two or three persons, it is prudent to allow a little more— say 15 feet. More than this is unnecessary, and less than 9 or 10 feet is not much good.

It is essential to examine your rope from time to time to see that it is in good condition. If you are wise you will do this yourself every day. Latterly, I have examined every inch of my rope overnight, and upon more than one occasion have found the strands of the Manilla rope nearly half severed through accidental grazes.

* For example, when the leader suspects crevasses, and *sounds* for them, in the manner shown in the engraving, he usually loses half a step or more. The second man should take a turn of the rope around his hand to draw it back in case the leader goes through.

Thus far the rope has been supposed to be employed upon level, snow-covered glacier, to prevent any risk from concealed crevasses. On rocks and on slopes it is used for a different purpose (namely, to guard against slips), and in these cases it is equally important to keep it taut, and to preserve a reasonable distance one from the other. It is much more troublesome to keep the rope taut upon slopes than upon the level ; and upon difficult rocks it is all but impossible, except by adopting the plan of moving only one at a time (see p. 170).

There is no good reason for employing a rope upon easy rocks, and I believe that its needless use is likely to promote carelessness. On difficult rocks and on snow-slopes (frequently improperly called ice-slopes) it is a great advantage to be tied together, provided the rope is handled properly ; but upon actual ice-slopes, such as that on the Col Dolent (p. 351), or upon slopes in which ice is mingled with small and loose rocks, such as the upper part of the Pointe des Ecrins (p. 214), it is almost useless, because the slip of one person might upset the entire party.* I am not prepared to say, however, that men should not be tied together upon similar slopes. Being attached to others usually gives confidence, and confidence decidedly assists stability. It is more questionable whether men should be in such places at all. If a man can keep on his feet upon an *escalier* cut in an ice-slope, I see no reason why he should be

---

* When several persons are descending such places, it is evident that the *last man* cannot derive any assistance from the rope, and so might as well be untied. Partly upon this account, it is usual to place one of the strongest and steadiest men last. Now, although this cannot be termed a senseless precaution, it is obvious that it is a perfectly useless one, if it is true that a single slip would upset the entire party. The best plan I know is that which we adopted on the descent of the Col Dolent, namely, to let one man go in advance until he reaches some secure point. This one then detaches himself, the rope is drawn up, and another man is sent down to join him, and so on until the last. The last man still occupies the most difficult post, and should be the steadiest man ; but he is not exposed to any risk from his comrades slipping, and they, of course, draw in the rope as he descends, so that his position is less hazardous than if he were to come down quite by himself.

debarred from making use of that particular form of staircase. If he cannot, let him keep clear of such places.*

There would be no advantage in discoursing upon the use of the rope at greater length. A single day upon a mountain's side will give a clear idea of the value of a good rope, and of the numerous purposes for which it may be employed, than any one will obtain from reading all that has been written upon the subject ; but no one will become really expert in its management without much experience.

From the Col d'Olen we proceeded down the Combe of the same name to the chalets of Prerayen, and passed the night of the 6th under the roof of our old acquaintance, the wealthy herdsman. On the 7th we crossed the Va Cornère pass, *en route* for Breil. My thoughts were fixed on the Matterhorn, and my guides knew that I wished them to accompany me. They had an aversion to the mountain, and repeatedly expressed their belief that it was useless to try to ascend it. " *Anything* but Matterhorn, dear sir ! " said Almer ; " *anything* but Matterhorn." He did not speak of difficulty or of danger, nor was he shirking *work*. He offered to go *anywhere ;* but he entreated that the Matterhorn should be abandoned. Both men spoke fairly enough. They did not think that an ascent could be made ; and for their own credit, as well as for my sake, they did not wish to undertake a business which, in their opinion, would only lead to loss of time and money.

---

* Upon this subject I refer the reader back to p. 113. If you are out upon an excursion, and find the work becoming so arduous that you have great difficulty in maintaining your balance, you should at once retire, and not imperil the lives of others. I am well aware that the withdrawal of one person for such reasons would usually necessitate the retreat of a second, and that expeditions would be often cut short if this were to happen. With the fear of this before their eyes, I believe that many amateurs continue to go on, albeit well convinced that they ought not. They do not wish to stop the sport of their comrades ; but they frequently suffer mental tortures in consequence, which most emphatically do not assist their stability, and are likely to lead to something even more disagreeable than the abandonment of the excursion. The moral is, take an adequate number of guides.

3 c

I sent them by the short cut to Breil, and walked down to Val Tournanche to look for Jean-Antoine Carrel. He was not there. The villagers said that he, and three others, had started on the 6th to try the Matterhorn by the old way, on their own account. They will have no luck, I thought, for the clouds were low down on the mountains; and I walked up to Breil, fully expecting to meet them. Nor was I disappointed. About half-way up I saw a group of men clustered around a chalet upon the other side of the torrent, and, crossing over, found that the party had returned. Jean-Antoine and Cæsar were there, C. E. Gorret, and J. J. Maquignaz. They had had no success. The weather, they said, had been horrible, and they had scarcely reached the glacier du Lion.

I explained the situation to Carrel, and proposed that we, with Cæsar and another man, should cross the Theodule by moon-light on the 9th, and that upon the 10th we should pitch the tent as high as possible upon the east face. He was unwilling to abandon the old route, and urged me to try it again. I promised to do so provided the new route failed. This satisfied him, and he agreed to my proposal. I then went up to Breil, and discharged Almer and Biener—with much regret, for no two men ever served me more faithfully or more willingly.* On the next day they crossed to Zermatt.

The 8th was occupied with preparations. The weather was stormy; and black, rainy vapours obscured the mountains. Towards evening a young man came from Val Tournanche, and reported that an Englishman was lying there, extremely ill. Now was the time for the performance of my vow;† and on the morning of Sunday the 9th I went down the valley to look after the sick man. On my way I passed a foreign gentleman, with a mule and several porters laden with baggage. Amongst these men were Jean-

---

* During the preceding eighteen days (I exclude Sundays and other non-working days) we ascended more than 100,000 feet, and descended 98,000 feet.

† See p. 122.

Antoine and Cæsar, carrying some barometers. " Hullo !" I said,
"what are you doing?" They explained that the foreigner had
arrived just as they were setting out, and that they were assisting
his porters. " Very well ; go on to Breil, and await me there ; we
start at midnight as agreed." Jean-Antoine then said that he
should not be able to serve me after Tuesday the 11th, as he was
engaged to travel "with a family of distinction" in the valley of
Aosta. " And Cæsar?" " And Cæsar also." "Why did you not
say this before?" "Because," said he, "it was not settled. The
engagement is of long standing, but *the day* was not fixed. When
I got back to Val Tournanche on Friday night, after leaving you, I
found a letter naming the day." I could not object to the answer ;
but the prospect of being left guideless was provoking. They
went up, and I down, the valley.

The sick man declared that he was better, though the exertion
of saying as much tumbled him over on to the floor in a fainting fit.
He was badly in want of medicine, and I tramped down to Chatillon to get it. It was late before I returned to Val Tournanche,
for the weather was tempestuous, and rain fell in torrents. A figure
passed me under the church-porch. " *Qui vive?* " " Jean-Antoine."
I thought you were at Breil." " No, sir : when the storms came on
I knew we should not start to-night, and so came down to sleep
here." " Ha, Carrel !" I said ; " this is a great bore. If to-morrow
is not fine we shall not be able to do anything together. I have
sent away my guides, relying on you ; and now you are going to
leave me to travel with a party of ladies. That work is not fit for
you (he smiled, I supposed at the implied compliment) ; can't you
send some one else instead?" " No, monsieur. I am sorry, but
my word is pledged. I should like to accompany you, but I
can't break my engagement." By this time we had arrived at the
inn door. " Well, it is no fault of yours. Come presently with
Cæsar, and have some wine." They came, and we sat up till
midnight, recounting our old adventures, in the inn of Val
Tournanche.

The weather continued bad upon the 10th, and I returned to Breil. The two Carrels were again hovering about the above mentioned chalet, and I bade them adieu. In the evening the sick man crawled up, a good deal better ; but his was the only arrival. The Monday crowd* did not cross the Theodule, on account of the continued storms. The inn was lonely. I went to bed early, and was awoke the next morning by the invalid inquiring if I had "heard the news." "No ; what news ?" "Why," said he, "a large party of guides went off this morning to try the Matterhorn, taking with them a mule laden with provisions."

I went to the door, and with a telescope saw the party upon the lower slopes of the mountain. Favre, the landlord, stood by. "What is all this about ?" I inquired, "who is the leader of this party ?" "Carrel." "What! Jean-Antoine ?" "Yes ; Jean-Antoine." "Is Cæsar there too ?" "Yes, he is there." Then I saw in a moment that I had been bamboozled and humbugged ; and learned, bit by bit, that the affair had been arranged long beforehand. The start on the 6th had been for a preliminary reconnaissance ; the mule, that I passed, was conveying stores for the attack ; the 'family of distinction' was Signor F. Giordano, who had just despatched the party to facilitate the way to the summit, and who, when the facilitation was completed, was to be taken to the top along with Signor Sella ! †

I was greatly mortified. My plans were upset ; the Italians had clearly stolen a march upon me, and I saw that the astute Favre chuckled over my discomfiture, because the route by the eastern face, if successful, would not benefit his inn. What was to be done ? I retired to my room, and soothed by tobacco, re-studied my plans, to see if it was not possible to outmanœuvre the Italians. "They have taken a mule's load of provisions." That is *one* point

* Tourists usually congregate at Zermatt upon Sundays, and large gangs and droves cross the Theodule pass on Mondays.

† The Italian Minister. Signor Giordano had undertaken the business arrangements for Signor Sella.

in my favour, for they will take two or three days to get through the food, and, until that is done, no work will be accomplished." " How is the weather ?" I went to the window. The mountain was smothered up in mist. " Another point in my favour." " They are to facilitate the way. Well, if they do that to any purpose, it will be a long job." Altogether, I reckoned that they could not possibly ascend the mountain and come back to Breil in less than seven days. I got cooler, for it was evident that the wily ones might be outwitted after all. There was time enough to go to Zermatt, to try the eastern face, and, should it prove impracticable, to come back to Breil before the men returned ; and then, it seemed to me, as the mountain was not padlocked, one might start at the same time as the Messieurs, and yet get to the top before them.

The first thing to do was to go to Zermatt. Easier said than done. The seven guides upon the mountain included the ablest men in the valley, and none of the ordinary muleteer-guides were at Breil. Two men, at least, were wanted for my baggage, but not a soul could be found. I ran about, and sent about in all directions, but not a single porter could be obtained. One was with Carrel ; another was ill ; another was at Chatillon, and so forth. Even Meynet, the hunchback, could not be induced to come ; he was in the thick of some important cheese-making operations. I was in the position of a general without an army ; it was all very well to make plans, but there was no one to execute them. This did not much trouble me, for it was evident that so long as the weather stopped traffic over the Theodule, it would hinder the men equally upon the Matterhorn ; and I knew that directly it improved company would certainly arrive.

About midday on Tuesday the 11th a large party hove in sight from Zermatt, preceded by a nimble young Englishman, and one of old Peter Taugwalder's sons.* I went at once to this gentleman to learn if he could dispense with Taugwalder. He said that he

* Peter Taugwalder, the father, is called *old* Peter, to distinguish him from his eldest son, *young* Peter. In 1865 the father's age was about 45.

could not, as they were going to recross to Zermatt on the morrow, but that the young man should assist in transporting my baggage, as he had nothing to carry. We naturally got into conversation. I told my story, and learned that the young Englishman was Lord Francis Douglas,* whose recent exploit—the ascent of the Gabelhorn—had excited my wonder and admiration. He brought good news. Old Peter had lately been beyond the Hörnli, and had reported that he thought an ascent of the Matterhorn was possible upon that side. Almer had left Zermatt, and could not be recovered, so I determined to seek for old Peter. Lord Francis Douglas expressed a warm desire to ascend the mountain, and before long it was determined that he should take part in the expedition.

Favre could no longer hinder our departure, and lent us one of his men. We crossed the Col Theodule on Wednesday morning the 12th of July, rounded the foot of the Ober Theodulgletscher, crossed the Furggengletscher, and deposited tent, blankets, ropes, and other matters in the little chapel at the Schwarzsee.† All four were heavily laden, for we brought across the whole of my stores from Breil. Of rope alone there was about 600 feet. There were three kinds. First, 200 feet of the Manilla rope ; second, 150 feet of a stouter, and probably stronger rope than the first ; and third, more than 200 feet of a lighter and weaker rope than the first, of a kind that I used formerly (stout sash-line).

We descended to Zermatt, sought and engaged old Peter, and gave him permission to choose another guide. When we returned to the Monte Rosa Hotel, whom should we see sitting upon the wall in front but my old *guide chef*, Michel Croz. I supposed that he had come with Mr. B——, but I learned that that gentleman had arrived in ill health, at Chamounix, and had returned to England. Croz, thus left free, had been immediately engaged by the Rev. Charles Hudson, and they had come to Zermatt with the

---

* Brother of the present Marquis of Queensberry.

† For route, and the others mentioned in the subsequent chapters, see map of the Matterhorn and its glaciers.

same object as ourselves—namely, to attempt the ascent of the Matterhorn !

Lord Francis Douglas and I dined at the Monte Rosa, and had just finished when Mr. Hudson and a friend entered the *salle à manger*. They had returned from inspecting the mountain, and some idlers in the room demanded their intentions. We heard a confirmation of Croz's statement, and learned that Mr. Hudson intended to set out on the morrow at the same hour as ourselves. We left the room to consult, and agreed it was undesirable that two independent parties should be on the mountain at the same time with the same object. Mr. Hudson was therefore invited to join us, and he accepted our proposal. Before admitting his friend—Mr. Hadow—I took the precaution to inquire what he had done in the Alps, and, as well as I remember, Mr. Hudson's reply was, " Mr. Hadow has done Mont Blanc in less time than most men." He then mentioned several other excursions that were unknown to me, and added, in answer to a further question, " I consider he is a sufficiently good man to go with us." Mr. Hadow was admitted without any further question, and we then went into the matter of guides. Hudson thought that Croz and old Peter would be sufficient. The question was referred to the men themselves, and they made no objection.

So Croz and I became comrades once more ; and as I threw myself on my bed and tried to go to sleep, I wondered at the strange series of chances which had first separated us and then brought us together again. I thought of the mistake through which he had accepted the engagement to Mr. B——; of his unwillingness to adopt my route ; of his recommendation to transfer our energies to the chain of Mont Blanc ; of the retirement of Almer and Biener ; of the desertion of Carrel ; of the arrival of Lord Francis Douglas ; and, lastly, of our accidental meeting at Zermatt ; and as I pondered over these things I could not help asking, " What next ?" If any one of the links of this fatal chain of circumstances had been omitted, what a different story I should have to tell !

CHAPTER XXI.

THE ASCENT OF THE MATTERHORN.

"Had we succeeded well,
We had been reckoned 'mongst the wise : our minds
Are so disposed to judge from the event."
EURIPIDES.

"It is a thoroughly unfair, but an ordinary custom, to praise or blame designs (which in themselves may be good or bad) just as they turn out well or ill. Hence the same actions are at one time attributed to earnestness and at another to vanity."
PLINY MIN.

WE started from Zermatt on the 13th of July, at half-past 5, on a brilliant and perfectly cloudless morning. We were eight in number—Croz, old Peter and his two sons,* Lord F. Douglas, Hadow, Hudson,† and I. To ensure steady motion, one tourist and

* The two young Taugwalders were taken as porters, by desire of their father, and carried provisions amply sufficient for three days, in case the ascent should prove more troublesome than we anticipated.

† I remember speaking about pedestrianism to a well-known mountaineer some years ago, and venturing to remark that a man who averaged thirty miles a-day might be considered a good walker. "A fair walker," he said, "a *fair* walker." "What then would you consider *good* walking?" "Well," he replied, "I will tell you. Some time back a friend and I agreed to go to Switzerland, but a short time afterwards he wrote to say he ought to let me know that a young and delicate lad was going with him who would not be equal to great things, in fact, he would not be able to do more than fifty miles a-day!" "What became of the young and delicate lad?" "He lives." "And who was your extraordinary friend?" "Charles Hudson." I have every reason to believe that the gentlemen referred to *were* equal to walking more than fifty miles a-day, but they were exceptional, not *good* pedestrians.

Charles Hudson, Vicar of Skillington in Lincolnshire, was considered by the mountaineering fraternity to be the best amateur of his time. He was the organiser and leader of the party of Englishmen who ascended Mont Blanc by the Aig. du Goûter, and descended by the Grands Mulets route, without guides, in 1855. His

one native walked together.   The youngest Taugwalder fell to my share, and the lad marched well, proud to be on the expedition, and happy to show his powers.   The wine-bags also fell to my lot to carry, and throughout the day, after each drink, I replenished them secretly with water, so that at the next halt they were found fuller than before !   This was considered a good omen, and little short of miraculous.

On the first day we did not intend to ascend to any great height, and we mounted, accordingly, very leisurely ; picked up the things which were left in the chapel at the Schwarzsee at 8.20, and proceeded thence along the ridge connecting the Hörnli with the Matterhorn.*   At half-past 11 we arrived at the base of the actual peak ; then quitted the ridge, and clambered round some

long practice made him surefooted, and in that respect he was not greatly inferior to a born mountaineer.   I remember him as a well-made man of middle height and age, neither stout nor thin, with face pleasant—though grave, and with quiet unassuming manners.   Although an athletic man, he would have been overlooked in a crowd ; and although he had done the greatest mountaineering feats which have been done, he was the last man to speak of his own doings.   His friend Mr. Hadow was a young man of nineteen, who had the looks and manners of a greater age.   He was a rapid walker, but 1865 was his first season in the Alps.   Lord Francis Douglas was about the same age as Mr. Hadow.   He had had the advantage of several seasons in the Alps.   He was nimble as a deer, and was becoming an expert mountaineer.   Just before our meeting he had ascended the Ober Gabelhorn (with old Peter and Jos. Viennin), and this gave me a high opinion of his powers ; for I had examined that mountain all round, a few weeks before, and had declined its ascent on account of its apparent difficulty.

My personal acquaintance with Mr. Hudson was very slight—still I should have been content to have placed myself under his orders if he had chosen to claim the position to which he was entitled.   Those who knew him will not be surprised to learn that, so far from doing this, he lost no opportunity of consulting the wishes and opinions of those around him.   We deliberated together whenever there was occasion, and our authority was recognised by the others.   Whatever responsibility there was devolved upon us.   I recollect with satisfaction that there was no difference of opinion between us as to what should be done, and that the most perfect harmony existed between all of us so long as we were together.

* Arrived at the chapel 7.30 A.M. ; left it, 8.20 ; halted to examine route 9.30 ; started again 10.25, and arrived at 11.20 at the cairn made by Mr. Kennedy in 1862 (see p 97), marked 10,820 feet upon the map.   Stopped 10 min. here.   From the

3 D

ledges, on to the eastern face. We were now fairly upon the mountain, and were astonished to find that places which from the Riffel, or even from the Furggengletscher, looked entirely impracticable, were so easy that we could *run about.*

Before twelve o'clock we had found a good position for the tent, at a height of 11,000 feet.* Croz and young Peter went on to see what was above, in order to save time on the following morning. They cut across the heads of the snow-slopes which descended towards the Furggengletscher, and disappeared round a corner ; but shortly afterwards we saw them high up on the face, moving quickly. We others made a solid platform for the tent in a well-protected spot, and then watched eagerly for the return of the men. The stones which they upset told that they were very high, and we supposed that the way must be easy. At length, just before 3 P.M., we saw them coming down, evidently much excited. " What are they saying, Peter ?" " Gentlemen, they say it is no good." But when they came near we heard a different story. " Nothing but what was good ; not a difficulty, not a single difficulty ! We could have gone to the summit and returned to-day easily !"

We passed the remaining hours of daylight—some basking in the sunshine, some sketching or collecting ; and when the sun went down, giving, as it departed, a glorious promise for the morrow, we returned to the tent to arrange for the night. Hudson made tea, I coffee, and we then retired each one to his blanket-bag ; the Taugwalders, Lord Francis Douglas, and myself, occupying the tent, the

Hörnli to this point we kept, when possible, to the crest of the ridge. The greater part of the way was excessively easy, but there were a few places where the axe had to be used.

    * Thus far the guides did not once go to the front. Hudson or I led, and when any cutting was required we did it ourselves. This was done to spare the guides, and to show them that we were thoroughly in earnest. The spot at which we camped was just four hours' walking from Zermatt, and is marked upon the map—CAMP (1865). It was just upon a level with the Furggengrat, and its position is indicated upon the engraving facing p. 285 by a little circular white spot, in a line with the word CAMP.

others remaining, by preference, outside. Long after dusk the cliffs above echoed with our laughter and with the songs of the guides, for we were happy that night in camp, and feared no evil.

We assembled together outside the tent before dawn on the morning of the 14th, and started directly it was light enough to move. Young Peter came on with us as a guide, and his brother returned to Zermatt.* We followed the route which had been taken on the previous day, and in a few minutes turned the rib which had intercepted the view of the eastern face from our tent platform. The whole of this great slope was now revealed, rising for 3000 feet like a huge natural staircase.† Some parts were more, and others were less, easy ; but we were not once brought to a halt by any serious impediment, for when an obstruction was met in front it could always be turned to the right or to the left. For the greater part of the way there was, indeed, no occasion for the rope, and sometimes Hudson led, sometimes myself. At 6.20 we had attained a height of 12,800 feet, and halted for half-an-hour ; we then continued the ascent without a break until 9.55, when we stopped for 50 minutes, at a height of 14,000 feet. Twice we struck the N.E. ridge, and followed it for some little distance,‡—to no advantage, for it was usually more rotten and steep, and always more difficult than the face.§ Still, we kept near to it, lest stones perchance might fall. ‖

* It was originally intended to leave both of the young men behind. We found it difficult to divide the food, and so the new arrangement was made.

† See pp. 285-9.

‡ For track, see the lower of the outlines facing p. 288.

§ See remarks on arêtes and faces on pp. 265-6. There is very little to choose between in the arêtes leading from the summit towards the Hörnli (N.E. ridge) and towards the Col du Lion (S.W. ridge). Both are jagged, serrated ridges, which any experienced climber would willingly avoid if he could find another route. On the northern (Zermatt) side the eastern face affords another route, or any number of routes, since there is hardly a part of it which cannot be traversed ! On the southern (Breil) side the ridge alone, generally speaking, can be followed ; and when it becomes impracticable, and the climber is forced to bear down to the right or to the left, the work is of the most difficult character.

‖ Very few stones fell during the two days I was on the mountain, and none came

We had now arrived at the foot of that part which, from the Riffelberg or from Zermatt, seems perpendicular or overhanging, and could no longer continue upon the eastern side. For a little distance we ascended by snow upon the arête*—that is, the ridge —descending towards Zermatt, and then, by common consent, turned over to the right, or to the northern side. Before doing so, we made a change in the order of ascent. Croz went first, I followed, Hudson came third ; Hadow and old Peter were last. " Now," said Croz, as he led off, " now for something altogether different." The work became difficult, and required caution. In some places there was little to hold, and it was desirable that those should be in front who were least likely to slip. The general slope of the mountain at this part was *less* than 40°, and snow had accumulated in, and had filled up, the interstices of the rock-face, leaving only occasional fragments projecting here and there. These were at times covered with a thin film of ice, produced from the melting and refreezing of the snow. It was the counterpart, on a small scale, of the upper 700 feet of the Pointe des Ecrins,—only there was this material difference; the face of the Ecrins was about, or exceeded, an angle of 50°, and the Matterhorn face was less than 40°.† It was a place over which

near us. Others who have followed the same route have not been so fortunate ; they may not, perhaps, have taken the same precautions. It is a noteworthy fact, that the lateral moraine of the left bank of the Furggengletscher is scarcely larger than that of the right bank, although the former receives all the débris that falls from the 4000 feet of cliffs which form the eastern side of the Matterhorn, whilst the latter is fed by perfectly insignificant slopes. Neither of these moraines is large. This is strong evidence that stones do *not* fall to any great extent from the eastern face. The inward dip of the beds retains the detritus in place. Hence the eastern face appears, when one is upon it, to be undergoing more rapid disintegration than the other sides : in reality, the mantle of ruin spares the mountain from farther waste. Upon the southern side, rocks fall as they are rent off ; " each day's work is cleared away " every day ; and hence the faces and ridges are left naked, and exposed to fresh attacks.

* The snow seen in the engraving facing p. 285, half-an-inch below the summit, and a little to its left.

† This part was less steeply inclined than the whole of the eastern face.

any fair mountaineer might pass in safety, and Mr. Hudson ascended this part, and, as far as I know, the entire mountain, without having the slightest assistance rendered to him upon any occasion. Sometimes, after I had taken a hand from Croz, or received a pull, I turned to offer the same to Hudson ; but he invariably declined, saying it was not necessary. Mr. Hadow, however, was not accustomed to this kind of work, and required continual assistance. It is only fair to say that the difficulty which he found at this part arose simply and entirely from want of experience.

This solitary difficult part was of no great extent.* We bore away over it at first, nearly horizontally, for a distance of about 400 feet ; then ascended directly towards the summit for about 60 feet ; and then doubled back to the ridge which descends towards Zermatt. A long stride round a rather awkward corner brought us to snow once more. The last doubt vanished ! The Matterhorn was ours ! Nothing but 200 feet of easy snow remained to be surmounted !

You must now carry your thoughts back to the seven Italians who started from Breil on the 11th of July. Four days had passed since their departure, and we were tormented with anxiety lest they should arrive on the top before us. All the way up we had talked of them, and many false alarms of " men on the summit" had been raised. The higher we rose, the more intense became the excitement. What if we should be beaten at the last moment ? The slope eased off, at length we could be detached, and Croz and I, dashing away, ran a neck-and-neck race, which ended in a dead heat. At 1.40 P.M. the world was at our feet, and the Matterhorn was conquered. Hurrah ! Not a footstep could be seen.

It was not yet certain that we had not been beaten. The summit of the Matterhorn was formed of a rudely level ridge,

---

* I have no memorandum of the time that it occupied. It must have taken about an hour and a half.

about 350 feet long,* and the Italians might have been at its farther extremity. I hastened to the southern end, scanning the snow right and left eagerly. Hurrah! again; it was untrodden. "Where were the men?" I peered over the cliff, half doubting, half expectant. I saw them immediately—mere dots on the ridge,

"CROZ! CROZ!! COME HERE!"

at an immense distance below. Up went my arms and my hat.

* The highest points are towards the two ends. In 1865 the northern end was slightly higher than the southern one. In bygone years Carrel and I often suggested to each other that we might one day arrive upon the top, and find ourselves cut off from the very highest point by a notch in the summit-ridge which is seen from the Theodule and from Breil (marked **D** on the outline on p. 128). This notch is very conspicuous from below, but when one is actually upon the summit it is hardly noticed, and it can be passed without the least difficulty.

"Croz! Croz!! come here!"   "Where are they, Monsieur?"
"There, don't you see them, down there?"   "Ah! the *coquins*,
they are low down."   "Croz, we must make those fellows hear us."
We yelled until we were hoarse.   The Italians seemed to regard us
—we could not be certain.   "Croz, we *must* make them hear us ;
they *shall* hear us!"   I seized a block of rock and hurled it down,
and called upon my companion, in the name of friendship, to do
the same.   We drove our sticks in, and prized away the crags, and
soon a torrent of stones poured down the cliffs.   There was no
mistake about it this time.   The Italians turned and fled.*

Still, I would that the leader of that party could have stood
with us at that moment, for our victorious shouts conveyed to him
the disappointment of the ambition of a lifetime.   He was *the* man,
of all those who attempted the ascent of the Matterhorn, who most
deserved to be the first upon its summit.   He was the first to
doubt its inaccessibility, and he was the only man who persisted in
believing that its ascent would be accomplished.   It was the aim
of his life to make the ascent from the side of Italy, for the honour
of his native valley.   For a time he had the game in his hands :
he played it as he thought best ; but he made a false move, and he
lost it.   Times have changed with Carrel.   His supremacy is questioned in the Val Tournanche ; new men have arisen ; and he is no
longer recognised as *the* chasseur above all others : but so long as
he remains the man that he is to-day, it will not be easy to find his
superior.

The others had arrived, so we went back to the northern end
of the ridge.   Croz now took the tent-pole,† and planted it in the
highest snow.   "Yes," we said, "there is the flag-staff, but where
is the flag?"   "Here it is," he answered, pulling off his blouse and

* I have learnt since from J.-A. Carrel that they heard our first cries.   They
were then upon the south-west ridge, close to the 'Cravate,' and *twelve hundred and
fifty* feet below us ; or, as the crow flies, at a distance of about one-third of a mile.

† At our departure the men were confident that the ascent would be made, and
took one of the poles out of the tent.   I protested that it was tempting Providence ;
they took the pole, nevertheless.

fixing it to the stick.. It made a poor flag, and there was no wind
to float it out, yet it was seen all around. They saw it at Zermatt—
at the Riffel—in the Val Tournanche. At Breil, the watchers
cried, " Victory is ours!" They raised ' bravos' for Carrel, and
' vivas' for Italy, and hastened to put themselves *en fête*. On the

THE SUMMIT OF THE MATTERHORN IN 1865 (NORTHERN END).

morrow they were undeceived. " All was changed ; the explorers
returned sad—cast down—disheartened—confounded—gloomy."
" It is true," said the men. " We saw them ourselves—they hurled
stones at us! The old traditions *are* true,—there are spirits on
the top of the Matterhorn !"*

* Signor Giordano was naturally disappointed at the result, and wished the men
to start again. *They all refused to do so, with the exception of Jean-Antoine.* Upon
the 16th of July he set out again with three others, and upon the 17th gained the

We returned to the southern end of the ridge to build a cairn, and then paid homage to the view.* The day was one of those superlatively calm and clear ones which usually precede bad weather. The atmosphere was perfectly still, and free from all clouds or vapours. Mountains fifty—nay a hundred—miles off, looked sharp and near. All their details—ridge and crag, snow and glacier—stood out with faultless definition. Pleasant thoughts of happy days in bygone years came up unbidden, as we recognised the old, familiar forms. All were revealed—not one of the princi-

summit by passing (at first) up the south-west ridge, and (afterwards) by turning over to the Z'Mutt, or north-western side. On the 18th he returned to Breil.

Whilst we were upon the southern end of the summit-ridge, we paid some attention to the portion of the mountain which intervened between ourselves and the Italian guides. It seemed as if there would not be the least chance for them if they should attempt to storm the final peak directly from the end of the 'shoulder.' In that direction cliffs fell sheer down from the summit, and we were unable to see beyond a certain distance. There remained the route about which Carrel and I had often talked, namely, to ascend directly at first from the end of the ' shoulder,' and afterwards to swerve to the left—that is, to the Z'Mutt side—and to complete the ascent from the north-west. When we were upon the summit we laughed at this idea. The part of the mountain that I have described upon p. 388, was not easy, although its inclination was moderate. If that slope were made only ten degrees steeper, its difficulty would be enormously increased. To double its inclination would be to make it impracticable. The slope at the southern end of the summit-ridge, falling towards the north-west, was *much* steeper than that over which we passed, and we ridiculed the idea that any person should attempt to ascend in that direction, when the northern route was so easy. Nevertheless, the summit was reached by that route by the undaunted Carrel. From knowing the final slope over which he passed, and from the account of Mr. F. C. Grove—who is the only traveller by whom it has been traversed—I do not hesitate to term the ascent of Carrel and Bich in 1865 the most desperate piece of mountain-scrambling upon record. In 1869 I asked Carrel if he had ever done anything more difficult. His reply was, "Man cannot do anything much more difficult than that!" See Appendix.

* The summit-ridge was much shattered, although not so extensively as the south-west and north-east ridges. The highest rock, in 1865, was a block of mica-schist, and the fragment I broke off it not only possesses, in a remarkable degree, the *character* of the peak, but mimics, in an astonishing manner, the details of its form. (See illustration on page 395.)

3 E

pal peaks of the Alps was hidden.* I see them clearly now—the great inner circles of giants, backed by the ranges, chains, and *massifs*. First came the Dent Blanche, hoary and grand ; the Gabelhorn and pointed Rothhorn ; and then the peerless Weisshorn : the towering Mischabelhörner, flanked by the Allaleinhorn, Strahlhorn, and Rimpfischhorn ; then Monte Rosa—with its many Spitzes—the Lyskamm and the Breithorn. Behind were the Bernese Oberland, governed by the Finsteraarhorn ; the Simplon and St. Gothard groups ; the Disgrazia and the Orteler. Towards the south we looked down to Chivasso on the plain of Piedmont, and far beyond. The Viso—one hundred miles away—seemed close upon us ; the Maritime Alps—one hundred and thirty miles distant—were free from haze. Then came my first love—the Pelvoux ; the Ecrins and the Meije ; the clusters of the Graians ; and lastly, in the west, gorgeous in the full sunlight, rose the monarch of all—Mont Blanc. Ten thousand feet beneath us were the green fields of Zermatt, dotted with chalets, from which blue smoke rose lazily. Eight thousand feet below, on the other side, were the pastures of Breil. There were forests black and gloomy, and meadows bright and lively ; bounding waterfalls and tranquil lakes ; fertile lands and savage wastes ; sunny plains and frigid *plateaux*. There were the most rugged forms, and the most graceful outlines—bold, perpendicular cliffs, and gentle, undulating slopes ; rocky mountains and snowy mountains, sombre and solemn, or glittering and white, with walls—turrets—pinnacles—pyramids —domes—cones—and spires ! There was every combination that the world can give, and every contrast that the heart could desire.

We remained on the summit for one hour—

> " One crowded hour of glorious life."

It passed away too quickly, and we began to prepare for the descent.

---

* It is most unusual to see the southern half of the panorama unclouded. A hundred ascents may be made before this will be the case again.

THE ACTUAL SUMMIT OF THE MATTERHORN IN 1865.

CHAPTER XXII.

DESCENT OF THE MATTERHORN.*

HUDSON and I again consulted as to the best and safest arrangement of the party. We agreed that it would be best for Croz to go first,† and Hadow second ; Hudson, who was almost equal to a guide in sureness of foot, wished to be third ; Lord F. Douglas was placed next, and old Peter, the strongest of the remainder, after him. I suggested to Hudson that we should attach a rope to the rocks on our arrival at the difficult bit, and hold it as we descended, as an additional protection. He approved the idea, but it was not definitely settled that it should be done. The party was being

* The substance of Chapter XXII. appeared in a letter in the *Times*, August 8, 1865. A few paragraphs have now been added, and a few corrections have been made. The former will help to make clear that which was obscure in the original account, and the latter are, mostly, unimportant.

† If the members of the party had been more equally efficient, Croz would have been placed *last*.

arranged in the above order whilst I was sketching the summit, and they had finished, and were waiting for me to be tied in line, when some one remembered that our names had not been left in a bottle. They requested me to write them down, and moved off while it was being done.

A few minutes afterwards I tied myself to young Peter, ran down after the others, and caught them just as they were commencing the descent of the difficult part.* Great care was being taken. Only one man was moving at a time ; when he was firmly planted the next advanced, and so on. They had not, however, attached the additional rope to rocks, and nothing was said about it. The suggestion was not made for my own sake, and I am not sure that it even occurred to me again. For some little distance we two followed the others, detached from them, and should have continued so had not Lord F. Douglas asked me, about 3 P.M., to tie on to old Peter, as he feared, he said, that Taugwalder would not be able to hold his ground if a slip occurred.

A few minutes later, a sharp-eyed lad ran into the Monte Rosa hotel, to Seiler, saying that he had seen an avalanche fall from the summit of the Matterhorn on to the Matterhorngletscher. The boy was reproved for telling idle stories ; he was right, nevertheless, and this was what he saw.

Michel Croz had laid aside his axe, and in order to give Mr. Hadow greater security, was absolutely taking hold of his legs, and putting his feet, one by one, into their proper positions.† As far as I know, no one was actually descending. I cannot speak with certainty, because the two leading men were partially hidden from my sight by an intervening mass of rock, but it is my belief, from

---

* Described upon pp. 388-9.

† Not at all an unusual proceeding, even between born mountaineers. I wish to convey the impression that Croz was using all pains, rather than to indicate extreme inability on the part of Mr. Hadow. The insertion of the word 'absolutely' makes the passage, perhaps, rather ambiguous. I retain it now, in order to offer the above explanation.

the movements of their shoulders, that Croz, having done as I have said, was in the act of turning round to go down a step or two himself; at this moment Mr. Hadow slipped, fell against him, and knocked him over. I heard one startled exclamation from Croz, then saw him and Mr. Hadow flying downwards; in another moment Hudson was dragged from his steps, and Lord F. Douglas immediately after him.* All this was the work of a moment. Immediately we heard Croz's exclamation, old Peter and I planted ourselves as firmly as the rocks would permit :† the rope was taut between us, and the jerk came on us both as on one man. We held; but the rope broke midway between Taugwalder and Lord Francis Douglas. For a few seconds we saw our unfortunate companions sliding downwards on their backs, and spreading out their

---

* At the moment of the accident, Croz, Hadow, and Hudson, were all close together. Between Hudson and Lord F. Douglas the rope was all but taut, and the same between all the others who were *above.* Croz was standing by the side of a rock which afforded good hold, and if he had been aware, or had suspected, that anything was about to occur, he might and would have gripped it, and would have prevented any mischief. He was taken totally by surprise. Mr. Hadow slipped off his feet on to his back, his feet struck Croz in the small of the back, and knocked him right over, head first. Croz's axe was out of his reach, and without it he managed to get his head uppermost before he disappeared from our sight. If it had been in his hand I have no doubt that he would have stopped himself and Mr. Hadow.

Mr. Hadow, at the moment of the slip, was not occupying a bad position. He could have moved either up or down, and could touch with his hand the rock of which I have spoken. Hudson was not so well placed, but he had liberty of motion. The rope was not taut from him to Hadow, and the two men fell ten or twelve feet before the jerk came upon him. Lord F. Douglas was not favourably placed, and could neither move up nor down. Old Peter was firmly planted, and stood just beneath a large rock which he hugged with both arms. I enter into these details to make it more apparent that the position occupied by the party at the moment of the accident was not by any means excessively trying. We were compelled to pass over the exact spot where the slip occurred, and we found—even with shaken nerves—that it was not a difficult place to pass. I have described the *slope generally* as difficult, and it is so undoubtedly to most persons; but it must be distinctly understood that Mr. Hadow slipped at an easy part.

† Or, more correctly, we held on as tightly as possible. There was no time to change our position.

hands, endeavouring to save themselves.   They passed from our sight uninjured, disappeared one by one, and fell from precipice to precipice on to the Matterhorngletscher below, a distance of nearly 4000 feet in height.   From the moment the rope broke it was impossible to help them.

So perished our comrades!   For the space of half-an-hour we remained on the spot without moving a single step.   The two men, paralysed by terror, cried like infants, and trembled in such a manner as to threaten us with the fate of the others.   Old Peter rent the air with exclamations of " Chamounix! Oh, what will Chamounix say?"   He meant, Who would believe that Croz could fall?   The young man did nothing but scream or sob, " We

are lost! we are lost!"   Fixed between the two, I could neither move up nor down.   I begged young Peter to descend, but he dared not. Unless he did, we could not advance.   Old Peter became alive to the danger, and swelled the cry, " We are lost! we are lost!"   The father's fear was natural—he trembled for his son ; the young man's fear was cowardly—he thought of self alone. At last old Peter summoned up courage, and changed his position to a rock to which he could fix the rope ; the young man then descended, and we all stood together.

ROPE BROKEN ON THE MATTERHORN.

Immediately we did so, I asked for the rope which had given way, and found, to my surprise—indeed, to my horror—that it was the weakest of the three ropes.   It was not brought, and should not have been employed, for the purpose for which it was used.   It was old rope, and, compared with the others, was feeble.   It was intended as a reserve, in case we had to leave much rope behind, attached to rocks. I saw at once that a serious question was involved, and made him give me the end. It had broken in mid-air, and it did not appear to have sustained previous injury.

For more than two hours afterwards I thought almost every moment that the next would be my last ; for the Taugwalders, utterly unnerved, were not only incapable of giving assistance, but were in such a state that a slip might have been expected from them at any moment. After a time, we were able to do that which should have been done at first, and fixed rope to firm rocks, in addition to being tied together. These ropes were cut from time to time, and were left behind.* Even with their assurance the men were afraid to proceed, and several times old Peter turned with ashy face and faltering limbs, and said, with terrible emphasis, "*I cannot !*"

About 6 P.M. we arrived at the snow upon the ridge descending towards Zermatt, and all peril was over. We frequently looked, but in vain, for traces of our unfortunate companions ; we bent over the ridge and cried to them, but no sound returned. Convinced at last that they were neither within sight nor hearing, we ceased from our useless efforts ; and, too cast down for speech, silently gathered up our things, and the little effects of those who were lost, preparatory to continuing the descent. When, lo ! a mighty arch appeared, rising above the Lyskamm, high into the sky. Pale, colourless, and noiseless, but perfectly sharp and defined, except where it was lost in the clouds, this unearthly apparition seemed like a vision from another world ; and, almost appalled, we watched with amazement the gradual development of two vast crosses, one on either side. If the Taugwalders had not been the first to perceive it, I should have doubted my senses. They thought it had some connection with the accident, and I, after a while, that it might bear some relation to ourselves. But our

---

* These ends, I believe, are still attached to the rocks, and mark our line of ascent and descent.

movements had no effect upon it. The spectral forms remained motionless. It was a fearful and wonderful sight ; unique in my experience, and impressive beyond description, coming at such a moment.*

I was ready to leave, and waiting for the others. They had recovered their appetites and the use of their tongues. They spoke in patois, which I did not understand. At length the son

* See Frontispiece. I paid very little attention to this remarkable phenomenon, and was glad when it disappeared, as it distracted our attention. Under ordinary circumstances I should have felt vexed afterwards at not having observed with greater precision an occurrence so rare and so wonderful. I can add very little about it to that which is said above. The sun was directly at our backs ; that is to say, the fog-bow was opposite to the sun. The time was 6.30 P.M. The forms were at once tender and sharp ; neutral in tone ; were developed gradually, and disappeared suddenly. The mists were light (that is, not dense), and were dissipated in the course of the evening.

It has been suggested that the crosses are incorrectly figured in the Frontispiece, and that they were probably formed by the intersection of other circles or ellipses, as shown in the annexed diagram. I think this suggestion is very likely correct ; but I have preferred to follow my original memorandum.

In Parry's *Narrative of an Attempt to reach the North Pole*, 4to, 1828, there is, at pp. 99-100, an account of the occurrence of a phenomenon analogous to the above-mentioned one. "At half-past five P.M. we witnessed a very beautiful natural phenomenon. A broad white fog-bow first appeared opposite to the sun, as was very commonly the case," etc. I follow Parry in using the term fog-bow.

It may be observed that, upon the descent of the Italian guides (whose expedition is noticed upon p. 393, and again in the Appendix), upon July 17th, 1865, the phenomenon commonly termed the Brocken was observed. The following is the account given by the Abbé Amé Gorret in the *Feuille d'Aoste*, October 31, 1865 :— " Nous étions sur l'épaule (the ' shoulder') quand nous remarquâmes un phénomène qui nous fit plaisir ; le nuage était très-dense du côté de Valtornanche, c'était serein en Suisse ; nous nous vîmes au milieu d'un cercle aux couleurs de l'arc-en-ciel ; ce mirage nous formait à tous une couronne au milieu de laquelle nous voyions notre ombre." This occurred at about 6.30 to 7 P.M., and the Italians in mention were at about the same height as ourselves—namely, 14,000 feet.

said in French, "Monsieur." "Yes." "We are poor men; we have lost our Herr; we shall not get paid; we can ill afford this."* "Stop!" I said, interrupting him, "that is nonsense; I shall pay you, of course, just as if your Herr were here." They talked together in their patois for a short time, and then the son spoke again. "We don't wish you to pay us. We wish you to write in the hotel-book at Zermatt, and to your journals, that we have not been paid." "What nonsense are you talking? I don't understand you. What do you mean?" He proceeded—"Why, next year there will be many travellers at Zermatt, and we shall get more *voyageurs*." †

Who would answer such a proposition? I made them no reply in words,‡ but they knew very well the indignation that I felt. They filled the cup of bitterness to overflowing, and I tore down the cliff, madly and recklessly, in a way that caused them, more than once, to inquire if I wished to kill them. Night fell; and for an hour the descent was continued in the darkness. At half-past 9 a resting-place was found, and upon a wretched slab, barely large enough to hold the three, we passed six miserable hours. At daybreak the descent was resumed, and from the Hörnli ridge we ran down to the chalets of Buhl, and on to Zermatt. Seiler met me at his door, and followed in silence to my room. "What is the matter?" "The Taugwalders and I have returned." He did not need more, and

MONSIEUR ALEX. SEILER.

burst into tears; but lost no time in useless lamentations, and set to work to arouse the village. Ere long a score of men had started

---

* They had been travelling with, and had been engaged by, Lord F. Douglas, and so considered him their employer, and responsible to them.

† Transcribed from the original memorandum.

‡ Nor did I speak to them afterwards, unless it was absolutely necessary, so long as we were together.

to ascend the Hohlicht heights, above Kalbermatt and Z'Mutt, which commanded the plateau of the Matterhorngletscher. They returned after six hours, and reported that they had seen the bodies lying motionless on the snow. This was on Saturday; and they proposed that we should leave on Sunday evening, so as to arrive upon the plateau at daybreak on Monday. Unwilling to lose the slightest chance, the Rev. J. M'Cormick and I resolved to start on Sunday morning. The Zermatt men, threatened with excommunication by their priests if they failed to attend the early mass, were unable to accompany us. To several of them, at least, this was a severe trial, and Peter Perrn declared with tears that nothing else would have prevented him from joining in the search for his old comrades. Englishmen came to our aid. The Rev. J. Robertson and Mr. J. Phillpotts offered themselves, and their guide Franz Andermatten;[*] another Englishman lent us Joseph Marie and Alexandre Lochmatter. Frédéric Payot, and Jean Tairraz, of Chamounix, also volunteered.

We started at 2 A.M. on Sunday the 16th, and followed the route that we had taken on the previous Thursday as far as the Hörnli. From thence we went down to the right of the ridge,[†] and mounted through the *séracs* of the Matterhorngletscher. By 8.30 we had got to the plateau at the top of the glacier, and within sight of the corner in which we knew my companions must be.[‡] As we saw one weather-beaten man after another raise the telescope, turn deadly pale, and pass it on without a word to the next, we knew that all hope was gone. We approached. They had fallen below as they had fallen above—Croz a little in advance, Hadow near him, and Hudson some distance behind; but of Lord F. Douglas we could see nothing.[§] We left them where they fell;

[*] A portrait of Franz Andermatten is given in the engraving facing p. 262.

[†] To the point marked Z on the map.　　　　[‡] Marked with a cross on the map.

[§] A pair of gloves, a belt, and boot that had belonged to him were found. This, somehow, became publicly known, and gave rise to wild notions, which would not have been entertained had it been also known that the *whole* of the boots of those who had fallen *were off*, and were lying upon the snow near the bodies.

buried in snow at the base of the grandest cliff of the most majestic mountain of the Alps.

All those who had fallen had been tied with the Manilla, or with the second and equally strong rope, and, consequently, there had been only one link—that between old Peter and Lord F. Douglas—where the weaker rope had been used. This had a very ugly look for Taugwalder, for it was not possible to suppose that the others would have sanctioned the employment of a rope so greatly inferior in strength when there were more than 250 feet of the better qualities still remaining out of use.* For the sake of the old guide (who bore a good reputation), and upon all other accounts, it was de-

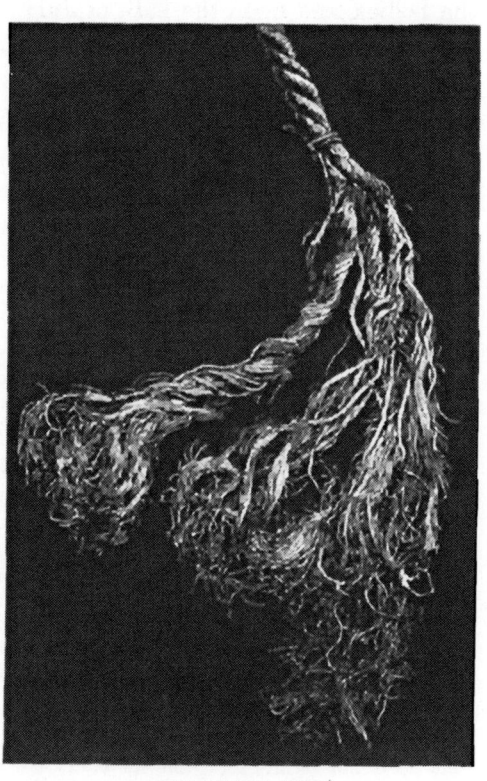

THE MANILLA ROPE.†

sirable that this matter should be cleared up; and after my examination before the court of inquiry which was instituted by the Government was over, I handed in a number of questions which were framed so as to afford old Peter an opportunity of exculpating himself from the grave suspicions which at once fell upon him.

* I was one hundred feet or more from the others whilst they were being tied up, and am unable to throw any light on the matter. Croz and old Peter no doubt tied up the others.

† The three ropes have been reduced by photography to the same scale.

The questions, I was told, were put and answered ; but the answers, although promised, have never reached me.*

Meanwhile, the administration sent strict injunctions to recover the bodies, and upon the 19th of July, twenty-one men of Zermatt accomplished that sad and dangerous task.† Of the body of Lord Francis Douglas they, too, saw nothing ; it is probably still arrested on the rocks above.‡ The remains of Hudson and Hadow

* This is not the only occasion upon which M. Clemenz (who presided over the inquiry) has failed to give up answers that he has promised. It is greatly to be regretted that he does not feel that the suppression of the truth is equally against the interests of travellers and of the guides. If the men are untrustworthy, the public should be warned of the fact ; but if they are blameless, why allow them to remain under unmerited suspicion ?

Old Peter Taugwalder is a man who is labouring under an unjust accusation. Notwithstanding repeated denials, even his comrades and neighbours at Zermatt persist in asserting or insinuating that he *cut* the rope which led from him to Lord F. Douglas. In regard to this infamous charge, I say that he *could* not do so at the moment of the slip, and that the end of the rope in my possession shows that he did not do so beforehand. There remains, however, the suspicious fact that the rope which broke was the thinnest and weakest one that we had. It is suspicious, because it is unlikely that any of the four men in front would have selected an old and weak rope when there was abundance of new, and much stronger, rope to spare ; and, on the other hand, because if Taugwalder thought that an accident was likely to happen, it was to his interest to have the weaker rope where it was placed.

I should rejoice to learn that his answers to the questions which were put to him were satisfactory. Not only was his act at the critical moment wonderful as a feat of strength, but it was admirable in its performance at the right time. I am told that he is now nearly incapable for work—not absolutely mad, but with intellect gone and almost crazy ; which is not to be wondered at, whether we regard him as a man who contemplated a scoundrelly meanness, or as an injured man suffering under an unjust accusation.

In respect to young Peter, it is not possible to speak in the same manner. The odious idea that he propounded (which I believe emanated from *him*) he has endeavoured to trade upon, in spite of the fact that his father was paid (for both) in the presence of witnesses. Whatever may be his abilities as a guide, he is not one to whom I would ever trust my life, or afford any countenance.

† They followed the route laid down upon the map, and on their descent were in great peril from the fall of a *sérac*. The character of the work they undertook may be gathered from a reference to p. 155.

‡ This, or a subsequent party, discovered a sleeve. No other traces have been found.

were interred upon the north side of the Zermatt Church, in the presence of a reverent crowd of sympathising friends. The body of Michel Croz lies upon the other side, under a simpler tomb ; whose inscription bears honourable testimony to his rectitude, to his courage, and to his devotion.*

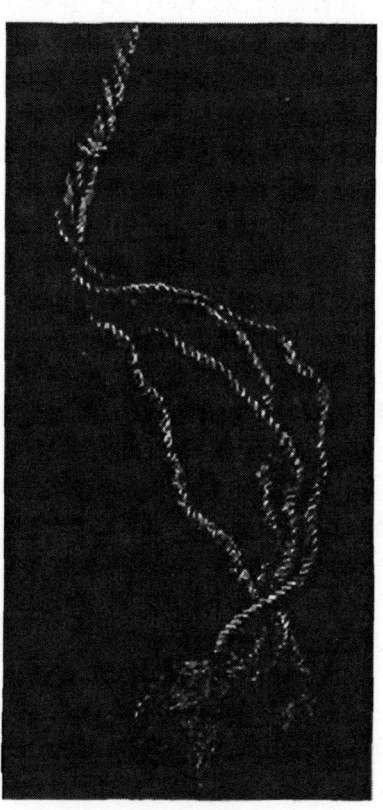

THE SECOND ROPE.

So the traditional inaccessibility of the Matterhorn was vanquished, and was replaced by legends of a more real character. Others will essay to scale its proud cliffs, but to none will it be the mountain that it was to its early explorers. Others may tread its summit-snows, but none will ever know the feelings of those who first gazed upon its marvellous panorama ; and none, I trust, will ever be compelled to tell of joy turned into grief, and of laughter into mourning. It proved to be a stubborn foe ; it resisted long, and gave many a hard blow ; it was defeated at last with an ease that none could have anticipated, but, like a relentless enemy—conquered but not crushed—it took terrible vengeance. The time may come when

* At the instance of Mr. Alfred Wills, a subscription list was opened for the benefit of the sisters of Michel Croz, who had been partly dependent upon his earnings. In a short time more than £280 were raised. This was considered sufficient, and the list was closed. The proceeds were invested in French Rentes (by Mr. William Mathews), at the recommendation of M. Dupui, at that time Maire of Chamounix.

the Matterhorn shall have passed away, and nothing, save a heap
of shapeless fragments, will mark the spot where the great mountain stood ; for, atom by atom, inch by inch, and yard by yard, it
yields to forces which nothing can withstand. That time is far
distant ; and, ages hence, generations unborn will gaze upon its
awful precipices, and wonder at its unique form. However exalted
may be their ideas, and however exaggerated their expectations,
none will come to return disappointed !

The play is over, and the curtain is about to fall. Before we
part, a word upon the graver teachings of the mountains. See
yonder height ! 'Tis far away—unbidden comes the word " Impossible !" " Not so," says the mountaineer. " The way is long,
I know ; it's difficult—it may be—dangerous. It's possible, I'm
sure ; I'll seek the way ; take counsel of my brother mountaineers,
and find how they have gained similar heights, and learned to avoid
the dangers." He starts (all slumbering down below) ; the path is
slippery—may be laborious, too. Caution and perseverance gain
the day—the height is reached ! and those beneath cry, " Incredible ; 'tis superhuman ! "

We who go mountain-scrambling have constantly set before us
the superiority of fixed purpose or perseverance to brute force. We
know that each height, each step, must be gained by patient, laborious toil, and that wishing cannot take the place of working ; we
know the benefits of mutual aid ; that many a difficulty must be
encountered, and many an obstacle must be grappled with or
turned, but we know that where there's a will there's a way : and
we come back to our daily occupations better fitted to fight the
battle of life, and to overcome the impediments which obstruct our
paths, strengthened and cheered by the recollection of past labours,
and by the memories of victories gained in other fields.

I have not made myself an advocate or an apologist for mountaineering, nor do I now intend to usurp the functions of a moralist ;
but my task would have been ill performed if it had been concluded

without one reference to the more serious lessons of the mountaineer. We glory in the physical regeneration which is the product of our exertions ; we exult over the grandeur of the scenes that are brought before our eyes, the splendours of sunrise and sunset, and the beauties of hill, dale, lake, wood, and waterfall ; but we value more highly the development of manliness, and the evolution, under combat with difficulties, of those noble qualities of human nature—courage, patience, endurance, and fortitude.

Some hold these virtues in less estimation, and assign base and contemptible motives to those who indulge in our innocent sport.

" Be thou chaste as ice, as pure as snow, thou shalt not escape calumny."

Others, again, who are not detractors, find mountaineering, as a sport, to be wholly unintelligible. It is not greatly to be wondered at—we are not all constituted alike. Mountaineering is a pursuit essentially adapted to the young or vigorous, and not to the old or feeble. To the latter, toil may be no pleasure ; and it is often said by such persons, " This man is making a toil of pleasure." Let the motto on the title-page be an answer, if an answer be required. Toil he must who goes mountaineering ; but out of the toil comes strength (not merely muscular energy—more than that), an awakening of all the faculties ; and from the strength arises pleasure. Then, again, it is often asked, in tones which seem to imply that the answer must, at least, be doubtful, " But does it repay you ?" Well, we cannot estimate our enjoyment as you measure your wine, or weigh your lead,—it is real, nevertheless. If I could blot out every reminiscence, or erase every memory, still I should say that my scrambles amongst the Alps have repaid me, for they have given me two of the best things a man can possess—health and friends.

The recollections of past pleasures cannot be effaced. Even now as I write they crowd up before me. First comes an endless series of pictures, magnificent in form, effect, and colour. I see the great peaks, with clouded tops, seeming to mount up for ever and ever ; I hear the music of the distant herds, the peasant's jodel, and the solemn church-bells ; and I scent the fragrant breath of the pines : and after these have passed away, another train of thoughts succeeds—of those who have been upright, brave, and true ; of kind hearts and bold deeds ; and of courtesies received at stranger hands, trifles in themselves, but expressive of that good will towards men which is the essence of charity.

Still, the last, sad memory hovers round, and sometimes drifts across like floating mist, cutting off sunshine, and chilling the remembrance of happier times. There have been joys too great to be described in words, and there have been griefs upon which I have not dared to dwell ; and with these in mind I say, Climb if you will, but remember that courage and strength are nought without prudence, and that a momentary negligence may destroy the happiness of a lifetime. Do nothing in haste ; look well to each step ; and from the beginning think what may be the end.

APPENDIX.

A. Progress of the Great Tunnel through the Alps.

The advanced galleries of the Mont Cenis tunnel were successfully joined upon Dec. 26, 1870.* Their progress in 1870 was unusually rapid. In the first eleven months, 1511 mètres were driven ; whereas in the whole of 1869 they progressed only 1431 mètres. At the end of 1870 about 1000 mètres of the tunnel still remained to be lined with masonry, and it was anticipated that it could be quite finished, ready for use, by July or August 1871. The railway from Susa to Bardonnêche will also be completed by that time, but the line that is to connect Modane with St. Michel will not be ready until about the end of the year, so that the opening of the tunnel will probably be delayed until this latter period.

Signor F. Giordano (inspector of Italian mines) made some observations upon the natural temperature of the rock in the tunnel, at the end of 1870 ; and I learn that the highest reading he obtained (near the centre) was 85°·1 Faht. The temperature of the air at the same part was slightly above 86°. About 85° will doubtless be the temperature of the middle of the tunnel for a considerable time, although it is sure to cool gradually. Travellers who go through it in the winter time will, therefore, pass from an almost arctic climate to a sub-tropical one in a distance of three and a half miles.†

The following paragraph (appended as a note to pp. 78-9) explains itself :—

A Coal-pit on Fire.—On Friday morning, Jan. 13, it was discovered that one of the coal-pits at West Ardsley, near Leeds, belonging to the West Yorkshire Iron and Coal Company, had taken fire, and the most serious consequences were imminent. The men and boys, amounting to several hundreds, were drawn out of the pit with the utmost rapidity, and the usual measures taken for extinguishing such fires. This pit is fortunately worked by machine coal-cutters, driven by compressed air. The pipes which convey the compressed air into the workings were promptly connected with the water reservoir at the surface, and the water transmitted through the pipes to the place where the fire was raging. Through the great pressure of the water, the shaft being 170 yards deep, there was a powerful stream steadily playing upon the burning matter, and in less than an hour the fire was subdued and all danger overcome. It seems that at the spot where the fire took place there is a 'throw,' or 'fault,' and some gas had accumulated, which, on the firing of a shot, was ignited, and thus set fire to the coal and waste. The fortunate circumstance that the pit is worked by air-machinery has saved the proprietors from the loss of many thousands of pounds, which otherwise would have been inevitable, and a very large population would have been thrown out of employment during this very inclement season.—*Standard*, Jan. 17, 1871.

* According to a letter in the *Standard*, Jan. 6, 1871, there was a mistake in the determination of the length of the tunnel to the extent of sixteen mètres.

† The temperature of the interior may, possibly, be reduced by artificial ventilation·

B. THE DEATH OF BENNEN.[*]

On February 28, 1864, Mr. P. C. Gosset and Mr. B—— started from the village of Ardon (about mid-way between Sion and Martigny), to make the ascent of the Haut-de-Cry (9688 feet), with the guides J. J. Nance, F. Rebot, A. Bevard, and J. J. Bennen. They arrived within a few hundred feet of the summit before mid-day, and determined to complete the ascent by following the crest of a ridge leading towards the east. Before this could be done it was necessary to cross some steep snow ; and, while passing this, an avalanche was unfortunately started. Bennen and Mr. B—— perished ; the others happily escaped. The following narrative, from the pen of Mr. Gosset, illustrates, in a very impressive manner, the danger of traversing new-fallen snow at considerable inclinations :—

" We had to go up a steep snow-field, about 800 feet high, as well as I remember. It was about 150 feet broad at the top, and 400 or 500 at the bottom. It was a sort of couloir on a large scale. During the ascent we sank about one foot deep at every step. Bennen did not seem to like the look of the snow very much. He asked the local guides whether avalanches ever came down this couloir, to which they answered that our position was perfectly safe. We had mounted on the northern side of the couloir, and having arrived at 150 feet from the top, we began crossing it on a horizontal curve, so as to gain the E. arête. The inflexion or dip of the couloir was slight, not above 25 feet, the inclination near 35°. We were walking in the following order :—Bevard, Nance, Bennen, myself, B., and Rebot. Having crossed over about three-quarters of the breadth of the couloir, the two leading men suddenly sank considerably above their waists. Bennen tightened the rope. The snow was too deep to think of getting out of the hole they had made, so they advanced one or two steps, dividing the snow with their bodies. Bennen turned round and told us he was afraid of starting an avalanche ; we asked whether it would not be better to return and cross the couloir higher up. To this the three Ardon men opposed themselves ; they mistook the proposed precaution for fear, and the two leading men continued their work. After three or four steps gained in the aforesaid manner, the snow became hard again. Bennen had not moved—he was evidently undecided what he should do ; as soon, however, as he saw hard snow again, he advanced and crossed parallel to, but above, the furrow the Ardon men had made. Strange to say, the snow supported him. While he was passing I observed that the leader, Bevard, had ten or twelve feet of rope coiled round his shoulder. I of course at once told him to uncoil it and get on the arête, from which he was not more than fifteen feet distant. Bennen then told me to follow. I tried his steps, but sank up to my waist in the very first. So I went through the furrows, holding my elbows close to my body, so as not to touch the sides. This furrow was about twelve feet long, and as the snow was good on the other side, we had all come to the false conclusion that the snow was accidentally softer there than else-

[*] See p. 86.

where. Bennen advanced ; he had made but a few steps when we heard a deep, cutting sound. The snow-field split in two about fourteen or fifteen feet above us. The cleft was at first quite narrow, not more than an inch broad. An awful silence ensued ; it lasted but a few seconds, and then it was broken by Bennen's voice, ' We are all lost.' His words were slow and solemn, and those who knew him felt what they really meant when spoken by such a man as Bennen. They were his last words. I drove my alpenstock into the snow, and brought the weight of my body to bear on it. I then waited. It was an awful moment of suspense. I turned my head towards Bennen to see whether he had done the same thing. To my astonishment I saw him turn round, face the valley, and stretch out both arms. The snow on which we stood began to move slowly, and I felt the utter uselessness of any alpenstock. I soon sank up to my shoulders, and began descending backwards. From this moment I saw nothing of what had happened to the rest of the party. With a good deal of trouble I succeeded in turning round. The speed of the avalanche increased rapidly, and before long I was covered up with snow. I was suffocating when I suddenly came to the surface again. I was on a wave of the avalanche, and saw it before me as I was carried down. It was the most awful sight I ever saw. The head of the avalanche was already at the spot where we had made our last halt. The head alone was preceded by a thick cloud of snow-dust ; the rest of the avalanche was clear. Around me I heard the horrid hissing of the snow, and far before me the thundering of the foremost part of the avalanche. To prevent myself sinking again, I made use of my arms much in the same way as when swimming in a standing position. At last I noticed that I was moving slower ; then I saw the pieces of snow in front of me stop at some yards' distance ; then the snow straight before me stopped, and I heard on a large scale the same creaking sound that is produced when a heavy cart passes over frozen snow in winter. I felt that I also had stopped, and instantly threw up both arms to protect my head in case I should again be covered up. I had stopped, but the snow behind me was still in motion ; its pressure on my body was so strong, that I thought I should be crushed to death. This tremendous pressure lasted but a short time ; I was covered up by snow coming from behind me. My first impulse was to try and uncover my head —but this I could not do, the avalanche had frozen by pressure the moment it stopped, and I was frozen in. Whilst trying vainly to move my arms, I suddenly became aware that the hands as far as the wrist had the faculty of motion. The conclusion was easy, they must be above the snow. I set to work as well as I could ; it was time, for I could not have held out much longer. At last I saw a faint glimmer of light. The crust above my head was getting thinner, but I could not reach it any more with my hands ; the idea struck me that I might pierce it with my breath. After several efforts I succeeded in doing so, and felt suddenly a rush of air towards my mouth. I saw the sky again through a little round hole. A dead silence reigned around me ; I was so surprised to be still alive, and so persuaded at the first moment that none of my fellow-sufferers had survived, that I did not even think of shouting for them. I then made vain efforts to extricate my arms, but found it impossible ; the most I could do was to join the ends of my fingers, but they could not reach the snow any longer. After a few minutes I heard a man shouting ; what a relief it was to know that I was not the sole survivor ! to know that perhaps he was not frozen in and could come to my assistance ! I answered ; the voice approached, but seemed uncertain where to go, and yet it was now quite near. A sudden exclamation of surprise ! Rebot had seen my hands. He cleared my head in an instant, and was about to try and cut me out completely, when I saw a foot above the snow, and so near to me that I could touch it with my arms, although they were not quite free yet. I at once tried to move the foot ; it was my poor friend's. A pang of agony shot through me as I saw that the foot did not move. Poor B. had lost sensation, and was perhaps already dead. Rebot did his best : after some time he wished me to help him, so he freed my arms a little more so that I could make use of them. I could do but little, for Rebot had torn the axe from my shoulder as soon as he had cleared my head (I generally carry an axe separate from my alpenstock—the blade tied to the belt, and the handle attached to the left shoulder). Before coming to me Rebot had helped Nance out of the snow ; he was lying nearly horizontally, and was not much covered over. Nance found Bevard, who was upright in the snow, but covered up to the head. After about twenty minutes the two last-named guides came up. I was at length taken out ; the snow had to be cut with the axe down to my feet before I could be pulled out. A few minutes after one o'clock P.M. we came to my poor friend's face. . . . I wished the body to be taken out completely, but nothing could induce the three guides to work any longer, from the moment they saw that it was too late to save him. I acknowledge that they were nearly as incapable of doing anything as I was. When I was taken out of the snow the cord had to be cut. We tried the end going towards Bennen, but could not move it ; it went nearly straight down, and showed us that there was the grave of the bravest guide the Valais ever had, and ever will have. The cold had done its work on us ; we could stand it no longer, and began the descent."

C. STRUCK BY LIGHTNING UPON THE MATTERHORN.[*]

[Mr. R. B. Heathcote, of Chingford, Essex, whilst attempting to ascend the Matterhorn by the southern route, was unfortunately used as a lightning-conductor, when he was within 500 feet of the summit of the mountain. It may be observed that the Matterhorn (like all isolated Alpine rock summits) is frequently struck by lightning. Signor Giordano has pointed out elsewhere that he found numerous traces of electric discharges upon the top of the mountain.][†]

"On July 30, 1869, in company with Peter Perrn, Peter Taugwalder junior, and Jos. Maquignaz, I commenced the ascent. The atmosphere was clear, and the wind southerly. When very near to the summit an extremely loud thunder-clap was heard, and we thought it prudent to descend. We commenced the descent in the following order :—Taugwalder first, myself next,

* See p. 175.　　† Malte-Brun's *Annales des Voyages*, April 1869.

then Perrn, and Maquignaz last. On approaching the Col de Felicité* I received a sharp, stinging blow on the leg, and thought, at first, that a stone had been dislodged ; but a loud thunder-clap at once told me what it was. Perrn also said that he had been hit on the leg. In a few moments I received a hit on the right arm, which seemed to run along it, and resembled a shock from a galvanic battery. At the same time all the men gave a startled shriek, and exclaimed that they were hit by lightning. The storm continued near us for some little time, and then gradually died away. On arriving at the *cabane* I found that Perrn had a long sore on his arm ; next morning his leg was much swollen and very weak. We descended to Breil on the following day, and crossed to Zermatt. The same day my hand began to swell, and it continued very weak for about a week. Maquignaz's neck was much swollen on each side ; the lightning hitting him (according to his account) on the back, and upon each side of the neck. Taugwalder's leg was also slightly swollen. The thunder was tremendous—louder than I have ever heard it before. There was no wind, nor rain, and everything was in a mist."

D. Note to Chapter VIII. p. 179.

It was stated in the commencement of this chapter that the Pointe des Ecrins was the highest mountain in France. I have learned, since that paragraph was written, that Captain Mieulet has determined that the height of the Aiguille Verte is 13,540 feet ; that mountain is consequently 78 feet higher than the Pointe des Ecrins, and is the highest in France.

E. Subsequent History of the Matterhorn.†

The Val Tournanche natives who started to facilitate the way up the southwest ridge of the Matterhorn for MM. Giordano and Sella, pitched their tent upon the third platform, at the foot of the Great Tower (12,992 feet), and enjoyed several days of bad weather under its shelter. On the first fine day (13th of July) they began their work, and about midday on the 14th got on to the 'shoulder,' and arrived at the base of the final peak (the point where Bennen stopped on July 28, 1862). The counsels of the party were then divided. Two—Jean-Antoine Carrel and Joseph Maquignaz— wished to go on ; the others were not eager about it. A discussion took place, and the result was they all commenced to descend, and whilst upon the 'cravate' (13,524) they heard our cries from the summit.‡ Upon the 15th they went down to Breil and reported their ill-success to M. Giordano (see p. 392). That gentleman was naturally much disappointed, and pressed the men to set out again. § Said he, " Until now I have striven for the honour

* A place on the final peak, about half-way between the 'Shoulder' and the summit.

† We resume here the account of the proceedings of the Italians who started from Breil on the 11th of July 1865. See p. 380.

‡ The foregoing particulars were related to me by J.-A. Carrel.

§ The following details are taken from the account of the Abbé Amé Gorret (published in the *Feuille d'Aoste*, Oct, 1865), who was at Breil when the men returned.

of making the first ascent,—fate has decided against me,—I am beaten. Patience ! Now, if I make further sacrifices it will be on your account, for your honour, and for your interests. Will you start again to settle the question, or, at least, to let there be no more uncertainty ?" The majority of the men (in fact the whole of them with the exception of Jean-Antoine) refused point-blank to have anything more to do with the mountain. Carrel, however, stepped forward, saying, " As for me, I have not given it up ; if you (turning to the Abbé Gorret) or the others will come, I will start again immediately." " Not I !" said one. " No more for me," cried a second. " If you would give me a thousand francs I would not go back," said a third. The Abbé Gorret alone volunteered. This plucky priest was concerned in the very first attempts upon the mountain,* and is an enthusiastic mountaineer. Carrel and the Abbé would have set out by themselves had not J. B. Bich and J.-A. Meynet (two men in the employ of Favre the innkeeper) come forward at the last moment. M. Giordano also wished to accompany them, but the men knew the nature of the work they had to undertake, and positively declined to be accompanied by an amateur.

These four men left Breil at 6.30 A.M. on July 16, at 1 P.M. arrived at the third tent-platform, and there passed the night. At daybreak on the 17th they continued the ascent by the route which had been taken before ; passed successively the Great Tower, the ' crête du coq,' the ' cravate,' and the ' shoulder,' † and at 10 A.M. gained the point at the foot of the final peak from which the explorers had turned back on the 14th. ‡ They had then about 800 feet to accomplish, and, says the Abbé, " nous allions entrer en pays inconnu, aucun n'étant jamais allé aussi loin."

The passage of the cleft which stopped Bennen was accomplished, and then the party proceeded directly towards the summit, over rocks which for some distance were not particularly difficult. The steep cliffs down which we had hurled stones (on the 14th) then stopped their way, and Carrel led round to the left or Z'Mutt side. The work at this part was of the very greatest difficulty, and stones and icicles which fell rendered the position of the party very precarious ; § so much so that they preferred to turn up directly towards the summit, and climb by rocks that the Abbé termed " almost perpendicular." He added, " This part occupied the most time, and gave us the greatest trouble." At length they arrived at a fault in the rocks which formed a roughly horizontal gallery. They crept along this in the direction of a ridge that descended towards the north-west, or thereabouts,

* See Appendix F, attempt No. 1.

† These terms, as well as the others, Great Staircase, Col du Lion, Tête du Lion, Chimney, and so forth, were applied by Carrel and myself to the various points, in consequence of real or supposed resemblances in the rocks to other things. A few of the terms originated with the author, but they are chiefly due to the inventive genius of J.-A. Carrel.

‡ This point is marked by the red letter E upon the lower of the two outlines facing p. 83.

§ I have seen icicles more than a hundred feet long hanging from the rocks near the summit of the Matterhorn.

and when close to the ridge, found that they could not climb on to it ; but they perceived that, by descending a gully with perpendicular sides, they could reach the ridge at a lower point. The bold Abbé was the heaviest and the strongest of the four, and he was sacrificed for the success of the expedition. He and Meynet remained behind, and lowered the others, one by one, into the gully. Carrel and Bich clambered up the other side, attained the ridge descending towards the north-west, shortly afterwards gained an " easy route, * they galloped," and in a few minutes reached the southern end of the summit-ridge.

The time of their arrival does not appear to have been noticed. It was late in the day, I believe about 3 P.M. Carrel and his comrade only waited long enough to plant a flag by the side of the cairn that we had built three days previously, then descended at once, rejoined the others, and all four hurried down as fast as possible to the tent. They were so pressed for time that they could not eat ! and it was 9 P.M. before they arrived at their camp at the foot of the Great Tower. In descending they followed the gallery above mentioned throughout its entire length, and so avoided the very difficult rocks over which they had passed on the ascent. As they were traversing the length of the ' shoulder' they witnessed the phenomenon to which I have already adverted at the foot of p. 400.

When Carrel and Bich were near the summit they saw our traces upon the Matterhorngletscher, and suspected that an accident had occurred ; they did not, however, hear of the Matterhorn catastrophe until their return to Breil, at 3 P.M. upon the 18th. The details of that sad event were in the mouths of all, and it was not unnaturally supposed, in the absence of correct information, that the accident was a proof that the northern side was frightfully dangerous. The safe return of the four Italians was regarded, on the other hand, as evidence that the Breil route was the best. Those who were interested (either personally or otherwise) in the Val Tournanche made the most of the circumstances, and trumpeted the praises of the southern route. Some went farther, and instituted comparisons between the two routes to the disadvantage of the northern one, and were pleased to term our expedition on the 13-14th of July precipitate, and so forth. Considering the circumstances which caused us to leave the Val Tournanche on the 12th of July, these remarks were not in the best possible taste, but I have no feeling regarding them. There may be some, however, who may be interested in a comparison of the two routes, and for their sakes I will place the essential points in juxtaposition. We (that is the Taugwalders and myself) were absent from Zermatt 53 hours. Excluding halts and stoppages of one sort or another, the ascent and descent occupied us 23 hours. Zermatt is 5315 feet above the level of the sea, and the Matterhorn is 14,780 ; we had therefore to ascend 9465 feet. As far as the point marked 10,820 feet the way was known, so we had to find the way over only 3960 feet. The members of our party (I now include all) were very unequal in ability, and none of us could for a moment be compared as cragsmen with Jean-Antoine Carrel. The four Italians who started from Breil on the 16th of July were absent during 56½

* The words of the Abbé. I imagine that he meant *comparatively* easy.

3 H

hours, and as far as I can gather from the published account, and from conversation with the men, excluding halts, they took for the ascent and descent 23¾ hours. The hotel at Breil is 6890 feet above the sea, so they had to ascend 7890 feet. As far as the end of the ' shoulder ' the way was known to Carrel, and he had to find the way over only about 800 feet. All four men were born mountaineers, good climbers, and they were led by the most expert cragsman I have seen. The weather in each instance was fine. It is seen, therefore, that these four nearly equally matched men took a *longer* time to ascend 1500 feet *less* height than ourselves, although we had to find the way over more than four times as much untrodden ground as they. This alone would lead any mountaineer to suppose that their route must have been more difficult than ours.* I know the greater part of the ground over which they passed, and from my knowledge, and from the account of Mr. Grove, I am sure that their route was not only more difficult, but that it was *much* more difficult than ours.

This was not the opinion in the Val Tournanche at the end of 1865, and the natives confidently reckoned that tourists would flock to their side in preference to the other. It was, I believe, the Canon Carrel of Aosta (who always takes great interest in such matters) who first proposed the construction of a *cabane* upon the southern side of the Matterhorn. The project was taken up with spirit, and funds for its execution were speedily provided—principally by the members of the Italian Alpine Club, or by their friends. The indefatigable Carrel found a natural hole upon the ledge called the ' cravate ' (13,524), and this, in course of time, was turned, under his direction, into a respectable little hut. Its position is superb, and gives a view of the most magnificent character.

Whilst this work was being carried out, my friend Mr. F. Craufurd Grove consulted me respecting the ascent of the Matterhorn. I recommended him to ascend by the northern route, and to place himself in the hands of Jean-Antoine Carrel. Mr. Grove found, however, that Carrel distinctly preferred the southern side, and they ascended accordingly by the Breil route. Mr. Grove has been good enough to supply the following account of his expedition. He carries on my description of the southern route from the highest point I attained on that side (a little below the ' cravate ') to the summit, and thus renders complete my descriptions of the two sides.

" In August 1867 I ascended the Matterhorn from Breil, taking as guides three mountaineers of the Valtournanche—J. A. Carrel, J. Bich, and S. Meynet,—Carrel being the leader. At that time the Matterhorn had not been scaled since the famous expedition of the Italian guides mentioned above.

" Our route was identical with that which they followed in their descent when, as will be seen, they struck out on one part of the mountain a different line from that which they had taken in ascending. After gaining the Col du Lion, we climbed the south-western or Breil *arête* by the route which has been described in these pages, passing the night at the then unfinished hut con-

---

* The pace of a party is ruled by that of its least efficient member.

structed by the Italian Alpine Club on the ' cravate.' Starting from the hut at daylight, we reached at an early hour the summit of the ' shoulder,' and then traversed its *arête* to the final peak of the Matterhorn. The passage of this *arête* was perhaps the most enjoyable part of the whole expedition. The ridge, worn by slow irregular decay into monstrous and rugged battlements, and guarded on each side by tremendous precipices, is grand beyond all description, but does not, strange to say, present any remarkable difficulty to the climber, save that it is exceedingly trying to the head. Great care is of course necessary, but the scramble is by no means of so arduous a nature as entirely to absorb the attention ; so that a fine climb, and rock scenery, of grandeur perhaps unparalleled in the Alps, can both be appreciated.

" It was near the end of this *arête*, close to the place where it abuts against the final peak, that Professor Tyndall's party turned in 1862,* arrested by a cleft in the ridge. From the point where they stopped the main tower of the Matterhorn rises in front of the climber, abrupt, magnificent, and apparently inaccessible. The summit is fully 750 feet in vertical height above this spot, and certainly, to my eye, appeared to be separated from me by a yet more considerable interval ; for I remember, when at the end of the *arête*, looking upward at the crest of the mountain, and thinking that it must be a good 1000 feet above me.

" When the Italian guides made their splendid ascent, they traversed the *arête* of the shoulder to the main peak, passed the cleft which has been mentioned (p. 133), clambered on to the tremendous north-western face of the mountain (described by Mr. Whymper at pp. 388 and 393), and then endeavoured to cross this face so as to get on to the Z'Mutt *arête*.† The passage of this slope proved a work of great difficulty and danger. I saw it from very near the place which they traversed, and was unable to conceive how any human creatures managed to crawl over rocks so steep and so treacherous. After they had got about half-way across, they found the difficulties of the route and the danger from falling stones so great, that they struck straight up the mountain, in the hope of finding some safer way. They were to a certain extent successful, for they came presently to a small ledge, caused by a sort of fault in the rock, running horizontally across the north-western face of the mountain a little distance below the summit. Traversing this ledge, the Italians found themselves close to the Z'Mutt *arête*, but still separated from it by a barrier, to outflank which it was necessary to descend a perpendicular gully. Carrel and Bich were lowered down this, the other two men remaining at the top to haul up their companions on their return, as otherwise they could not have got up again. Passing on to the Z'Mutt *arête* without further difficulty, Carrel and Bich climbed by that ridge to the summit of the mountain. In returning, the Italians kept to the ledge for the whole distance across the north-western face, and descended to the place where the *arête* of the shoulder abuts against the main peak by a sort of rough ridge of rocks between the north-western and southern faces. When I ascended in 1867, we followed this route in the ascent and in the descent. I thought the ledge difficult, in some places decidedly dangerous, and should not care to set foot on it again ; but

* See pp. 126-9, and pp. 133-4.

† A ridge descending towards the Z'Muttgletscher.

assuredly it neither is so difficult nor so continuously dangerous as those gaunt and pitiless rock-slopes which the Italians crossed in their upward route.

"The credit of making the *Italian* ascent of the Matterhorn belongs undoubtedly to J.-A. Carrel and to the other mountaineers who accompanied him. Bennen led his party bravely and skilfully to a point some 750 feet below the top. From this point, however, good guide though he was, Bennen had to retire defeated ; and it was reserved for the better mountain-craft of the Valtournanche guide to win the difficult way to the summit of the Matterhorn."

Mr. Craufurd Grove was the first traveller who ascended the Matterhorn after the accident, and the natives of Val Tournanche were, of course, greatly delighted that his ascent was made upon their side. Some of them, however, were by no means well pleased that J.-A. Carrel was so much regarded. They feared, perhaps, that he would acquire the monopoly of the mountain. Just a month after Mr. Grove's ascent, six Valtournanchians set out to see whether they could not learn the route, and so come in for a share of the good things which were expected to arrive. They were three Maquignaz's, Cæsar Carrel (my old guide), J.-B. Carrel, and a daughter of the last named ! They left Breil at 5 A.M. on Sept. 12, and at 3 P.M. arrived at the hut, where they passed the night. At 7 A.M. the next day they started again (leaving J.-B. Carrel behind), and proceeded along the 'shoulder' to the final peak ; passed the cleft which had stopped Bennen, and clambered up the comparatively easy rocks on the other side until they arrived at the base of the last precipice, down which we had hurled stones on July 14, 1865. They (young woman and all) were then about 350 feet from the summit ! Then, instead of turning to the left, as Carrel and Mr. Grove had done, Joseph and J.-Pierre Maquignaz paid attention to the cliff in front of them, and managed to find a means of passing up, by clefts, ledges, and gullies, to the summit. This was a shorter (and it appears to be an easier) route than that taken by Carrel and Grove, and it has been followed by all those who have since then ascended the mountain from the side of Breil.* Subsequently, a rope was fixed over the most difficult portions of the final climb.

In the meantime they had not been idle upon the other side. A hut was constructed upon the eastern face, at a height of 12,526 feet above the sea, near to the crest of the ridge which descends towards Zermatt (north-east ridge). This was done at the expense of Monsieur Seiler and of the Swiss Alpine Club. Mons. Seiler placed the execution of the work under the direction of the Knubels, of the village of St. Nicholas, in the Zermatt valley ; and Peter Knubel, along with Joseph Marie Lochmatter of the same village, had the honour of making the second ascent of the mountain upon the northern side with Mr. Elliott. This took place on July 24-25, 1868.† Since then

---

* Joseph and J.-Pierre Maquignaz alone ascended ; the others had had enough and returned. It should be observed that ropes had been fixed, by J.-A. Carrel and others, over *all* the difficult parts of the mountain as high as the shoulder, *before* the ascent of these persons. This explains the facility with which they moved over ground which had been found very trying in earlier times. The young woman declared that the ascent (as far as she went) was a trifle, or used words to that effect ; if she had tried to get to the same height before 1862, she would probably have been of a different opinion.

† It was supposed by Mr. Elliott that he avoided the place where the accident

numerous ascents have been made, and of these the only one which calls for mention is that by Signor Giordano, on September 3-5, 1868. This gentleman came to Breil several times after his famous visit in 1865, with the intention of making the ascent, but he was always baffled by weather. In July 1866 he got as high as the ' cravate' (with J.-A. Carrel and other men), and *was detained there five days and nights, unable to move either up or down !* At last, upon the above-named date, he was able to gratify his desires, and accomplished the feat of ascending the mountain upon one side and descending it upon the other. Signor Giordano is, I believe, the only geologist who has ascended the Matterhorn. He spent a considerable time in the examination of its structure, and became benighted on its eastern face in consequence. I am indebted to him for the valuable note and the accompanying section which follow the Table of Ascents.*

The two tables upon pp. 422-23 explain themselves. The first exhibits at a glance all the attempts which were made to ascend the Matterhorn before July 1865, whether by natives or whether by stranger-amateurs ; and the second, all of the ascents which have been actually made since that date. Besides these successes, there have been a large number of failures. I have been compelled to omit all mention of the latter, merely on account of their number. Great trouble has been taken to make the following tables accurate ; but it is, of course, possible that some names have been omitted which should have been inserted.

The ascents have been equally divided between the two routes. The northern one still remains, I believe, just what it was in 1865, with the exception of the hut built upon the eastern face. The southern route, however, has been rendered very much easier by the ropes which have been placed over all the difficult places. It is another thing whether it is *safer* than it was. Unless a greater amount of supervision is given to these ropes than I expect will be given to them, and unless they are replaced from time to time by new ones, they will be likely to render it more, rather than less, hazardous. In *difficulty*, there is now probably little or no difference between the routes. Very poor climbers may make, and have made, the ascent. Novices, in my opinion, ought to be invariably deterred from attempting it, and if it ever becomes fashionable (like the ascent of Mont Blanc, for example), the most disastrous consequences may be anticipated.

occurred on July 14, 1865, and improved the route. Others who have made the ascent by the northern route have thought the same ; but, as far as I can learn, there has not been any material deviation from the route we took over the small difficult part of the mountain ; and my information leads me to believe, that most of those who have ascended or descended the northern route have passed over the exact place where the accident occurred.

* Signor Giordano carried a mercurial barometer throughout the entire distance, and read it frequently. His observations have enabled me to determine with confidence and accuracy the heights which were attained upon the different attempts to ascend the mountain, and the various points upon it which have been so frequently mentioned throughout this volume. He left a minimum thermometer upon the summit in 1868. This was recovered by J.-A. Carrel in July 1869, and was found to register only 9° Fahrenheit below the freezing point. It was supposed that it was protected from the winter cold by a deep covering of snow. The explanation is scarcely satisfactory.

F. TABLE OF ATTEMPTS MADE TO ASCEND THE MATTERHORN PREVIOUS TO THE FIRST ASCENT.

No. of Attempt.	Date.	Names.	Side upon which the attempt was made, and place arrived at.	Greatest height attained.	REMARKS.
1	1858-9.	J.-Antoine Carrel. J.-Jacques Carrel. Victor Carrel. Gab. Maquignaz. Abbé Gorret.	Breil side . "Chimney."	12,650	Several attempts were made before this height was attained; the men concerned cannot remember how many. See p. 84.
2	1860. July .	Alfred Parker. Charles Parker. Sandbach Parker.	Zermatt side. East face.	11,500 ?	Without guides. P. 85.
3	August .	V. Hawkins. J. Tyndall.	Breil side . Hawkins got to foot of "Great Tower," Tyndall a few feet higher.	12,992 13,050 ?	Guides — J. J. Bennen and J.-Jacques Carrel. Pp. 85-7.
4	1861. July .	Messrs. Parker .	Zermatt side. East face.	11,700 ?	No guides. P. 87.
5	Aug. 29 .	J.-Antoine Carrel. J.-Jacques Carrel.	Breil side . "Crête du Coq."	13,230	See p. 95.
6	Aug. 29-30	Edward Whymper .	Breil side . "Chimney."	12,650	Camped upon the mountain, with an Oberland guide. Pp. 90-5.
7	1862. January .	T. S. Kennedy .	Zermatt side. East face.	11,000 ?	Winter attempt. Pp. 96-7.
8	July 7-8 .	R. J. S. Macdonald. Edward Whymper.	Breil side . Arête below "Chimney."	12,000	Guides — Johann zum Taugwald and Johann Kronig. Pp. 102-3.
9	July 9-10	R. J. S. Macdonald. Edward Whymper.	Breil side . "Great Tower."	12,992	Guides—J.-A. Carrel and Pession. P. 104.
„	July 18-19	„　　„	Breil side . Somewhat higher than the lowest part of the "Cravate."	13,400	Alone. Pp. 105-119.
10	July 23-24	„　　„	Breil side . "Crête du Coq."	13,150	Guides—J.-A. Carrel, Cæsar Carrel, and Luc Meynet. P. 123.
11	July 25-26	„　　„	Breil side . Nearly as high as the highest part of the "Cravate."	13,460	With Luc Meynet. Pp. 125-6.
12	July 27-28	J. Tyndall . .	Breil side . "The Shoulder," to foot of final peak.	13,970	Guides—J. J. Bennen and Anton Walter; porters—J.-Antoine Carrel, Cæsar Carrel, and another. Pp. 126-9, 133-4.
13	1863. Aug. 10-11	Edward Whymper .	Breil side . "Crête du Coq."	13,280	Guides—J.-A. Carrel, Cæsar Carrel, Luc Meynet, and two porters. Pp. 169-176.
14	1865. June 21 .	„　　„	South-east face	11,200 ?	Guides — Michel Croz, Christian Almer, Franz Biener; porter—Luc Meynet. Pp. 290-3.

TABLE OF ASCENTS.

G. ASCENTS OF THE MATTERHORN.

No. of Ascent	Date.	Names.	Route taken.	REMARKS.
	1865.			
1	July 13-15	Lord Francis Douglas. D. Hadow. Charles Hudson. Edward Whymper.	Zermatt . . (Or Northern route.)	Guides—Michel Croz, Peter Taugwalder *père*, Peter Taugwalder *fils.* See pp. 384-94.
2	July 16-18	Jean-Antoine Carrel. J. Baptiste Bich. Amé Gorret. J.-Augustin Meynet	Breil . . (Or Southern route.)	The first two named only ascended to the summit. See pp. 393, 416-7.
	1867.			
3	Aug. 13-15	F. Craufurd Grove .	Breil . .	Guides—J.-A. Carrel, Salamon Meynet, and J. B. Bich.
4	Sept. 12-14	Jos. Maquignaz. J.-Pierre Maquignaz. Victor Maquignaz. Cæsar Carrel. J.-B. Carrel.	Breil . .	An easier route was discovered by this party than that taken upon July 17, 1865. The first two named only ascended to the summit.
5	Oct. 1-3 .	W. Leighton Jordan	Breil . .	Guides—the three Maquignaz's just named, Cæsar Carrel, and F. Ansermin. The Maquignaz's and Mr. Jordan alone reached the summit.
	1868.			
6	July 24-25	J. M. Elliott . .	Zermatt .	Guides—Jos. Marie Lochmatter and Peter Knubel.
7	July 26-28	J. Tyndall . . .	Up Breil side and down Zermatt side.	Guides—Jos. and Pierre Maquignaz, and three others.
8	Aug. 2-4 .	O. Hoiler. F. Thioly.	Seem to have ascended from Zermatt and descended to Breil.	Account given in hotel-book at Breil is not very clear. Guides seem to have been Jos. and Victor Maquignaz and Elie Pession.
9	Aug. 3-4 .	G. E. Foster . .	Zermatt .	Guides—Hans Baumann, Peter Bernett, and Peter Knubel.
10	Aug. 8* .	Paul Guessfeldt .	Zermatt .	Guides—Jos. Marie Lochmatter, Nich. Knubel, and Peter Knubel.
11	Sept. 1-2 .	A. G. Girdlestone. F. Craufurd Grove. W. E. U. Kelso.	Zermatt .	Guides—Jos. Marie Lochmatter and the two Knubels.
12	Sept. 2-3 .	G. B. Marke . .	Zermatt .	Guides—Nich. Knubel and Pierre Zurbriggen (Saas).
13	Sept. 3-5 .	F. Giordano . .	Ascended Breil side and descended to Zermatt.	Guides—J.-A. Carrel and Jos. Maquignaz.
14	Sept. 8-9 .	Paul Sauzet . .	Breil . .	Guides—J.-A. Carrel and Jos. Maquignaz.
	1869.			
15	July 20 .	James Eccles . .	Breil . .	Guides—J.-A. Carrel, Bich, and two Payots (Chamounix).
16	Aug. 26-27	R. B. Heathcote .	Breil . .	Guides—the four Maquignaz's (Val Tournanche).
	1870.			
17	July 20 (?)	?	Zermatt .	One ascent only was made in 1870. No details have come to hand.

* Although *one* day only is named for this and for a subsequent ascent, I have reason to believe that two or more days have been occupied upon all ascents which have, as yet, been made.

H. COURTE NOTE SUR LA GÉOLOGIE DU MATTERHORN. Par SIGNOR
F. GIORDANO, Ingénieur en Chef des Mines d'Italie, etc. etc.

Le Matterhorn ou Mont Cervin est formé depuis la base jusqu'au sommet
de roches stratifiées en bancs assez réguliers, qui sont tous légèrement rélevès
vers l'Est, savoir vers le Mont Rose. Ces roches quoiqu'evidemment d'origine
sédimentaire ont une structure fortement cristalline qui doit être l'effet d'une
puissante action de métamorphisme très-développée dans cette région des
Alpes. Dans la serie des roches constituantes du Mont Cervin l'on peut faire
une distinction assez marquée, savoir celles formant la base inférieure de la
montagne, et celles formant le pic proprement dit.

Les roches de la base qu'on voit dans le Val Tournanche, dans le vallon
de Z'Mutt, au col de Théodule et ailleurs, sont en général des schistes talqueux,
serpentineux, chloriteux, et amphiboliques, alternant fort souvent avec des
schistes calcaires à noyeaux quartzeux. Ces schistes calcaires de couleur
brunâtre alternent ça et la avec des dolomies, des carguelues, et des quartzites
tegulaires. Cette formation calcaréo-serpentineuse est très etendue dans les
environs. Le pic au contraire est tout formé d'un gneiss talqueux, souvent à
gros éléments, alternant parfois à quelques bancs de schistes talqueux et
quartzeux, mais sans bancs calcaires. Vers le pied ouest du pic, le gneiss est
remplacé par de l'euphotide granitoïde massive, qui semble y former une grosse
lentille se fondant de tous côtés dans le gneiss même. Du reste les roches du
Cervin montrent partout des exemples fort instructifs de passages graduels
d'une structure à l'autre, résultant du métamorphisme plus ou moins avancé.

Le pic actuel n'est que le reste d'une puissante formation géologique
ancienne, triasique peut-être, dont les couches puissantes de plus de 3500
mètres enveloppaient tout autour comme un immense manteau le grand massif
granitoïde et feldspathique du Mont Rose. Aussi son etude détaillée, qui par
exception est rendue fort facile par la profondeur des vallons d'ou il surgit,
donne la clef de la structure géologique de beaucoup d'autres montagnes des
environs. On y voit partout le phénomène assez curieux d'une puissante
formation talqueuse très-cristalline, presque granitoïde, régulièrement superposée
à une formation schisteuse et calcarifère. Cette même constitution géologique
est en partie la cause de la forme aigue et de l'isolement du pic qui en font la
merveille des voyageurs. En effet, tandis que les roches feuilletées de la base
étant facilement corrodées par l'action des météores et de l'eau ont été facilement creusées en vallées larges et profondes, la roche supérieure qui constitue
la pyramide donne lieu par sa dureté à des fendillements formant des parois
escarpées qui conservent au pic ce profil elancé et caractéristique alpin. Les
glaciers qui entourent son pied de tous les côtés en emportant d'une manière
continue les débris tombant de ses flancs, contribuent pour leur part à main-
tenir cet isolement de la merveilleuse pyramide qui sans eux serait peut-être
deja ensevelie sous ses propres ruines.

GEOLOGICAL SECTION OF THE MATTERHORN. (MONT CERVIN)

BY SIGNOR F. GIORDANO.

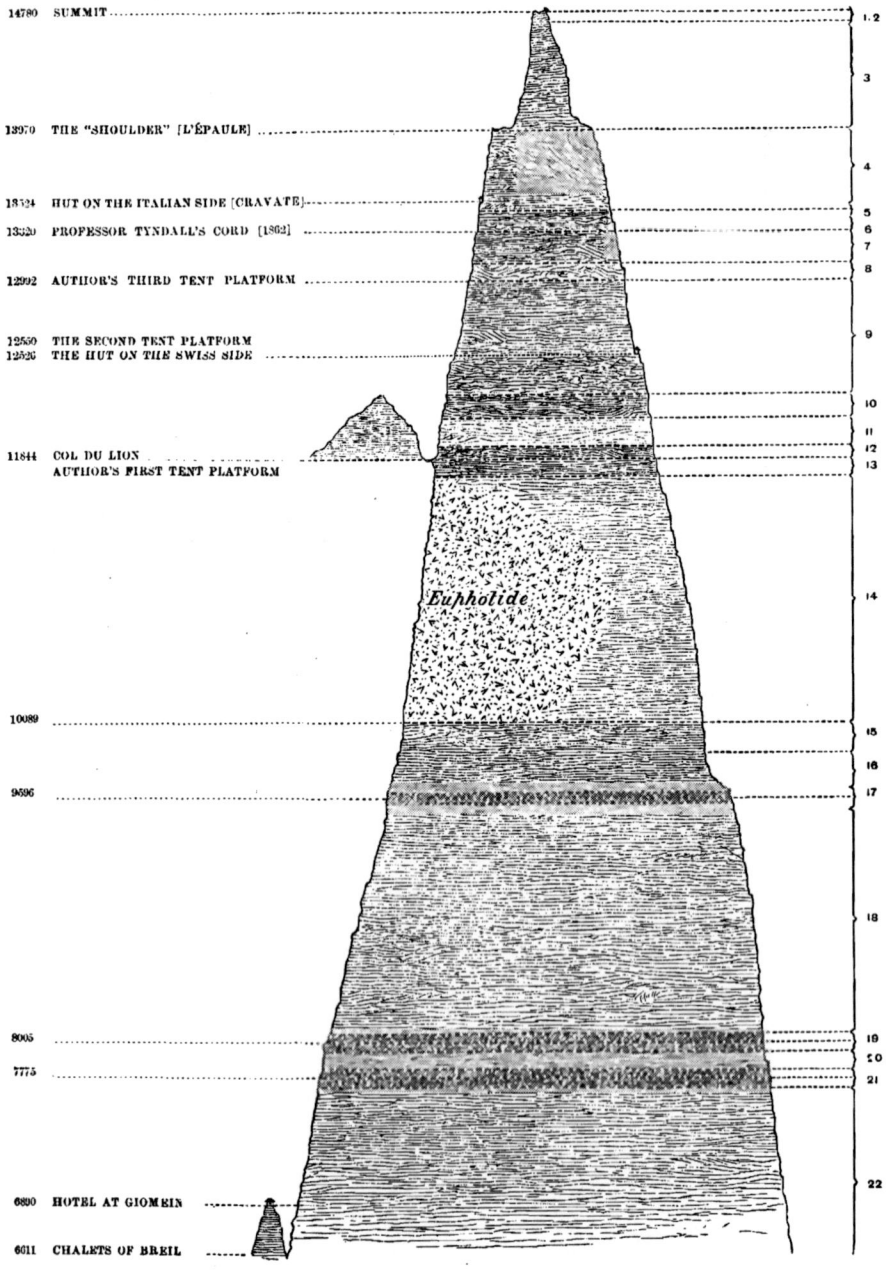

14780   SUMMIT 1. 2

   3

13970   THE "SHOULDER" [L'ÉPAULE]   4

13524   HUT ON THE ITALIAN SIDE [CRAVATE]..............   5
13320   PROFESSOR TYNDALL'S CORD [1862]   6
   7

12992   AUTHOR'S THIRD TENT PLATFORM   8

12550   THE SECOND TENT PLATFORM
12526   THE HUT ON THE SWISS SIDE   9

   10

   11
11844   COL DU LION   12
       AUTHOR'S FIRST TENT PLATFORM   13

Euphotide

   14

10089   15

   16

9596   17

   18

8005   19

7775   20
   21

   22

6890   HOTEL AT GIOMEIN ....

6011   CHALETS OF BREIL ....

REFERENCES TO THE GEOLOGICAL SECTION OF THE MATTERHORN.

I. Gneiss talqueux quartzifère.   Beaucoup de traces de foudres.
II. Banc de 3 à 4 mètres de schistes serpentineux et talqueux verts.
III. Gneiss talqueux à éléments plus ou moins schisteux, avec quelque lit de quartzite.
„ Gneiss et micaschistes ferrugineux à éléments très-fins, beaucoup de traces de foudre.
IV. Gneiss alternant avec des schistes talqueux et à des felsites en zones blanches et grises.
V. Petite couche de schistes serpentineux, vert sombre.
VI. Gneiss et micaschiste avec zones quartzifères rubanées.
VII. Gneiss talqueux à éléments schisteux.
VIII. *Id.   id.*   verdâtre, porphyroïde à éléments moyens.
IX. Gneiss talqueux granitoïde à gros éléments et avec des cristaux de feldspath.
X. Schistes grisâtres.
XI. Micaschistes ferrugineux.
XII. Gneiss talqueux vert sombre.
XIII. Gneiss et schistes quartzeux, couleur vert clair.
XIV. Euphotide massive (feldspath et diallage) à éléments cristallins bien développés, traversée par des veines d'eurite blanchâtre. Cette roche forme un banc ou plutôt une lentille de plus de 500 mètres de puissance intercalée au gneiss talqueux.*
XV. Gneiss talqueux alternant avec des schistes talqueux et micacés.
XVI. Schistes compactes couleur vert clair.
XVII. Calcaire cristallin micacé (calcschiste) avec veines et rognons de quartz. Il alterne avec des schistes verts chloriteux et serpentineux.
XVIII. Schistes verts chloriteux, serpentineux et talqueux, avec des masses stéatiteuses.
XIX. Calcschistes (comme ci-dessus) formant un banc de plus de 100 mètres.†
XX. Schistes verts chloriteux.
XXI. Calcschistes (comme ci-dessus).
XXII. Il suit ci dessous une série fort puissante de schistes verts serpentineux, chloriteux, talqueux et stéatiteux alternant encore avec des calcschistes. En plusieurs localités les schistes deviennent très-amphibologiques à petits cristaux noirs. Cette puissante formation calcaréo-serpentineuse repose inférieurement sur des micaschistes et des gneiss anciens.

* Cette roche granitoïde paraît surtout à la base ouest du pic sous le col du Lion tandis qu'elle ne paraît pas du tout sur le flanc est où elle paraît passer au gneiss talqueux.

† En plusieurs localités des environs, cette zone calcarifère présente des bancs et des lentilles de dolomie, de cargueule de gypse et de quartzites.

I. Stratification of Snow and Formation of Glacier-Ice.

In the spring of 1866, the late Principal J. D. Forbes urged me to endeavour to find out more about the ' veined structure' of glaciers, which he then, and, I believe, until his death considered, was very much in want of elucidation. After thinking the subject over, it seemed to me that its difficulties were so considerable that it would be useless to attempt to grapple with them except in a thorough manner, and that it would be necessary to scrutinise and to follow out the gradual transition of snow into glacier-ice, from beginning to end, in at least *one* glacier. Superficial examination was almost worthless, for it was well known that the veined structure, or structures, existed in glacier-ice above the snow-line ; and hence it appeared that the only effectual procedure would be to sink a number of pits or trenches through the superincumbent snow, commencing at the very birth-place of the glacier, and watching its growth and structural development as it descended to the lower regions. This opinion I still entertain.

I left England at the end of July, with the intention of sinking several pits in the Stock glacier, which descends towards the north-east from the Col de Valpelline.* In the first instance it was desirable that a trench should be made in some position that was free from local interference, and in this respect the Col de Valpelline was an excellent station. It was a snowy plateau—almost a plain (without any protruding ridges or rocks)—which gave birth to two great glaciers—one (the Stock glacier) descending gently towards the north-east, the second (the Valpelline glacier) falling away rather more rapidly to the south-west. Wretched weather and miserable workmen retarded the work, and only one pit was sunk in the time at my disposal. This was a little more than 22 feet in depth ; and, although it threw scarcely any light upon the veined structure, it yielded some information respecting stratification of snow and the formation of glacier-ice. I will describe, first of all, how the work was done ; and secondly, what we observed.

I arrived at Zermatt on the 30th of July, possessed of a pickaxe (one end of the head pointed and the other adze-shaped) and a couple of shovels ; engaged three common peasants as labourers, and Franz Biener as guide, and waited some days for the weather to improve. On the afternoon of August 2 we started, and camped on the rocks of the Stockje,† at a height of about 9000 feet. It was a very gusty night, and snow fell heavily. Great avalanches poured down incessantly from the surrounding slopes into the basin of the Tiefenmatten glacier, and minor ones from the slopes of our tent. We left our camp at 9.20 A.M. on the 3d, and proceeded to the summit of the Col (11,650) against a bitterly cold wind, and with the clouds embracing everything. I marked out a place for excavation, immediately at the summit of the pass, ‡ 24 feet long by 5 wide, and the men soon threw out enough snow to protect themselves from the wind. Two walls of the pit

* See map of the Valpelline, etc.

† Marked on the map of Matterhorn and its glaciers, Camp (1866).

‡ The pit was made about mid-way between the Tête Blanche and the nameless point marked on the Dufour map 3813 mètres.

were dressed tolerably smooth, a third was left rough, and the fourth was occupied by an inclined plane that led from the surface to the workers. Two men were always at work ; one hewing with the pick, and the other throwing out with the shovel. The others rested, and relieved the workers about every fifteen minutes. For seven or eight feet down they got along rapidly, as the stuff could be thrown out ; but after a time the progress became much slower, for the snow had to be carried out in baskets.

After 5 hours' exposure to the wind and drifting snow I was half frozen, and in a much worse state than the men, who kept themselves alive by their work. All our faces were massed with icicles. At length I beat a retreat, and descended to the tent with Biener. The mists were so dense that we dared not use either veils or spectacles, and I was snow-blind in consequence for two days afterwards. On the morning of the 4th my eyelids refused to open, and the light was painful even when they were closed. The men started off at 6.45, leaving me with my head tied up in a handkerchief, unable to eat or even to smoke ! Biener came back at 4.30 p.m. and reported that the snow seemed to be getting softer rather than harder the farther they descended. On the 5th (Sunday) my condition was slightly improved, and on Monday morning I was able to make a start, and ascended to the Col to see what the labourers had done in my absence. They certainly had not overworked themselves ; for while on the first day they had got down more than 9 feet in 5 hours, they had, during the time I had been away, only accomplished 4 feet more. They said that on Sunday night 3 feet of snow had drifted into the pit, and almost as much on Friday night. This, of course, had considerably added to the work. They were extremely anxious to get away ; which was not surprising, as the wind was blowing ferociously from the north-west, and was tearing away sheets of snow from the summit of the pass. It was impossible to stand against it, and in a single hour we should have been all frozen if we had remained upon the surface. I told them (rather jesuitically) that they had only to reach glacier, and the work would be over at that spot. This consoled them, and they promised to work hard during our absence.

Biener and I passed the night of the 6th at Prerayen, and upon the 7th we went down the Valpelline to Biona upon other business. On the 8th we returned to the summit of the Col, and found all three men sitting on the nearest rocks smoking their pipes. They admitted that they had done nothing on that day, but excused themselves by saying that they had got down to glacier. I found that the wretches had only gone down another foot during our thirty-six hours' absence. My wrath, however, was somewhat appeased when I went down into the pit. They had struck a layer of ice of much greater thickness than any which had been previously met with. It extended all round the floor of the pit to a depth of 6¼ inches. The men went to work again, and soon reached another stratum of ice of formidable thickness ; or, rather, three layers which were barely separated from each other. After this, the snow seemed to be no denser than it was above the great layer. I waited some time ; but my eyes were still very weak, and could not be exposed for many minutes together, so at length Biener and I went down to Zermatt through a terrific thunderstorm and very heavy rain.

On the 9th we returned again to the Col, and whilst climbing the rocks of the Stockje, discovered the dead chamois which was mentioned upon p. 156.   It rained as far as our camp, and thenceforward we had to fight our way up through continuously falling snow, against an easterly gale.   It blew dead in our teeth, and our progress was painfully slow.   The snow was writhing all around, as if tormented ; or caught by whirlwinds, and sent eddying high aloft ; or seized by gusts and borne onwards in clouds which seemed to be driven right through us.   The wind was appalling ; once I was fairly blown down, although tied to Biener, and many times we were sent staggering back for ten or a dozen paces against our will.   Our track was obliterated at the summit, and we could not find the pit.   We tried east, west, north, and south, to no purpose.   At last we heard a shout !   We halted, panting for breath.   Another !   It came with the wind, and we had to face the storm again.   After a long search we arrived at the pit, which by this time was a huge hole twenty feet deep.   The inclined plane had had to be abandoned, and a regular staircase led down to the bottom.   The men had again struck work, having, they said, arrived at glacier ; the fact was, they were completely cowed by the weather, and had taken to shouting, expecting that we should be lost.   I descended, and with two strokes of the pick went through their glacier, which was only another thick stratum of ice.

The last day had arrived, and the next was to see me *en route* for London. I drove them to their work, and stood over them once more.   The stuff which came up in the baskets was different to that which I had seen last !   It was not ice of a compact kind like the horizontal layers, still it was not snow. Sometimes one could say, This is snow ; but at others no one would have said that it was snow.   On inquiry, they said that it had been like this for several feet.   I went down, took the tools in my own hands, and hewed the walls smooth.   It was then apparent that vertical glacification (if I may be permitted to use such an expression) had commenced (see **A A** on section).

The men were anxious to leave, for the weather was terrible.   The wind howled over our heads in a true hurricane.   I was unwilling to go until it was absolutely necessary.   At length they refused to work any longer ; I concluded the measurements ; we tied in line, and floundered downwards, and at 9 P.M. arrived at Zermatt.

I will now proceed to describe what we saw.[*]   For 11 inches from the surface the snow was soft and white, or what is usually termed *new* snow. There was then a very decided increase in density, and all the snow beneath had a slight bluish tint.[†]   At 21 inches from the surface the tone of the snow seemed somewhat deeper than that which was above, but below this point there was little or no increase in colour until the depth of 15 feet was passed.   The density of the snow naturally increased as we descended, although much less rapidly than I expected.   Down to the depth of 13½ feet (or to just above the broad blue band on the right-hand column of the section) the mass was decidedly and unmistakably *snowy ;* that is to say,

---

[*] The reader is now referred to the section at the end of the volume, drawn to a scale of one inch to a foot from actual measurement.

[†] Compared with the 11 inches of snow at the surface, that beneath seemed dirty. I hesitate, however, to term it dirty.   We did not anywhere detect grit or sand.

lumps could readily be compressed between the hands. This was also the case in some places *below* the depth of 15 feet. For example, at **B B**, on the section, the snow was not perceptibly denser than it was six or eight feet higher up. In other places, **A A**, it could not be termed snowy ; it could not be readily compressed in the hands ; and it looked and felt like an imperfect or wet and spongy form of ice. The colour at **B B** was perceptibly stronger than at **A A**, but it should be said that the colour here, and of the horizontal strata of ice, has been intentionally exaggerated upon the section for the sake of clearness.

The entire mass was pervaded with horizontal strata of pure ice. In the 22 feet that we penetrated there were 75 such layers, varying from one-tenth of an inch in thickness to $6\frac{1}{4}$ inches, which amounted in the aggregate to $25\frac{5}{8}$ inches of solid ice. These strata were parallel to the surface of the snow, and to each other. Not perfectly so ; sometimes they approached, and sometimes receded from each other. Neither was their substance (thickness) constant. In some places they were more, and in others less thick. For example, the stratum which is between the brackets marked 1863-4 ? and 1864-5 ? was in some places an inch and a half thick, but in others scarcely an eighth of an inch. Upon the whole, the stouter strata were continued completely round the sides of the pit, and were tolerably uniform in thickness. The finer strata, on the other hand, frequently died out in short distances, and seldom or never could be traced completely round the walls. The finer strata also were much more numerous towards the surface than towards the bottom of the pit, and they were readily obscured by the drifting snow. It was obvious, yet important to observe, that the strata or layers of pure ice became fewer in number as one descended, and that they constantly, although not regularly, became thicker.

I attempted to gain an idea of the temperature of the snow at different depths, but I do not care to quote my readings, as they were, without a doubt, falsified by the wind. I am not sure, moreover, that it is possible under any circumstances to obtain correct readings of snow temperature in the way that they were taken. The recorded temperatures, anyhow, must have been influenced by the surrounding air. If they were correct they proved that the lower strata were warmer than the upper ones.

We must now quit the region of facts, and descend to that of surmises and conjectures. The differences in the quality and in the tone of the snow of the first three feet below the surface were sufficiently marked to suggest that we saw in them snow belonging to three different years. The unanimous opinion of the four men was, that the uppermost 11 inches belonged to 1865-6, the next 10 inches to 1864-5, and the next 16 inches to 1863-4. In this matter they were not, perhaps, altogether incompetent judges. I am doubtful, however, whether their opinion was correct, and incline to the idea that the uppermost 11 inches had fallen during the summer of 1866, and that the succeeding 10 inches *may* have been all that remained of the preceding winter's snow. Whatever surprise may be felt at so small a depth being considered as representing a year's fall, must be modified when it is remembered that the position at which the pit was sunk could scarcely have been more exposed. We had evidence that a mere fraction only of the snow that fell remained *in situ*—the wind tore it away in sheets and streams. It will be remembered, too, that no inconsiderable amount passes off by evaporation. If other pits had been sunk to the north and to the south of the pass, we should probably have found in them a greater depth of snow between each of the horizontal layers of pure ice. This is mere conjecture, and it may be taken for what it is worth. It is more important to note—1. (*a*) That the fine layers or strata of pure ice were *numerous* towards the surface ; (*b*) *disappeared* as we descended ; (*c*) and that the lower strata were, upon the whole, much thicker than those towards the surface. 2. That the thickness of these strata of pure ice amounted to nearly one-tenth of the mass that we were able to penetrate. 3. That, below the depth of 15 feet, vertical glacification began to show itself. Upon each of these subjects I will now venture to offer a few remarks.

1 (*a.*) *The fine horizontal layers or strata of pure ice were numerous towards the surface.* All of these layers had been formed by weathering *at* the surface. It is usual, even during the winter, for considerable periods of fine weather to succeed heavy snow-falls ; and in these periods the surface of the snow is alternately melted and refrozen, and, at length, is glazed with a crust or film of pure ice. This, when covered up by another snow-fall, and exposed as in the section, appears as a bluish horizontal line drawn through the whiter mass. The snow between any two of these layers (near the surface) did not therefore represent a year's snow, but it was the remnant, and only the remnant, of a considerable fall, between whose deposition, and that of the next stratum above, a considerable interval of time had probably elapsed.

(*b.*) *The fine strata disappeared as we descended.* I imagine that this was a result of pressure from the superincumbent mass, but I leave to others to show the exact manner in which these finer strata were got rid of. Is it possible to liquefy by steady pressure a plate of ice (say, one-tenth of an inch in thickness) placed in the interior of a mass of snow, without liquefaction of the snow ?

(*c.*) *The lower strata of pure ice were, upon the whole, thicker than those towards the surface.* This, doubtless, was a result of vertical pressure. The strata grew under pressure. But why should some grow and others disappear ? I presume that the *finest* ones disappear, and that the stouter ones grow. Can it be shown experimentally that it is possible to liquefy by steady pressure a fine plate of ice placed in the interior of a mass of snow, and at the same time, under the same conditions, to thicken another and stouter plate of ice ?

2. *These horizontal strata of pure ice amounted in the aggregate to nearly one-tenth of the thickness of the mass that we penetrated.* It was perfectly well known prior to 1866 that the upper snows (which give birth to glaciers) were pervaded with strata of pure ice, and a host of observers had written before that date upon stratification of snow and of glacier. It may be questioned, however, whether any had an idea of the very important amount of glacification that is effected by superficial weathering, and subsequent thickening of the strata through vertical pressure. A search through the works of the principal writers on glaciers has failed to show me that any person imagined that one-tenth of the mass, or anything like that amount, was composed of strata of pure ice.

PINNACLES NEAR SACHAS, IN THE VALLEY OF THE DURANCE;   FORMED FROM AN OLD MORAINE.

There are two points in regard to these horizontal strata of pure ice that are worthy of consideration :—(a) Does not their existence, and especially the existence of the fine layers towards the surface, conclusively disprove the idea that the production of glacier-ice is greatly promoted by infiltration of water from the surface ? (b) Can these numerous strata of pure ice (some of which are of such considerable thickness, and extending over large areas) be *obliterated* in the subsequent progress of the glacier ? If so, how are they obliterated ? Or is it not reasonable to suppose that these thick strata of solid ice must continue to exist, must continue to thicken under pressure, and must supply many of those plates of pure ice which are seen in the imperfect ice of the glacier, and which have been referred to at different times and by various persons as the ' veined structure ?'

3. *Below the depth of* 15 *feet the appearances which I have ventured to term vertical glacification were first noticed.* Were they accidental ? or will they be found at or about the same depth in all other places ? Into what would those appearances have developed at a greater depth ? What produced them ? These questions may perhaps be answered one day by future investigators. I cannot answer them except by guesses or conjectures. Most unwillingly I left the excavation just at the time when it promised to yield more valuable information than it had done previously ; and since then I have never been able to resume the work. I believe that the exposure of considerable sections of the interior of a glacier, at different parts of its course, would yield information of extreme interest ; and that more light would be thrown in such way upon the doubts and difficulties which attend the formation of glacier-ice and the ' veined structure,' than will ever be thrown upon those vexed subjects by idle wandering upon the surface of glaciers and by peering into crevasses.

J. Denudation in the Valley of the Durance.

In the summer of 1869, whilst walking up the Valley of the Durance from Mont Dauphin to Briançon, I noticed, when about five kilomètres from the latter place, some pinnacles on the mountain-slopes to the west of the road. I scrambled up, and found the remarkable natural pillars which are represented in the annexed engraving.* They were formed out of an unstratified conglomerate of gritty earth, boulders, and stones. Some of them were more thickly studded with stones than a plum-pudding usually is with plums, whilst from others the stones projected like the spines from an echinoderm. The earth (or mud) was extremely hard and tenacious, and the stones, embedded in it, were extricated with considerable difficulty. The mud adhered very firmly to the stones that were got out, but it was readily washed away in a little stream near at hand. In a few minutes I extracted fragments of syenite, mica-schist, several kinds of limestone and conglomerates,

---

* They were 750 feet (by aneroid) above the road, and were not far from the village of Sachas. There were a dozen of about the size of those shown in the engraving, and also numerous *stumps* of other minor ones. There may have been more, and more considerable ones, farther behind. I was pressed for time, and could not proceed beyond the point shown in the illustration. I have thought the above imperfect account of these pinnacles worth recording, as I believe they have never been described or observed before.

and some fossil plants characteristic of carboniferous strata. Most of the fragments were covered with scratches, which told that they had travelled underneath a glacier. The mud had all the character of glacier-mud, and the hill-side was covered with drift. From these indications, and from the situation of the pinnacles, I concluded that they had been formed out of an old moraine. The greatest of them were 60 to 70 feet high, and the moraine had therefore been at least that height. I judged from appearances that the moraine was a frontal-terminal one of a glacier which had been an affluent of the great glacier that formerly occupied the Valley of the Durance, and which, during retrogression, had made a stand upon this hill-side near Sachas. This lateral glacier had flowed down a nameless *vallon* which descends towards the E.S.E. from the mountain called upon the French Government map Sommet de l'Eychouda (8740).

Only one of all the pinnacles that I saw was *capped* by a stone (a small one), and I did not notice any boulders lying in their immediate vicinity of a size sufficient to account for their production in the manner of the celebrated pillars near Botzen. The readers of Sir Charles Lyell's *Principles* (10th ed. vol. i. p. 338) will remember that he attributes the formation of the Botzen pillars chiefly to the protection which boulders have afforded to the under-lying matter from the direct action of rain. This is no doubt correct—the Botzen pinnacles are mostly capped by boulders of considerable dimensions. In the present instance this does not appear to have been exactly the case. Running water has cut the moraine into ridges (shown upon the right hand of the engraving), and has evidently assisted in the work of denudation. The group of pinnacles here figured, belonged, in all probability, to a ridge which had been formed in this way, whose crest, in course of time, became sharp, perhaps attenuated. In such a condition, very small stones upon the crest of the ridge would originate little pinnacles ; whether these would develop into larger ones, would depend upon the quantity of stones embedded in the surrounding moraine-matter. I imagine that the largest of the Sachas pinnacles owe their existence to the portions of the moraine out of which they are formed having been studded with a greater quantity of stones and small boulders than the portions of the moraine which formerly filled the gaps between them ; and, of course, primarily, to the facts that glacier-mud is extremely tenacious when dry, and is readily washed away. Thus, the present form of the pinnacles is chiefly due to the direct action of rain, but their production was assisted, in the first instance, by the action of running water.

Lightning Source UK Ltd.
Milton Keynes UK
27 November 2009

146770UK00001B/253/P